THE PHILADELPHIA READER

THE PHILADELPHIA
READER

EDITED BY ROBERT HUBER AND BENJAMIN WALLACE
FOREWORD BY BUZZ BISSINGER

Temple University Press
Philadelphia

Temple University Press
1601 North Broad Street
Philadelphia PA 19122
www.temple.edu/tempress

Published 2006
Printed in the United States of America

Text design by Andrew Zahn

Philadelphia® magazine is a registered trademark of Metro Corp.

The paper used in this publication meets the requirements of the American National Standard for Information Sciences—Permanence of Paper for Printed Library Materials, ANSI Z39-48-1992

Library of Congress Cataloging-in-Publication Data

The Philadelphia reader / edited by Robert Huber and Benjamin Wallace; foreword by Buzz Bissinger.
p. cm.
Articles originally published in Philadelphia magazine.
Includes bibliographical references and index.
ISBN 1-59213-460-2 (cloth : alk. paper)
ISBN 1-59213-461-0 (pbk. : alk. paper)
1. Philadelphia (Pa.)—Biography. 2. Celebrities—Pennsylvania—
Philadelphia—Biography. 3. Philadelphia (Pa.)—History—20th century.
I. Huber, Robert, 1954- II. Wallace, Benjamin, 1968- III. Philadelphia (1967)

F158.53.P47 2006
920.0748'11—dc22

2006005728

2 4 6 8 9 7 5 3 1

CONTENTS

FOREWORD

by Buzz Bissinger

rying to capture the essence of Philadelphia in fewer than 1,500 words is both an honor and a plague. The honor part comes in being asked by the editors of *Philadelphia* magazine to come up with some snazzy and clever insights into the heart of this place. The plague part comes in actually doing it with some modicum of accuracy, in finding the heart when there are so many different veins within the heart itself—beautiful, blown-out, bucolic, bereft, bountiful, bare, buoyant, brutal, booming, bust. After all, what city in the country, what city in the world, has an art museum as beloved for the steps outside that the great Rocky graced as it is for the priceless works that hang inside? The Louvre in Paris? The Metropolitan in New York? The Tate in London?

Yo, get a frigging life. And the Phillies stink.

But surely there must be a common artery, a universal Philadelphia truth whether it's North Philly or North Wales, Manayunk or the Main Line, Brewerytown or Bryn Mawr. I've thought about this for months, and every time I think I've got it, something else comes into my head that delightfully screws it up. I consider *The Philadelphia Story*, the quintessential Katharine Hepburn film based on the life of the quintessential Main Line Queen, Hope Montgomery Scott. Then I think of *Rocky*, because how can you be a Philadelphian and not think of Rocky in his gray and soiled sweatshirt on top of those Art Museum steps with those upraised arms and the exquisite panorama of the Ben Franklin Parkway stretching beneath him? I think of Frank Rizzo when he was the police commissioner of this raging and racially divided city in the 1970s with a nightstick stuck into his cummerbund. Then I think of Ed Rendell 20 years later when he was the mayor and had the city in the palm of his hands with his rumpled irreverence and sat at his desk one day trying to figure out a baseball team fielded entirely by local sports mascots. I think of David Brenner and Will Smith, Mike Douglas and Mike Schmidt. I think of a mayor with a street for a last name and a film director with a night for his middle one. It's confusing, wonderfully confusing. I think maybe there is no Philadelphia It, no communal heart, but then I think of Frank E. Reighter.

Who?

It's part of the reason I like him, an anonymous man in a city that has never been about the silly gloss of celebrity. I like what he represents—humble, funny, feisty, a day at a time in this city of rowhouses and corner bars and luncheonettes and cars parked in the middle of Broad Street. Reighter's take on the city, made several years ago in a newspaper story, came in the context of describing the impact and importance of another quintessential Philadelphian.

His name was Larry Feinberg, and he was born in a rowhouse in South Philly in 1902. He died 73 years later in Los Angeles, but in between he was simply known as Larry, the Larry of the Three Stooges, the Larry who spent so much of his life getting the stuffing slapped out of him by the sadistic and Hitlerian Moe and trying to answer back. In 1999, a push started in Philadelphia to honor Larry with a mural, and it was then that Reighter, an avid collector of Three Stooges memorabilia in between his regular gig as a stocker of shelves at a local grocery, came up with a quote that is still on the front of my refrigerator. "He is a perfect type of Philadelphian," said Reighter of Larry's Stoogerian plight, "always fighting the level of people above him. Stocking shelves at night, I think about this stuff."

I still smile whenever I read Reighter's description. I appreciate it in particular, having spent five-and-a-half years of my life probing the belly of Philadelphia in a book I wrote called *A Prayer for the City*. I had 402 pages, and I only wish I had a phrase in there as dead-on as what Reighter said in 27 words. It isn't perfect—there are many exceptions to it—but it's good. Because Philadelphia is an underdog city, constantly (and unnecessarily) feeling it has to justify itself in the shadows of New York to the north and Washington to the south. It is a city of scrappers and streetfighters at every level whether it's politics, business, or that ultimate cockfight known as a Philadelphia courtroom. It is a city that wears a chip on its shoulder with such warrior fierceness I sometimes think we're all equipped with spears.

I realize I am playing into a certain stereotype of the city, the beer and a lunch bucket city, the ham-fisted city, the pretzel city, the hoagie city, the city that cheered Kiteman when he crashed at the Vet because let's cut the crap, the frigging guy stunk. Philadelphia is more than that, much more, not just a city, of course, but a wide and expansive region of three million. It is a place with the most beautiful neighborhoods in the world, from Society Hill to Chestnut Hill to the royal estates of the Main Line. It is a place of funk and culture from the jazz joints of North Philly to the Philadelphia Orchestra. It is a place with the greatest urban resource known to man, the splendor of Fairmount Park and the Wissahickon Creek.

The sensory extravaganza of Philadelphia comes every time I walk through it or ride through it. It's exciting and refreshing, but it's still not enough. I want secrets both delicious and dark. I want the intimacies of the people who make this city so unlike any other. Which is where *Philadelphia* magazine comes in. The magazine has been a precious resource for me ever since I was a student at Penn in the early 1970s. Its journalism is the best of any urban magazine in the country, tough when it has to be, unflinching when it has to be, compassionate when it has to be.

The collection of profiles in these pages only reinforces even more the futility of what I have just tried to do: If you want to know the heart of Philadelphia, the complete heart with all the different veins, sit back and enjoy, and read these wonderful pieces about such diverse forces as Julius Erving, M. Night Shyamalan, and Ed Rendell. Revel in them as I did when I read them. And feel special afterwards. Feel proud to live in a city that may not be the biggest in the world, or the most glamorous, but has enough individuality and idiosyncrasy to circle the globe a hundred times over.

INTRODUCTION

n the 1960s and 1970s, *Philadelphia* magazine was a pioneer of the so-called New Journalism, and largely defined the template of what a city or regional magazine can be. At a time when most city magazines were Bibles of Babbitt, peddling gaseous boosterism and selling content to advertisers, *Philadelphia* was breaking china in Main Line drawing rooms, shining light into the smoky back rooms of Old Philadelphia power, and writing unflinchingly about the city's seamy underbelly. Among its coups: Exposing the *Philadelphia Inquirer*'s top investigative reporter as a shakedown artist. He was fired and spent the rest of his life in prison. A 1966 article called "The Dancing Master" led to the closing of the Pearl Buck Foundation. It was a story that detailed how an Arthur Murray dance instructor had taken over the famous author's life, and was abusing Korean war orphans that the foundation was supposed to help. Both stories made national news.

One of the staples of the magazine has always been the profile, an in-depth prose portrait of a newsmaker or larger-than-life character who in some way defines Philadelphia. This volume brings together, for the first time, some of the best of these pieces just as they first appeared in the magazine. The subjects are among the brightest lights in the recent history of Philadelphia—with a handful of infamous charmers and oddballs included for good measure—captured with a greater depth and intimacy than in any other local medium. Since these pieces were written, some of the subjects' circumstances have changed, of course, but the profiles are meant to reflect the subjects in that moment and milieu.

Mark Kram Jr.'s piece on Robert Montgomery Scott, for example, was the portrait of a man out of time, the grandson of über-WASP Hope Montgomery Scott and standard-bearer for a patrician way of life long associated with the Main Line and in its twilight. Spending a single, revealing day with Ed Rendell, then riding high as "America's Mayor," Lisa DePaulo famously captured a man who puts the animal back in political animal. In his 1997 profile of

Comcast's Brian Roberts, Larry Platt trapped in amber a business titan on the cusp of greatness.

Yet the fame that comes with greatness—especially in this city—can be a double-edged sword, as another Platt profile, of Phillies third baseman Mike Schmidt in 1995, makes painfully clear:

> It was about 7 o'clock one morning during the winter following the 1983 World Series, the one in which Schmidt had managed just one bloop single in 20 at-bats as the Phillies lost in five games to the Baltimore Orioles. It had been snowing most of the night, so Schmidt wasn't surprised when the phone rang and he learned that the school bus carrying his kids—Jonathan and Jessica—had gotten stuck. He got in his four-wheel drive and braved the slick suburban streets around Media before pulling up alongside a yellow bus on the side of the road. Rolling down his window, he realized it wasn't his kids'.
>
> "I saw all these cute grade-schoolers on the bus," he recalls today, sitting behind the wheel of his emerald green Lexus on his way to pick up Jonathan, now 15, from school. "All of a sudden, one of these really cute little kids recognized me—I see him point and yell. They must have been in fourth grade. Then the whole damn bus, every one of these kids, just starts booing me."

Likewise, the other profiles collected here resonate with a sense of the subjects living in—and interacting with—this city. Tracking the careers, lives, and foibles of 29 Philadelphians over the last two decades substantiates what a wonderfully rich and odd and sometimes difficult place this is.

THROUGHOUT the collection, we've also interspersed "My Philadelphia Story" as a quick interlude. It's a form—the subjects speaking directly to the reader, in their words only—that yields startling insights and revelations. Terry Gross, we learn, is quite content to have many of her radio listeners think she is gay. Former mayor W. Wilson Goode, who presided over the bombing of an entire city block, offers that "In the whole scheme of things, MOVE was a bad day. But it's not something that has ever, or that ever does, weigh me down." Only in Philadelphia.

Yet it's the in-depth teasing out of the arresting and mighty by our finest writers that makes this collection such a varied walk through this city. Here is Stephen Rodrick's opening paragraph of his funny and telling profile of renowned playboy Harry Jay Katz:

> It's a sultry summer evening, and the pulse of Philadelphia night life is flat-lining. By dusk on this Monday, most of the dwellers of America's fifth largest city have already tramped home. Jaywalkers on Broad Street pause in the middle of the city's most famous boulevard for aimless chitchat without fear of vehicular homicide. A valet stands idle, rhythmically tossing and catching a lone set of keys. It's no different inside the Palm, a sirloin and

potato establishment popular with the folks who rule this town. But at 8 p.m. sharp, the mood goes from tepid to warm. Harry Jay Katz has arrived.

We're off and running into the night meanderings of one of the most charmingly shameless rogues this town has known. Or, consider Christopher McDougall's ride into the workaday world of a very different sort of Philadelphia legend:

> Nearly every house on the block is still dark at this miserable hour of a wet spring morning when Mayor John Street comes double-timing down the steps of his North Philadelphia rowhome, coatless in the fine, needling rain. Street's face is stony, but his body jitters with energy as he rams a Hefty bag into a trash can and speedwalks down the driveway.
>
> "Okay, Bush," he orders his driver by way of greeting. "Office."
>
> Marion Winbush slides open the side door of an all-black van that from the outside could pass for the A-Team command vehicle; inside, with its deep crimson upholstery and dim yellow lighting, it feels more like a hearse.

The richness of the characters in this collection stretches in surprising directions: Here is M. Night Shyamalan, right before his career-making *Sixth Sense* hit theaters; Olympic rowing coach Mike Teti en route to the Gold; legendary (and legendarily difficult) lawyer Richard Sprague in the autumn of his career; Curtis Institute piano prodigy Lang Lang when he's just beginning. Some of our subjects were embraced by the city (Sound of Philadelphia producer Kenny Gamble), while others were shunned (including Schmidt, merely baseball's greatest third baseman ever). Here, too, are figures of varying degrees of notoriety: We charted the rise of convicted murderer and self-proclaimed "political prisoner" Mumia Abu-Jamal to international cause célèbre; discovered how whiz kid Wharton dropout Mark Yagalla embezzled $30 million of investors' money and lavished it on high-priced hookers; took a hard look at world-class race-card player Richard Glanton, then-head of the embattled Barnes Foundation.

Collectively, a group snapshot of a place and a time emerges: Philadelphia around the turn of the twenty-first century. The men and women behind the proverbial camera, including Lisa DePaulo, Buzz Bissinger, and Chris McDougall, are among the finest chroniclers our city has known. They give us Philly and its variegated resident species: The Philadelphian.

THE PHILADELPHIA READER

PART 1

1988 – 1994

By Lisa DePaulo
June 1988

MRS. NOSE BUILDS HER DREAM CLOSET

andra Newman is leaning dangerously over a second-story balcony, waving her 20-carat diamond ring, and screaming, "Five!" to the auctioneer.

"But Saaaan-dra," pleads Karl Krumholz, her decorator, "we don't have *room* for a brass bed."

"I don't care," says Sandra Newman. "The bedding alone's worth $500!"

It's just another wild and crazy night with Sandra and Julius "Dr. Nose" Newman—and their decorator—this one at the March of Dimes gala furniture auction. Sandra, who's dressed more like the March of Diamonds, simply *has* to buy something.

"Six hundred!" calls the auctioneer. "Do I hear $650?"

"Six fifty!"

Karl puts his hand on his hip. "Saaaan-dra," he whines, "where are we gonna *put* it?"

Karl Krumholz is Sandra's and Julius's date for the night. From the moment they hired him as interior designer of their new $4 million-plus home out in Gladwyne, he's been in attendance whenever there was furniture to be bought.

"I suppose," he says, "we *could* put it in the maid's room."

"Not a chance!" says Sandra. "I'm giving it to the kids. Jonathan and Nancy would *love* a brass bed. Seven fifty!" she shouts.

"Is she the cutest or what?" says her husband, as Sandra comes *this close* to tumbling over the balcony, champagne flute in one hand, extra-long More cigarette burning in the other. She's wearing her usual 4-inch heels and a dress that's half leopard miniskirt and half cleavage with black sequins. She may be 49, but all her husband, the much-hyped plastic surgeon, has ever had to fix was her nose. The rest is the original model.

"Do I hear nine?" asks the auctioneer.

"Nine!" shouts Sandra.

"Do I hear $950?"

"One thousand!" she yells.

Behind her, Dr. Nose bursts out laughing. "She just outbid herself!" he roars. "Did I tell you she was the cutest?"

"We got it!" says Sandra, dropping ashes on the floor. "Quick, honey! Call the kids! Tell them what we bought for them!"

"OK," says Dr. Nose. "And don't you worry, dear, a thousand sounds better than $900 anyway."

"YOU want the truth about the house? I'll tell you the truth." Today, Sandra Newman is sitting behind her desk in the posh Bala Cynwyd offices of Astor, Weiss, & Newman, the law firm where she reigns as the highest-paid—and only female—partner.

"I just woke up one day and said, *This...is...ridiculous*! I have no room for my shoes, I have no room for my dresses..."

She reaches for a cigarette. Brown, the same shade as today's outfit. Chocolate brown dress, brown suede boots, a brown fedora hat tipped dramatically and deliberately over her forehead. Her copper-red Medusa hair is frizzed down to her shoulders. Her lips are carefully outlined in matching pencil. She looks exactly like the kind of person—part woman/part tigress—you wouldn't want representing your husband in a divorce. On her finger, she's wearing nothing but a thin gold wedding band.

"I never wear my jewelry to work," she says. "Because that's the *last* thing my clients need to see. Besides, their wives already think, 'That bitch! She has everything in the world and I'm gonna end up starving.' Of course, my response to that is, 'So, why aren't you working?'...Oh, and I never drive my Rolls to work either....

"So where were we? The house. Well, first I called my architect. I said, 'Vince, I need more closet space!' Well, he came over and drew up all these elaborate plans, then said, 'We're gonna have to put another story on the house.' It was going to be fabulous—with a spiral staircase leading up from my bathroom and a greenhouse all around it—but I wasn't getting too excited about it. I said, 'Vince, I lead a busy life. Can you picture me every morning climbing up to get to my clothes?'"

So that night Sandra Newman wrote a very business-like letter to her husband. "None of this you-better-do-this-'cause-you-love-me crap. Just a very business-like letter about why this was ridiculous and how we'd have to build a new house. And the next day, he said, 'All right, let's build a house.' We're calling it Casablanca—did I tell you that?"

She picks up the phone and punches in the numbers to dial her chauffeur. "Let me take you out there now. I'll tell ya, it better be done by June, 'cause we already sold the old house. And believe me, my builder will not want to pay to have *me* somewhere else until it's finished. I have dogs that have to go into a kennel. I have nine cars to put in garages...."

"Cathy? How are you dear?...do me a favor, and tell Bob to come over to the office. I need him to drive me someplace..."

In seconds we are being whisked—first to the Newmans' old house in Penn Valley, which sold for over $1 million, then to Casablanca. In the driveway of the house she's outgrown sit five of the Newmans' cars, including the limo and one of the Rollses—the one with "Dr. Nose" on the vanity license plate.

Inside, Alison the maid is cleaning the kitchen floor, Cathy the full-time bookkeeper is working in the home office, and Bob is on the way downstairs to the gym to polish some of Dr. Newman's shoes.

"What do you want first?" asks Sandra. "The house tour or the clothes tour?"

IF THE unofficial motto of the 1980s is that, in the end, Whoever Has the Most Toys Wins, then the Newmans are going to come close. How they've played the game is another story altogether. It's a story of what happens when your husband has done more than 17,000 nose jobs (but who's counting?) and you've risen to the top of the divorce law profession, leaving plenty of male competitors in the dust.

By now the legend of her husband, Dr. Nose—with his fur coats, his Vegas-style offices, his nurses who get called Newman's Angels, and his blatant style of promoting himself—has become as much a part of Philadelphia folklore as the statue of Rocky. And if you don't believe it, just ask him. But just like with Rocky, no one's ever been quite sure if we should be proud of this flamboyant tribute to excess or appalled by the...well, the chutzpah of it all.

They have built their considerable fortune on the vanities—and the weaknesses—of others. She splits them, he fixes them. And if now they seem to have chosen to live their lives like the embodiment of those vanities, well isn't that what the 1980s was all about? If you've got it, get more?

The neighbors may hiss, but they still call Sandra Newman for their 8-figure divorce settlements. And they still count on her husband to readjust their noses—if only so they can keep them in the air.

"I don't even think about what people think of me," says Sandra. "Because I learned a very important lesson many years ago. A friend I had in college said to me, 'Sandra, if people don't either love you or hate you, you haven't left your mark on the world.'"

"BOY, SHE'S something, ain't she?" says Bob. Bob is Sandra Newman's chauffeur. "I know what you're thinking," says Bob. "You know how those rich people are. But I gotta tell ya, not this one. She's real. And I'll tell ya how I know. I belong to the Main Line Chauffeurs Society. There's 26 of us. And if you wanna hear *stories*! We meet once a month. And they don't even believe me when I tell them what the Newmans are like to work for.

"Wherever they go—wherever—they make sure that I go out to eat. I drove them last week to Washington, they get out at this fancy restaurant, and you know what she does? She hands me a $100 bill and says, 'Get a decent meal.' So I went to McDonald's and brought her the change. She couldn't understand what I ate. I said, 'Mrs. Newman, that's where I eat.'

"For Christmas—she never even *met* my sons—and they all got these beautiful gifts. My wife got this beautiful watch. I don't even want to tell you what I got.

"You wanna know the kinds of things she does? My wife and I were going on vacation last year. She said, 'Bob, where you going?' I said, the Trump Hotel in Atlantic City. We got this package deal. The room, the meals, and the shows. And she says, 'Bob, you mind me asking what it costs?' So I told her, $422. And she went into her office and came out with a check for $500. She said, 'Now this isn't from the Nose, it's from me, Bob, so don't even argue.' *That's* what Mrs. Newman's like. The other guys, they don't believe me."

The funny thing is, no matter who you ask about the Newmans—even those who aren't on the payroll—they can't help but mention the tabs she picks up, the lavish parties they get invited to, the gifts she sends, all carefully handpicked and planned, and the spreads of champagne and smoked salmon she brings to settlement negotiating sessions. The Newmans are hardly the only ones enjoying their money.

Several weeks after Bob the chauffeur delivers his monologue on Sandra, he is driving the Newman limousine, with the boss lady in tow, through heavy Manhattan traffic as part of the annual ritual of Putting Mrs. Newman's Furs in Storage. Bob hates Manhattan, and his hands get sweaty just thinking of the wildlife kingdom stashed in the trunk—17 pelts he must deliver personally to her midtown furrier.

A block away from the Helmsley Palace he loses his cool.

"Oh, *go to hell*!" the Newman chauffeur is screaming to a New York traffic cop. "That's right, buddy, go to hell!"

At which point Mrs. Newman lowers the window that separates him from us, and raises her voice to her chauffeur.

"Go get 'em, Bob!" she yells.

THIRTY YEARS ago, when Sandra was 19, she went to a bar mitzvah and a waiter served her a knish. Eight months later she married the waiter. No, there weren't any dollar signs in Sandra Eileen Schultz's eyes when she became Mrs. Julius Newman.

In fact he was, if you'll pardon the expression, a nose below what Sandra had been used to. Not that the Schultzes of Wynnefield were *rich* rich, as she likes to put it, but they were comfortable enough to send their only daughter off to "typical Jewish kid camp" in the summers—where she led the raids on the boys bunks—and to clothe her in her first fur-lined coat at the age of eight. Still, her mother worked full time all her life in the family business, a string of food store/luncheonettes.

By age 17, while a freshman at Drexel, Sandra joined the Young Republicans—a decision, she says, that was made in deliberate defiance of her father's liberal Democrat view. "I was a capitalist even then," she says. "Though, to my father, becoming a Republican was the worst thing I could do."

Jules had a much different upbringing. His mother died when he was six, and his father remarried three times, with two of those marriages ending in divorce. "He used to think," says Sandra, "that 1801 Vine [Family Court] was his second home." And though the Newmans weren't exactly *poor* poor, they were poor whenever it seemed to matter. His father, who had a food store in Atlantic City, did well some years and did miserably the rest. The youngest of four boys, Jules watched his two oldest brothers be put through college and grad school (one became a podiatrist, the other a dentist), but by the time he was of age, there wasn't any money left. And so he went to work for a catering company to pay for every nickel of tuition through college and med school at Temple.

When he met Sandra Schultz, he was 29, doing his internship, and just beginning to entertain the notion of going into cosmetic surgery. She was a fourth-year student at Drexel, majoring in audiology. When she brought him home, her mother said, "Sandra, he's too old for you. When he's 50 everyone will think that *you're* 50, too. Besides, he's probably been married before and he's not telling you."

(Actually it was Sandra who had broken an engagement just four days before she met Jules, returning a nice-size rock.)

When Jules proposed, he brought her to his apartment at St. Mary Hospital where he was interning, and offered her his medical fraternity pin.

They married on a Saturday in July, and two days later, Jules started his residency. No honeymoon, not even a motel room. They spent their wedding night in the efficiency apartment they rented near Graduate Hospital. Sandra put up a screen so the bed would be separate from the living room.

They had their first big fight the following week when Jules came home with a bloody surgeon's outfit and Sandra told him. "Wash it yourself!" "I'll never forget that bloody outfit floating in our bathtub," says Sandra. "*That* was my honeymoon!"

She admits she used to go out with her old college friends (she'd graduated two weeks before the wedding) while he worked long hours as a resident and a waiter, and wonder what the hell she had gotten herself into. "The first year of marriage was the worst year of my life," says Sandra. In the sixth week she got pregnant, and cried for three months, wondering every night how they'd ever support a child on the $250 per month her husband brought home. But somehow her pregnancy became a sign of hope for both of them. "Jules desperately wanted a little girl," says Sandra. After carrying full term, Sandra delivered a stillborn daughter.

Sandra saw a shrink for the first and last time in her life. When, years later, her firstborn son would take his bride-to-be home—a fellow Penn law student whose mother had recently died—Sandra welcomed her as though she were her own, instructing family and friends never to call Nancy the Newmans' daughter-in-law, just daughter. And Nancy has called her "Mom" since almost the first date. But for a long time the loss of that child was something Sandra never thought she'd shake. Even when her sons went off to college, she'd call them—and hang up—just so she knew they were safe. "Mom," they learned to say, "I know it's you."

When Sandra was 22 and had just given birth to her first son, Jonathan, Jules went into the Army. "We could have gone anywhere in the world," says Sandra, "and he chose Fort Dix." If there seemed to be a lack of focus and security in their lives, it was a feeling Sandra Newman was determined never to have again.

ACCORDING to the architects of Sandra Newman's new house, the first thing she told them was that the closet had to be big enough for 1,000 dresses.

Just how big is it?

"Ever see *Mommie Dearest*?" replies Vince Rivera, her architect.

Actually, it's the same size as one of the four-car garages; it's 800 square feet—200 square feet larger than the average one-bedroom apartment. It is arranged supermarket style, by aisle—scarf aisle, hat aisle, shoe aisle (the jewelry closet is separate)—so Sandra can compose her outfit as she goes along.

Once the closet was designed, the Newmans sat down to figure out what to do with the rest of the house—all 20,000 square feet of it. Jules drew up his vision on a cocktail napkin on a flight to L.A. and the architects went to work. An entry rotunda with a neon-lit dome. A "floating" grand staircase (the supports are an optical illusion). Hand-pressed terra-cotta tiles from Spain, marble from Italy, a whole kitchen being shipped from Germany, and a dining room table made of the largest piece of glass commercially available. At one point, during one of the architects' weekly meetings with the Newmans, someone dared mention that the house had everything but an indoor swimming pool. "Well, why the hell not?" asked Sandra, and in went the 20- by 40-foot glass-enclosed pool with a roof that disappears with the press of a button.

But today, as Sandra floats through her old house, opening doors and pointing to her clothes collection, one can't help but wonder: Will 1,000 hangers ever be enough?

"These are my work dresses for winter," she says at one door. "In this closet, I keep my winter hats. Here's a shoe closet. And here's another shoe closet...."

"You don't want to know how many pairs of shoes I have, do you? Two hundred pairs of boots and 350 pairs of shoes. I had to count them for the new closet."

Upstairs, invading her kids' bedrooms, is another wall full of shoes and a half-dozen more closets filled with Sandra's designer gowns. "My favorites are Galanos, Zandra Rhodes, and Fabrice, but if I had to pick a fourth, I'd probably pick Blass...Though I just bought a Scaasi that I'm mad for."

Sandra does most of her clothes shopping at Giorgio on Rodeo Drive. When she's back in Philadelphia, her girl there ships her new designer gowns, three and four at a time. When pressed she goes directly to the designer. Upon meeting Zandra Rhodes at a party in Manhattan, she couldn't help but order three new dresses made-especially-for-Sandra Newman.

Everything they say about her shopping sprees is true. On one recent trip to New York, it took her just one minute and 32 seconds to drop $1,950 on a Judith Lieber evening bag at Bergdorfs. She spent another 10 minutes sitting with her legs crossed in a skin-tight leather mini in a dressing room at hoity-toity Martha on Park Avenue, as a salesgirl brought out dress after $10,000 dress.

"Now this is my art hallway," Sandra is saying, continuing the tour of her clothes. She enters a second-floor foyer whose walls are covered with, among other things, two original Salvador Dalis. Between them stands a clothes rack on wheels. On it hangs the 17 fur coats (three belong to Jules). "Would you believe I have to keep these in the hallway because I ran out of space?

"Now do you see why I need a new house?"

THE ARMY was, well...interesting for the Newmans. Starting with the day Jules had to go to a surplus store on Broad Street and pick up his uniforms. "I thought we were going shopping!" says Sandra. She marched up to the counter, with her husband in tow, and asked the officer what kind of outfits they had in his size. He handed her a stack of standard-issue shirts and pants and one pair of black shoes.

"I'm not crazy about this style," said Sandra. "Do you have anything else?"

It was in the Army, though, that Jules really began to make his mark as a plastic surgeon. He'd enlisted on a plan whereby doctors who gave the government two years of service would never have to worry about being yanked out of practice later on—and he began to serve his country doing nose jobs for officers and face lifts for their wives.

"Every big, fat sergeant had a little pug nose when my husband got through," says Sandra, proudly. His big moment, though, was when he did the nose of the woman who became Miss McGuire Air Force Base. Shortly after, he was summoned on his day off. The general's wife needed a new chin.

By the time the Newmans left Fort Dix, Jules had done enough nose jobs to think about a practice. The top cosmetic surgeon in Philly at the time, who has since died, offered him the chance to join him in his practice. Jules declined, much to Sandra's worry—the thought of a steady paycheck seemed wonderful to her. Especially since they'd just made a down payment on a $22,500 house in Wynnefield that they knew they couldn't afford. But in his first year in practice for himself, Jules made 70 percent more than the $35,000 he'd been guaranteed as a salaried partner. Sandy and Jules were on their way to Casablanca.

IF JULES'S rise to fame, fortune, and flamboyance was impressive, it was nothing compared to Sandra's own rise.

She was 28, had two children, a master's degree in audiology from Temple, was working part time for her husband, and was beginning to study at night for her Ph.D, when she drove by Villanova Law School and thought, "What I really want to be is a lawyer."

She walked in, filled out an application, took the LSATs that Saturday, and started law school the very day she dropped her five-year-old off for his first day of kindergarten. She had her classes scheduled so she could deliver a hot lunch at noontime to her second-grader; she certainly wasn't going to let her son eat cold peanut butter and jelly every day. When stuck with a late afternoon class, she sometimes took her children to law school with her—a practice that stopped when she learned that one of the other law students had taught her seven-year-old how to play gin.

She continued full time and was one of eight women to finish law school in the 1972 'Nova class whose graduates included tough-nuts prosecutor Barbara Christie and judge-turned-informant Mary Rose Fante Cunningham. ("They were *like this* in law school," Sandra remembers.)

Her first year out, she became the first female assistant D.A. in Montgomery County in over 30 years. And it didn't take long for her to make her mark. The first case she prosecuted was a fornication and bastardy case. Dressed to kill, Sandra stood in front of the jury, and held up the one-year-old child in question. "Winston Churchill once said that every baby looked like him," she said. "But I ask you, ladies and gentlemen of the jury, doesn't this baby look like the defendant?" It was vintage Sandra Newman—part woman/part tigress, part mother/part bitch—and the jury bought it all.

She made a name for herself quickly with her ballsy confidence and outrageous style, showing up for court as if she were auditioning for *Dynasty*.

As a colleague would later say, "She never felt, like other women lawyers did, that she had to out-macho the male lawyers to get her point across. She was a woman first, but that didn't mean she wasn't tough as nails."

Judge Vincent Cirillo, now president judge of the Superior Court, remembers the first case she tried before him, early on in her career. She was prosecuting a man charged with drunken driving whose defense was that he'd run out of aftershave and put bourbon on his face instead.

"She stood in my courtroom, opened a bottle of Jack Daniels and splashed it on her face," Cirillo remembers. Of course it dissipated and you couldn't smell a thing. "She walked up to the jury," Cirillo remembers, "and said, 'Ladies and gentlemen, I ask you. Is this the same strong smell of bourbon the officer described?' The jury deliberated for about three minutes. And I have to say, I was mighty impressed. If there's one thing she has that has always put her far above the rest, that Sandra is a *salesperson*."

Cirillo has since become one of Sandra's closest friends. In fact, it's a longstanding tradition between Sandra and the judge—who weighs in at about 300 pounds—to throw each other into the swimming pool at friends' parties. "I can't remember a party where Sandra and I didn't end up in the pool," says Cirillo.

"I lose about a gown a year on that thing!" says Sandra.

At one point while her kids were in high school, Sandra considered running for public office. She'd gotten chummy with Faith Whittlesley before Whittlesley's appointment as U. S. ambassador to Switzerland, and had campaigned for many Republicans. People thought that with her skills and her ability to raise money, maybe she should take a shot, starting with a judgeship. So Sandra sat down with her inner circle of friends, law partners, and family and thrashed it out. "It wasn't a simple decision, but I figured—and they agreed—my image is just not right. I mean, I couldn't wear my clothes, I couldn't wear my jewelry…It just wouldn't be any *fun*!"

By the time Sandra left the D. A.'s office for private practice, she already had a reputation as a heavy-hitter. And so it was that with less than a decade of experience, the Main Line plastic surgeon's wife with the penchant for fancy clothes was called on to handle some of the biggest criminal cases in town, the kind that win plenty of publicity.

Though she'd only been a prosecutor in rape cases before, it was Sandra Newman who defended Dr. Panayotis Apostoledes, the Lankenau Hospital gynecologist who was charged with four counts of rape by his patients, all of whom remained silent for years before filing charges. "I defended him," says Sandra, "because as a woman, I couldn't imagine that you could return a year later to a doctor who had raped you." With the prosecution marching witness after witness to the stand, and Women Organized Against Rape marching outside the courtroom, Newman got the doctor off on the criminal charge.

Yet that year, she decided to give up criminal defense work for a strictly matrimonial practice—something she'd been doing more and more of anyway. Back then divorce law was a lot like criminal defense work—with wiretaps and bedroom videos yet to be ruled illegal—and as her reputation grew, so did the size of her clients' bankrolls.

When the laws of equitable distribution came about—and divorce became more a search for hidden assets, and less a search for body parts—she found herself in even greater demand: Finding bank accounts and hidden funds suited Mrs. Nose well. Her representation has cost clients up to $125,000, but her settlements have reached well into eight figures. Even her most competitive rivals admit, "No one can negotiate a settlement like Sandra Newman."

She represented Barbara Katz, filing an injunction to prevent Harold Katz from buying the Philadelphia '76ers until he put his wife's settlement money in escrow. She's representing a common-law wife of Muhammad Ali who, as the undisputed mother of one of his children, is suing him for a piece of the action. And years earlier, after getting chummy with fellow Villanova Law School grad Susan Tose Fletcher, she was called in to settle Leonard Tose's sticky divorce from his second wife Andrea.

But business is business. A few years after representing Tose, she sued her former client—and squelched her friendship with Susan (who was once close enough to Sandra to name her guardian to her daughter in a will)—in the well-publicized attempt by the Newmans and two other investors to buy the Philadelphia Eagles. Charging that Tose reneged on a contract to sell the team, the Newmans and their pals landed a $1.75 million settlement.

"I am a devil Scorpio," says Sandra Newman. And if you believe in astrology as she does—to the point of having had her babies' charts read 20 minutes after she gave birth—you'd know that means more than having your sun and moon in Scorpio.

"If someone does me one good, I'll do them a thousand goods," she explains. "But if someone does me a wrong, they're in trouble."

In her practice, she's earned the luxury of being able to turn down cases—and colleagues say she does that frequently, particularly custody cases where she does not agree that the potential client is the parent who should have the child. If Meryl Streep had come to her in *Kramer vs. Kramer*, for instance, Newman says she would have told her to find another lawyer. "I have no compassion whatsoever for a parent who walks out on a kid," she says. "But I also don't take cases I don't think I can win."

Hers is hardly a lady-of-luxury career. Just like her husband, who does nearly 30 cosmetic operations a week, Sandra works like she still needs the money. She settles more than 100 cases a year, and averages well over 50 billable hours a week. She also represents more men than women, because as she figures, "Wouldn't it seem logical to get a woman who has a career to stand up there and argue that your wife has earning ability?" Or maybe it's just the way a client once explained it, that "only a woman could be as big a bitch as my wife!"

But in fact, it may just be that more men can afford her.

At $225 an hour, she's one of the highest-paid divorce lawyers in town. Only Al Momjian, who charges $250, is believed to be on a higher scale than Newman, though she insists that she gets better retainers—$7,500 to $20,000.

One woman who hired Sandra Newman after her husband of 22 years announced that he wanted out, says the $60,000 in legal fees was worth it just to see the look on her husband's face when she told him, "I got Sandra Newman."

"My wife positively hated her," says another client, who forked over $50,000 for the pleasure. When, as part of the settlement, his ex-wife was asked to return his 100 credit cards, she sent them, one at a time, in envelopes to Sandra Newman.

"In the Delaware Valley, there are ten divorce lawyers who are very, very good," says Neil Hurowitz, president of the Pennsylvania Chapter of the American Academy of Matrimonial Lawyers, whose members are elected by their peers.

"There are only a handful who are exceptional. Sandra is one of them."

"MY EARLIEST recollection of Sandra was years ago," says Diane Biefeld, Sandra's best friend and jeweler. "Our boys were in Little League together and there I was sitting in the bleachers in jeans and a warm-up top, like all the other mothers, and in walks this powerhouse, who we all knew was the D.A., in a white cashmere dress. We were so impressed.

"She is not a lady who lunches," says Diane. "She has no time whatsoever for the nonsense of women. But she'll think nothing of spending $10,000 on a dress. I wouldn't spend that in a million years. I sit with her in a dressing room and all I can says is, 'Are you *crazy*?' The price tags look like telephone numbers. Then she'll go out and buy two Chanel bags, one for herself, one for [her daughter-in-law] Nancy. I say, 'Sandra? Are you *crazy*? You're gonna turn her into a monster.'"

"And did she tell you how she got the ring?" Diane is referring to Sandy's flawless 20-carat diamond, which Sandra says she won when she stopped smoking once.

"Hmm," says Diane, "Well, now I'm gonna tell you the truth."

Diane says when the stone went on the market she only wanted to *show* it to Sandra ("They're my friends, I'm not out to make a profit from them") but when she brought it over to their house, Sandra slipped it on her finger, and declared, "I gotta have it."

"Jules was sitting in a lounge chair in the bedroom saying, 'I'm not buying it, I'm not buying it.' And it took her about a minute. She said, 'Jules, I'll quit smoking!' And he said, 'You got a deal!'"

When Sandra started smoking again, Jules put the ring in a vault for six months, says Diane. So how'd she get it back? "All she has to do is smile at him." (Sandra won't tell, but she says smiling wasn't what did it.)

"I have to tell you something else," says Diane. "They ought to make a statue out of him, to put up with her. She's gonna kill me for saying this. I can hear her now—'You bitch!' But Jules is a doll, a living doll. The man calls her from the operating room! He runs home to her bedside if she has a sniffle. I've never seen anything like the love affair between those two people, and Sandra is *not* an easy person to live with. She likes everything *just so*.

"I tell her all the time, 'You're gonna have to stand him up in the operating room at four in the morning to pay for what you're buying.'"

But while Sandra Newman went about selling herself (and OK, also buying for herself), she also had quite a bit to say in the successful—and very calculated—selling of her husband. She had decided early on in their marriage that Jules wasn't going to be just any old cosmetic surgeon, and set out to help him in creating his image. (She insists that they've "never paid a dime to a PR person, which nobody believes.")

"I knew Jules could do it with his talent," explains Sandra. "Nobody does a nose like Jules! But I also knew that this had to be a splash."

First she decided "that we had to get out to the right balls and the right social events." Problem is, her husband may have an ego the size of her old nose when he's with clients, but socially, the man is *shy* to the point of being introverted. It takes at *least* two or three meetings for Jules to loosen up. But if you'd never guess it from Julius Newman's image, maybe it's because his wife has done such a good job. It was Sandra who ordered the license plates (the new one says "Dr. Lipo," as in liposuction). And it was Sandra who created his flashy offices. Jules says she phoned him in his old office in Upper Darby one day and said, "Honey, you're just too *good* to be out there! We're gonna move your offices."

"Actually, I was kind of content where I was," says Jules, "but when she makes up her mind to do something, it's done."

Sandra decided that her husband had to be at "the number one traffic area in Philadelphia," and when waiting one day in bumper-to-bumper traffic at a light at City and Haverford avenues, she caught herself staring at an empty gas station and decided that was it. "I couldn't believe it," says Jules. "The property was in litigation, but she went to the owners and wheeled and dealed until they sold it to her." He suggested they use the existing structure. Sandra had it bulldozed.

The huge electric sign out front that says Newman Cosmetic Surgery Center? Her idea. The inside decor—complete with the custom-made wallpaper in "The Mirrored Room" that says, in little hearts, "I love my cosmetic surgeon"…? Sandra's idea. She worked with the decorator through every last piece of glitz.

By this point Dr. Nose had become a media darling. But Sandra's job hardly ended there. Not only does Mrs. Newman lay out her husband's clothes—arranging a week's worth of outfits, right down to the hanky, belt, shoes, and tie, every Saturday afternoon—but she purchases all of his clothes. Including an entire wardrobe selected specifically for his TV appearances.

"THEY'RE NO dummies, I'll tell you that," says Lou Guida. "The two of them—sharp as a tack." Guida, the former senior V.P. of Merrill Lynch, and the man who tried to purchase the Eagles with the Newmans, should know. In the last few years, he's been their investment partner on some very profitable deals. Never in the stock market, because if Sandra can't touch it, Sandra doesn't trust it. Instead, they've hit pay dirt in the very risky business of purchasing racehorses. Two of the horses the Newmans put their money on, the father and son horse team of Nihilator and Niatross, turned out to be the greatest pacers in the 157-year history of harness racing. A third, Mack Lobell, is considered by industry publications to be the single greatest trotter. We're talking *thousands* of nose jobs: Nihilator, which they purchased on gut instinct for $100,000, they sold with their fellow investors 14 months later for $19.2 million.

They also own a fifth of Laurel Racetrack in Maryland, a business that, since they purchased it, has profited nicely from the troubles at Garden State, and according to Guida, is now making $8 million a year. And with that nice little sum they got from Leonard Tose, they invested in a ski mountain in Vermont.

SUCCESS, Success, Success, Money, Money, Money. OK, but how did she manage to find time to work, go to school, shop, dress her husband—and still raise a family?

"People make such a big deal out of it," says Sandra. "But I did have live-in help. And Jules was like a cheerleader. 'Do it, Sandra! You always wanted it, Sandra!' And he'd usually cook dinner, because we never wanted the kids to come home from school and have supper with the maid." Just in case, she prepared three of the week's meals in advance every Sunday.

It was always a rule in the Newman household that the family have dinner together every night—no matter what. And it's something Sandra still does—afterward, she and her husband work at adjoining desks in their bedroom.

Their sons (who both had their noses done by Daddy) say that neither parent ever missed a rugby game or a school play. And there were plenty to attend. Jonathan, who is 26 and a lawyer with La Brum & Doak, graduated summa cum laude from Bowdoin College, co-founded a conservative newspaper on campus and started the school's croquet club. David, who's 24, is head of artists and repertoire for a record company in L.A., graduated magna cum laude from Bowdoin, starred in tennis, and performed in musical productions.

"I never, ever felt the lack of her being there," says David. "She's always had an unbelievable knack of doing 2,000 things at once."

Well into her career, Sandra tried desperately to have more children, the one thing she says she wishes could have been different in her life. In bringing up her two sons, she somehow managed to give them the good life that she never had without raising a pair of brats. Though they always knew which parent to go to for a raise in their allowance, they were never allowed to watch TV during the week, and when they turned 16, and their pals at Penn Charter got brand new cars, the Newman kids did not. They had to make honors at Bowdoin before they got a Buick and a Datsun. "I just didn't think it was appropriate," says Sandra, "for a kid to be driving a BMW." Still, she'd let David tool around in her Porsche, and when Jonathan's pet snake got sick, he was taken to the vet in a limo.

Growing up Newman certainly had its moments. Jonathan remembers how mortified he was when his mother sent him off to summer camp—with a set of matching designer luggage. All the other kids had duffel bags.

"That's nothing," says David. "They drove me up to my *bunk* in a Rolls Royce. Was I embarrassed? Big time. In elementary school, I used to make my father drop me off a few blocks away, 'cause it was so uncomfortable pulling up in the Rolls."

"I tried," Sandra sighs. "I even bought a separate wardrobe just for PTA meetings."

"My mother has quite a few sides to her," says David. "She has the princess side that wants to be pampered and taken care of, and then she has the shrewd business woman/career woman side. But either way she has to be *in control* of everything."

He's not just referring to Sandra's compulsiveness: She arranges her scarves and underwear by color, and draws up long checklists every night for the help. He's referring to what he calls his mother's "*Dynasty* fantasy."

"Her main goal in life is to have us all under one roof," says David. "I live in L.A., but she's building me my own suite in the house in Gladwyne. I'd say she brings up my moving back home about 35 times a week. She'd even settle for me moving to New York."

David thinks that what is often perceived as extravagance on Sandra's part is often just her need to be surrounded by her husband and sons. "They're coming out here tomorrow," he says one night on the telephone from L.A. "Now I have an *apartment* here, but my mother calls and tells me she took a room for me at the Beverly Hills Hotel, where they always stay. I said, 'Mom, that's a waste of money.' But again, she goes to major extremes to keep the family together." (Eventually, they compromised: He slept on a cot in their hotel bungalow.)

SANDRA Newman is sitting at a table at the Four Seasons, dressed in a Valentino trimmed in fox. She was in court at 8:30 this morning, but ran home to change "because I didn't want to walk in my court clothes." After lunch she has an appointment with the trustees of one of her scholarship funds; three universities have full scholarships in Sandra's mother's name, and she always insists on meeting the Villanova Law School recipient, to say that they can have it under one condition: that they promise to do the same when they're big-buck lawyers. At 6:30 this morning, before she went to court, she got up, sauteed a brisket and made matzo balls. "David's coming in this weekend," she explains. "I can't send him back to L.A. without my matzo balls."

I ask Sandra Newman if her parents were this way.

"My mother had a wonderful sense of style and elegance. She was also my best friend," says Sandra. Her mother also had a rare kind of cancer for 22 years. During Sandra's first month in law school, she had the operation that ended up being the beginning of the end. She died right after Sandra graduated, at the age of 56.

"This was 15 years ago," says Sandra. "And Jules was doing well by then. But I wish she could have seen what I've done. She was always so worried about my going to law school, though she worked her entire life. She was convinced I was going to ruin my marriage. To the man she warned me not to marry! They ended up having a beautiful relationship, you know. Jules really adored her. When she was sick, he literally carried her around. When I'd be in class, he'd be sitting by her side in the hospital. You know, I think he was to her everything she would have liked in a husband…"

It was the first time she had brought up her father without having been asked.

"My father was," she says slowly, "a very difficult person. I mean, he was not an affectionate person. He was very old-world. I mean, I wish I could tell you more about him, I really do. But I don't think I'll ever know what he thought or felt. It was funny when you asked about the kids and their grade school plays.

Because I remember the time when I was in a ballet recital. My father went to the bathroom and missed me." She pauses. "It was the only thing he ever showed up for."

The plates are cleared and Sandra, who's constantly dieting, passes on dessert. So far, she's admitted that what she'd really like to do—if she could do anything at all—is be a race car driver. (She signed up for lessons but "Jules went bonkers.") And that the only thing she's afraid of is elevators. But then, she divulges something else.

"Jules will tell you," she whispers, "that I spend money like a drunken sailor, and I don't know the value of a dollar. But you know, I use toothpaste until there's nothing left in the tube, I'll yell at poor Jules if he throws it away, and then I'll go out and buy a gown for umpteen thousand dollars. I don't understand it either."

Hmmm. Anything besides elevators?

"Dying," says Sandra. "That's the only other thing. You know, I wouldn't even care if we lost all our money tomorrow. I mean, sure it would be an *adjustment*, but we'd be fine. We'd really be fine. I made drapes in Fort Dix, I could do it again. I mean, we've planned so well, that unless the economy went to hell, it probably wouldn't happen. But if it did? Guess what? I wouldn't shoot myself. Though sometimes I wonder how the world would react to us poor...."

SANDRA has decided that he'll be Rick and she'll be Ilsa and they'll star in their own version of *Casablanca* no matter what the world thinks.

The idea came to her one morning while her husband was at work doing nose jobs and she was at work splitting people up. "I got it," she told Jules when he called her from the operating room, as is his custom between procedures (though he does wait till the patients are asleep). Since they were going to call the new house Casablanca anyway, why not do a family portrait for the great room? She could be Ilsa, he could be Rick, their son David could be Sam, the piano player. And Jonathan could be the French lieutenant, and Jonathan's new wife Nancy could be...oh, she'd figure something out. And the dogs could be in it too, since they're already named Humphrey and Bogart. It is her favorite movie.

"Sandra," said Jules, "you're brilliant."

And so now the top divorce lawyer in town and the top cosmetic surgeon are posing for pictures as Ilsa and Rick—except that Ilsa probably didn't wear a black enamel choker covered with clusters of diamonds.

"Sandy," says Sue Horvitz, the portrait artist, whose mission it is to turn this idea into a 20- by 40-foot canvas to hang in the main room of the house. "Let's show a *little* more leg."

The last project Sue did for the Newmans was a 72- by 44-inch portrait Sandra commissioned for Jules's office—of his wife in, and only in, high heels, tights, and a fur coat, showing not a little bit of leg, but most of it. "See," says Jules, whenever he shows it off, "she's the sexiest divorce lawyer in the country." (He believes that enough to have used part of his wife's anatomy in a recent advertisement. "When you've got the best, why not use the best?" says Jules.)

"Is there lipstick on my teeth?" asks Sandra.

"Don't worry," says Sue. "I can touch that up. Now, let's try to look like you did at the last sitting. Remember how you were looking at him as though he were Humphrey Bogart?"

Sandra stares deep into her husband's eyes, across a table set up like the one at Rick's Cafe, and says smiling through clenched teeth, "Like this?"

"No, no, no," says Sue. "You're looking at him like you've been married forever."

"We have been," says Jules. To think, of all the bar mitzvahs in all the cities in the world, she had to walk into his.

"Think Humphrey Bogart, Sandy," says Sue.

"That's easy for me to do," says Sandra. "Tell him to think Ingrid Bergman."

"Sandra," says Jules, "you're prettier than Ingrid Bergman."

"Oh, Jules."

"Now, *that's* it," says Sue. "Perfect! Just a *little* more leg…"

By Alicia Mundy
March 1992

THE TRANSMOGRIFICATION OF ARLEN SPECTER

n 30 years you can make a lot of enemies, if you work at it. And Arlen Specter is one of the hardest workers anyone knows.

Tonight many of his enemies are gathered inside a small auditorium for an Arlen Specter Open House. It's a cold evening in Center City, but inside the Drake Tower, the temperature's rising. In other days, in other incarnations, Specter might have had this crowd of about 150 constituents, reporters and activists eating out of his hand. Tonight they're eating him alive.

WE BELIEVE ANITA signs are in the front. Chanting erupts with almost every Anita Hill question. And the anger is coming at Specter in waves. Not long into the session, when an elderly man dons his coat, walks down the center aisle, and passes right in front of Specter to leave the room, the senator manages a smile: "I wish *I* could go." But right at the outset, when Specter asked everyone with a question to raise a hand, 28 went up, and now he is committed to staying for 28 questions.

As the questions and hostility mount, his face turns increasingly red. Gravity has not been kind to the 62-year-old former district attorney. His forehead still marks him as patrician, but the once-handsome face is being pulled down. His jowls hang like storage bins, the bags beneath his eyes could hold a change of underwear, and his hair seems to be making the leap from shaggy to unkempt.

"Senator Specter," a nicely dressed matron begins, "I admire you for coming here tonight and explaining your decision on the Judiciary Committee." She probably went to one of Philly's Catholic schools, where they teach girls to try to accommodate. "And I respect your views on the subject." Yep, St. Joe's or Chestnut Hill. "But I was appalled at the way you treated Anita Hill in the hearing."

The first direct blow has been struck, and the crowd applauds and cheers wildly. When the noise stops, a female voice in the back of the room calls out the question that may save Specter's career: "What are you going to do, vote for Stephen Freind?"

"No," says the matron, "no one in their right mind would vote for Stephen Freind." She turns back to Specter, her words still polite, her tone still strained. "But, Senator, I'd like to vote for you, as I have before, because I want you for my senator—not because you're the lesser of two evils."

The crowd thunders back: first the applause, then the foot-stomping, and then the chant—"Shame! Shame! Shame!" The senator stands there and takes it. He looks down at the card he's crumpled in his palm, where he's keeping a running count of the questions asked so far—the only notes he's taking. He searches the crowd for a smile that will not grow fangs and bite him. But on this night, Specter's advance team has not managed to plant even one friendly face. "Shame! Shame! Shame!"

Finally the chant subsides long enough for him to call for a question. "Number six," he calls out, "on the way to 28." The Anita Hill comments keep coming, the most strident focusing on his accusation that Hill committed perjury at the hearing—not the first time in his career that Specter issued a perjury accusation that defies explanation. "Professor Hill's testimony established perjury," he answers, standing his ground, "whether you like it or not."

As the challenges continue, the senator falls back on what has proved to be his most effective explanation—the Nina Defense. "Waah!," he twangs with that Kansas accent that still surprises, "Nina Totenberg says my questioning of Anita Hill was proper." More and more, he's taken to waving the National Public Radio reporter's words like a string of garlic, to ward off vampires.

He will change no minds tonight, but the Nina Defense—one Totenberg herself will have some interesting thoughts on later—allows him to press on. For more than an hour the questions, the chants, the derisive applause continue, until his escape is just about in sight. "Number 27," Specter calls, once again ignoring a demonstrator from the gay rights lobby Act Up who has been heckling him all evening, "on the way to 28."

"Then I'm 27a," says the man from Act Up.

"Waah!," says Specter, who has kept his cool so far, "in your case we all know what the 'a' stands for."

The crowd gasps. Is Frank Rizzo back, and did someone invite him to speak? Is a U.S. senator really calling this man an asshole? "What *does* it stand for?" calls out the man. The stomping and chanting resume. "What *does* it stand for, Senator?"

Again Specter just stands there, this time with a smirk on his face, as the crowd screams wildly. When the din finally subsides, Specter, ignoring number 27a, answers the final two questions and then makes his way through the crowd, through the hall, to the front door, where a car is waiting.

This group may not be representative of the Pennsylvania electorate, or indicative of what will happen when Specter meets Freind in the April 28th primary, but this is Center City, Specter's home turf, scene of his glory days as a young, crusading D.A. In fact, this is the 8th Ward, which is precisely where, some three decades ago, Arlen Specter began his political career—as a Democratic committeeman.

It has been a long, tortured path from earnest liberal to right-wing hatchet man. And never in all his years has Specter stood so alone as he stands now. He is not, however, a normal politician. He has been accused of choosing the politically expedient option at every turn. He has survived the loss of elections for D.A., mayor, senator and governor by learning to play politics deftly and at times viciously. And the smart money is betting he will survive Anita Hill, too—if only because of lightweight opposition. His primary opponent, Freind, is widely dismissed as a one-issue (anti-abortion) candidate. His most likely opponent in the general election, Lieutenant Governor Mark Singel, doesn't even have the support of his own two-time running mate, Governor Casey. "Arlen Specter," Democratic consultant Neil Oxman likes to say, "is the Richard Nixon of Pennsylvania politics. To kill him, you've got to put a stake through his heart."

For all his enemies, including those who cheer during the *JFK* scene where he's labeled a liar, it's hard to escape the conclusion that this man's most formidable enemy—perhaps the only one who can stop him—is Arlen Specter himself.

ARLEN Specter arrived in Philadelphia in 1956 as a liberal democrat. He grew up in Russell, Kansas, a town with about 6,000 folks, one of whom was Robert Dole, now the Senate GOP leader. The perfect debater, Specter—who declined to be interviewed for this story—trundled off to Yale Law School, where, to no one's surprise, he excelled. Armed with credentials and a few connections, he landed a job at the prestigious Philadelphia firm of Dechert Price & Rhoads.

Almost from the beginning, he was telling people he wanted to be a U.S. senator. Ambitious? If Cassius had a lean and hungry look, Arlen was positively anorexic. In 1959 he took a job as an assistant prosecutor in James Crumlish's district attorney's office, where he advanced rapidly, where he began to lay the foundation for his political career, and where his legend began to grow. The first person he rolled over was his mentor, Crumlish, who quickly and memorably labeled Specter "a calculating calculator."

By 1965, the assistant prosecutor had already made himself a national figure. First he got to know Attorney General Robert Kennedy (who had his sights set on Jimmy Hoffa), by taking on the Teamsters in a well-publicized racketeering case. When Specter won convictions for all six defendants, he got some great press, and name recognition in Camelot—which soon paid off with a junior counsel spot on the Warren Commission. By the end, Specter *was* the Warren Commission, the proud papa of the single-bullet theory, that notorious feature of physics that would have awed Einstein. What was Specter thinking?

Those who give him the benefit of the doubt believe he seized upon the improbable theory to try to soothe a wounded country. It took almost 30 years for Oliver Stone and the conspiracy theorists to catch up with him. Meanwhile, Specter's political career was launched by the single bullet and the publicity it engendered. He was known, according to a former *Inquirer* editor, for calling reporters at night to discuss the commission: "He was collegial, confidential, off-the-record."

Back then, in 1965, Specter wanted to run for D.A. as a Democrat. He was supposed to replace his mentor Crumlish, who was ready to step aside, but then Crumlish changed his mind and decided to run again. Put off by his own party, Specter turned to GOP boss Bill Meehan, who set him up as the Republican candidate—against Crumlish. And Specter won. What people remember about the election isn't the numbers or the endorsements. It's that Specter remained a registered Democrat until *after* he won.

Right from the start, he cut a fierce, independent, dynamic figure. He held a lot of press conferences, and his office—especially his even fiercer first assistant, Richard Sprague—won a lot of high-profile cases. And, in stark contrast to a traditional D.A., he quickly earned a well-deserved reputation for attracting highly competent lawyers regardless of political affiliation. (The city's top two Democrats today, Mayor Ed Rendell and D.A. Lynne Abraham, were Specter hires.)

The reviews were so good that after only two years, Specter decided to challenge the incumbent mayor, Jim Tate, in a race that still resonates. For years the lazy, lethargic Democratic machine had tolerated, even encouraged, incompetence and corruption throughout City Hall. The result was a 1967 race that pitted a man who couldn't win—the aging mayor—against a man who couldn't lose—the dashing D.A. But Tate was not a fool. He understood that two issues mattered most—keeping hard-nosed folk hero Frank Rizzo as police commissioner, and supporting aid to the city's massive parochial school system. Tate promised both. Specter, troubled by the constitutional pitfalls of funding religious schools, not wanting to be backed into a corner on future appointments—even though he said privately he had no intention of replacing his friend Rizzo—took a stand, on principle. He also lost—by just 11,000 votes. "It was," says attorney Gregory Harvey, a Democratic committeeman, "the last election in which he took a stand on principle."

When Specter ran for reelection as D.A. in 1969, he took no chances and no prisoners. He ran on a ticket with popular local jock Tom Gola, and their billboards are still considered the finest political ads the city has seen: THEY'RE YOUNGER. THEY'RE TOUGHER. AND NOBODY OWNS THEM.

It's the image Specter's friends prefer to remember. "I still get goose pimples when I think about it," says Elliott Curson, the ad man who wrote the slogan with political consultant David Garth. "That's what Arlen represented to all of us."

But something happened just before the election that would forever change the way some people saw Specter. To those who remember and were offended by it, this topped even Specter's questioning of Anita Hill for pure ruthlessness. Two weeks before the election, Specter obtained grand jury indictments of two close Tate associates. The grand jury presentment, which grew out of a Specter investigation of the then-incomplete Centre Square development, also called for the resignation of Tate's Redevelopment Authority chairman, sharply rebuked the lead developer, who happened to be one of Tate's leading fund-raisers—and dropped the names of a lot of other people close to Tate.

"It's difficult to understand why a man would stoop this low," said one of those indicted, a lawyer who, like most of those singled out, happened to be a leading figure in the city's Jewish community. "I can only observe that this is October 21st, and Election Day is November 4th." Gil Stein, a former assistant prosecutor who spearheaded the Centre Square investigation, says the charges were well-founded, and the timing of the indictments—two weeks before the election—coincidental.

On Election Day, the crusading, corruption-hunting D.A. easily defeated attorney David Berger. Not long thereafter, the charges against Tate's friends disappeared. The indicted lawyer went on to have an outstanding career, but the memory lingered—especially within the Jewish community. Eventually, however, Specter became a senator and established a strongly pro-Israel voting record, and a new generation of local Jewish leaders emerged. "Before Specter got elected to the Senate," says a former congressman, "he wasn't well accepted by the Philadelphia Jewish community. Then he took the right position on Jewish affairs, and now he's well supported."

"You know, being D.A. is a mixed bag," says Ed Rosen, a former president of the Jewish Federation and a longtime Specter friend. "You have the key to the jail house, but you don't make a lot of friends when you indict people. I'm sure there are some people who remember the bad old days and still bear a grudge. Listen, the particular leader [indicted] at that time happens to be a friend of mine for whom I have great respect. I have always felt badly about that."

For Philadelphians, Specter's questioning of Anita Hill may have triggered memories of the early '70s, when Specter first displayed his unique uses of perjury law. He once leveled the charge against two cops who'd been convicted of extorting a numbers runner and then were summoned to a political-corruption grand jury. During their testimony, for which both cops were given immunity, they told the grand jury that they were innocent of the extortion accusation. It was for that protestation of innocence—at a time when their cases were under appeal—that Specter accused them of perjury.

"Specter made a *big* case and a *big* announcement and a *big* grand jury, and then farted," says attorney A. Charles Peruto Sr., who defended both policemen. "He says he knows perjury when he sees it, but he wouldn't know a case of dog-bite if the dog was still attached to his leg when he got to court."

In a similar case in December 1973, Specter's office granted a Democratic politico immunity to testify before a political-corruption grand jury after he'd been cleared in court of running a smuggling ring. Specter then accused the unfortunate politico of perjury, because he first testified that he understood the terms of his immunity agreement and then said—*outside* the grand jury—that he *didn't* understand the agreement. "It was outrageous," says a former assistant prosecutor, "to fall back on such a shoddy perjury rap. It wasn't anything like perjury. The guy said two different things to two different people because he didn't understand what his lawyer had signed for him. It was crazy."

Midway through his second term, Specter seemed to lose his fire. In 1971 he began another run for mayor, but then backed down. He earned a reputation for humiliating his subordinates—although many of those who worked for him remain intensely loyal. "Arlen wasn't a boss you'd want to have a drink with," says former assistant prosecutor Ed Rendell, "but the staff respected his intelligence and his competence. He made us feel like heroes. Every day I went to work, I felt like it was the D.A. against the forces of evil."

Specter became embroiled in some bitter, long-running feuds with the *Philadelphia Inquirer*, which at one point started running a daily note on its editorial page demanding that Specter make public a certain file the paper wanted for an investigation. In 1973 the *Inquirer* computer-analyzed Specter's performance and concluded that despite his press-conference hype, he had "posted one of the poorest conviction rates in the nation."

In the months leading up to the '73 election for D.A., Specter—echoing his erstwhile mentor, Crumlish—said first that he would not run again, and then changed his mind. His Democratic opponent was a former assistant prosecutor, Emmett Fitzpatrick—a sacrifice, everyone agreed. But Watergate had tarnished many GOP candidates across the country, and Specter had just been the subject of ridicule and rumor on the op-ed page of the *Inquirer*. There was also, says Fitzpatrick, the problem of Specter's personality. In a shocker, Fitzpatrick won. "I didn't beat Arlen," he says. "I couldn't. He beat himself."

Specter went back to Dechert Price, where he made a lot of money and continued to hone his Harold Stassen imitation. He went on to lose the 1976 Senate primary to John Heinz, and the 1978 gubernatorial primary to Dick Thornburgh. At that point he all but retired from politics, moving to Atlantic City in 1979 to open a satellite Dechert office. "The thing about Arlen," says one of his former Dechert partners, "is that even though he's all of the things people say—he's obviously an opportunist, and he's calculating and pragmatic to the extreme—he also has a great deal of charm and humor. Occasionally he comes back to our firm to some sort of dinner, and when he stands up and talks, he says things that are extremely funny and sometimes self-deprecating, and he gets a lot of laughs. The people who worked with Arlen while he was here came to feel he was extraordinarily bright, and an extraordinarily quick study. But I think he was probably a little bored by private practice. He really likes action."

Deciding to take one last shot, Specter ran in the 1980 Republican primary for retiring Senator Richard Schweiker's seat. He ran even though Heinz, Thornburgh and the Philadelphia GOP all endorsed his opponent, Delaware County businessman Bud Haabestad. If only because his frequent defeats had bought him name recognition, Specter won. In the general election he beat another longtime loser: Pete Flaherty, the former mayor of Pittsburgh.

Thus in 1980, the year of the Reagan landslide, Specter became the junior Republican senator from Pennsylvania. But his odd, arm's-length relationship with his party—which has not rushed to embrace him in his post-Anita hour of need—had already been established: "I felt strongly that I had been given short shrift by the Republican Party," Specter told Richard Fenno Jr., a University of Rochester political science professor who wrote a book about Specter's first Senate term. "I was once a Democrat, as you know. And the [local] party was very willing to use that fact, to use my connections in liberal circles, in the Jewish community, in the black community, and let me run for mayor of Philadelphia. They were willing to use me to pull all those groups in. But when it came to the choice plums, they reserved them for [others]."

Specter also told Fenno, "I didn't come in on Ronald Reagan's coattails. Our election patterns were completely different. I carried Philadelphia; he lost Philadelphia. He carried Pittsburgh; I lost Pittsburgh.... I don't feel I owe Reagan anything."

Twelve years later, few Republicans feel they owe Specter something.

———

THE most peculiar aspect of Specter's Anita Hill debacle was its timing. It followed, almost instantaneously, what may have been the zenith of the man's time in the Senate.

Although widely considered one of Congress' most brilliant members, Specter has no major legislative accomplishments to boast, and it has taken him most of his second term to overcome the damage done by a spate of silly, camera-grabbing hearings he held during his first term. But toward the end of the pre-Anita phase of the Clarence Thomas hearings, Specter was roundly congratulated for his questioning. However flawed the confirmation process, for one brief moment he was working with his president, trying on the role of elder statesman. "He's a very able guy," says Philip Kalodner, a longtime Specter watcher who has been part of Democratic administrations in both Philadelphia and Harrisburg since the mid '60s. "None of his critics have ever suggested any limitations on his ability. The criticism is that somebody with that ability should do more with it."

If the lasting image of Specter as D.A. is of an opportunist, the dominant reputation he seems to have forged in the Senate is that of a fence-sitter. Even his friends have noticed. "He's *very* cautious," says Utah Senator Orrin Hatch, who has nothing but praise for Specter. "And independent. Did I mention that he is independent?"

Specter's caution showed in July 1989, when the Judiciary Committee was considering a ban on the sale of assault rifles. The debate raged in Congress—with the troops from the National Rifle Association in full formation—shortly after a crazed Vietnam veteran killed five children in a California school yard. The committee members had been postponing the vote, and it was becoming obvious that they might tie, with Specter—not for the first time—the lone undecided.

On the day the committee finally voted, it was forced to await the arrival of Senators Specter and Patrick Leahy, who were in another chamber attending hearings on the impeachment of a federal judge. When Leahy showed up, he tipped the pending count to 7–6 in favor of banning the guns. A tying vote by Specter would kill the ban in committee; a "yes" would set him squarely against the NRA, which has contributed thousands of dollars to his campaigns. Specter finally walked in and noted the other hearing apologetically—without explaining how Leahy had made it on time—just as the rifle vote went around the table.

And then committee chairman Joe Biden asked for Specter's vote. "Specter was stunned," says a former Judiciary Committee staffer. "I think he thought he had timed it so he would arrive after the vote. But his staff screwed up. He got there too soon. When he walked in and Biden asked him for his vote, he was just shocked." Specter requested extra time. Biden said no. Specter abstained.

WHEN Specter first arrived in Washington in 1980, he chose to keep a low profile. This was in dramatic contrast to his press-happy days as D.A., when his buddy Bill Meehan was moved to tell the *Inquirer*, "Someone spills a can of beans, Arlen'll issue a statement." After a couple of years, however, Specter reverted to form. He told Professor Fenno in 1982, "I'm groping to find a major, substantial issue that could become the subject of an investigation. I want to find something that would command attention."

The grope continued for three years. As chairman of the Senate Subcommittee on Juvenile Justice, Specter held a bizarre series of hearings that convinced some people he was auditioning to be a talk-show host. There were hearings on Nazi war criminal Dr. Josef Mengele—ostensibly because Mengele had conducted experiments on children. And there were hearings on pornography, during which porn queen Linda Lovelace testified that a boyfriend had forced her into her career at gunpoint. Other porn stars said they enjoyed their work: "I am the love toy," Veronica Vera told the committee, "the object of your desires, exposed and vulnerable. Picture yourself tying the ropes, keeping me as your prisoner, to be taken whenever you want, always open to...should I go on?"

"You certainly may," said Chairman Specter.

Specter has also gained a reputation for attempting to upstage his colleagues—especially when the cameras are running. In 1988, for instance, Congressman

Tom Foglietta and John Heinz planned a workers' appreciation award for the Naval Yard, and arranged a press conference. But Specter showed up a day early, got the glory, and, despite security restrictions on press around the base, got the Navy commander to let the media follow him around. The incident was an eerie replay of a similar Specter maneuver at the Naval Yard in 1985. That time Foglietta had been planning a press conference for weeks—to denounce a previous attempt to shut down the yard—only to have Specter call a last-minute conference one hour before Foglietta was due to speak.

Washington hasn't made Specter any more desirable as a boss. One former staffer says Specter used to insist that aides escorting him from his office in the Hart Building to the adjacent Dirksen Building plot the route in advance. Since the floors in the two buildings don't meet, Specter's aides were required to make sure that when the senator got off the elevator, he was half a flight *up* from the floor he wanted, not half a flight down—because it's quicker to walk *down* stairs. "We used to get reamed out in staff meetings if we messed up," says the former staff member. Specter is also known as the senator whose own aides refused to let him stay in their homes while his apartment was being redecorated.

The incidents sound petty, but Specter's personality quirks may have undermined his effectiveness. On Capitol Hill, getting work done means getting along. When Specter joined the Senate, he was given a couple of prestigious committee appointments—Appropriations and Judiciary. He was a moderate Republican who was expected to find allies among Democrats. He had everything going for him—except that he is Arlen Specter. He has few friends in the Senate, though a supporter insists he's close to Dole. "Arlen *who*?" laughs a Dole staffer. "Arlen Specter," says a Democratic senator, "is the single most obnoxious man in the Senate."

His isolation has at times worked to the detriment of Philadelphia. He maintains a home here, in East Falls, with his wife Joan, the City Councilwoman (one of their two sons, Shanin, is an adviser in Specter's campaign), but he has been criticized for not doing enough to help his city. "You want to talk about the senator from Philadelphia?" asks a staffer on the Appropriations Committee. "Sure, I'll talk about Frank Lautenberg." The guy who's done the most for Philadelphia—apart from the late John Heinz, says the Appropriations staffer—is Lautenberg, the junior senator from New Jersey: "Lautenberg sees we get dredging funds for the Delaware, SEPTA money, and he's worked for the Naval Yard—*with* the rest of Congress."

A former Heinz aide agrees: "Even with Specter on Appropriations, it was the senior players from the rest of the delegation—McDade, Murtha, Gray—who made the difference."

Two years ago, then-Congressman William Gray III introduced a bill intended to secure dedicated funding for SEPTA. "It was the last thing Gray did," says Gray's former chief of staff, J. Whyatt Mondesire. "And Specter blocked it. He was siding with the fat cats who didn't want to give more money to SEPTA." Specter eventually backed down, and SEPTA got the funding.

It's possible, though, that Specter's abrasive personality keeps him from getting credit he deserves. "He fights like a dog for some of that federal stuff," says a Democratic pol who has held positions in both city and state administrations. "I'm not ready to vote for Arlen Specter—don't misunderstand me—and I'm not wild about what he did in the [Thomas] hearing, and I think he's done a lot of opportunistic things, but it's been 12 years that he's been in the Senate, and he's always been ready to get things done for the city. I think I've mellowed on Arlen a bit. Sometimes I temper my rage."

SPECTER'S supporters tend to praise the same aspects of his record:

• His independence. In his book, Professor Fenno relates an incident where the Reagan administration was putting heavy pressure on Specter—including threatening not to raise money for him—to vote for the MX missile. Specter wound up voting in favor of the MX, but announced he would turn down the president's campaign support to prove he hadn't caved in. "I just died when I heard that," Specter's campaign manager told Fenno. "It cost us a million dollars."

• His voting record on Israel, civil rights, and women's issues. "He's got a 96 percent record on our issues," says an official at Planned Parenthood. "He has fought the gag rule and supported funding for poor women's abortions in D.C."

• His ability to ask questions. When conservative William Bradford Reynolds was nominated to be associate attorney general in 1985, Specter led the charge. At the confirmation hearings, the former D.A. used a memo the nominee had written to undercut Reynolds' own testimony. "As usual," says Nina Totenberg, the NPR correspondent, "Specter read all of Reynolds' handwritten comments and nailed him for misleading the committee."

One of Specter's best-known performances came during Robert Bork's doomed Supreme Court confirmation hearings in 1987. *The New York Times* called Specter's interrogation "brilliant." "There are some times when I regard him in awe," says Senator Alan Simpson. "He has an extraordinary mind. That morning in the Bork hearings should have been taped for a debate on constitutional law."

Not surprisingly, Bork wasn't as impressed. "I spent almost seven hours all told with Senator Specter, at the hearings and in his offices, discussing constitutional law," Bork wrote in his book, *The Tempting of America.* "Because I was, out of necessity, patient with him, a lot of people not versed in constitutional law got the impression that this was a serious constitutional discussion."

Specter cast the vote that sank Bork. It was a vote that made him a hero to a lot of people who now can't believe what he did to Anita Hill. "I think history will judge that Arlen made the most important decision of his career for the court, when he decided against Bork," says Mark Gitenstein, former chief counsel to the Judiciary Committee. "I think it was more important than voting for Thomas. Specter saw Bork as dangerous because his views were so extreme." Of course, Specter's vote infuriated conservatives.

On a warm October day last fall, Specter may have seen an opportunity to make amends. The prosecutorial zeal with which Specter attacked Hill, especially his perjury accusation, may have stunned people across the nation—but not everyone in Philadelphia. "When I saw him go after that woman, and I saw that expression on his face and heard the tone in his voice, it all came back to me," says a woman who worked in Specter's D.A. office. "That was the real him. He's a cold, intelligent, honest beast."

Those sympathetic to Specter say he was a trained prosecutor given a job to do. Says Orrin Hatch, the Judiciary Committee member who waved his copy of *The Exorcist* at Hill, "He felt it was a terrific honor, a recognition of his skills, a recognition of the respect [of his peers]."

But why did he perform the job so aggressively? Was the exhibition simply an attempt to mend fences with conservatives for his primary? "Don't be ridiculous," says Mayor Rendell. "Stephen Freind was never a threat to him. Obviously, he did it because he thought it was the right thing to do."

"Think of what was at stake," says Bruce Kauffman, the former state Supreme Court justice and longtime GOP fund-raiser. "You had a man's life at stake. More importantly, you had a presidential nomination to the Supreme Court of the United States. You don't handle a situation as explosive as that with white gloves. He was there to get Clarence Thomas confirmed, and he did it. Whether you like it or not, he did a fabulous job at the hearings. I think a lot of people got confused, particularly some women. They have equated Arlen's questioning with an anti-women's rights attitude. Arlen has an outstanding record on women's rights."

"That he should be the whipping boy for women now," says Philadelphia businessman Ed Rosen, one of Specter's closest friends, "is an exquisite irony. His position has been so caring for women's rights. He was way ahead of his time. I don't think he knew the kind of reaction he was going to get, and possibly he got a little carried away in his zeal, but he was given an assignment."

For Specter, damage control has not been easy. He suddenly found himself rounding up moderate GOP women in Washington and Pennsylvania to come to his aid. Elsie Hillman, the grande dame of Pennsylvania Republicans, arranged a gathering for him in Pittsburgh. After more than an hour at a similar meeting in Harrisburg, says one participant, the women present began to feel they were getting through to him: "He realized he couldn't keep intellectualizing what he'd done with Hill. He'd attacked her and in a way attacked all of us. I think he understands that now. But he can't apologize, because he doesn't know how."

Wherever he speaks these days, Specter pulls out the Nina Defense. Totenberg, however, says she was surprised to learn she had become a political talisman for Specter: "I said his questioning was proper, which it was. But his conclusion was political. And I also said he went too far. There's not a reputable prosecutor anywhere who would bring a perjury charge on that."

Specter tried a conciliatory approach at a meeting last November at Philadelphia's Har Zion synagogue. "He admitted he hadn't understood the depths of feelings," says Evelyn Bodek Rosen, an English professor at the Community College of Philadelphia who is married to Ed Rosen. "He was willing to listen to the feelings, and listen to the women. By the time the meeting was over, many of the people weren't hostile anymore."

SPECTER once again got caught in the bizarre cross fire of Anita Hill and the Magic Bullet at a January open house in Germantown. The conspiracy theorists in the back were passing out diagrams of the bullet's path—the final victim being, of course, Specter. And the crowd broke into sustained, rhythmical applause when someone criticized Specter's perjury accusation. "Now, how many of you here," a smiling Specter asked when the applause faded, "take the other side of that issue?" An elderly man and his wife applauded. Then another couple across the room joined in. Specter's smile faded.

Nonetheless, it seems likely that Specter can count on his core constituents, the pro-choice moderates, to back him against Freind. "We'll fight for Arlen," says one Planned Parenthood leader, "but if he loses, Singel's our candidate. We have to hold something back, in case Arlen loses, to help the Democrats."

But even if Specter survives once again, it seems likely the Anita Hill episode will be seen as the crowning moment of a career built on political expediency. The charge is one even Specter's friends have trouble rejecting outright.

"To say that Arlen is doing what is politically expedient," says Ed Rosen, "is to say that Arlen is a politician."

"If you really think about it," says Bruce Kauffman, "he should be congratulated for his ability to remain open-minded. Here's a public servant who listens carefully to the public and is sufficiently secure intellectually to be able to change his views from time to time."

Others see the senator's open mind differently. Elliott Curson—the consultant who coauthored the "younger, tougher, nobody owns them" slogan—has been approached to work for Stephen Freind. Curson says he hasn't signed on, but he is willing to suggest a new slogan, one written for Freind but once again capturing Specter:

VOTE FOR FRIEND. YOU KNOW WHERE HE STANDS.

By Devin Leonard
December 1993

PRESUMED INNOCENT

n a rainy night in New York City, nearly three dozen people have slogged through the puddles, climbed four flights of stairs and paid $6 to get into a West Village loft and watch a grainy video of a handcuffed man speaking from behind a thick Plexiglas barrier in Huntingdon State Prison near Altoona, Pennsylvania. A handsome 39-year-old with an engaging grin and waist-length dreadlocks that dangle from his head like dark vines, the unrepentant death-row inmate asserts that he's behind bars because of his revolutionary beliefs. "I'm fighting my conviction, fighting the sentence, fighting for my life," says Mumia Abu-Jamal, a former WHYY-FM reporter convicted in 1982 of the murder of a Philadelphia cop. "Yes, I am a political prisoner."

After the amateurish video, which was shot in 1990 and lasts only 13 minutes, the host, Kate Holum of Queer Women and Men United in Support of Political Prisoners, pleads for more cash from her audience of aging radicals and their bright-eyed young followers. "A death warrant can be signed at any time," Holum warns. "So can people, like, pass the cans around?" Or perhaps they would be willing to spend $15 for one of the black Mumia Abu-Jamal T-shirts being modeled by Holum, a young woman with the milky skin, earnest blue eyes and guileless voice of a Midwestern farm girl.

The shirt goes perfectly with Holum's black jeans, black sneakers and black baseball cap.

The can is passed—even though you'd think many of these Queer Women and Men would think twice about supporting a man who's openly opposed to homosexuality. In fact, Holum reads a letter in which Jamal salutes the radical zeal of her organization, but says he's a follower of another radical—MOVE founder John Africa, who preached that the "male-female hookup" is the natural way to go. "We had a lot of discussions about that in our group," Holum admits with a pained expression. But she asserts that Jamal's sexual philosophy is outweighed by his credentials as a black revolutionary—and his presumed innocence. "His case points out the nature of this vicious society," she says. "He is part of a struggle that has pushed along all other struggles. The most progressive times have followed the struggle in the black community—women's liberation, gay rights. His death would be a blow to us all, and that's why we need to stand by him." By the end of Holum's speech, people are cheering and the money cans are stuffed with bills.

It is a common event these days—and not just among fringe groups. Eleven years after his conviction for killing police officer Daniel Faulkner, Jamal is rapidly gaining currency around the world as America's political prisoner, the first to face execution since Ethel and Julius Rosenberg and a man whose mistreatment symbolizes something dark and evil in this country. Once a brilliant journalist with a golden tongue, Jamal has helped legitimize his own cause with radio commentaries taped on death row and articles published in the *Yale Law Review* and *The Nation* in which he says he's been a government target ever since he was a teenage Black Panther in West Philadelphia. And he has found many believers. Dr. Benjamin Chavis, executive director of the National Association for the Advancement of Colored People, spoke out about Jamal's imprisonment at an international black issues conference held earlier this year in Africa. Leonard Weinglass, the prominent attorney and activist who assisted William Kuntsler in the legendary Chicago Seven trial, signed on last year to handle Jamal's appeal. "We are in a race against time," Weinglass wrote in the *Philadelphia Tribune*, "to save this innocent and eloquent spokesman of the African-American community."

Even police officers have rallied behind Jamal. Ronald Hampton, director of the 35,000-member National Black Police Association, has spoken at a number of the "Free Mumia" rallies that are now held routinely from Hawaii to San Francisco to Germany to solicit funds for a new investigation planned by Weinglass. So far, supporters say, nearly $70,000 has been raised—with roughly one-third of that coming from Germany, where almost 2,000 admirers took to the streets last year to protest when then-President George Bush paid a visit.

Perhaps predictably, Jamal is now finding support in Hollywood. Actors Whoopi Goldberg, Ed Asner and Mike Farrell have all joined the cause. The curious thing is that in the 11 years since Daniel Faulkner died, Mumia Abu-Jamal has offered little, if any, reason to doubt that he executed the policeman with a cold-blooded shot between the eyes.

ON THE radio, there was something about Jamal's voice that grabbed people. When his sister Lydia used to walk through North Philadelphia, the neighborhood girls would stop her and say, "Oh, that *voice*! What's he *like?*"

He had a similar effect on executives at WUHY-FM, the city's National Public Radio affiliate, which has since changed its call letters to WHYY. "Anybody who heard Mumia's voice on the radio was transfixed," says the station's former news director, Nick Peters, who hired Jamal in 1979. "He had one of the greatest voices I've ever heard." Bill Siemering, WUHY's station manager at the time, was convinced Jamal had a brilliant future. "I found him to be a superb reporter," Siemering says now. "He was very gifted. He could have been an anchor at NPR."

Born Wesley Cooke, Jamal grew up at 7th and Wallace in the Spring Garden Street projects. The other kids thought he was a nerd, always asking questions and reading books about stuff outside their world of low-rise apartments and cement playgrounds. Even his own brothers and sisters weren't sure what to make of him. "We were just project kids," says Lydia Wallace. "We weren't interested in what was outside of the projects."

But Wesley Cooke was. He became a revolutionary, he has written, at age 13, when he was kicked in the face by a police officer after he and a group of friends disrupted a 1968 George Wallace for President rally. "I was always grateful to that cop," he wrote. "He kicked me straight into the Black Panther Party."

Jamal wrote for the Panther newspaper, fed children at a Panther soup kitchen in North Philadelphia and was soon named the local chapter's minister of information. In January 1970, Jamal made the front page of the *Inquirer* for the first time, in an article about police attacks on local Panthers. "Black people," he was quoted as saying, "are facing the reality that the Black Panther Party has been facing: Political power grows out of the barrel of a gun." Later that year, he was kicked out of Benjamin Franklin High School for organizing a series of unsuccessful demonstrations seeking to change the school's name to Malcolm X High. Then he left the party and changed his own name to Mumia Abu-Jamal, an African name that he told his family meant "prince." In the years that followed, he had little to say about the Panthers. But on death row, he would write scornfully of how Bobby Seale and Eldridge Cleaver had rejected the party and sold out.

After graduating from Overbrook High School, Jamal went off to study broadcast journalism at Goddard College in Vermont. He ran out of money before finishing his final year, but returned to Philadelphia and made a quick splash with commentaries on black issues for Temple University's WRTI-FM. After that he landed paying jobs at WHAT, WCAU-FM, WPEN, and WDAS. In 1979, he won a prestigious position on WUHY-FM's *91 Report*, the local version of NPR's *All Things Considered*.

There was little question that he was headed for stardom. Former news director Peters remembers network officials in Washington snickering when he told them he was sending the new guy with the African name to cover the striking police officers parading around City Hall, but Jamal came back with a tape that made them believers. "Three minutes after they heard it," says Peters, "they went wild and said, 'Who *is* that?'"

Jamal won awards in 1979 for a piece on how a group of black men in a North Philly pool hall viewed Pope John Paul II's visit to Philadelphia. Jamal found and conveyed something profoundly disturbing in the distance these men felt from the televised hoopla. And station officials say they are still haunted by his interviews with public housing residents caught in the crossfire of a drug war. More awards followed, and Jamal was elected president of the Philadelphia chapter of the Association of Black Journalists. In 1981, *Philadelphia* magazine praised both Jamal and fellow WUHY reporter America Rodriguez: "Their eloquent, often passionate, and always insightful interviews bring a special dimension to radio reporting."

Later, however, there were instances in which Jamal may have brought too much passion to his reporting. During the trial of nine MOVE members who were convicted of killing police officer James J. Ramp in the 1978 Powelton Village shootout, Jamal began to identify with the radical group. While many journalists saw MOVE as a nihilistic cult that provoked both that incident and the infamous 1985 bomb-dropping, Jamal came to embrace the members' self-images as victims of a repressive government plot. "This man," says Pam Africa, a MOVE member and now leader of the Philadelphia-based Concerned Family and Friends of Mumia Abu-Jamal, "came out of his reporter role and turned into something else."

One day when she was tired during a MOVE trial, Africa says Jamal took over for her at the microphone outside City Hall to solicit donations for the group. "Some of his colleagues came down," says Africa, "and they were looking at him like 'Mumia done flipped.'" Then there was the hot summer day outside the courthouse when Africa and other members took a break from protesting another MOVE trial to cool off in a nearby fountain. "I happened to turn around," she says, "and look who was jumping around in the fountain with his pants rolled up, but Mumia. I mean, he was so *real.*"

At the time, WUHY officials were unaware of these incidents, but they began to have problems with Jamal. While they'd always known he had a formidable ego, they began to see him as a cultlike figure of his own creation who was surrounded by admirers, many of them women. MOVE, meanwhile, had become his obsession, the only thing he was interested in covering. "He became an advocate," says Peters. "It wasn't even advocacy journalism. It was pure advocacy." For a time, the station simply balanced Jamal's MOVE stories for him. But the situation kept getting worse—Peters says he was startled one day in 1981 to hear Jamal's unmistakable baritone saluting Lucien Blackwell in a radio campaign ad. Peters collared Jamal and told him he could be fired for lending his voice to politicians.

Jamal apologized and kept his job. But the following March, he disappeared for two days. On the third day, he walked into Peters' office and coolly announced, "I'm gone." Jamal typed up a quick resignation letter and strolled out. When he failed to win a full-time job at WDAS, Jamal claimed it was because his probing accounts of "the MOVE reality" were too much for the corporate powers. "I'm probably thought of, and rightly so, as a troublemaker," he told *Community*, a now-defunct Center City weekly. "Someone who raises his voice, someone who doesn't buy what he's told."

By the time Daniel Faulkner was shot, Jamal was driving a cab and freelancing part-time for WDAS. News of the shooting shocked Peters. But Peters couldn't help wondering if Jamal had become so absorbed in some interior drama that he might have shot the cop to make a political statement. "I don't know," says Peters, now vice president of operations for Medialink, a New York City company. "But my reaction was that that was not out of the realm of possibility in the strange mosaic that was and is this guy."

JUST BEFORE midnight on December 9, 1981, five hours before his death, Daniel Faulkner said goodbye to his wife, Maureen, in their Southwest Philadelphia rowhouse and headed off into the cold, windy darkness.

Only 25 years old, Faulkner was already a seasoned cop, a decorated five-year veteran the rookies looked up to. He and his partner, Officer Garry Bell, had made names for themselves in Center City's 6th District as a wagon team assisting other cops with their arrests and by making more than a few of their own. Then manpower problems took their wagon off the street and split up the two cops, who were so tight they shared a house in Avalon each summer. Faulkner was assigned to a squad car by himself; Bell got a foot patrol on Market Street.

Bell was walking the beat at 3:50 that morning when he heard Faulkner radio for backup from 13th and Locust, a dingy corner frequented by drug dealers and prostitutes who did business outside the topless bars. "He sounded real calm and casual, like he had it all under control," Bell says.

But then Bell's radio crackled with reports of an officer shot at 13th and Locust. He charged down 13th Street only to see a police wagon fly by carrying Faulkner to Thomas Jefferson Hospital. As Bell flagged a taxi, it never occurred to him that his partner might be hurt badly—until a grim-faced surgeon cautioned him outside the emergency room not to go any farther. Bell ignored him. "I saw him lying there," he says. "I saw all the blood and I couldn't even recognize him, because he'd been shot in the face." Minutes later, more cops burst through the entrance carrying the alleged gunman, a dreadlocked man in an army jacket who was bleeding from a bullet wound in the chest.

When Jamal's sister Lydia arrived, she found her brother handcuffed, his face wrapped in bloody bandages. Suffering from delirium, he was in critical condition but was refusing surgery. He whispered to his sister that the police had beaten him and would try to kill him on the operating table. He also told her, she says, "I didn't shoot the cop." At the urging of his sister and his wife, Marilyn, Jamal eventually allowed doctors to operate and remove the bullet.

Even then, the police were certain they had their man. By dawn, the department was feeding the following story to the news media: Officer Faulkner had been driving down Locust Street when he saw a blue Volkswagen headed the wrong way on 13th Street. The driver was William Cooke, a 25-year-old street vendor and Jamal's brother. After Faulkner stopped his car and attempted to search him, Cooke punched Faulkner in the face. As the two men started fighting, Jamal emerged from the darkness of a parking lot across the street with a .38-caliber pistol. He shot Faulkner in the back, spinning the cop around to face him. Faulkner squeezed off a shot to Jamal's chest before tumbling over on his back. Standing over Faulkner's body, the journalist shot him four more times, including once between the eyes. Then he sat down on the curb and awaited the police, his gun lying nearby on the pavement.

Months later, after Jamal had filed a police-brutality complaint, Garry Bell and several other officers added to their story. They suddenly remembered that while he was awaiting surgery, Jamal had blurted out a confession: "Yeah, I shot the motherfucker and I hope he dies!" For some reason, they had forgotten to mention this on the night of the murder.

THE DUBIOUS confession further encouraged friends of Jamal who were already disinclined to believe a police department well known for its poor relations with Philadelphia's black community. A committee was formed to raise money for his defense. State Representative David Richardson and then-state Senator T. Milton Street testified on Jamal's behalf at a bail hearing. Attorney Anthony E. Jackson, who had defended MOVE members and served as director of the Public Interest Law Center's police abuse project, signed on as Jamal's court-appointed attorney. Jackson quickly discovered that Jamal had his own plans. "It became obvious," he says, "that it wasn't going to be my show."

Instead of simply mounting a defense against the first-degree murder charge, Jamal seemed more intent on using the trial as a political forum. Although he was facing the death penalty, he decided that rather than using Jackson, he would prefer to represent himself with the assistance of Vincent Leaphart, better known as John Africa, the elusive founder of MOVE. Though not a lawyer, Africa had represented himself the year before in a federal trial and managed to get himself acquitted of charges that he had stockpiled guns and bombs in Powelton Village. Still, the decision prompted some members of the Mumia Abu-Jamal Defense Committee to resign in disgust.

Jamal responded in a scathing letter to his supporters in May 1982. "I am taking my direction from John Africa, a committed, wise, dedicated revolutionary—not Marx, Engels, or Mao Tse-Tung," he wrote. "So, [if] any of you have a problem with

MOVE, kindly move out of the way." Jamal also refused help from his colleagues in the local association of black journalists. "We talked to him and his family, and he told us to go fuck ourselves," says J. Whyatt Mondesire, then an editor at the *Inquirer* and now editor of the *Philadelphia Sunday Sun*. "The guy was looking to be a martyr. He didn't have to be a martyr. He was *looking* to be a martyr."

What unfolded in Courtroom 253 that June was somewhat bizarre. Jamal prepared his own defense, but his tactics didn't play well with Common Pleas Court Judge Albert F. Sabo, a notoriously pro-prosecution jurist who's been dubbed "King of Death Row" for doling out more death sentences than any other judge in Pennsylvania. Sabo denied Jamal's request to have John Africa at the defense table, because Africa wasn't an attorney, and he ordered the reluctant Jackson to take over the case. "It seems real clear to me," responded Jamal, who refused to cooperate with Jackson, "and it should be clear to everyone else in this court that you're afraid of having John Africa's presence in this courtroom, even though it's in my defense, in defense of my life."

After that outburst, Sabo had Jamal carried off to a holding cell and began the trial without him. He would return, however, to disrupt the five-week trial repeatedly. The prosecutor, Assistant District Attorney Joseph J. McGill, says he believes Jamal was doing everything in his power to divert the jury from the facts of the case. "He's no dummy," says McGill. "Many defense attorneys try to do that."

But Jamal's outbursts put Jackson in a tough position. "I was representing him for a murder charge," says Jackson. "I wasn't defending his political views. Even now, I'm not altogether certain what his political views were. To this day, I'm not entirely sure what MOVE's politics are. And he wasn't even a MOVE member."

Still, Jackson says he did his best to save his uncooperative client. He produced witnesses who said they had seen shadowy figures running away from the crime scene and suggested that *they* might have been the killers. He grilled the prosecution's key witnesses—an admitted prostitute with an extensive rap sheet and a cabdriver with a conviction for tossing a Molotov cocktail into Bartram High School for money. But Jamal refused to take the witness stand and give his version of what happened that night, and he told Jackson not to call his brother to testify. Under those constraints, it was difficult for Jackson to get around the troubling fact that Jamal was found with the .38 sitting next to a dying cop. Ballistics tests failed to prove conclusively that the five mangled bullets that killed Faulkner had come from Jamal's pistol, but the gun did contain five spent shell casings. On July 2nd, having deliberated for five hours, the jury found Jamal guilty.

The following morning, he refused to present any evidence at his sentencing hearing. Instead, he read a speech. He called Jackson a "worthless sellout and shyster" and branded Judge Sabo a "black-robed conspirator." Then he turned to the jury of ten whites and two blacks and said, "I am innocent despite what you 12 people think. This jury is not composed of my peers, for those closest to my life experience were systematically excluded, peremptorily excused. Only those prosecution-prone, some who began with a fixed opinion of guilt, some related to city police, mostly white, mostly male. May they one day be so judged." Hearing the diatribe, Jackson's heart sank. "I thought Mumia really got up and killed himself when he attacked the jury," he says. "He essentially told them, 'Ya'll ain't shit.'"

Then assistant D.A. McGill cross-examined Jamal. Hoping to provoke even more inflammatory remarks, McGill held up a copy of the 1970 *Inquirer* story about the Black Panthers and said, "You've often been quoted as saying this: 'Political power grows out of the barrel of a gun.' Do you remember saying this?"

"It's very clear that political power grows out of the barrel of a gun, or else America wouldn't be here today," Jamal replied. "It is America who has seized political power from the Indian race, not by God, not by Christianity, not by goodness, but by the barrel of a gun." After McGill asserted that Jamal had been dreaming of killing a cop for years, the jury deliberated for four hours and then sentenced him to death.

Faulkner's family praised the verdict. "Thank God Danny shot him, got a bullet in him, so he couldn't run away," Kenneth Faulkner, the officer's brother, told reporters. "Or else we'd never have gotten him at all." Jamal's relatives, however, were devastated. "I think that was the thing that broke my mother's spirit," says his sister Lydia. "I know for Billy, my baby brother, he could never get his life together again." Though William Cooke was also arrested the night of the murder, charges against him were later dropped. He went back to work as a street vendor, Lydia says, but ultimately fell into a nightmare of homelessness from which he has yet to escape.

JAMAL was shipped off to Huntingdon State, a maximum security prison that is Pennsylvania's death row. In obscure black newspapers and leftist journals, he continued to spin his courtroom arguments. In 1989, the Pennsylvania Supreme Court turned down Jamal's appeal. By then he had been largely abandoned by his local supporters, many of whom were disillusioned by his fervent adherence to MOVE. But then an odd thing happened: Through his writings, Jamal began to attract supporters from outside Philadelphia—people who, not without reason, were ready to believe the worst about Philadelphia's cops and justice system and who may not have fully appreciated the more nettlesome aspects of Jamal's case. The Free Mumia movement was born.

In 1990, the Partisan Defense Committee, a group of New York Trotskyites, started organizing protests in America and Europe. The committee, which provides monthly stipends to other convicted cop killers, including jailed MOVE members, started to spread the word: "His name should be a rallying cry in the fight against racist injustice," argued a PDC tract. "Mumia Abu-Jamal—synonymous with the fight against the barbaric death penalty. Mumia—the name of resistance to brutal prison conditions. The state has shackled his limbs, but they cannot break his spirit or silence his voice."

Next came the Quixote Center, a group of dissident Catholics in Hyattsville, Maryland, best known for sending millions of dollars to Nicaragua when the

Reagan administration was backing the Contras. Jamal's case became the focal point of Equal Justice USA, a Quixote Center project created to fight the death penalty. Equal Justice's coordinator, Jane Henderson, says Jamal's predicament illustrates how the court system and capital punishment are stacked against minorities, particularly those who espouse radical politics. "We figured that if this could happen to Mumia," she says, "it could happen to anybody."

One after another, increasingly mainstream groups joined the cause. Amnesty International petitioned Governor Casey, urging clemency. The American Civil Liberties Union and the National Conference of Black Lawyers filed amici briefs in his appeal. The American Friends Service Committee lent its name to rallies. State Representative Richardson introduced a resolution last year calling for a federal investigation. The initiative stalled in the Assembly, but the Philadelphia Democrat hasn't given up. He's convinced Jamal simply isn't the kind of guy who'd kill a cop. "I not only think he's innocent," Richardson says. "I *know* he's innocent." In some instances, Jamal's supporters have seized upon legitimate concerns about the way he was treated in court. But they also have seemed willing to dismiss things others find unsettling. Asked to explain why Jamal didn't testify, Jane Henderson says, "You have to put yourself in his place. Mumia was probably very upset."

The movement continues to snowball. Perhaps most odd is the support Jamal has won from, of all things, an organization of police officers. "Jamal was someone who had spoken out against the police department and its practices," says Ron Hampton, a District of Columbia cop and director of the National Black Police Association. "So he could very well have been victimized by the police department. That's not unheard of."

At the same time, Jamal has found increasing demand for his essays, which have been appearing in publications such as the *Nation*, the *Inquirer*, and the *Yale Law Journal*. In a 1991 *Law Journal* article, Jamal wrote impressively about what's wrong with the death penalty. He also complained that his telephone privileges had been denied because he refused to cut his dreadlocks. "I found him to be very articulate, especially in today's debate about habeas corpus," says Christopher Gilkerson, the former Yale law student who commissioned the piece.

In 1992, Jamal returned to the airwaves. In commentaries taped at Huntingdon State by San Francisco journalist and Jamal supporter Noelle Hanrahan, he weighed in on Operation Desert Storm, the Rodney King beating, the Clarence Thomas hearings, the MOVE bombing, the flow of drugs into black neighborhoods—all of which he portrayed as pieces of a global conspiracy directed against people like him. The commentaries were heard on stations in New York and San Francisco, but also in England, Cuba, the Philippines, Canada, Australia, France, and Germany. "Don't expect the big networks or mega-chains of Big Mac media to tell you," he informed his listeners in comments now available on tape, along with the T-shirts and buttons. "Because of the incestuousness of the media and the government and big business, which they both serve, they can't. I can. Even if I must do so from the valley of the shadow of death, I will. From death row, this is Mumia Abu-Jamal."

In part because Jamal's voice hasn't lost its power, Governor Casey's office has been deluged with thousands of letters calling for the staying of his execution. In October 1992, Jamal supporters—"Stop the legal lynching!"—joined forces with abortion-rights demonstrators to disrupt a pro-life speech Casey tried to give in New York. The *Village Voice* wrote before a Free Mumia benefit concert that it "seems like every left-leaning performer in town is kicking in to save this radical journalist and former Black Panther."

And then came Hollywood. Mike Farrell, an outspoken liberal best known for playing B.J. Honeycutt on *M.A.S.H.*, says he learned of Jamal from attorney Leonard Weinglass, a personal friend. Farrell is no lawyer, but he plans to play Clarence Darrow soon in a one-man theater production. He says he's read the trial transcript and reached a partial verdict: "I don't know if Mumia is innocent or guilty. What's clear is that this man was subjected to the deplorable use of political and racial scare tactics which have no place in an American courtroom."

Among those Farrell has enlisted are fellow actors Ed Asner and Whoopi Goldberg. While Goldberg has simply lent her name to the cause, Asner has written a letter to Governor Casey seeking a stay of Jamal's execution. "I feel," he says, "that the fact that not one black sat on the jury in the City of Philadelphia becomes a highly suspicious factor."

Actually, there were two black jurors.

"Well," says Asner, "let me review my information. It still sounds like a fast job was done."

AND YET, years after he refused to testify at his trial, Jamal still has not offered evidence of his innocence—apparently not even to his family. "He still feels all that stuff has to come out in court," says his sister Lydia. That doesn't bother some of his supporters, who say they don't need to hear Jamal's story; they believe the prosecution's evidence was so flimsy he *couldn't* have been the gunman. "There are a lot of people out there who don't believe he shot that officer and has spent a lot of time in prison for nothing," says E. Steven Collins, a friend of Jamal's and host of WDAS's "News Magazine." "I think there's a tremendous amount of support from people who know him from the radio, who knew he was an advocate of the downtrodden."

Some supporters are convinced lawyer Weinglass will unearth important new evidence in his investigation, but at the moment, that doesn't look promising. Weinglass, whose client list includes Angela Davis, Jane Fonda, and Amy Carter, declined to be interviewed for this article, but he has written in the *Philadelphia Tribune* that the trail has grown cold after more than a decade. Originally planned to be completed last spring, the investigation drags on, and supporters lament that they have raised only about a third of the $150,000 Weinglass says he needs.

While there have been no executions in Pennsylvania since 1962, the state's death penalty was reinstated in 1978. Equal Justice's Jane Henderson says Governor Casey's former general counsel, James Haggerty, told her in September 1992 that the governor might sign Jamal's death warrant in the following six months. That never happened, but Casey spokesman John Taylor suggests Casey's failing health had a lot to do with it. "I can't predict with any certainty if this case is going to be presented to the governor before he leaves office," Taylor said more recently. "But I'll tell you this: The governor does not sign death warrants for anyone who has an appeal outstanding."

That doesn't bode well for Jamal. The U.S. Supreme Court rejected his most recent appeal in 1992. Weinglass plans to seek a new trial, but supporters say there's no point in going back to court until Weinglass completes his investigation. That means more rallies, more fund-raising, and more T-shirts. But even as Hollywood opens its hearts and wallets, many Philadelphians remain uneasy about the case. "The black clergy ain't down with this," says *Sunday Sun* editor Jerry Mondesire. "The [local] NAACP ain't down with this. I don't get the sense that mainstream organizations, black, white or whatever, are down with this." Then how do you explain the Free Mumia movement? "Those people in New York don't know the first thing about what happened in Philadelphia at 13th and Locust," says Mondesire. "They're just trying to relive the '60s." Ironically, Mondesire doesn't think Jamal did it either. But he's convinced Jamal's covering up for the real killer. Just who that might be the newspaper editor won't say.

Not surprisingly, Faulkner's friends on the police force find the whole situation extremely galling. "It makes me sick to my stomach," says Officer Bill Frazier, one of those who found Faulkner bleeding to death. "I can't believe this guy hasn't gotten the death penalty yet."

"I'd be happy to send Whoopi or Ed Asner some of the transcripts or some of the newspaper headlines to tell them what went on," says Garry Bell, who still maintains that Jamal confessed that night at the hospital. "I wonder if they have all the facts of the case or whether they really care about facts."

THE FACTS don't seem to bother anybody much on the sweltering July day when almost 300 protesters show up at Independence Mall for a Mumia rally. It is July 3rd, the 11th anniversary of Jamal's sentencing and one day before the city will award its Liberty Medal to Nelson Mandela and South African President F.W. de Klerk. The crowd is a multiracial mix of Trotskyites, graying hippies, anarchist punks, gay activists, and black militants, most of them New Yorkers. The organizers, mystified that Jamal is more popular in Germany than in his own hometown, can't hide their disappointment that there are so few Philadelphians among the demonstrators.

They have arrived on the mall this afternoon after marching south on Broad Street to the scene of the shooting. Leading the strange parade were a group of dreadlocked women pounding on drums and a carload of bullhorn-wielding

MOVE members chanting "Stop the plot, stop the plan, stop the death of an innocent man!" The marchers carried banners with slogans like FREE ALL POLITICAL PRISONERS and FREE THE L.A. FOUR—JAIL THE COPS. They called out to people on the sidewalk to join them in the street.

Now, as tourists line up across Market Street to see the Liberty Bell, the demonstrators set up a public-address system at the top of the hot concrete steps behind a dry fountain. The Mumia T-shirts are selling briskly, and the faithful keep coming to the mike. Again and again, Jamal is compared to Malcolm X, Martin Luther King Jr., Nelson Mandela. "You freed Mandela," the protesters chant. "Now free Mumia!"

A dark-haired young woman from Penn State tells of her pilgrimage to see Jamal in Huntingdon. "My first reaction was not just that he was a great guy, but that he was a revolutionary!" she announces. "I found out what the state was really all about. He gave me the encouragement and the knowledge that what they are doing to him, what they did to Malcolm X, what they did to MOVE, what they are doing to all of our communities will be avenged. He said all those bosses, all those people who have oppressed us, we're going to put them in jail, we're going to put them in the gallows, we're going to put them on death row!"

The threats and the chants echo through the concrete mall, but they disappear into the din of the Market Street traffic. A few bewildered pedestrians stop and listen for a moment before continuing on their way. An aging black militant with sunglasses and a black skull cap takes the microphone and offers what is either a bald-faced lie or startling new evidence of Jamal's innocence. "His gun was still in his cab—in its holster!" the militant yells, shaking his fist. "It was never used! Listen up, all you people thinking about doing away with our brother. We will burn Philadelphia to the ground if you-all kill Mumia. God is my witness."

Across Market Street, the tourists continue to file in to see the Liberty Bell, oblivious to it all.

W. WILSON GOODE SR.

Preacher, former mayor, 65; Overbrook Farms

I moved here exactly 50 years ago and thought it was like Heaven. All of us who were old enough to work got jobs, and eventually we bought a house. It was the first time my family had ever owned a house.

I don't know of any day of any week of any month of any year that I didn't try as hard as I could to be a good servant of the people.

I feel respected, I feel loved, I feel admired by a lot of people in this city. They recognize that I gave everything that I had.

In the whole scheme of things, MOVE was a bad day. But it's not something that has ever, or that ever does, weigh me down.

When I left office, I knew for sure that preaching was the one thing I was not going to do. I had my watch up, wasn't letting God in. But in a moment of weakness, he snuck up on me.

I wish I had listened to God 25 years ago. If I had a choice between being mayor and being a preacher, I would take preacher. I enjoy it much more.

It's unfortunate that as mayor, I viewed John Street as an enemy rather than someone who was doing his job. He's my friend now. I would be the most surprised person in the world if he ever did anything illegal.

There is clearly a difference in the way the media covered Ed Rendell and John Street. In what way? The question is, in what way is it not different?

Philadelphia is one of those cities that would rather see a white man as mayor. I could feel it when I was mayor, and it's the same now.

I'm not complaining about that—I'm saying that that's the way it is.

I'm an avid Eagles fan. I love Donovan McNabb. I just can't watch every game because they're on Sundays, when I'm preaching.

Now I always have to say I'm W. Wilson Goode Sr., because my son worries I'll mess things up for him.

I have two lovely granddaughters who I spoil in every way I can. If I knew that grandfatherhood was this good, I would have skipped fatherhood altogether.

My favorite place in the city is the Free Library. I like to just go there and read. We didn't have libraries when I was growing up in North Carolina—at least, not that I could go to. The first one I ever went to was the Paschalville branch in Southwest Philadelphia. I fell in love with it.

The best piece of advice I ever got was from former mayor Bill Green: Never write a letter, and never throw one away. He meant don't ever put anything in writing that you wouldn't want anyone to read, and don't ever throw anything away that you might need. I still follow it.

The worst piece of advice I ever got was not to run for mayor because I couldn't win. I'm not going to tell you who it was from.

I don't hear a lot of folks beyond my son and maybe Michael Nutter talking about issues, about how they can bring about change.

If every state rep in this city did the kind of job that Dwight Evans does for his district, the city would be far better off.

I don't see any progress on race relations in this city. Very few people of different races go to church together, very few live in the same neighborhood, very few attend the same schools. If they don't go to school together, live together and go to church together, then where's the change going to take place?

But I'm hopeful. I have no reason to be. But I'm always hopeful.

By Lisa DePaulo
March 1993

BOBBY SIMONE'S LAST 1,000 MARTINIS

"When you look at the destructive things the mob has done, Exhibit A is Bobby Simone."
—Louis Pichini, of the U.S. attorney's office
"Gimme a fuckin' break."—Robert F. Simone

'm bummed," Simone says as he falls into the front seat of my car one night in January. It's been 23 days since the verdict. "That fuckin' broad's coming tomorrow."

We're heading up Walnut Street trying to decide where to have dinner.

"I just don't like the idea of *that fuckin' broad* comin' into *my* apartment."

That Fuckin' Broad is his probation officer. It's standard procedure after a conviction like his to get a visit from one before being sentenced to prison, to establish "residency" and so forth. "Like I don't live where I say I live," he mumbles. He lives in Independence Place, as odd as that may sound.

"I gotta stop thinkin' about it. It's gonna make me nuts."

We decide not to go to the Palm.

"And *then* I'm told I gotta dig up my divorce decree, my marriage license, my birth certificate.... Like I wasn't fuckin' born!"

"Veranda?"

"Nah, I was there last night."

He lights a cigarette.

"She's gotta come and go through *my* closets to prove that's where I live!" he rails. "They didn't go to Philip Leonetti's fuckin' house, a *murderer*, killed 12 people, and they didn't go through *his* goddamn closets!" He's referring to his former client, his former friend who danced at his wedding, whose testimony as a mobster-turned-informant helped convict Simone on five federal counts, counts that could get him sentenced this month to jail for the rest of his life.

"You know, I'm gonna *ask* that fuckin' broad, 'Why aren't you goin' through Philip Leonetti's closets?'"

"Morton's?"

"Yeah, let's go to Morton's."

He tells me to take a right.

"Fuckin' broad," he mutters. "So how was your day?"

I'M DRIVING because Simone doesn't have a car. Sometimes he borrows the one that belongs to Jennifer, his 32-year-old girlfriend. But the lease on his steel-blue Jaguar expired in December. "You have to lease them for at least a couple of years," he explains. "And I might not be driving much pretty soon, ya know what I mean?"

It is the first indication he has given, in the weeks that I have spent with him, that he is actually making plans to go to prison. His 24-year-old daughter, Kim, who has been living with him in his rented three-bedroom condo for the past six years, says the lease is up in July, and she feels that it's time to get her own place anyway, but they haven't yet discussed where she'll go. "I've been told he's told other people he's worried about where I'm going to live," says Kim. "I'm worried, he's worried, every-body's worried, but nobody talks about it." His son, Scott, who's 28 and does tele-marketing in Vegas, talks to his father just about every day. "But the word *jail* never comes up," Scott says. "It's not like he's saying, 'What will I do with my furniture?'"

"Mr. Simone." The maître d' at Morton's delivers this more like a salute than a greeting. Without a reservation, Simone is escorted to the best table in the house.

And the usual scene occurs. Everywhere he goes he's treated like a rock star, or the corpse at his own funeral. The mumbling, the stares, the pointing—then they start coming toward him with condolences. "Hey, I'm really sorry." "We're praying for you."

"You got screwed."

Tonight, it's more the rock star thing. What other convicted criminal gets treated like this everywhere from Morton's to IHOP? The fawning, the touch-ing, the we-love-yous. The waiter who's "honored" to be waiting on him. The customer who lit a candle for him. The other waiter who can cite all the flaws in Philip Leonetti's testimony. The tripping all over themselves to bring him his Bombay gin martini with olive. If he had a ring, they'd kiss it.

"To health and freedom," he says, raising his glass. The same toast he made to the jury with a paper cup of water.

Then he slides his hands under the table and slaps it several times. Just a little joke he has when he sits down in restaurants: checking for electronic bugging devices.

SIMONE'S drink of choice is the gin martini. But only when he wants to "get nuts." When he *doesn't* want to get nuts, he drinks vodka martinis or scotch. "I never get drunk when I drink scotch," he explains, "no matter how many I have."

Tonight is a Bombay gin martini night.

We decide to talk about jail.

"When I was going to go to trial in '86, my second case [he was acquitted of perjury, regarding his alleged knowledge of the mob], I thought the worst was gonna happen. I could lose and go to jail, and go to jail for *a long time....*

"That's very fast." He's talking to the waiter who brought his second martini. "What's your name? ... Scott? My son's name is Scott. You know what it means? Wanderer."

Is that why he named him that?

"I'm not that deep. Now Scott, no more martinis after this, okay? Because two, I'm fine. Three, I start to get giddy. And four, *forget about it.*

"So. I thought the worst could possibly happen," he goes on, taking a long drag on his cigarette. "And now I represented lots of people charged with serious crimes over a lot of years. And I won a lot and lost a lot. Some went and did their time ... *like men.* And some bitched and complained about every little thing. I considered a lot of them babies.

"So, I'm thinking about the possibility of the worst, and I hear all these guys complaining about all this *bullshit jail.* So I started reading these books about people who went through hell. I read *Papillon,* about all he went through on Devil's Island. How he fought it and survived insurmountable odds, and escaped from Devil's Island, after all the indignities that he went through, all the torture that he went through—and *that* was torture. Not like these guys who are complaining about how they can't make a fucking phone call. Gimme a break."

Frank Sinatra's "That's Life" is playing. He tells me he likes Sinatra and Bob Marley, and lights another Merit 100.

"So then," he says, "I read Willie Sutton's story about the Northeastern State Penitentiary, and how he got tortured and escaped. And then I read a book by a Chinese woman who was a victim of the Cultural Revolution in China. When the Communists took over the country, they killed her daughter, they put her in prison, in solitary confinement, and she went through hell." He sips his drink. "She lives in Washington now."

Is that the moral of the story? Escaping?

He winces. Simone basically has four facial expressions: Gimme a fuckin' break, tortured agony, puppy dog or devilish smile. Right now it is all four.

"I *read* these books for my own head, to get myself accustomed. So that I could prepare myself mentally for the worst—that no matter what they did to me, it couldn't be as bad as what they were doing to these people. Here, eat this, it's good for you."

He's piling spinach on my plate.

So no matter what happens, you plan to handle it gracefully?

"It's not that I want to go gracefully. It's that, you know, I'll do whatever I have to do. I'm a little bit of a fatalist. Whatever happens, you know, happens. But I also feel that things usually happen for the best."

That's pretty Catholic.

"I was just thinking about Christ on the cross." He smiles.

"*Scott!*"

"*Sir!*"

"All right, I want *one* more. Now, after that, that's *it*."

"One more of these, then after that no more," Scott the wandering waiter repeats dutifully.

"Lemme tell you a story," he says, tugging Scott's sleeve. "I used to bet on a horse many years ago. The name of the horse was Third Martini. It was the fastest horse that ran. There's a moral there."

"Stop after three," says Scott.

"You can count past three, right?" says Simone. "Well, I don't want you to do that."

"One two three. One two three," says Scott.

"Right. Now Scott—the waiter with the glasses? The young guy over there. I forget his name."

"Rick, sir," he whispers.

"*Don't* tell him I asked you his name. Because *if you do that*, you betray my trust."

Scott wanders away. Sinatra's "My Way" is playing in the background.

It seems as good a time as any to ask him about his relationship with Angelo Bruno, the late Mafia don who was boss when Simone represented his first mob client, in 1973. Simone got Frank Sindone off on loan-sharking charges (twice), even though the way he *met* Sindone was by being one of his customers. He was into Sindone for thousands when he represented him. The way the story goes, Bruno called him after the first acquittal and said, "You know who this is. I told him not to hire you. You have a friend for life."

Bruno became "like a father to me." It was Angelo Bruno who tried the hardest to get Simone to stop gambling through a two-decade tear during which he pissed away a fortune and wound up with his first federal indictment, for tax evasion, in 1984. Simone filed timely tax returns and accurate tax returns. He just didn't pay in full. Representing himself, he won the case by basically telling the jury what a pig he was when it came to gambling, parading friend after friend to the witness stand to attest to his out-of-control behavior. ("I believe he plays to lose," said one. "He is a demolition expert.") He then explained to the jurors that he owed about a million to the government and a million to the loan sharks, so he paid the loan sharks since they, as one friend put it, "had more-efficient means of collecting." The jury deliberated for less than 30 minutes before finding him not guilty.

"Angelo Bruno," he says, deciding which anecdote to deliver. "Remember the 500 Club? Skinny D'Amato's place in Atlantic City? Well, one night Sinatra was playing—"

What was he like?

"Dead drunk. So Sinatra's playing at the 500 Club, and Angelo Bruno was there. And Sinatra was trying to impress Angelo Bruno. But what happened was, what happened was *nuts*. He was drunk and he was carrying on and he was insulting the waitress. And Angelo, who was a great man—"

"Would you like to take your steak home, Mr. Simone?" asks Scott. Simone always eats exactly half of what's on his plate, then abruptly pushes the dish across the table, simultaneously firing up a cigarette.

"I have no place to take it, Scott. I have no home. I'm a homeless person."

Scott wanders away.

"So, Sinatra—he insults the waitress. And Angelo Bruno says, 'Come here.' And Sinatra comes over to Ange and Ange says, '*Sit over there.*' And he made him sit there. And Sinatra said, 'Why am I sitting here?' And Ange said, 'Because you don't know how to *treat* people.'" Simone drains the martini, then pushes the glass away. "Angelo Bruno was a *gentleman*."

The third martini arrives.

"You know, I was thinking about something you said to me today. *What am I doing here?* Why don't I just go away? Money. I need money. I have to get money. Can't go away without money." He sips his drink. "But I'm workin' on that now. And then, *See ya later!*"

He catches my look.

"I'm not gonna be a *fugitive*. I'm just gonna go away. For a little vacation."

More fans stop by the table. "How ya doin'?" "Hangin' in there." It's a group of well-heeled men leaving the restaurant who think he got screwed, are praying for him and want him to know that they are sure he will win on appeal.

"What do you mean?" I ask when they leave. "You're 'working on that now'?"

"I'm just workin' on it," he says.

There is always a threshold with Bobby Simone, a point when he is done, when he's answered enough, a point when he turns to stone. His daughter Kim explains it well when she says, "He doesn't get *mad*, really. He just shuts off. And that means he's pissed off." She says he does it sometimes at home in the apartment, when she and his girlfriend Jennifer, who've gotten very chummy, have water fights, as they sometimes do. Or whipped-cream fights. "We have these great whipped-cream fights," says Kim, "and he'll be having lots of fun, and then, all of a sudden, he'll just *stop* having fun. He'll say, '*Look!* It's all over the floor, look at this carpet! You guys are assholes!' We have fun with him. Till *he's* had enough."

And then, just as quickly, he's into it again.

"All right. Today was a good day because I talked to my client in Fort Lauderdale. He said, 'Fuck the government. I still want you to represent me.' That was before lunch. After lunch, the guy in North Carolina, a very serious case, a CCE [continuing criminal enterprise] case, said the same thing. 'Fuck the government.' Because I'm one of the few people that stands up to them. Which is really absolutely the truth."

And why, he explains, he has always been "a target" of the federal government.

This is a theme that dominates so many of our conversations together, tonight I try to move on to something else.

"Tell me more about growing up," I say, knowing he hates such questions.

"I'm still growing up."

I try again. Tell me about your brothers, your mother who's in the nursing home, your father who died in 1962. It was written once that his father, a Calabrese Italian—"hard heads," Simone explains—used to honk his car horn to call his sons to dinner, and the boys (he was the second) used to fight over who would sit next to him. "Nobody wanted to sit at the right hand of my father," he was once quoted as saying, because they were afraid he might strike them.

"Your childhood," I remind him.

"It was like all childhoods."

"Were you close to your father?"

"Oh, *great.* More psycho*logi*cal questions," he says with his gimme-a-fuckin'-break look, until I give up.

Scott wanders by and Simone points to his empty glass. Without saying a word, the waiter disappears and the fourth martini arrives. The choice of topics is his. He chooses Delilah's Den.

Earlier this morning, while tossing coins to the bums outside his office, he told me that one of the things he did in the nights after the verdict was go to Delilah's Den, the "gentlemen's club" at Front and Spring Garden. He described the entertainment there this way: "They have girls, but they aren't really naked. They're lightly dressed."

Lightly dressed.

"Maybe we'll go there after this," he's saying now. "You have the *balls to* walk in?"

He studies me, baiting me.

"Nah," he says. "You don't have the balls."

ON DECEMBER 15th, when Simone walked out of the federal courthouse on Market Street, it seemed like the ongoing saga of Bobby v. Them had finally reached its end. At 59, he'd spent a lifetime fending off the feds—both on his own behalf and on behalf of his notorious clients, many of whom showed their appreciation for the brilliant lawyer who got them off all those messy mob charges by showing up in court this fall as mobsters-turned-informants, to testify against him as part of their cushy plea agreements. Simone ended up with the biggest conviction ever handed to a prominent mob lawyer: up to 100 years for racketeering, conspiring with mob figures in the Willard

Rouse extortion, having knowledge of mob hits and using the threat of the mob to shake someone down. In other words, what the feds had been saying all along: that even though Simone was not a "member" of the mob, he was more than the mob's lawyer.

But with Bobby Simone it's never over, even when it's over.

No sooner was the ink dry on press reports of the jury's decision when one anguished juror by the name of Dennis Kline was slobbering all over the local news about how he didn't really think Simone was guilty, but got peer-pressured into convicting him and now wanted to kill himself. Another came forward, blaming the verdict on Judge James T. Giles, who she said gave the impression, when they were at a stalemate midway through nine days of deliberations, that there couldn't be a hung jury. (The note passed to the judge that day said some jurors didn't believe "the testimony of the criminals.") Kline even confessed that the jurors had read newspapers during the trial, in violation of their oath.

The "jurors' behavior," as Simone calls it, is just one of a half-dozen arguments that make up the post-trial motions Simone filed after the verdict, paving the way for an appeal. And it is likely that on March 11th, his scheduled sentencing date, he could be placed on bail for up to a year pending that appeal. Or he could be incarcerated immediately. But in either event, you can bet he'll keep on fighting. "Bobby is a warrior," says his pal Bruce Cutler, attorney for New York mob boss John Gotti, who thinks Simone will be "vindicated on appeal."

Immediately after the verdict, Simone retired to Bookbinders, his longtime haunt, with Jennifer, Kim, co-counsel Ed Jacobs and longtime pal Luther Fleck. "Everyone tried not to talk about it," says his daughter.

"Had a bottle of wine, some nice seafood," says Simone. "I've been going there for 30 years, and it was the first time they ever picked up the check. So something good came of the verdict."

He says he didn't cry when the verdict came in, "until I looked at my daughter and saw her crying."

His 86-year-old mother heard the news on KYW radio. "They're pickin' on you, Bobby," she told him when he visited her at the nursing home, as he always does, on Sunday.

The day after the verdict, December 16th, he was in his office fielding calls from all over the country. His secretary B.J. had gone to work every day throughout the trial just to man the phones. Some of the letters wouldn't arrive until days later. In Lee Beloff's, sent from Loretto prison, he wrote that he still planned to have "my first 1,000 drinks with you." The former councilman and former client of Simone's is serving a 10-year sentence for his role in the Rouse extortion, and is up there on Simone's Most Loyal list. "All he had to do to get out of jail was say one bad thing about me," says Simone. "That's a friend."

So is his number-one client, jailed mob boss Nicky Scarfo, who sat in his cell in solitary confinement on Christmas Eve and wrote a letter to Simone. It was sitting on his desk in January, several pages of Nicky script under a pile of other messages.

"I can't show it to you because it's privileged," says Simone, waving the letter in front of me. "But basically what he says is how bad he feels and how responsible he feels for his nephew [Leonetti] coming in and lying on me."

He folds up the letter. "He was kind of upset. He was very upset. He feels worse about the case than I do."

On December 22nd, one week after the verdict, Simone was in attendance at the Boardroom party, an orgy of criminal defense attorneys that's been a Christmas tradition for twenty some years. He started the night deep in conversation in a downstairs booth, then moved into the crowds, then ended up at the upstairs bar—alone with his glass of scotch and his painfully sad expression, as crowds hovered around, drinking and dancing and swaggering.

"I don't mean to interrupt you," I said.

"Please do," he said.

After the party he went to the Palm for dinner with friends. At the end of their meal, he was told he had a phone call. His friend Stanley Branche had just died of a heart attack. Branche was a longtime civil rights leader who'd served three years in prison on mob-related extortion charges. Simone's friends and family say he took Branche's death harder than he took the verdict.

Two days later, on Christmas Eve, Simone went Christmas shopping, as he always does, at the last minute. He bought both of his women—Jennifer and Kim—expensive outfits at Nan Duskin. His daughter, whom he calls "the strong one"—"I'm like my dad," she explains, "I bury everything deep inside"—couldn't bring herself to put up a tree in their apartment, but forced herself to go out and buy a few presents for her father: a clock radio, a sweater, and a shirt. Together, they spent Christmas day with Jennifer's parents in New Jersey.

December 29th. Simone is sitting at the downstairs bar at Le Bec-Fin. It is our first scheduled meeting. He tells me that the night before, he prepared himself by watching *Absence of Malice*, the film in which reporter Sally Field betrays her subject, Paul Newman. In the first five minutes, I ask him to repeat something he's said. "Why don't you just turn up the tape recorder?" he says, convinced my purse is wired. Later in the evening, he's sure that some suits standing near the bar are federal agents. It won't be until a week or so later, when we both make an amusing discovery, that his paranoia seems justified.

That night was also the evening before Stanley Branche's funeral, which I discover when I ask him who his closest friend is.

"My best friend's laying in a coffin," he says. He reaches for his drink. "Philip Leonetti was my friend.... Nicky Scarfo was my friend...."

For much of the remainder of the night, Simone discusses the biggest mistake he ever made. It is a theme that will drift into all of his thoughts, all of his profanities. He says it's "the one mistake I will take to my grave. Juror Number One"—aka "that fuckin' engineer." This is not the juror who cried on the local news—though

Simone has mixed emotions about him: Simone told the TV cameras he felt worse for him than he did for himself, but he also resents him for "caving in."

Juror Number One is another story. Simone says that after 35 years of picking juries, he'd never pick an engineer, which was this man's profession, or a Mason, which was this man's "fraternal order," because they are "too pro-government." "What possessed me?" he asks himself, holding his head at the bar. Five minutes later: "Eh, what's done is done, I'm not gonna dwell on it." Ten minutes later: "Fuckin' engineer." He's convinced that Juror Number One "retried the case in the jury room. I know it."

How do you know it?

"I just know it."

The following day, December 30th, Simone went to Stanley Branche's funeral, sat in his chair and wept.

Then he hopped on a plane with Jennifer to spend New Year's Eve on Sanibel Island.

"NICE tan."

"You sound like my probation officer."

Highlights from the dreaded visit: "We start talking about my finances and how much I owe, and I'm telling her how this has ruined my practice—who's gonna hire me when they know I'm dealing with this shit? I can't blame them. And she says, 'Nice tan, by the way.' Like I'm not gonna take a vacation after this!

"And *then*—you're gonna love this—she says, 'You know, one of our parole officers saw you the other night at Le Bec-Fin.' Like, I can't go to fuckin' Le Bec-Fin. So I told her, 'Well, that woman I was with was a reporter, and she paid. And in case you didn't get your report in from this week, I ate at Morton's with her, too.' Like they have nothing better to do than follow me to fuckin' restaurants."

He's sitting, then pacing, then smoking, then sitting in his office near Rittenhouse Square, with papers for his appeal piled all around him. It's an office that has seen more wires than Silo, if you just count the undercover agents who've visited over the years. Simone thinks he's been tapped, bugged or otherwise surveilled for about 20 years. The feds say he's wrong: "I don't think we actually installed bugs in his office," says one.

"So tell me about Florida," I say.

"I feel relaxed," he says.

Not that relaxed.

"Not only was he an *engineer!* And a *Mason*, for chrissakes. He was an engineer and a Mason who had worked for a nuclear plant!"

He sits. "But I don't want to talk that much about him."

He stands. "The bottom line is, *he* retried the case. I know that the jury would have at least been hung, and probably I would have been acquitted if I didn't have that guy on the jury."

But how does he *know*?

"Well, first of all, when the jury came out with questions [midway through deliberations] his sleeves were rolled up and his vest was open and he looked like he had been working *very hard*. Then, when they came out with the verdict and the jury was polled, one of the jurors made a mistake by giving the wrong verdict. And this guy, the engineer, *leaned over*, from his seat *three seats over*, and *gave* that juror *his* verdict slip. So he was not only controlling the jury in the deliberation room, he controlled them in the courtroom."

He lights a smoke.

"I mean, it was there to see, you know? I've been doing this for 35 years."

("It's unfortunate that Mr. Simone feels that way," says Juror Number One, Richard Emery, a soft-spoken nuclear engineer from Allentown. "I think if I were facing 100 years, I might be mad at somebody too. But I would think if Mr. Simone has any cause for complaint, it's against the government for bringing these charges. *They* started it." Him *too*?)

Simone's office is decorated in Bobby v. Them. On one wall, the framed sheet music of "Somebody's Watching Me," the song he recited to the jury in his income tax case ("Oh, what a mess, it must be the IRS ...") to drive home his depiction of the government as Big Brother, in a closing argument that George Orwell would have envied. That was the same case in which he discovered that the government had gone through the trash outside his home every day for four years. They didn't come up with anything damning, but he did. He read the personal notes that the agents had rifled through—notes to his wife, to his children—aloud to the jurors, who sat in horror. Simone says he later moved into a high-rise condo with trash chutes, so the feds could *really* have a field day.

"That was my daughter's idea, to use the lyrics from the song."

Underneath it is a collection of AP bulletins announcing his acquittal in his perjury case, beautifully framed and given to him by Jerry Blavat.

On the opposite wall, a poster says SILENCE MEANS SECURITY. Next to it is a 1973 article from the *Bulletin*, the first time he was publicly labeled a "mafia attorney." "Bobby Simone," the caption says, "is on his way to becoming a legend in his own time."

On the mantel, two of his favorite pictures. One is of him sitting next to Nicky Scarfo, who is wearing white shoes and testifying before a U.S. Senate hearing into organized crime in 1982. Scarfo's testimony was mostly the Fifth Amendment. "Just one of the things I did for him." Next to it is a photo of Simone with five other defense lawyers, celebrating after Nicky and the boys were found not guilty in a huge CCE case in 1987. "Look at that. I won that case for him and I couldn't win my own fuckin' case, pardon my French."

Pardon his *French*?

"That case was one of the reasons the government got a little pissed at me."

And we're onto his favorite topic: how the government targeted Bobby Simone. And made a deal with the devil—eight of them, all witnesses at his trial—to get him.

"Does it make any *sense*," rails Simone, "to let eight criminals—murderers and liars—go free to get me? I mean, am I a bigger target than a Philip Leonetti, who killed 12 people? Who's better off in jail? For *society's* sake? Philip Leonetti or me?"

He paraphrases Oscar Wilde: "Many times, the people who are supposed to take care of the justice system and handle the problems of crime often do more harm than the criminals themselves."

By Simone's estimate, the government spent $1.4 million "just on houses and gifts for these guys, forget the millions spent on investigations and trials." And, he says, "I defy them to prove there wasn't at least $10 to $15 million spent just on cases and investigations into *me*." He cites chapter and verse the cost of relocating criminals in the Federal Witness Protection Program, "not to mention the cost of hookers," referring to the now-infamous report of Thomas DelGiorno having a hooker provided for him, while in the custody of the New Jersey state police.

The feds point out that the witnesses—Leonetti in particular—sank a lot more people than Simone. They credit Scarfo's nephew's various turns on the witness stand since he flipped in 1989 for the final dismantling of the Philadelphia mob, and also for John Gotti's conviction. Sure, they argue, Leonetti *did* get out after just five and a half years—for what they say was only *ten* gangland murders. "But what kind of freedom is it," asks one fed, "when you're constantly being stalked, when John Gotti has said he wants you dead?" Which might be a compelling argument except for one thing: Aren't these guys supposed to be protecting him?

Simone says that he was approached three times by federal agents asking him to "cooperate." Usually they'd ask him to meet them in Rittenhouse Square, "and they'd tell me that Nicky Scarfo was about to kill me."

Did he ever believe them?

"I'm here, aren't I?"

He pauses.

"See, I never fell for any of their bullshit programs. 'Oh, you're gonna be killed, you better talk to us.' They wanted me to violate my lawyer-client privilege, and that's just not my bag. That's why I'm where I am right now."

His face reddens. "You know, as much as I'm accused of—really, convicted of—associating with these guys, who were my *clients*, who did *they* befriend? Who are *they* in bed with now?" He smiles. "I might have romanced them," he says, "but they fucked them."

"When we met, he'd write me these beautiful letters and send them to me Federal Express."
—Jennifer, Simone's girlfriend

JENNIFER sits in a cherry-red suit and black tights in the fireplace bar at the Ritz-Carlton, her legs crossed daintily like a young lady who's been raised in boarding schools, which she has.

She has delicate features and natural blond hair, and calls him Robert.

He has asked me to delete only one thing from the record, after all of our conversations, and that is the name of the company where Jennifer works. "It's hard enough for her," he explains.

She met Robert Simone in an elevator at Independence Place. She didn't know he had spotted her four months before, right after his second wife left him, then spent countless nights staring out the window, hoping to see her walking through Washington Square Park.

"We would sit in front of the window and look for Jennifer," says Kim.

When he finally found her again, in the elevator, "I walked off, and he came running after me and pulled my arm," she says, blushing, until she told him her name. Ten minutes later he was calling her in her apartment, which was on the floor below his. She called her mother: "Can you believe this guy in the elevator called me?" The phone calls didn't stop until she agreed to go out with him. "He was pretty persistent," she says.

After I meet Jennifer, I look up a story about Simone in the *Inquirer* from 1989 in which he and his now-estranged second wife, Rita, talked about how they met in a hotel lobby in Miami. "This beautiful girl walks through. I grabbed her by the arm," he said. "He sort of tugged on my arm, he was insistent," she said.

Jennifer sips a glass of chardonnay.

Anyway, she's telling me, "I had no idea who he was. I looked him up in the phone book to see if he was really a lawyer."

On their first date "he was so nervous. After dinner we went to the Four Seasons and danced. His friends say he doesn't dance, but he did that night."

The next day, he flew off to Chicago to represent Jesse Jackson's half-brother, Noah Robinson, on a murder rap. Then he handled a mob case there with Bruce Cutler. He was gone for another six months, bonding with Brucie. "Every night," says Cutler, "we'd go to the gym, have a drink, have dinner, then go back to our rooms at the Ritz."

Where Simone would write love letters on Ritz-Carlton stationery and Federal Express them to Jennifer. "And every morning," she remembers, "I'd get my package and read it as I walked through the Square. They were *unbelievable* letters. I think that's what did it."

When he returned, they took golf lessons together. They took up jogging together. They like to listen to reggae and watch Italian films with subtitles. He goes to Termini's every Sunday morning, then makes breakfast for her and Kim. And a couple nights a week, he "makes his peppers" on the stove. There was a three-month spell when they played Scrabble every night.

They've been together two years, and her eyes fill with tears at the mere mention of the verdict.

"We used to go to the shore and walk on the beach, and he'd tell me stories and I'd laugh. He makes me laugh," she says, about to cry.

"There's one thing you gotta always remember about Bobby Simone. He is a dichotomy. Bobby Simone has a very dark side. You gotta wonder: What was it that attracted Bobby Simone and Nicky Scarfo to each other?"
—Louis Pichini

TWENTY-SEVEN days after the verdict against him, Simone is headed for court again, to go to bat for Nicky Scarfo.

Scarfo—who can't be here today because he's out in a federal prison in Marion, Illinois, serving a zillion or so consecutive sentences for his role as the head of the Philadelphia mob during its bloodiest reign. Scarfo, who once said that if he needed brain surgery, he'd want Bobby Simone to operate.

Which doesn't seem, right now, to be above and beyond the call of duty.

Today is a status call at the Camden state courthouse—basically a check-in before the judge regarding Scarfo's pending RICO (Racketeer-Influenced and Corrupt Organizations statute) indictment as "the first person ever to be charged with the crime of heading an organized-crime family," says Simone with his gimme-a-fuckin'-break look. "With all his problems, it's kind of ridiculous for them to charge him with this. But that's America. They want to use him as a guinea pig to try out this statute."

Today's mission is to find an approximate date of trial and to figure out when they can get Little Nicky—who travels with more armor than the Bosnian troops—back here from Illinois.

"And I suspect there'll be an inquiry about me," says Simone. "And my 'continued representation.' But knowing Nicky Scarfo, he'll want me to represent him no matter what."

He's riding shotgun in an old Oldsmobile, owned and driven by his longtime friend and investigator, Ed Harrell, a cool-looking black guy in a brown fedora. In the old days, Ed got to cart Simone around in much flashier wheels. Now it's just Ed and his burgundy-vinyl Olds, with Dunkin Donuts wrappers scattered in the back, but Simone is still being chauffeured.

They're laughing as the Olds is careening over the Ben Franklin Bridge, Simone smoking his Merit 100s and reading Ed the headlines from today's *Daily News.* Ed drops him at the curb and wishes him luck.

Simone swaggers into the courthouse in his long black leather coat with the fur collar, ashes falling behind him, and the usual scene occurs. This time the condolences come from the mouths of lawyers, court reporters and handcuffed men in elevators.

"'In the halls of justice the only justice is in the halls.' Lenny Bruce said that," says Simone.

But he's not the only celebrity in the courtroom today.

"Nicodemo Scarfo Jr.?" says Judge Isaiah Steinberg.

"Here, your honor." The voice comes from the second row in the half-filled courtroom, where Little Nicky's son is here for his own status call, and looking rather dapper, we might add, for a guy who three Halloweens ago ate nine bullets at Dante & Luigi's. He and Simone smile and wave across the courtroom.

Seated next to Nicky Jr., and sporting silver hair and matching windbreaker, is Anthony "Tony Buck" Piccolo—"Cousin Anthony" to Nicky Jr., "the acting boss of the family" to the Pennsylvania Crime Commission. He and Simone smile and wave across the courtroom.

"Nicodemo Scarfo?" says the judge.

And Simone stands.

The judge advises both of his celebrities that he'll see them later, and individually, in chambers, and moves on to his list of common criminals.

Simone makes his way toward Nicky and Tony. First there are hugs, then mumbled sympathies. "Eh," Simone is saying, "whatta ya gonna do?" Then someone cracks a joke and they're laughing raucously in the courtroom, as Steinberg looks at them wearily.

And then Simone and the Scarfo mob, or what's left of it, move into the hallway. Together they fire up cigarettes, puffing coolly under the NO SMOKING signs, then stamp them out in the burnt-orange carpet. There are about a handful of them—the handful not dead, in jail, in the Witness Protection Program or still being praised by the government for the testimony they gave against Bobby Simone.

"So, how was Florida, Bob?" asks Nicky Jr.

"Got a letter from your old man," says Simone, and then they're off into a corner for some muffled conversation.

After Simone emerges from the judge's chambers—where it's decided they will try to try Scarfo before Simone is sentenced—Nicky Jr. has his arm around him. "It's not often that I'm graced with your presence," he tells Simone, and they both flash their gimme-a-fuckin'-break look. Then Simone gets semi-serious. "You know, I might be in jail when they try this case. They'll have to bring me in handcuffs."

"Whoa," says Nicky Jr., his arm on Bobby's back. "Donchoo be ridiculous. *Doan be* ri*dick*yalus."

"Yeah," says Simone. "Hey, listen. Say hello to your grandmother."

"In their hearts, they know they screwed me."
    —Bobby Simone
"In his heart, he knows he crossed the line."
    —Louis Pichini

MY LAST meal with Bobby Simone takes place in late January. I suggest Sfuzzi for lunch. He rolls his eyes. I suggest Cutter's. "They're yuppie places, aren't they?" he growls. We end up at Bogart's in the Latham.

He's drinking martinis—but they're vodka, so he won't "get nuts."

He's comparing himself to Clarence Darrow—the first famous lawyer "who got punished for representing the dregs of society." Any lawyer can represent popular people, says Simone. But it's a real test of your devotion to the justice system to represent the dregs—albeit dregs who danced at your wedding.

He even compares himself to the lawyer who represented Louis XVI and Marie Antoinette. After they both got tried and beheaded during the French Revolution, as Simone tells it, "the French government, who was a lot like these goddamn prosecutors, said, 'Now who can we get? I know! Let's get the goddamn lawyer who had the balls to represent them!'"

Of course this argument—which two other juries bought—infuriates the feds. "There's only one reason why we prosecuted Bob Simone," says former U.S. Attorney Michael Baylson. "One word: the evidence." "He knows deep down that this vendetta stuff is bullshit," adds Louis Pichini, the suit with the most passion, who as a leader of the Organized Crime Strike Force in the '80s went up against Simone in the courtroom more than any other prosecutor, and has great regard for him as a lawyer. "I really like Bobby," says Pichini. "We all do. Which is why it made it even harder to prosecute. But we had to separate our feelings for him from the fact that he broke the law."

I mention something else Pichini said. That "the only person [Simone] should be mad at is Nicky Scarfo."

"Well, I guess he feels that Nicky put me in the position to be a target. So no matter who was Nicky's lawyer, he'd be a target. So he's saying what I've been saying! Anyone who represented him—and represented him adequately—would be a target. They wanted me to lay down and play dead!"

On the second martini, he brings Pichini's comment up again.

"You know, that's interesting he would say that. I would think he would say that the only person I should be angry with is myself."

Are you?

"Nah...Well, just about that one thing."

Juror Number One.

No matter how many ways you phrase the question, that's the only regret he can come up with from his long, and admittedly indulgent, life. The rest he explains in a rare moment of introspection, deep in the booth at Bogart's:

"Yeah, I was a compulsive gambler. I consider it to have been an 'out,' like a way of blowing off steam rather than keeping it inside my head. I drank. I ran around on a lot of women. I did everything that I could do—as an *out*. To get away from, I guess, reality. And then you find out that you can't get away from it."

He sips his vodka.

"Angelo Bruno used to tell me that moderation was the key. But nobody could really tell me. You gotta learn, you gotta live it, you know? And, uh, I have this problem, I guess—well, I don't think it was a problem, because I enjoyed my life—but I do things, instead of in moderation, *excessively*."

I mention one of the stories I heard about his life in the fast lane. *Really* in the fast lane. The night he was speeding down Kelly Drive and a cop stopped him. "Bobby," said the cop, "you're speeding, you're drunk, you don't have a license ..." And Simone pulled a $100 bill out of his pocket and said, "Here, make it bribery, too."

"*Not* true," says Simone. "It wasn't Kelly Drive. It was the Expressway."

He smiles.

"But I'm not into that now. I mean, I'll go out and have a few drinks, but...one thing I think that's keeping me from doing that is, I don't really have anybody to do it with. A lot of my friends are either dead, in jail, in the Witness Protection Program, or some of them have even, I won't say have turned their back on me, but, well, some of them have."

Who betrayed him the most?

"I'd rather keep that to myself."

He orders another martini. He's done with this conversation.

"But by the way," he says, "I think everybody has a dark side. Lou Pichini has a dark side. Ask him what attracted him to going after me."

I ask him if he really likes Nicky Scarfo.

"Yeah, by and large, I like him as a person." He likes "his loyalty, which is very rare these days." He thinks "he's basically an honest person, believe it or not."

How does he see Scarfo—a man convicted of ordering the murders of most of his friends—as loyal and honest?

"I don't think that he conceals how he feels about things, or people. I think he's upfront about it. If he doesn't like somebody, he doesn't con him. He either won't associate with him or he'll be rude to him."

Which is one way of looking at it.

We move on to The Money. Why *didn't* he charge Nicky Scarfo legal fees? "I don't know, I guess I got too friendly with him to just make it, like, lawyer-client, 'You owe me X number of dollars.' And there were things that made up for it," he says.

Things, say the government, like Scarfo forgiving all of Simone's gambling debts.

Simone still owes the government more than $2 million—from the case he *won* in 1984. And his problems with the IRS are far from over. He has another indictment pending on new tax charges.

His son Scott says he "should have been a multimillionaire."

"No question about it," says Simone. "But I had a good time spending it."

IT'S THE morning of the president's inauguration, a day filled with promise, with hope—that Simone will be able "to get some guy his Porsche back." It is hardly the kind of case that makes Bobby Simone Bobby Simone. But he needs the money—and he needs to be in court. Which is why he is here in City Hall today representing Dennis, a handsome computer salesman who just happened to be in North Philly one day with a passenger who just happened to have coke in his pocket. Simone got Dennis off the drug charge months ago, but the authorities still have his red Porsche.

They spend most of the morning in the hall waiting for the judge, who is two hours late. Simone kills the time chain-smoking and cursing under his breath. His client, who repeatedly calls him Mr. *Shi*mone, is bouncing around the corridors like a wet noodle.

"Maybe we should make a deal," Dennis says.

"Dennis. It's a *car*," says Simone. "What kind of deal should we cut? You want half a car, Dennis?"

Two hours later, Simone has eviscerated the state's witness, a cop with "a hiding place," and won Dennis his car back, even though his client said three things on the witness stand that were completely contradictory to what his *own* witness had said moments earlier.

Dennis is overjoyed. In the hallway, he throws his arms around Simone. "I love ya, I love ya. You're a fuckin' *killer*!"

"Yeah," says Simone. "I been accused of *that* before."

And with that, he dons his brown fedora, lights another smoke and strolls out of City Hall. We have a new president and Dennis has his Porsche back. "A great day for America," says Simone.

As he walks up Market Street toward his last days of freedom, he stops to buy more cigarettes—two packs of Merit 100s, three lighters—when he spots a sign for lottery tickets.

"Eh, what the hell. Gimme $10 of those."

"Who knows?" he says, tossing me a lighter. "Maybe I'll get lucky."

By Lisa DePaulo
April 1994

"HOW MANY ED RENDELLS ARE THERE?"

merica's Mayor is riding shotgun on FDR Drive in New York City, on his way to see Rudy. Gimme that, says Ed Rendell, grabbing the driver's car phone so he can call and tell Rudy Giuliani that he's running a little late. He is in New York to do what he does best these days—become more popular. And so far, that's exactly what he's accomplished. He has just spent the morning wowing the New York business community on the joys of privatizing city services, and now he's off "to some dumb photo op" with the newly elected mayor of New York City.

"Frank," Eddie says to the driver, who's about to become his new best friend, "this is not to put any pressure on you, but how long will it take us to get to City Hall?"

"I'm not sure," says Frank Guido from Staten Island. "I've never been to City Hall."

"*All right, Frank!*" says Eddie, laughing and slapping. "But you do know where it is?"

Rendell punches in the number for directory assistance, asks for Mayor Giuliani's office and ends up in voice mail hell with the "Mayor's Action Line."

"Rudy didn't give you a *private* line?" asks Frank.

"No, Frank," says Eddie. "And this operator didn't even give me the mayor's *office*. Now I have to listen to this fucking recorded message."

Rendell bangs down the phone. "Screw it. We're almost there. And if we miss it, no big deal, Frank. It's justa buncha mayors."

"You want me to try and get through?" asks Frank.

"Nah," says Ed Rendell. "No one in New York speaks English anyway."

Moments later, the car carrying America's Mayor arrives in front of New York City Hall. Rendell marvels at the scene. "Look at all these foreign fucking cars," he says. He swings through the doors of City Hall like he always does, *like a bull*, pausing only to pass through the metal detector.

Unfortunately, the guest he's brought with him, this particular female reporter, beeps several times. At which point Rendell decides to show off that special subtle charm: "Take it off, Lis! Take *everything* off!" our mayor is laughing and yelling to me, as the security guards raise their eyebrows.

"I'm sorry," says one of the guards. "Your name is, again?"

"Ed Ren-*dell*," says our mayor.

He is quickly escorted into a flag-draped blue room filled with formal portraits of every mayor of New York (except for Koch, who insisted on a photograph). In the front of the room, Rudy Giuliani is sitting at a table, flanked by several of America's not-so-famous mayors. They are staring at a room full of press, including four TV cameras, waiting for Ed Rendell.

It turns out this is not just a dumb photo op.

"Glad they told me," mutters Rendell, who had "no idea" that Rudy gathered them here, in view of the entire New York press corps, to draft a letter to President Clinton to beg for more cops for the cities.

Rudy is sitting with his hands strangely clenched together, his mouth a thin straight line, in a crisp white shirt and cufflinks, white silk hankie in the pocket. When he spots Rendell barreling through the door, he bares his teeth. That's the way Rudy smiles.

Then what does our fine mayor do? Well, he does what he always does. He knocks their socks off.

First he waits, occasionally making faces, while the other mayors from towns like Houston and Indianapolis take their turns speaking. Then he smoothly ad-libs the best and most sensible sound bites of the session. When it's over the New York press has questions—almost all of them for Philadelphia's mayor. One reporter decides to challenge him. "At a breakfast here a few weeks ago," she reminds him, "you said you didn't want more cops..."

"First of all," says Eddie, "we'll take anything we can get." Laughter. So, yeah, he'll sign the letter, but "you're right," he tells her, more cops isn't the first thing on his wish list from Washington. "Because in the long run, all the cops in the world will do no good if we don't get our *people* back to work..."

As always, his answers begin as ad-libs and end up like campaign speeches.

"Because if we don't, we'll just have armed camps."

The press nods and scribbles. Rudy bares his teeth. They love him.

Afterward Rudy lets the other mayors leave, then invites Rendell back to his office.

Giuliani invoked Rendell's name all through his messy campaign—promising New Yorkers that he would do for their city "what Ed Rendell did for Philadelphia." The line got Rudy his biggest applause. He said it so many times that Ed's relatives in New York, where he was born, would call him up after watching the news and say, "He mentioned you again."

Giuliani's opponent, David Dinkins, managed to squeeze a sort-of statement of endorsement out of fellow Dem Rendell, literally on the eve of the election. "Because I think he's one of the finest individuals I ever met in politics," says Eddie. "But I agreed with Giuliani on most of the issues." And it was Giuliani who, literally the day after the election, had his staff make one of their first calls to Ed Rendell—asking "for all of our written stuff" (the five-year plan, etc.).

"This was LaGuardia's desk," says Rudy, proudly showing it off as Eddie rubs his fat fist across the surface.

"No kidding," says Rendell.

"When you were born," says Rudy, beaming, "he was mayor of New York."

"So," says Ed, "where's your real office?"

Giuliani smiles, this time a real one. "You want to see it?" he says eagerly.

He leads Rendell out of the fancy ceremonial office, through a small kitchen and down a narrow flight of wood stairs to a room that could pass for an office in an insurance agency: mini-blinds, ceiling fan, industrial carpet, glass shelves— empty except for a few framed family pictures. In office two and a half weeks, Rudy is still unpacking boxes.

"This is where Dinkins and Koch worked too," says Rudy.

Rendell checks it out, peering through the blinds. "So this is actually on the first floor," he observes. "Ya paranoid?"

"Well, not really," mutters Rudy.

"Good," says Rendell. "You shouldn't be. Before I got elected, the Philadelphia mayor's office was like a bomb shelter. And like I told my staff: 'If somebody's gonna shoot me, they're not gonna do it through my *office* window.'"

Rudy chuckles with him, though his eyes dart to the windows a bit nervously.

"So," says Rendell, slapping him on the shoulder. "How does it feel?"

"It feels *great*," says Rudy, awkwardly returning the slap. "It's a great job. *You* know that."

"Yeah," says Rendell. "And you're *doing* a great job, Rudy. You've been mayor for two weeks and the Rangers are already headed for their first Stanley Cup!"

As he says goodbye, Rendell promises Giuliani what he's promised every group he's spoken to in New York. That the mayor of Philadelphia—and who would have believed these words just a few years ago?—will continue to help New York in any way he can.

As he leaves New York City Hall, he stops to talk to a janitor, then playfully slaps the guy at the metal detector. "Don't worry," says Ed. "She didn't kill him."

"So," says Frank, as America's Mayor tumbles back into the car. "How'd it go?"

Rendell considers all the possible Giuliani stories he could share with Frank Guido from Staten Island, then picks this:

"Lis must have a spiked metal bra on or something, 'cause we almost didn't get in," he says, laughing.

"So how was Rudy?" Frank wants to know.

Rendell tells him how he wasn't expecting a press conference.

"So ya got duped," says Frank.

Rendell laughs. "Rudy's a good guy," he says. "And I think he'll build an effective coalition. Because New Yorkers are smart people, Frank, and they know they're up shits creek."

"I don't know about Giuliani," says Frank.

"Yeah," says Eddie. "We told him you didn't like him."

"Oh, *man*."

"Yep. Gave him your plates and everything."

They both crack up. And so it went—with no surprise that our Ed Rendell would bond as easily with Frank Guido as with Rudy Giuliani. That's part of what makes him so effective: The man has broad tastes indeed.

In the 24 hours I spent with Ed Rendell in late January, I watched him charm three groups of jaded New Yorkers, invite Frank the driver to join him at a game if the Phillies make the World Series this year, eat a hot dog in two bites, deliver a speech so eloquent audible "wows" could be heard, and speculate on how I might be in bed.

America, meet your mayor.

OF COURSE, this particular trip to New York was just one blip on his radar screen of "personal appearances." Since Ed Rendell became a national sensation, he's been logging more miles than the average Miss America—all to spread the good word of how he rescued Philadelphia from financial and moral despair, and how *you too* can make your city great.

Why, he's even starting to talk like a Miss America.

"One day in October," he tells me, "I had to be in Albany for some 'restructuring government' thing. My presentation was over at 9:50 a.m. I hopped a 10:10 flight to Phoenix to speak at a panel for the Association of Transit Administrators—you know, streets department people, stuff like that. I got finished at 2 Phoenix time, then I had to speak *again* in Phoenix, then I took a red-eye back to Philly. I got in the middle of the night."

Since he took office 15 months ago, he's been traveling to other cities, by his own estimation, three times a month; is a regular visitor at the White House; and is currently being booked three months in advance. He's been everywhere from Reno to Dallas. Mayors conferences alone—where he is invariably a speaker—have eaten up four trips. He's in Cambridge giving pointers to 44 first-time mayors at Harvard's Kennedy School of Government. He's in New York—and later, the *New Yorker*—to deliver the prestigious Wriston Lecture. He's in D.C. to dazzle the cynical Washington Press Club.

And rarely does a day go by when some other mayor, or some other "reinventing government" disciple, isn't on the phone with him asking for more advice. He's particularly chummy with Mayor Richard Daley of Chicago and Mayor Kurt Schmoke of Baltimore, both of whom are his age and, like him, former prosecutors. Schmoke, who's a big fan of Ed's, says he and Rendell "have stolen so many ideas from one another that we don't remember who thought them up first. We talk about everything from law enforcement to federal housing policy. We [also] talk a great deal about baseball." Schmoke says Rendell likes to "remind me of my lack of clout in my own city." Turns out, when Schmoke was the state's attorney of Baltimore, he had to call Ed Rendell in Philadelphia to get tickets to a World Series game between the Orioles and the Phillies—at Memorial Stadium in Baltimore.

When L.A.'s Republican mayor, Richard Riordan, got elected, he flew to Philadelphia the following week—to get four hours of tips from Ed and chief of staff David Cohen. When Dennis Archer, the new Democratic mayor of Detroit, got elected, he flew to Boston—to pump Ed outside class at the Kennedy School. That Rendell is also every mayor's direct line to Bill Clinton—"We've become great friends," says Ed—hasn't hurt his stature either.

But it was really the press—the national press—that launched the Rendell Cross-Country Tour. The mayor says he wasn't surprised at all when he became the flavor of the month. Or rather, 15 months. "Because this is a faddish country," he says, "I knew that once the *New York Times* and the *Wall Street Journal* wrote a story about us, everyone would do a story about us."

Since then he's had his ass kissed in every media outlet from the *CBS Evening News* ("I hear Philadelphia is a great place to live, John," says the CBS anchor to the CBS reporter) to the *Las Vegas Review-Journal*. It has gotten so that the gushing he receives almost daily in the *Inquirer* and the *Daily News* seems like criticism compared to what the rest of America thinks.

"He's even been in our limelight in Oregon," as Portland's former Mayor Neil Goldschmidt put it, introducing Rendell to yet another fawning group of New Yorkers. "He has taken a fresh look at how we are doing *everything* in our cities."

Naturally it was only a matter of time before the rest of America would want to *meet* this Ed Rendell. "I get *tons* of invitations," he says, "and I turn down a ton. All because of the success of what we've done in Philadelphia."

Oh, right. Philadelphia.

No one can argue that Eddie's national exposure hasn't done wonders for the city's image—when was the last time a hotel doorman in New York said, "You're from Philadelphia? Wow. I hear it's a really nice place."

But as Rendell himself is the first to admit, there's still some work left to do around here. Yeah, he's balanced the budget, turned the deficit into a surplus, boosted the bond rating, strong armed the union workers and landed a part in the *Philadelphia* movie. But ours is still a city that is losing 2 percent of its jobs each year, we just had the biggest population loss of any major city, and while Center City's shining (almost), the worst neighborhoods have only gotten worse. Unfortunately, solving the whole urban crisis is not a ceremonial job.

Eddie likes to point out all the gigs he's turned down ("Ten for every one that I accept"). Yeah, he went to the White House to screen *Philadelphia* with the president and director Jonathan Demme. Yeah, he's had a roll in the Lincoln Bedroom. But when his new pal Bill invited him down to schmooze with Arafat and Rabin after "the handshake that shook the world," he turned it down. Some small business was opening in Philadelphia. And yeah, The Donald is another new pal—they have regular conversations about riverboat gambling, says Ed, and Trump does little favors for him, like promising to fly in Muhammad Ali and his family and pay all their expenses so Ali can appear at "Knockout Night" during our Welcome America party in July. But Eddie turned down an invitation to Donald and Marla's wedding: "It was our office party that night."

"The glamour part of it really doesn't do it for me," Eddie insists. "Really. I get a bigger kick out of that middle-aged man coming up and asking for an autograph for his mother," referring to one of the many fans who assaulted him at the train station, "than reading in the *Picayune Times* that I'm America's Mayor.

"And, well, one of the reasons is I *do* try to work. So I really limit my traveling. I mean, if I really wanted to whack off, I could be out of town five days a week."

Of course, he also has two valuable weapons. The first is David Cohen. Here in Philadelphia, it's become a joke that the man behind the curtain, the guy who *never* leaves town and rarely even leaves City Hall, is Eddie's chief of staff, the 38-year-old former Ballard Spahr partner who left a big-bucks law career to be Rendell's Boy Friday (through Thursday). Now, even the other mayors are starting to catch on. Eddie reveals that Richard Riordan, who has some personal wealth, "told David, 'If you come to L.A., I'll pay you $350,000 out of my own pocket.'" Cohen, who makes $90,500 in Philadelphia, turned it down.

Rendell laughs when he tells the story. "If he'd have asked *me*, I'd have gone."

His other weapon is his seeming ability to be everywhere. It's hard to imagine that he spends so much time in hotel rooms when his mug appears all over town—more often than not making all four news channels a night for his city-wide appearances. In fact, he's been such a ubiquitous presence around the city he claims to have rescued that, as one Philadelphian put it at a cocktail party, moments after seeing Ed at *another* cocktail party, "How many Ed Rendells are there?"

There's Ed at Wanamaker's for a fashion show. There's Ed taking drink orders in a waiter's uniform at the Palm for some charity event. There's Ed under the flash-bulbs at the reopening of New Market, as Society Hill residents line the sidewalks to get a glimpse. There's Ed feeding strawberries into the pouty mouths of Katmandu waitresses at a photo shoot for this magazine. There's Ed conducting the Philadelphia Orchestra before game four of the World Series. He jumps in pools, he cleans toilets, he cooks hot dogs outside City Hall, he stands on *Gay News* publisher Mark Segal's roof at midnight during a Christmas party and sings "Happy Birthday" to his secretary.

On an average day in Philadelphia, says Eddie—who claims to survive on four hours of sleep a night, "five tops"—he does one or two public appearances before 9:30 in the morning, and three to four a night, "except for the last two weeks of December and the dog days of summer. And I don't do *half* of the invitations I get here."

And, as anyone who's seen him in action knows, he loves every minute of it. "Yeah, I enjoy it," says Ed. "And I think it's an important part of being mayor. Everyone made fun of Wilson [Goode] for doing all those ribbon cuttings—and I was one of them. But I've learned that it's very important that the mayor makes these appearances, because they really buoy the spirit of the city. It's the cheapest currency you have. The only price I pay is vis à vis Jesse [his 14-year-old son] and Midge [his wife, the newly appointed federal judge]. But they're veterans."

He also justifies it in dollars and cents. His stories of personally raising money for the city have been heralded not just locally but in the pages of the *Wall Street Journal* (Chief Cheerleader, Chief Beggar). He does almost nothing without a payoff.

"Hatfield Meats was willing to give the Rec Department $5,000," explains Eddie, "if I'd declare it Hatfield Hot Dog Day and cook a hot dog outside City Hall." Hell, he'd have declared it Hot Dog Month. "It took 30 minutes of my time to raise $5,000!" he boasts. It's just one of the things he advises other mayors to do.

On the train ride up to New York the night before his meeting with Rudy, he was going through a stack of appearance requests for events back home in Philadelphia. One was for a sporting exhibit at the Franklin Institute— "Curt Schilling will be throwing out the first ball," he says, writing YES to that one. Another was Wawa's 30th anniversary celebration. He'll also go to that. "*Sure,*" says Ed. "Wawa probably gives us $75,000 to $100,000 a year in contributions to different events. Again, it's a tiny little investment of my currency to say thank you for all they've done for us." How does he know how much Wawa gave? "Because I raised it," says Eddie.

He estimates that since he's been in office he has personally raised $50 million for various city causes—mostly for the Avenue of the Arts, which Ed tells the New Yorkers "will be much nicer than Lincoln Center," and which he credits his wife Midge and Diane Dalto, the deputy city rep for arts and culture, for spearheading.

Local groups who book him to speak receive a letter that basically says: If you plan on buying the mayor a little thank you gift, please send a check instead to the library or the Rec Department. ("I don't need 30 clocks," says Rendell.)

"And guess what else I found out?" he says excitedly. "That I can *marry* people." For $500, you too can be married by Ed Rendell. "I've done about six or seven so far," he says. "I grouse when I see them on the schedule, but I like them when I get there. I'm an old softy. Sometimes I even get a little choked up doing it.

"But you have to pay $500, no matter who you are," he explains. "And the money goes to one of three things: The library, the Rec Department or the Avenue of the Arts. But Lis," he says, "if you get married, I'll up it to $5,000."

I tell him not to let the city's financial future depend on it.

And hopefully it also won't depend on the fees he gets from his out-of-town appearances. Though many of the groups he speaks to pay him an honorarium—which goes into the coffers of one of those three favorite groups—when asked how much he's raised on the road doing the Eddie Tour, he thinks for a moment, then says, quite proudly, "I'd guess about $40,000," which almost amounts to the annual salary of one cop.

"But," adds Ed, "that includes the weddings."

What Ed Rendell doesn't brag about is the money he's raised for Ed Rendell. Though the papers didn't cover this, isn't it a bit strange that three months before the gubernatorial primary, the biggest Democrats in town got together and raised more than $1 million for a mayor who won't be up for reelection until 1995?

In February, just days apart, there were *two $5,000-a-head* fund-raisers. One of them, which he himself threw, drew over a hundred worshipers for cocktails at the Convention Center. The other one, dinner at Susanna Foo, hosted by big-time money-raiser Bill Batoff, had 25 Rendell fans nibbling dim sum. Batoff says Eddie needs to "replenish" his war chest for the '95 mayoral race. "Let's face it," says Batoff, "he gave a lot of his money to [Russell] Nigro and [Bill] Stinson," respectively referring, of course, to the failed Democratic state Supreme Court candidate and the recently dethroned and indicted Democratic state senator, accused of stealing an election from scrapper Bruce Marks in the biggest political scandal in recent Philadelphia history. (You can bet Rendell will also give some of his stash to whoever runs against Marks in the next round.)

Though Rendell handled the Stinson affair badly by anyone's assessment—basically saying it was no big deal—he seems to have Tefloned his way out of that one. It was in the heat of the Stinson scandal that Philadelphians paid $5,000 each—more than most presidents have gotten here—to have a cocktail with him.

IN THE HOURS before he's to meet with Giuliani, Ed's booked as the guest speaker for the Carnegie Council Privatization Project—a think tank of gung-ho corporate types whom he will later refer to as "a little fanatical" and who have packed a room in an Upper East Side townhouse at 8:30 a.m. to hear his wisdom.

On the way over, Ed, who never prepares a speech, jots down a couple of notes in his tiny handwriting. "All right, what am I gonna say here?" he asks himself, chewing on his pen.

"*You're* the mayor?" asks a woman at the registration desk, as Ed, in all his rawness, barrels in. He's immediately introduced to Gloria, the woman running the event, whom he treats with grace and aplomb, and whom, he will later brag, he "totally charmed."

"So he grew up in New York. Well, that's interesting," says a woman from the United Nations who's sitting with a diplomat from Switzerland. "I met his predecessor," she adds. "The black man with the entourage."

"Philadelphia is quite nice now, no?" adds the diplomat.

Rendell, who's seated next to Gloria and some big shots from the new Giuliani administration, somehow refrains from scarfing down the plate of Danish they've laid in front of him. He has all of them laughing.

A stiff guy in horn-rims from Chase Manhattan Bank gets up to introduce him.

"I'm happy to introduce to you Edward G. *Ren*-dil," he says—repeatedly. And then he launches into Ed's bio, mentioning how he lost a race for governor, lost a race for mayor, then finally got elected to office with 68 percent of the vote.

Eddie gets up to the mike and says that he's achieved such fame in Philadelphia that "it's nice to come up here and have someone mispronounce my name....And by the way, Brian," he adds, "when I speak to groups in Philadelphia—especially if they want something—they go directly from my election victory as D.A. [in '77] to my election victory as mayor and *skip* all the losses."

They love him already.

And so he launches into his favorite How-I-Saved-Philadelphia anecdotes.

The union contract story.

The incentiveless workforce story.

The cleaning-up-City Hall story.

The tax-the-athletes story.

The parades-don't-need-a-thousand-cops story.

Later he'll even tell the fish-in-the-Delaware story. Oh, you didn't hear that one? That's when he took on the crazy environmentalists who wanted to waste city dollars on improving the oxygen level for fish in the Delaware River. "Are the fish dead?" he says he asked them. No, they said, but the water's still below the EPA standard for what's good for the fish. "How do you know? Did you interview the fish?" he says he said, as everyone roars. "I told them they could seek a court order and cite me for contempt," because Ed Rendell would go to jail before he'd waste Philadelphia's money on fish.

His speech is peppered with as-I-told-Rudys. As in, "As I told Rudy, one area where you can't miss: Collect taxes better."

He also fires off his best sound bites: "There is no liberal answer to picking up the trash!" Yeah! "Short of taking an Uzi and gunning down your co-workers, you couldn't lose your city job in Philadelphia!" Before *he* got there. Yeah!

Then he winds down, like he usually does. Just at the point where they're nodding so vigorously their horn-rims are sliding down their noses, he hits them with self-deprecation: "And it was *easy*! That's the funny part," he says, while some of them are actually taking notes. "This is not rocket science."

The United Nations lady leans over and whispers, "He's not very polished, but in his own simple way, he's very effective, don't you agree?"

Afterward, he agrees to take questions, and so many of the guests have one that he ends up spending an hour after the waiters leave indulging the line of people that formed in front of him. To some he hands out David Cohen's direct line. To some, he instructs them to drop Cohen a short note. To some, he promises to put together a group of Philadelphians that they can come and visit, who will "help them in any way they can."

"I grew up here," he tells them. "My *mom* lives here. So *any* way I can help New York..."

"Excuse me," says one Upper East Side type who's been waiting for 20 minutes. "I didn't pull either lever in November, because I didn't like either candidate. And I was wondering—why don't you come back and visit your mother on a full-time basis in about three years?"

Ed laughs. He also manages to point out that the *New York Times* got a letter to the editor that pretty much said the same thing. *But*, he says, "he's your *mayor*." And then he proceeds to do the best PR Rudy Giuliani can hope for. He tells the guy "you can't judge a mayor by a campaign." He explains that before his election, lots of Philadelphians thought he was just another pol "with bullshit campaign promises" too.

"Give Rudy a *chance*," he continues. "He's your *mayor*." The jaded New Yorker is silent.

"It doesn't matter what he did in the past." And with this he segues right into: "I couldn't care less what Bill Clinton did with the Arkansas state police. That's *history*. He's our *president!*"

Ed delivers this like he's trying it out. And he seems to get exactly the response he's after.

"I agree!" says the jaded New Yorker.

"So do I," shouts a woman in line.

"I have one burning question," says another woman in line, who promptly shifts the conversation from presidential affairs to municipal privatization.

When the line ends, Gloria, whom he'll later refer to as "a helluvan attractive woman," ushers him out. "Thank you *so much*," she gushes. "You were so *stimulating*."

MUCH OF THE source of Ed Rendell's power began in the back seat of a car. It was January 1992 when Bill Clinton, then a nobody from Arkansas, came to visit Philly to drum up support, and Eddie took a ride with him from the Ritz-Carlton to Penn, where Clinton was giving a speech. Our mayor ended up throwing his substantial weight behind Clinton—one of the first prominent politicians to do so—mostly because they hit it off so well in the car, says Ed. "He's really fun to be around." Eddie stood by Bill—even when nobody else did, especially when Clinton's libido was first called into question.

A month after their backseat bonding, "when all the shit hit the fan about him [and Gennifer Flowers]," says Ed, loosening up on the train ride up to New York, "I was at a dinner for the Italian American Society, and I was sitting next to [Italian ambassador to Washington] Boris Biancheri—and we must have spent an hour and a half talking. And we got into the presidential election, and he said, 'You know, mayor, no offense, but yours is a strange country.' And I said, 'How so?' And he said, 'All this talk of this Clinton and his love affairs. In our country it would only *enhance* his voter appeal.'"

The train passes Metro Park station.

"Have you met Biancheri?" asks Ed. "His wife is a great-looking woman."

Anyway, Ed stuck by Bill, and Midge got tight with Hillary. "They get along terrific, just *terrific*," says Ed. "And *I* like Hillary a lot. She's smart, she has a great sense of humor, and *I* think she's attractive. I know she gets beat up a little bit, but *I* think she's attractive.

"When we were at the White House for the *Philadelphia* screening," says Ed, "Bill took us on a tour of the Oval Office after the movie." And, well, Clinton got a little goofy, says Ed. "And Hillary stood in the back and made good-natured fun of him, just as Midge would do.

"I probably shouldn't say this," he adds, "because it might not be taken right. I don't want to sound conceited, but Clinton and I are very much alike." How so? "We're both gregarious and fun, we both love sports, we both have a genuine affection for politics and government and substance. We're both married to successful women lawyers, we both have one kid the same age, we're both lawyers and former prosecutors. We both have big hearts, we both love junk food and have problems with our weight. And," he adds, laughing, "you can draw some other conclusions."

The train slows down to a crawl and Ed is getting rammy. "This is *most* disappointing," he says. He looks at his watch. "What the fuck is taking so long with this train? We should be pulling into the station by now."

Earlier, he fretted that he might not get to see his mother on this trip. Ed's mother, Ruth, who lives on the Upper East Side, was stricken with Parkinson's in 1977, the year her son was elected D.A., "and that put her in a chair for the rest of her life." She's 79 now and hasn't been able to travel to Philadelphia since, so he often visits New York mainly to see his mother.

Rendell's friends say his father's death, when Eddie was 14, was the defining moment in his life. It's why, when a cop is killed in Philadelphia, Rendell seems genuinely shattered. It is not good PR that puts him in hospital wards in the middle of the night, holding sleeping children while their mothers decide how to wake them to tell them that their father has been killed. Anyone who's seen Rendell show up at the side of these families knows that every time a boy loses his father, he seems to relive it all over again.

Rendell grew up on the Upper West Side and in private schools. His mother's family had some bucks—they owned Sloat Skirts, a large women's sportswear company. And his mother worked for a while as a designer. His dad worked as a converter in the textile industry—essentially he was a middleman between the fabric mills and the clothes manufacturers. He died of a heart attack at 58. But Ed, who's 50 now, says it's not fear or a cholesterol count of 240 that drives him to spend 35 minutes six days a week on the Stairmaster at the Sporting Club—where he manages to schmooze and sweat at the same time. "Every other male in my family, including my two grandfathers, lived into their 90s." (Rendell has one sibling, an older brother who's an international lawyer in Dallas; he says they are not close.)

"The bad news was I lost my father at 14. The good news is that I lived with him long enough for him to have a profound impact on me." How so? "My love for sports, my love for politics, being a Democrat, caring about ordinary people, my love for my son—because I'm sure it's just a mirror image of how my father treated me. And he was a great believer in the golden rule."

He pauses, then volunteers: "That's why, when all this bullshit popped up during my campaigns, about me using my power position to abuse women ..." He shakes his head over the rampant rumors about *his* libido. "*That's* not true."

What's not true? "I've never done anything to hurt women—or men. And stop writing for a minute..."

When we go back on the record, I ask him about the topic he later brings up with the privatization fanatics: what he thought about Clinton and the state troopers. On the train, he rails back at me.

"It's absolutely *irrelevant* and *meaningless* and, you know, there's got to be a statute of limitations on this stuff! You gotta judge him on how he is as president. We're gonna *kill* public life if we keep getting intrusive, intrusive, intrusive..."

I tell him I agree.

"You *do?*"

I do.

We seem to relax.

Enough to toss around another theory—that most great leaders have been philanderers. He seems to warm to this subject. "When you think of all the great leaders in history," he says, "David Lloyd George, Konrad Adenauer—and just in America alone, FDR, JFK.... Even Dwight, everybody's *grandfather*, was having a long-running affair with one of his attachés."

We take this logic a step further. Not only were most of our great leaders philanderers, we decide, but the ones we really had a problem with *weren't*.

"Look at Nixon," says Eddie.

And Carter, I offer.

"Yeah. No question about it. It's so silly. Elizabeth," he says, looking out the window. "I think we're passing through Elizabeth."

A fellow passenger comes over to pay homage to Rendell. Ed responds in his usual charming way, then abruptly stands.

"Gotta hit the head," he says. "Be right back."

HOW DID we come to love Eddie—Fast Eddie, who in his years as D.A. was best known for kicking in walls and throwing snowballs at Eagles games and hanging out at Apropos and being big-hearted. Eddie, who it is said used to sit in the dark at night in his office at Mesirov, Gelman, Jaffe, Cramer and Jamieson—thinking about *what*, Eddie, what? Eddie, who when his temper flares, is about as charming as the Missing Link?

The local answer is easy. Wilson Goode. After eight stultifying years with Mr. Congeniality—who, if nothing else, succeeded in diminishing our expectations—is it any wonder that we love Eddie? Or perhaps more accurately, that we *want* to love Eddie. We want him to save the city! We want to "love ourselves," as he has actually put it. When did Philadelphians *ever* love themselves?

And don't count Rizzo out of the equation. When we lost the Big Bambino, we were starving for a new local hero. But what's amazing about Eddie is that while, like Rizzo, he is beloved, unlike Rizzo, nobody seems to hate him. Or at least no one is willing to admit it.

"I'm not Rizzo and I never can be," says Eddie, "But I am more like Rizzo than I am like Bill [Green] or Wilson." Does he think he'd be so popular if Wilson weren't so unpopular? "I don't think it's Wilson so much. I think in Philadelphia, that certainly contributes to my popularity. But not nationally. Nationally, it's just the dollars and cents, nuts and bolts recovery story."

And so far those stories are so positively flattering that one wonders how long this honeymoon can possibly last. Is he worried? "A little bit," says Ed. "But I have tried, as you've seen, not to let this stuff make me think I'm anything special. In eight years—and I hope I'll be there for eight years—I expect some downtime, some negative turns. Even now," he says, with the public and press image so high, "there are constant defeats, *constant defeats.*"

Of course, part of the appeal of Rendell is, for lack of a better comparison, not so different from the appeal of the Phillies: He has managed to be both larger than life and Every guy. He can be smooth and he can be crude. He can be charming and he can be boorish. He can be calculating and he can be reckless. He can be very smart and he can be very, very dumb.

It is hard to imagine, for example, Rudy Giuliani bonding with Frank Guido from Staten Island. Or conducting the New York Philharmonic, for that matter. Or singing on a gay leader's roof. But it is equally hard to imagine Mayor Giuliani sitting in a car with a female reporter and casually mentioning, as Ed Rendell did with me on a rather fascinating ride back home, in the presence of Frank the driver and prominent Philly lawyer Tom Leonard, one of Ed's best friends, that he heard "something very interesting" about me. Then proceeding to tell me, in raw and alliterative terms, how he presumes I am in bed. All of which he says I "should find flattering."

How does one respond to such a thing?

Does it really matter that a mayor who has clearly turned Philadelphia around can sometimes act more like an extra in *Animal House* than a public servant? Does it really matter that the national press, in the throes of its love affair with Ed, rarely sees the side of him that Philadelphia has come to accept? Does it really matter that America's Mayor is probably more like America than anyone wants to admit?

But the really scary question is: Will Ed Rendell's most notable attributes—that *raw*, unadulterated realness that makes everyone, this reporter included, a fan of his ability to govern—also be his undoing?

And who's going to tell him where to draw the line?

It was cute, for example, at the train station—after I noticed he'd forgotten his bag in the car—when he gave me a little hug and said, "Lis, you're a lifesaver. I owe you one." It was still pretty cute a few minutes later on the train platform: "*Anything* your heart desires. No task is too menial, too trivial or too abject." Later in the train, it's a little less cute as he's going through his itinerary: "They didn't schedule any time for me to do whatever you ask me to. Remember, I owe you one." Even the following morning, he's still on this rant: He hopes to squeeze in a workout at the Plaza Hotel, he tells me. "Or," he adds, "you can get your favor then."

Does it really matter?

IN THE HOURS after he meets with Rudy, America's Mayor is off to the Plaza Hotel, where he is also staying (on *Forbes*' dime), to be the star of a "Rebuilding America" panel summoned to discuss infrastructure in American cities.

Unlike the other notables gathered for this conference, Ed Rendell is traveling sans entourage. Like he always does, much to the chagrin of his chief of security, Anthony "Butch" Buchanico, who "feels responsible for him. Put in the article that he shouldn't be traveling alone." I tell Rendell I'm surprised he does.

"Why?" he asks. "It would be a total waste of money for me to take a policeman to New York and pay for him to stay in a hotel. *I'm* in no danger in New York."

But surely all these fancy groups he speaks to would pay for the extra room.

"It's not my style," he responds. "Wilson would bring security into the Sporting Club. I could never do that. I don't even let them come to Wanamaker's with me when I shop.

"I really don't go for the monuments of power or any of that stuff," he adds. "The Crown Victoria's as good as I need. As you've probably noticed, I don't dress very well, I don't give a shit how many shoes I have."

Between his privatization speech and his infrastructure speech, he is joined in the car by an old pal from the D.A.'s office—Rob Shepardson, a former Philly assistant D.A. now working in New York.

"The *Ren*-dil was deftly handled this morning," Rob tells Ed.

"You think I should have ignored it?"

"No! It was great," says Rob. "So, how's Jesse?"

Ed tells him about his son's love of sports.

"Is he fast?" asks Rob.

"No, unfortunately that's one thing he didn't inherit from me. But when he was nine, he made an unassisted triple play. His mother was crying."

Rob asks Ed if he's seen *The War Room*, the campaign documentary starring political guru James Carville.

"No," says Rendell. "Is it self-serving?"

"Sure," says Rob. "Carville is absolutely magnetic."

"James did an absolutely *miserable* job for Florio," offers Ed.

"Can I interject?" asks Frank the driver.

"Sure, you can interject, Frank," says Ed.

"Do you think Carville or the media won the election for Bill Clinton?"

Ed thinks about this seriously, then says if he had to pick one thing that put Clinton in office, it would be his ability—particularly in the debates and the town meetings—to connect with the people (something that is also Eddie's forte).

Later, Rob asks Rendell who he thinks will win the Democratic primary for governor. And Ed says, "If Yeakel raises the money, she'll win."

"What about O'Donnell?" Rob asks, referring to former state representative Bob, the candidate Ed sort of endorsed back before O'Donnell lost his power as speaker of the House.

"I think it'll be *embarrassing*," says Rendell. "So how's Jane?"

Jane is apparently a friend of theirs who has some acting ambitions. "I screwed up," says Eddie. "I got to be good friends with Demme from the start. I should have gotten her a speaking role."

"How was the White House?" asks Rob.

Ed replies that the bed in the Lincoln bedroom was "woeful." Too small and too old. And that being there didn't have the "awe" he had expected, because Clinton "is so much like us," he tells Rob. "Maybe if it were FDR or something."

"So it was more like a sleepover?" asks Rob.

"Yeah," says Eddie. "It was just like a sleepover."

Now Frank wants to know what Eddie thought of the showboating of Rudy Giuliani's son, Andrew, on Inauguration Day.

"That mother should have taken that kid by the scruff of the neck," says Ed. "*My* wife," he tells Frank, "would have taken our kid by the collar and put a stop to that, real fast."

As we're approaching the Plaza, Ed asks for one of Frank's cards so that he can use him the next time he's here "on personal matters." By the end of the day, Rendell has promised Frank that he will "personally make a call to Rudy" and suggest that Giuliani hire him full-time.

Frank flips a card across the front seat. In the corner it says ARMED DRIVERS AVAILABLE.

"Armed drivers?!" says Rendell. "I love it. What a horrible city this is, Frank. Look at this traffic. There's no excuse for this, Frank. It's 11 o'fucking clock in the morning."

Rendell's infrastructure talk is scheduled to begin at 2:30. Mario Cuomo will be speaking at noon to the same "Rebuilding America" conference, but Rendell plans to blow off Cuomo's speech, which he expects will be "a B.S. sort of thing," and have lunch with Tom Leonard instead.

In the meantime, he retires to his room at the Plaza "to make some phone calls." He says he wants to check in with the office.

Two hours later, when he emerges from the Plaza elevator, he's late for his lunch with Leonard in the Prince Edward Room, but manages to squeeze it in before the infrastructure panel.

The first thing Rendell does when he shows up in the ballroom where the panel is to be held is re-arrange the namecards at the head table—so he can go last. Then he greets the other mayors in attendance, as if he were the star of the day, which, of course, he is. There's Stephen Goldsmith from Indianapolis, who wears a Mickey Mouse watch and whom Ed refers to as one of the most innovative, progressive mayors in the country. Goldsmith also went to high school with David Letterman, whom Eddie loves, which leads to a ten-minute discussion on Letterman's Andy Giuliani jokes—all of which Ed knows by heart. There's Bob Lanier of Houston, a good ol' Southern boy whose speeches Rendell rolls his eyes through, but whom he slaps on the back like a long-lost friend. And there's Meyera Oberndorf of Virginia Beach, a feisty little lady who loves Virginia Beach almost as much as Ed loves Philly, and who clearly amuses our mayor.

The panel ends up running late because the audience is still upstairs listening to Cuomo. Rendell looks at his watch and laughs: "Mario must be waxing eloquent again."

When the infrastructure panel finally begins—before a packed ballroom of New York lawyers, businessmen and other suits—Rendell manages, once again, to steal the show. But first, just as the mayor is stepping up to the seat he so carefully rearranged, Mayor Oberndorf mentions that Amtrak is virtually shut down and that Ed might have a hard time getting back to Philadelphia.

Rendell is genuinely surprised. "Why's that?" he asks.

AND SO it was that the mayor of our fine city spent 24 hours in New York without the foggiest clue that back home, the city was in a state of emergency. It was the day after the L.A. earthquake—which explained why Riordan didn't show—and also the day the worst storm of the winter landed on Philadelphia, paralyzing the city for the next month.

But it isn't until Ed is in the car at 5 p.m., with his pal Tom Leonard, that he learns what's going on back home. Apparently, those two hours in the hotel suite didn't include a phone call to David Cohen.

"What is *happening* in Philadelphia?" Rendell barks into the car phone to Butch, his chief of security. "*Brownouts*? Why are there brownouts? And why are the trains having problems?...I might have to send David to this thing tonight. They *cancelled* it? What's going on?"

Frank offers to blow off his next two fares and drive Eddie back to Philadelphia. Eddie says okay—and he'll even throw in some Flyers tickets—but only if Gloria from the Carnegie Institute, who hired Frank for the day for Rendell, will pick up the tab.

He hangs up on Butch and calls Gloria's secretary.

"It's Ed Rendell, from this morning," he sweet-talks into the phone. "Listen, this is a great driver you got us....Yes, I feel very *safe* with him. Yes, you should be commended. He's a fine young man. And see, I have to get back to Philadelphia, but there's a delay on Amtrak....Yes, wonderful. Tell Gloria to call me if there's a problem."

Ed hangs up the phone and turns to Leonard.

"She'll pay for it," he says. "I *charmed* Gloria."

A few minutes later, he punches in Cohen's direct line. "David, I leave town for one day and you screw up so *badly*!" he says, laughing.

Cohen gives him the rundown: PECO is in such bad shape that they're blacking out parts of the city for half-hour intervals. Firms have closed. The governor has declared a state of emergency.

"Oh my God," says Ed.

In fact, says Cohen, the Packard Building, where Tom Leonard's office is, really had it bad. The elevators were shut down and everything.

Rendell finds this terribly amusing, since the Packard Building is also where Bill Batoff works, and as he and Leonard chuckled earlier, "The Bates" was supposed to be hosting a big luncheon with U.S. Representative Dick Gephardt there today.

"So," says Ed, "did Bates have to go home to Beverly [his wife]?"

They're laughing raucously, he and Leonard. And Frank.

Then Leonard pipes in, suddenly serious. "Uh, David, what if it gets worse?... Is there a priority list on the power? You know, to make sure kids get it first?"

Cohen assures him everything's under control. "David," says Ed, "why don't you go home, too? Save the energy." He puts his hand over the phone and laughs.

Now Ed wants to talk to Butch again. He wants to know if "Hillary's still coming tomorrow."

He's told that she's not.

"Because of the *weather*?" asks Ed. "What the fuck is happening to this world? Earthquakes in L.A., brownouts in Philly...I can't leave you guys alone for a minute."

He hangs up the phone and thinks for a moment.

Then he calls his wife. He assures Midge he's sticking to the low-fat diet she has him on, then hangs up and confides to Frank that "my wife is nearly perfect," except that she's a lousy cook. "She's gonna be a judge," he also tells Frank, "so all week she's been interviewing law clerks. And they're all 24 or 25. She's gonna get herself a 24-year-old guy, Frank, I just know it."

"Nah," says Frank. "How could she do better than you?"

"True, Frank, true," says Eddie, and for the next few miles, he's staring silently out the windows—thinking of *what*, Eddie, what?

The following morning, the Philadelphia papers will report, in excruciating front-page detail, how the mayor's office snapped into action to handle the state of emergency, without any mention that the mayor himself was out of town. In New York, the papers will have breathless front-page coverage on Rudy Giuliani's plans to save the city, plans that are almost verbatim Rendell.

But for now Ed Rendell turns and asks Frank if he'd mind pulling into the next rest stop.

America's Mayor would like a hot dog.

PART 2

1995 – 1999

By Mark Kram Jr.

August 1995

END OF THE LINE

ven the cows are vanishing, Scattered across the sloping hillsides of Ardrossan, the herd of 300 is being rounded up and sent to a ranch in Southern Colorado in spacious, air-conditioned vans—deluxe accommodations, but somehow appropriate considering that these are not just ordinary bossies. The old colonel, Robert Learning Montgomery, began raising them in 1912, then passed them on to his daughter, the fabulous Hope, who cultivated the bloodlines of the group and won blue ribbons with them at shows. When Hope died in January, she bequeathed them to her son, Robert Montgomery Scott, who, alas, has found the economics of dairy farming to be prohibitive and is selling them for $1,000 or so a head.

Far from just the commonplace sale of cattle, the dispersal of the Ardrossan Ayrshires would seem to connote the passing of an era. Harking back to the Edwardian days of England, the world the Montgomerys and the Scotts once occupied was one of sprawling estates, obsequious servants and lavish balls where the women wore wonderful dresses and the men fine evening clothes. Helen Hope Montgomery Scott, "The Last Debutante," had been the diva of Main Line society for better than 70 years and led a life that included dancing at the Stork Club with the Duke of Windsor and dining shipboard with Sir Winston Churchill. She was so dazzling, so utterly fascinating, that Hollywood based a 1940 Oscar-winning film on her exploits: *The Philadelphia Story*, starring Katharine Hepburn, Cary Grant and James Stewart. It was (as Hope would have had it) all so thoroughly divine.

Whatever else Robert Montgomery Scott ("Bobby" to friends) is, he is a captive of that era. Schooled at Groton, Harvard, and Penn Law, he had a successful law career with Montgomery, McCracken, Walker, and Rhoads, became special assistant to Walter Annenberg during his appointment as ambassador to Great Britain, and has served as president of both the Academy of Music and the Philadelphia Museum of Art. While he has been one of the leading shapers of Philadelphia culture and society, he has found himself both embroiled in a continuing battle with Mayor Ed Rendell over Museum funding and at odds with certain elements of the Museum board, which recently discussed removing him but has since given him a unanimous vote of confidence.

Sophisticated, courtly and, as a lady friend says, "oh so sweet," Bobby Scott, 66, has seen sweeping change come into his otherwise orderly life. Splitting time between his "pad" at Ardrossan and his apartment at the Warwick Hotel, he separated in 1993 from his wife of 42 years, the former Gay Elliot. Then, one by one, parents and relatives began to die off: Hope, at 90 (though it was "rather sudden to me"); then his aunt, Mary Binney, at 87; and then his father, Edgar Scott, 96, a founder of the Janney Montgomery Scott investment house. What once had seemed so invulnerable has disintegrated before his wonderfully cheerful eyes.

"Some interesting things have happened," says Scott, strolling through Ardrossan beneath old portraits of his ancestors. "It is the disappearance of an era. I look back on what I have lost in the last two years or so and, well...shall we add it up? One wife—plus the house—one mother, one father, one aunt..."

He pauses, then grins: "And 300 cows."

UP THROUGH a set of iron gates, then a curving drive with woodland on either side, the "big house" stands on 650 acres of Radnor Township real estate. While the walls in the back stairwells are in need of new paint and the cloth wallpaper in a couple of the sitting rooms is ripped in spots, Ardrossan had a certain sparkle to it on this cool spring evening as Scott stood in a receiving line at the door and welcomed the Patron Circle of the Museum Trustee Association. Spilling from the ornate living room onto the veranda with cocktails in hand, the 84 guests in attendance seated themselves at tables dressed in silver and exquisite china. Moving through the room with bowls of oyster stew and plates of lamb, servants in black dinner jackets had just ladled out an especially sinful raspberry dessert when Bobby Scott stood to speak. "This is an old house," he began, "but it is a house that has always enjoyed a good party." He held up a glass of white wine and added, "So...cheers."

Far removed from its halcyon days, when the house had a staff of 12 and was the hub of Main Line society, the 50-room Georgian manse dates to 1912. (The architect was the celebrated Horace Trumbauer, who also designed the Philadelphia Museum of Art.) Colonel Montgomery, who came from an old Philadelphia line that squandered much of its holdings, had grown up in what he called "shabby gentility" and resolved at 17 to restore the Montgomery name. By the time he turned 30, he not only had built a considerable fortune through the operation of his brokerage house, he was also ensconced at Ardrossan and had become a fixture in Philadelphia society. When daughter Hope debuted at the Philadelphia Assemblies Ball in 1922, she received no fewer than four marriage proposals. She waved each of them off with a flourish of her delicate hand.

It was the society wedding of the year when Hope and Edgar Scott exchanged vows in 1923. One of the heirs to the Pennsylvania Railroad fortune, Scott had attended Harvard with playwright Philip Barry (who would write *The Philadelphia Story*) and had leanings himself at one point to write plays; the only professional production of one of his works, *The Jumblies*, ran in Philadelphia for just three nights before closing. He joined his father-in-law to form the brokerage house Montgomery Scott and Co. (now Janney Montgomery Scott), and that same year—1929—Bobby was born. Older brother Edgar Jr., born four years earlier, remembers that as children he and Bob cultivated a passion for horsemanship in order to spend time with their mother. "Heck," Edgar Jr. laughs, "we were too young to dance with her."

Through the Roaring '20s and even well into the Depression, the dancing continued. "We ate divine food like terrapin and champagne," Hope told the *Inquirer*. "Oh, but we had fun." While the Depression cut deeply into the fortunes of the Montgomerys and the Scotts (Bobby is not sure how deeply, but says "they were chronically broke"), cutting back on their servants or their extravagant lifestyle was, well…unthinkable. It was the Golden Age of the Anglo-American ascendancy, and no one luxuriated in it with greater joy than Hope. Cecil Beaton photographed her, Augustus John did her portrait (three times), and her son Bobby found her thoroughly intriguing: "Glamorous and vibrant and something of a free spirit," he says, seated upstairs in a sitting room at Ardrossan. "She also had an astonishing ability to swear, and an extraordinary temper that she inherited from the colonel, who—I should add—I got on well with. We were pals. He had a cold side to him, but it never bothered me."

He pauses and adds with a chuckle: "Perhaps because I have that same coldness."

He is asked: You think of yourself as that? Cold?

"I can be," he says sharply.

His daughter explains. "Not….well…icy, but there is a part of him that is inaccessible—even to himself," says Janny, a reporter for the *New York Times*. "He can be charming and gregarious, but there is a certain part of him that is profoundly private."

Shielded from the less fortunate world outside Ardrossan, Bobby Scott was raised by a French governess and then Irish housekeepers. Something of a solitary child who remembers being "perfectly content to sit in a sandbox…or dam up a stream," he attended Episcopal Academy until Grade 7 and then boarded at Groton in Massachusetts, where he received something his parents could not provide, a "regulatory authority that was there all the time." He did well at Groton, and he remembers that when he was 15 or so, he summered with his Aunt Anna in Northeast Harbor, Maine, and found himself under the spell of a girl called Happy.

"We had a place two cottages down, and I remember I used to sit on the stone wall and watch her pass," says Scott. "I was desperately shy, but I had such a crush on her. Then, when the summer was over and I had to leave, the beautiful Happy came over and said, 'Bobby, you better kiss me goodbye.' I was horrified. She had that honey-colored hair and those honey-colored eyes and was wearing, I remember, she was wearing this green silk scarf, which I ended up kissing the back of."

Scott chuckles.

"The story has, well...some kind of sequel to it," he continues. "Twenty years later, when her brother Bill was taking her to be married to Nelson Rockefeller, the future Happy Rockefeller said, 'Tell me, Billy, how is Bobby Scott?'"

It is with a certain wry humor that Bobby Scott looks back on those days. He used to tell his children that he is an anachronism, "the last of a kind," and it was true. While his children still return to Ardrossan occasionally, and Janny observes that she still bears the indelible "stamp" of her ancestors, each has pursued lives far from the insular world of the Main Line: daughters Janny and Hope reside in New York, and son Elliot, an erstwhile actor, just completed his MBA at the University of Chicago. You wonder if Bobby Scott somehow regrets this, how the future has become so unglued from the past. The answer is...no. The answer is..."the world changes." The answer is...

"I thoroughly enjoyed the lifestyle...but there are things I have done in life that I would not particularly care to do again."

Such as?

"Such as hunting with the pack of hounds. I suppose I look back on the old days with the same nostalgia one would have for an old girlfriend."

How, exactly?

"She was kind of fun while she was there..." He pauses. "But one would not especially want her back."

IT WAS at the Academy of Music anniversary ball at the Bellevue this past January that Bobby Scott suddenly remembered: He had come without a handkerchief! It was just one of those things "well-bred boys" never did. A "well-bred boy" never allowed his escort to walk on the curbside (for "fear that she would be splashed by a passing conveyance"); never preceded a lady out of an elevator (though Scott says he never fully understood that one); and he never attended a dance without having a handkerchief, for as Scott explains: "Well-bred girls are not fond of sweaty, well-bred boys."

So he excused himself and walked back to the Warwick to retrieve a handkerchief. There, he had just entered the lobby when he heard a sudden crack. It was his leg. Something had popped. It was so pronounced that even the door-man looked up and said, "I heard that, Mr. Scott." (Grinning, he now recalls in that exquisite accent of his: "I suppose he thought it was a fart.") He collapsed to the floor.

What happened at this point is fascinating, and explains how truly captive Bobby Scott is to his upbringing: Instead of hobbling up to his eighth-floor apartment and crawling into bed, he had the doorman hail a cab, and he returned to the Bellevue. Walking one-legged onto the escalator ("it was okay so long as I kept it stiff"), he presented himself to his hostess and apologetically explained that he would be unable to attend the event. Only then did he repair to bed, where he spent a difficult night before he was taken to the hospital the following day with a ruptured quadriceps tendon. He subsequently underwent surgery. "It would not have occurred to me not to return to the Bellevue and explain what happened," says Scott. "Though I do find it somewhat amusing. It was a triumph of breeding over brains."

Sizing up Bobby Scott at 66, it could well be tempting to write him off as a dilettante, the beneficiary of high birth and easy opportunity. Close acquaintances contradict that, however, and say that beneath his urbane charm is a man of some substance. Montgomery, McCracken chairman Carter Buller says Scott had a "distinguished law career" and represented the "spirit...and conscience of the firm." In addition to handling corporate and estate work, Scott served on 17 boards in the Philadelphia area. "Even with the social connections he had—and this surprised me—he worked hard at it," says attorney William Klaus of Pepper, Hamilton and Sheetz, who served with Scott on the First Fidelity Bank board. Scott himself traces his public spiritedness back to Groton. "The privileged brats who attended there were inculcated with the idea of giving something back," he says. "I inherited a hair shirt, and I have been forever aware of the itch."

Quite entrenched during the 1950s and 1960s with his wife, Gay, and three children up at Ardrossan in a 17-room home on the estate not far from where his parents lived, Scott accepted a position in London as special assistant to old family friend Walter Annenberg, whom President Richard Nixon had appointed ambassador to Great Britain. Though Scott did not consider himself a Nixon supporter ("I was pro-Rockefeller," he says), he was delighted to serve under Annenberg, who he remembers had "extraordinary tentacles of intuition." In charge of paper flow for Annenberg—Scott says he fell "somewhere between his deputy and his dog"—Scott remembers shuddering whenever the eldest Nixon daughter, Tricia, would come to England and expect the staff to cater to her whims. "I was fond of her sister, Julie, but I could have lived without Tricia," he says. "She could be wonderfully condescending."

He pauses and snipes, "Of course, she was royal."

Scott returned to Philadelphia in 1973. While Janny remembers that she and her siblings "all seemed to head off in different directions at that point," that the ties were beginning to break even then, Scott proceeded with his law career and was elected president of the Academy of Music, home of the world-renowned Philadelphia Orchestra. Characterizing himself as "ape over symphony and operas," he spearheaded expansion of the backstage. He also "institutionalized" the fund-raising of the Academy and helped generate $5 million in contributions. He was appointed president of the Philadelphia Museum of Art in 1980.

Initially serving as a "volunteer" president, Scott resigned from the law firm in 1982 when the Museum job was offered as a salaried position. It was less than half of what he had been earning, but as he remembers, "I just became more interested in the problems of the Museum than the problems of the law firm." Working arm-in-arm with director Anne d'Harnoncourt—who has presided over collections, the organization of special exhibitions, the curatorial staff and so on—Scott has been responsible for finance, building operations, membership, marketing, and public relations. Both say that the relationship has "worked out wonderfully," but the question being asked is: How long will Bobby Scott remain at the Museum?

The issue came up at an executive session in June that centered on removing Scott. While board chairman Phil Berman will not comment on that—he says Scott has done a "wonderful job"— he does concede that he sees no reason to perpetuate the dual leadership positions. Where that would leave Scott is unclear, but Scott himself says he has no inclination to run the "art end" of the Museum, and sources indicate d'Harnoncourt was promised sole leadership of the Museum when she rejected an offer from the Museum of Modern Art in New York; d'Harnoncourt denies that, saying: "No promises were made, and none were asked."

Explanations for why Scott appeared vulnerable are not hard to divine: While the Barnes exhibit was an immense success, and contributions are up, the Museum is faced with dwindling support from the city and some wonder if Scott has lost his effectiveness with the mayor. Even as he was taking bows for shielding the Museum from the New Era Philanthropy scandal ("I asked where the repayment of the funds would come from and was told it was a series of donors known only to Mr. Bennett," says Scott. "That was not enough"), Scott was swapping philosophical blows over funding with Mayor Ed Rendell. When Rendell proposed in his initial five-year plan to cut subsidies to the Museum, Scott shot back that this "violated a long-standing contract." The existing five-year plan calls for the Museum to receive $2.25 million (plus utilities), but Rendell is certain that it could be doing more to sell itself to the public.

"I like Bob Scott," says Rendell. "He has been a campaign contributor and a friend. But the Museum has operated in a never-never land and could be doing more."

Scott questions that.

"Because we do not have a catalog, the mayor assumes we are not trying," says Scott, who concedes that more could be done. "Somehow, we seem to have this temptation to conclude that we can save ourselves by going into the retail business."

Scott chuckles.

"It gives me immense pleasure, this job," he says. "And pain."

Speaking of which...his leg has hampered him terribly since his January incident. It has deprived him of riding his bicycle (which had been one of his passions) and forced upon him the periodic use of crutches. "I even had to use that," he says, pointing to a cane in the corner of his apartment and adding with a boarding-school laugh: "To get up off the john."

HELLO, dear pop!" Bobby Scott shouts as he sweeps into the living room of Orchard Lodge, the house Bobby and Edgar grew up in and one of 40 dwellings on the Ardrossan grounds. "How are we today?"

In the corner sits Edgar Scott Sr. 2 weeks before his death. His legs covered with a shawl, the old man looks up and replies, "Bobby?"

"Are we warm enough?" Bobby asks as he draws closer. "Shall I get another blanket for you?"

"No..." his father answers in a hoarse voice. His eyes close, then open again.

"Pop, tomorrow I will be attending a wedding," says Bobby, as he kisses the old man on the cheek. "The weather is supposed to be hot. I shall see you again on Sunday."

"Tomorrow?" Edgar Scott says as his son strolls from the room. "Come back tomorrow when your mother is here."

Bobby Scott explains as he glances back into the room, where his father is now sleeping again: "He still thinks Mom is alive sometimes," says Bobby. "When she died in January, the life seemed to go out of him. His game plan is to sleep the days away."

Somehow, Bobby Scott had prepared himself for his father to die— "it was time for him to go"—but not Hope. Even at this age she seemed so...so vibrant and forceful and endlessly brimming with the joy of living. Although as a child he saw only passing glimpses of her, he found himself growing closer to her as the years passed. So he remembers that she loved a good time and how she enjoyed people who "thought she was funny and attractive." Hope had become a "terribly, terribly dear friend," says Bobby, who smiles sadly and observes, "Now when I have a dirty joke, and she loved them, I have no one to tell it to."

It left a hole in his life when Hope died just as surely as it had left one when he and Gay separated. It had been a relationship that commenced back in college, when Bobby was at Harvard and Gay was at Radcliffe. While Gay Scott prefers not to comment on her former husband ("I would feel awkward doing that," she says), Bobby once told an English friend in a letter that while it was not "the greatest union in the world," it was the only one he ever expected to have. He says it came as a shattering blow to him when it ended, although he concedes that he contributed to the dissolution. "My [infidelities] were not that frequent, that random or that profligate," he says. "Whatever the national average is for rich males—I think I read somewhere it was six—I am just under it."

So...what happened?

"It was wonderful...and then over the course of time it became less wonderful," says Scott. "Walls developed...We had a relationship from the beginning where each of us did different things, and I suppose in the end it just eroded. We were like a suit of clothes that just sort of wears. You never notice them wearing out until one day..."

Scott also concedes that he has had a drinking problem. He received treatment for it in 1991 and seems to be handling it well. "Faced with not drinking at all or drinking in controlled quantities...I have chosen the latter," he says, adding that his excessive drinking "just sort of crept up." Once, he added up the evenings in a year that he could have spent out on museum-related business, and it came to 230. He observes: "Museum life involves a lot of receptions...a social drink."

He has discovered that he enjoys the single life. Although he was "scared to death to be alone" in the beginning and had such trouble concentrating that even reading a *New Yorker* profile was too arduous, Scott has since settled into what he calls "bachelorhood" with increasing ease. He cooks for himself and derives immense pleasure from it, even though an upstairs neighbor at the Warwick who has eaten with him, Sue Peck Goldenberg, says with a laugh: "A lot of it is boiled Main Line...even the vegetables."

While Scott contends that he is far from lonely and rather enjoys "being sought after," a part of him mourns. Walking through the big house recently, he pauses before an antique table arrayed with old photographs: shots of Hope and Edgar, brother Ed and even himself. He glances down at it and observes, "I was cute once." Moving from room to room flipping on lights, he comes upon a huge oil portrait of Hope, dressed in a gown that seems to flow forever. He lingers on their parting.

Scott had been at a reception for the Museum in Meadowbrook and stopped at Orchard Lodge to see his parents. Told that Hope was upstairs—that she had fallen while leading the donkeys to the stable and was napping—Scott expected to see her stretched out on her daybed. Instead, he found her on the bathroom floor, slipping into unconsciousness. She looked up at him, confused, but then realizing who it was reached for his hand. She kissed it and then let it go. The Last Debutante fell into a coma and was dead the following day.

WHEN he is not kept in town at night on business, Bobby Scott drives home at the end of the day to Ardrossan. He is quite fond of it there, and says pointedly, "I have never once taken it for granted. It has always been impressive to me." Surrounded by deep foliage, every kind of fowl, and creamy sunlight, he peers out at the sweeping lawn that spills forth from the veranda and is overcome with a sharp sense of loss...not for a period that once was, but for the people he loved.

Up on the hillside the herd of cows is thinning: there are 30 fewer than there were the previous week. Still not sure what he plans to do with the land when the cows have been removed, Scott is considering raising a high grade of French beef cattle, Charolais. "I am planning an aristocratic group," he says with a laugh. "Smaller in number and not so demanding," While this is an exclusive piece of real estate and would be ripe for development, Scott hopes that it will remain open space.

"Which," he observes, "is to say it will become a golf course."

And the big house?

"Well..." he ponders, then smiles, "I suppose it would be an excellent club-house."

By Larry Platt
July 1995

THE UNLOVED

"Beyond all the years of practice and all the hours of glory waits the inexorable terror of living without the game."
  —Senator Bill Bradley, former New York Knick

 glove protrudes from his right rear pocket as Michael Jack Schmidt, gazing intently at the ball, wiggles his hips in anticipation just before uncoiling a compact textbook swing. The ball isn't just struck, it's launched.

"They don't get any better than that," he says as he follows through and watches the ball's flight before it kisses the green some 250 yards away. It is six summers since Mike Schmidt last watched the trajectory of a slightly larger ball after a similarly expert swing, six summers since the best third baseman baseball's ever known walked away from the game, six summers into a new life, one that seems more like a state of exile than retirement.

"You find yourself a retired person at the age of 39, and for 5 years before that you were told by everyone 'Whatever you want to do after you retire, you can do,'" he says, walking after his ball on the tenth hole of the exclusive Medalist Golf Club's course, co-designed by pro golfer Greg Norman. This is where Schmidt can be found most days, working alone on his game, harboring vague hopes of joining the PGA Senior Tour when he turns 50 in 1999. "You start believing there's always going to be something for you. Then you retire, and you're puttering around the house and the phone isn't ringing."

Since moving to Jupiter, Florida, three years ago, Schmidt has settled into a comfortable routine—he lives on the water, owns a boat and a boating business, coaches for his son's high school baseball team and works on his golf game. His ties to Philadelphia are tenuous; he and his wife, Donna, a South Philly native, return occasionally to visit her family, and he's an investor in a chain of hoagie shops bearing his name. He says he's happy now—"Where else can I just show up and have Greg Norman or Nick Price, the two best golfers in the world, come over and ask if I've got a game?"—but, as he prepares for his career's ultimate honor at Cooperstown this month, it's clear Mike Schmidt is haunted by the life that preceded this middle age, still scarred by the invective that assaulted him on countless summer nights inside the Vet, still wounded by the Phillies' refusal to find a place for him in the organization, still smarting from the by-now familiar raps on his game popularized by an often cynical press.

As he expertly whacks golf ball after golf ball with a smooth, easy swing on this gorgeous Florida day, Mike Schmidt grows increasingly morose as he talks about his former life. "I look back on that and sometimes I think it all happened to another person," he says, frowning. "You know, it's hard for me to be positive, to have real good things to say about a town that never did anything for me and in general made life miserable for me."

You wonder what it would take to bring Mike Schmidt a sense of contentment. He runs his hand through his thick, graying hair. He sighs and looks down, preparing to smack yet another ball. "I've never understood the concept of peace," he says.

IT WAS ABOUT 7 o'clock one morning during the winter following the 1983 World Series, the one in which Schmidt had managed just one bloop single in 20 at-bats as the Phillies lost in five games to the Baltimore Orioles. It had been snowing most of the night, so Schmidt wasn't surprised when the phone rang and he learned that the school bus carrying his kids—Jonathan and Jessica—had gotten stuck. He got in his four-wheel drive and braved the slick suburban streets around Media before pulling up alongside a yellow bus on the side of the road. Rolling down his window, he realized it wasn't his kids'.

"I saw all these cute grade-schoolers on the bus," he recalls today, sitting behind the wheel of his emerald green Lexus on his way to pick up Jonathan, now 15, from school. "All of a sudden, one of these really cute little kids recognizes me—I see him point and yell. They must have been in fourth grade. Then the whole damn bus, every one of these kids, just starts booing me."

Schmidt winces at the memory. I can't help but laugh at the image. "You think that's funny?" he asks pointedly. "I'll never forget that. I think it's sickening."

This is what comes to Mike Schmidt's mind when he is asked about his painful relationship with the Philadelphia fans. Over the years, as Schmidt is quick to point out, there have been many athletes driven from this town by the fanatics whose idea of rooting is to hurl obscenities at guys they will cheer with equal passion the moment a game-winning homer is hit or a shot sunk. Was there anything more hypocritical than the way, after Schmidt's 500th home run, the fans started cheering him? Even that was done grudgingly. Why, he even had the insult of watching his Center City restaurant, Michael Jack's, go belly-up.

Of course, he's not alone. The list of those athletes happy to escape Philly's antipathy reads like an all-time all-star team: Wilt Chamberlain, Dick Allen, Del Ennis, Charles Barkley. But Schmidt, the most accomplished jock Philadelphia's ever had, may have gotten the worst of it. Yes, despite the home runs, the MVPs, the Gold Gloves, Mike Schmidt's real legacy may lie in what his treatment says about Philly sports fans—that we're not as discerning or sophisticated as we think, that excellence isn't enough for us. He is a symbol of our shame, the Philly fan's Scarlet Letter.

"Forget about his dominance of the '80s—just look at what he did in the '70s," says sportscaster and baseball maven Bob Costas. "If he has *that* career in St. Louis [Costas' home], he's probably a god. For fans who pride themselves on their baseball smarts, it's a mystery to me why Philadelphia never really embraced the player who is the modern era's clear-cut choice as the best to ever play a position."

Of course, the conventional wisdom, which even Schmidt subscribes to, is that he didn't fit the Philly fan's shot-and-a-beer mold. "I was not the type of player who lit the fire of the average fan in Philly," Schmidt concedes. "I may have in Los Angeles, but in Philly, they want the brawler, they want the guy who doesn't wipe the blood off, who doesn't wipe the dirt off, who looks like he's having a tough time getting it done. They wanted Pete [Rose], they wanted Bobby Clarke. I'm the exact opposite."

Then again, there have been some quintessentially blue-collar types who also knew the fans' wrath—Ron Jaworski comes to mind. No, the vilification of Schmidt is really about a host of complex perceptions about him—and about the essential nature of a rabid core of fans.

"They want the rest of the country to know how they are, how they treat athletes like myself," he says. "That's what they want, that's their thing. That's their release. I don't remember that city doing a lot to make me think highly of it. I mean, they've got a statue up of Julius Erving, one of my favorite people, but he didn't even play his whole career there. Look, if that's the worst thing that happens in your life—having to deal with a city like that—then you've been pretty lucky. But I don't miss the town."

Schmidt was a perfect whipping boy. Throughout his career, there were the Roses, Bowas, and Luzinskis, the scrappy over-achievers, and there was Schmidt, the natural. Of course the fans would take someone like Luzinski under their wing: He looked like he lived for cheesesteaks, and he set up the Bull Ring, a section in left field for underprivileged kids, besides. Schmidt, on the other hand, never flaunted his charitable acts, and he had the ideal body for baseball along with the insouciance to convey that his on-field exploits were divinely inspired.

They weren't, not entirely. Back then, much was made of Bowa's having been cut from his high school team, but hardly anyone knew that Schmidt was a college walk-on. He'd had two knee surgeries while in high school in Dayton, Ohio, and as a result most scouts didn't think he'd last long in the majors. While countless column inches of area sports pages were devoted to Bowa's obsessive fielding of ground balls, Schmidt's intense preparation went unnoticed.

"Very few in the game worked as hard as I did, and I never got credit for that, because it went on behind the scenes and I never talked about it," he says as we idle in traffic before a drawbridge, one of Schmidt's few complaints about Florida living. "I'm talking about being consumed by the sport. Players today come to the park, watch some TV, read a newspaper, make a sandwich, have a few laughs, break out the cards, ease into their uniforms, and then it's time for batting practice. When I got to the park, I started preparing immediately. I was all business."

Schmidt was aloof, but over nearly 20 years in Philly's limelight there was not a single instance of what would now be considered conduct unbecoming a role model, no headlines recounting brushes with the law or loutish behavior in public places. Still, every time I wonder aloud to friends about the reasons behind the fans' mistreatment of Schmidt, there is a strange tendency to blame the victim: The guy was a jerk, they say, a verdict fueled by the press. When, for instance, Schmidt was elected to the Hall of Fame early this year, *Delaware County Daily Times* columnist Bill Brown wrote a nasty piece explaining the unexplainable: why he didn't vote for Schmidt. According to Brown, Schmidt was "arrogant," "egomaniacal" and "thoughtless," a self-obsessed "man who carried a bat to his hotel room at night and studied himself in the mirror."

Today, Schmidt is still bothered by perceptions of him that he couldn't control. "Hell, you could just listen to WIP and hear some guy call in to say his son asked for an autograph and I walked away," Schmidt says. "That's like a cancer. That goes out on the airwaves one time and I don't know how many people formulate an opinion about me. The truth is, there are players who the Philly fans loved who would push kids out of their way rather than sign an autograph. I never did that. In fact, I'd feel guilty if I had to refuse to sign a ball for a kid.

"When Jonathan was playing Little League, I tried to create a policy that I wouldn't sign autographs there, because if I signed one, it would lead to a mob scene and take away from the kids playing the game. Well, one time this cute little kid was sent over to me, on a mission from his mom, and he asked me to sign his ball. And I'm sitting there trying to explain to this little kid about my policy. I told him I couldn't sign the ball, but I'd take a handshake, and I patted his head. And then I watched him walk back to his mom. Now, can you imagine what that mother said when he came back without an autograph? You know what she felt: Who the hell does Mike Schmidt think he is?"

Even when he did sign autographs, Schmidt rarely showed enthusiasm. Often, he'd sign a ball or a program without looking a fan in the eye. It seemed like a chore to him when, in fact, it tested his lifelong shyness. He never really warmed up. In 1985, the fans started coming around to him when he donned a wild wig during infield practice to cut the tension after he had blasted the fans in the press. They cheered—Michael Jack was finally loosening up. "But that wasn't me. I was just trying to give the fans what they wanted," he says. "Larry Andersen reached into his bag of tricks and coerced me into doing it."

Away from the stadium was no different. "Schmitty hated crowds," recalls Phillies broadcaster Chris Wheeler. "I remember this one night, Jim Kaat, Tim McCarver, Schmitty and I had an appearance in Delaware, and then we were going to some bar in King of Prussia for a drink. On our way over, Schmitty asks, 'Are there going to be people there?' Kitty [Kaat] was like, 'No, Mike, we'll call ahead and have them clear the place out.'"

Schmidt laughs when Wheeler's anecdote is repeated. "It's true, I'm uncomfortable when I feel people staring at me like I'm on display," he says, as his son Jonathan, thin, blond-haired and tan, gets in the car. He's a good-looking kid wearing a T-shirt and khaki shorts who answers questions with one-word, soft-spoken replies. We're heading to Miami to watch the Phillies play the Marlins tonight, a rare return for Schmidt to a major-league ballpark. But at least in Florida he can maintain some degree of anonymity. "That's why I like living here so much. As soon as I get off an airplane in Philly, though, my heart starts pumping like crazy. Because they'll yell it out in Philly—'*Hey!! There goes Michael Jack!*' You know?"

Schmidt fiddles with the car radio, passing over his usual jazz and R&B in search of something he and Jonathan can agree on. He settles on a station that plays a lot of Joe Cocker and Crosby, Stills and Nash.

"You know, I can't help who I am. I don't have a painted-on smile, and I don't look like a real pleasant guy all the time," he says. "I'd love to be different than I am. But people forget that someone is the way he is, generally, because he had a father who was that way too. And my father was not a guy the Philly fans would have enjoyed watching. He was very unemotional."

When he played, Schmidt's unemotional nature was called "cool" at a time when the word had all sorts of implications, many of them racial. In the '70s, the Phillies were a racially segregated team in a racially segregated town, and Schmidt, with his slow, cocky swagger, tight Afro and collection of Earth, Wind and Fire albums, was an honorary brother, hanging with Dave Cash, Dick Allen and Garry Maddox. (Ironically, emotionalism in sports has become the province of the black athlete; now it's the white guys who are removed and repressed.) In other cities at other times, to be cool might have been an asset. New Yorkers worshiped Joe DiMaggio's classy, regal countenance in the '30s and '40s, for instance. But by the '70s in Philly, a whole host of attitudes went into the way we looked at our sports stars. It's not altogether far-fetched to wonder if some of the backlash against Schmidt in a town run by Frank Rizzo had to do with a demeanor recognized, on some level, as black.

"It ain't the color, it's the game, and Mike played black," says Dick Allen, now a roving hitting instructor for the Phillies. "He could gig, man, that's what we used to say. I was proud of that Afro he wore. He was the coolest white boy I ever played with. And the sportswriters knew what was going on in the clubhouse, and the fans picked it up from them."

At the time, Schmidt sought comfort from the black players in a locker room that had become a painful place for him. Bowa and Luzinski relentlessly teased him about his strikeouts, his pockmarked complexion, his "coolness." It may have been meant as good-natured locker-room banter, but Schmidt didn't see it like that. On almost a daily basis, Dave Cash would sit with Schmidt in front of his locker, massaging the slugger's battered ego, telling him to ignore his teammates' derision and repeating, over and over, "You're the man, Mike, you're the man."

"Bowa and Luzinski were unmerciful on me back then, and I sensed a lot of petty jealousy from them," Schmidt says. "I saw it as mean-spirited, no question. I found a solace from the black players, who, for some reason, took a liking to me. There was just a sensitivity there I felt very comfortable with."

Bowa, now a Phillies coach, smiles when asked about his riding of Schmidt. "A lot of that was because I kept reading about this shortstop they drafted who was supposedly going to be in the majors in three years," he says. "I had to let him know he'd have to play third if he wanted to make it in the big leagues. Come to think of it, I take some credit for him getting into the Hall of Fame, because if he'd taken my job, he would have been too tired to hit all those home runs."

Today, Schmidt says, his relationship with Bowa is better than ever. But the fans were a tougher problem to overcome. Even in the '80s, the decade Schmidt won his trio of MVP awards, there were nights that, when dredged up now, still send him into deep funks. One comes to mind as we pull into Joe Robbie Stadium.

Schmidt lowers his window, telling the guard "My name's Mike Schmidt" while Jonathan rolls his eyes—"He knows who you are, Dad." Just then, like the return of a bad dream, Schmidt is visited by a painful recollection.

It was a tight game at home against the Expos in 1983. Four times Schmidt comes up and four times he strikes out on consecutive pitches. Twelve pitches, four outs. Each time, walking back to the dugout, the boos get louder and angrier. Finally, in extra innings, he hits pitch number 13 off ace reliever Jeff Reardon for a game-winning home run and sprints around the bases, aware of the deafening cheers, his stomach churning. He runs past his teammates, into the dugout, down the runway to his locker, thinking about the fans, how they're not really ever with him, how quick they are to turn on him, how they don't deserve a slow trot and don't deserve a tip of the hat—why *should* he savor the moment?—and he grabs his keys without breaking stride, sprints to his car, and then he's on his way home, in full uniform, blasting hard-driving funk music all the way.

THE PHILLIES are taking batting practice, and Mike Schmidt, Jonathan close by his side, is sitting in the Phils' dugout. "This is neat," Jonathan says, watching light-hitting second baseman Mickey Morandini take his cuts. "But, Dad, how come they're all trying to go yard [hit it out of the park]?"

Schmidt smiles. "Because they get paid $5 million a year, they can do whatever they want," he says. "But I can tell you this: They wouldn't be doing that if I were out there working with them."

At the end of the dugout sits Phils general manager Lee Thomas, who looks over a number of times before approaching Schmidt. When he does, Thomas' gregariousness is overwhelming. "I hear you're broadcasting a couple of games for the Baseball Network? That's *terrific*, Mike, just *terrific*," Thomas says, pumping Schmidt's arm a little too enthusiastically.

Schmidt mumbles a thank you and, as he walks away after the brief exchange, raises his eyebrows. "That may have been the longest conversation we've ever had," he says as we make our way to the press box. "I can understand Lee being a little nervous around me, though. Everywhere that guy goes, he must hear 'Oh, you have Schmitty's job.' And, look, if I was hired as the general manager in St. Louis tomorrow, I don't know if the first thing I'd do is ask Stan Musial what job he'd want. But I'd also be damn sure he and I were on good terms and that Stan would be available if I needed him for something, whether it's teaching a minor-leaguer how to field ground balls or to do promotions."

In 1988, as his playing days were winding down, Schmidt asked Phils owner Bill Giles for the general manager's job. Four years before, Flyers owner Ed Snider promoted his superstar, Bobby Clarke, from center ice to the GM's office. Giles, who by no means considered the job Schmidt's for the taking, instead encouraged him to pursue a career in broadcasting and hired Thomas.

In 1991, a frustrated Schmidt told Ray Didinger of the *Daily News*, "Let me tell you ... there's only one guy in this town whose organization that is, and it's mine. Somebody else may own it, but it's mine."

"I don't think that went over too well with the people who actually own the team," Schmidt says today, laughing. Looking back, Schmidt concedes that he was a bit of a "lost soul" after his retirement and was hurt that the Phillies felt he should start by managing in the minor leagues, as if he needed to prove he knew the game.

A year later, though, he was ready to do just that. The Double A Reading Phils were looking for a manager. He called Del Unser, the team's director of player development, and expressed interest. "Del was my good friend," Schmidt says. "He and I had stayed up till 4 in the morning in many a hotel bar, talking baseball."

Nonetheless, Unser rebuffed his former teammate. A subsequent offer by Schmidt to go to Clearwater and work with the younger players was similarly declined.

"Maybe it's not like I perceive it to be," Schmidt says, grabbing a tray and getting in the crowded press room's cafeteria line. A lot of eyes are on him and he feels it. He begins to talk softly. "When I'm around the Phillies, everybody's so nice, it's always 'How's Donna and the kids?' and everybody's all lovey-dovey.

But maybe when those guys are upstairs at the Vet, thinking about the future, maybe they're saying 'We don't want Schmidt around.' See, Bill and Lee don't see me as a guy who would go to Spartanburg for a week and live in a Holiday Inn. The problem for me is that, generally, the people who run the game are almost all fringe players, guys who weren't stars. So they think I can't relate to the normal hitter."

"I don't think Mike had the people skills to be a manager or general manager," explains Giles. "I never thought he'd make a good leader. Besides, most great players who try to become managers don't do well because the game came so easily to them."

To Schmidt, Giles' reasoning amounts to once again being labeled "a natural," which he interprets as a knock against his work ethic. "I went from ducking every time they threw a breaking ball to being the best right-handed breaking-ball hitter in the league, because I had the patience and drive to learn the game," he says. "I climbed just about every fence, and people never want to give me credit for that. Do you ever hear anybody say 'That Mike Schmidt, he sure had baseball smarts'? They don't say that."

And yet, it was his analytical nature—not his natural talent—that was largely responsible for his Hall of Fame career. The history of baseball is littered with sluggers full of raw ability who dominate for a few years and then fade away. It wasn't so long ago, for instance, that Eric Davis was going to be the next Willie Mays. Now he's out of baseball. When Schmidt's career started to wane in the mid '80s, it was his studied approach to the art of hitting that resurrected him. He changed his style, began hitting down on the ball and started using the whole field.

"Early in my career, pitchers would have rather faced me with two outs, a runner on second and the game on the line than Bake McBride or big Bull Luzinski, because those guys would hit bloop singles in that situation and I'd strike out—I was trying too hard," he says. "But late in my career, I became a clutch hitter. And there's no question it was because of my desire to get into the dynamics of the swing and make adjustments. It's something Dale Murphy, for whatever reason, didn't do. But, still, you don't hear people saying 'Boy, Schmidt would make a great coach.'"

Even now, the perception that Schmidt was not a clutch hitter persists. Wheeler says that, when he speaks to area groups today, someone will invariably claim that Schmidt never drove in a big run. It's a rap that should have been dropped in 1980, when he hit four game-winning home runs during the pennant drive and was named MVP of the World Series after hitting .381. And the statistics bear out Schmidt's claim that, in the mid '80s, he began consistently delivering in crunch time. From 1984 to 1988, his overall average was .274, but he hit almost 20 points higher with runners in scoring position and in "late-inning pressure situations"—any at-bat in the last three innings with runners on base and his team trailing by three or fewer runs.

Far from being a hindrance, Schmidt's penchant for analysis enabled him to become a money player. "If I had been some dumb guy, one of those guys perceived as kind of country, they'd have said I was better than I was," he says, eating a side of popcorn with his pasta entree. "That's the perception—'If only he had been less sensitive and a little bit ignorant, imagine how good he could have been.' And you're powerless over things like that. It's probably something some announcer said to a writer and then that shit takes on a life of its own."

It is 20 minutes to game time, and broadcaster Harry Kalas ambles over to the table, intoning "*Michael Jack, how ya hitting 'em*?" and asking Jonathan what *he* hit during his recent high school season. ".333," Jonathan replies, barely audible. "He was two for six," Schmidt says, smiling, looking at his son. "Sorry, I had to tell him. You can tell I'm not *head* coach, or else he would have had at least 25 at-bats."

Kalas laughs and invites Schmidt up to the TV booth to broadcast a few innings. (In 1991, Schmidt did good color commentary on PRISM's Phillies telecasts; the team's brass, however, felt he was too critical.) Before going, Schmidt turns to me. "Baseball is what I know," he says, looking at Jonathan and breaking into a grin. "I have this reservoir of knowledge, but I'm coaching kids who can't turn a double play. I'm talking to them about the dynamics of the swing, so they can go ten for 14. But that's okay, because I'm teaching the game."

WANT TO see some homework being done back there," Schmidt says, looking in his rear-view mirror. Then, turning to me, he says, "If I were as hard on my kids as I want to be, they'd probably hate me. I'm not nearly as hard on them as my father was on me."

We are on the way home, and Jonathan dutifully opens his English book. Tomorrow morning, he will begin his day by eagerly turning to the sports section, where he will dissect the Phillies box score. But his father won't. The only sport Mike Schmidt goes out of his way to watch is golf; he hardly ever watches major league baseball, even on TV. It's not because he's lost his passion for the game. It's because the game has lost its passion for him.

It's been a long, emotional day for Schmidt, talking about his former life, opening up old wounds normally salved by his nine irons or his kids' needs. What do you do when, for well over a decade, you were the best in the world at what you did—yet felt unappreciated all the while? What if the thing you were meant to do—punish baseballs—brought you more pain than anything else in your life?

"You know, I've been real lucky, and I thank God for the fact that things are so great in my life right now—I get to spend time with my kids and play all the golf I want," he says softly. "So it's all worked out okay. I've accepted what happened. It's okay that the fans got on me the way they did, it's okay that the Phillies didn't hire me when I retired."

Mike Schmidt pauses. "But it would have been nice to have been wanted."

By Amy Donohue
June 1996

A PROPER DISTANCE

nne d'Harnoncourt was ready for her closeup. The director of the Philadelphia Museum of Art sat tall—six feet tall, to be exact—behind its president Bobby Scott, a bemused smile on her face, her hair escaping its usual graying knot, her skirt grazing the middle of her calves, a necklace of thick silver beads around her strong throat. As Scott announced his resignation on a cold February day to two dozen reporters and cameramen, something looked different about d'Harnoncourt: pinkish lipstick, even a hint of peachy blush, by God.

When Anne d'Harnoncourt gets out the Lancôme, you know something big is up.

Scott, *comme d'habitude*, was pink-cheeked and sprightly as he danced around reporters' questions, but he was obviously tired. Spent. The man looked ready for a beach and a drink with an umbrella in it.

"I once had a vacation of six weeks," he sang, "and I was enjoying it *more* at the end of the sixth week."

The announcement of 53-year-old d'Harnoncourt's ascendance—she will, by year's end, assume the additional title of CEO of the Museum—came as a surprise to no one. She is formidable, brilliant, internationally esteemed for her expertise in 20th-century art, and generally credited as the force behind the Philadelphia Museum's new prominence in the international art scene and such recent blockbuster shows as 1995s Barnes and Brancusi exhibitions and this month's Cézanne retrospective. She possesses a worldwide web of connections and a noble name; she works tirelessly and even looks the part, her astonishingly tall frame "walking the halls with impunity," as one observer puts it.

"She's a fabulous, capable girl," says Museum board vice chairman Ray Perelman from his winter lair in Palm Beach, summing up the board's position on d'Harnoncourt neatly, if not politically correctly.

"A very astute art person," adds chairman Phil Berman from his office in Allentown with equal lack of eloquence.

But the timing of Scott's abdication *was* interesting. Just a year and a half earlier, art circles buzzed with the news that Anne d'Harnoncourt was being courted heavily by New York's Museum of Modern Art to succeed retiring director Richard Oldenburg—a position of seemingly irresistible power and clout at one of the world's most exciting museums. Since d'Harnoncourt's father, Austrian-born aristocrat René, served as MoMA's director himself from 1949 to 1968, the move had seemed almost preordained—but Anne took herself off MoMA's list to stay here. Had d'Harnoncourt used the MoMA flirtation as leverage with her own board to exact a promise that it would depose Scott?

Then in late January, the city and the Museum received copies of the jointly commissioned Lord Study, a detailed analysis of PMA finances that recommended the city step up its $3.7 million yearly allotment to the institution. After several years of friction between Scott and Mayor Rendell and his chief aide David Cohen, there was no guarantee, of course, the Museum would receive more money. To culturati, the report seemed to give the Museum board the excuse it had been waiting for to ease Scott out.

Ask Anne d'Harnoncourt about any of this faintly murky business, however, and you'll receive an oblique, nonspecific, pro-Philadelphia, pro-PMA answer. Unlike Bob Scott, who is *always* Bob Scott, there is an opaqueness to d'Harnoncourt: She is fascinating and intimidating, by turns warm and cool and, like a white-on-white Malevich, open to interpretation.

"NOT AVAILABLE."

It is not easy to get close to Anne d'Harnoncourt.

"She has an hour on Wednesday, or maybe Thursday afternoon," muses her assistant. "No, she really only has a few minutes that day." Of course, I could have expected as much—the head of one of the top five museums in the country was bound to keep a tight schedule, especially in the midst of preparing for mega-show Cézanne. It was the other obstacles to getting to know Anne d'Harnoncourt (pronounced DARN-in-court) that took me more by surprise, despite how many warnings I had received from her friends and associates.

Take, for example, her comments about her plans for the future: "My sense of the next 10 years is building on the strength of what we have and building our audience. In the last calendar year we had almost a million people, which has been a goal of the Museum's for a long time.

"We can't stop," she continues in her queenly voice, sitting in her Museum office (just down the hall from Bob Scott's empty digs—he's gone to Europe) in a rather delicate green-velvet club chair that's too small for her, really. Her office is surprisingly tiny and filled with piles of paper and Bible-size art tomes. On one wall hangs a dark mauve-and-black Léger; a folksy canvas by Roy De Forest is across from it. The paint on the walls underneath is chipped and peeling.

As I listen to her speak—elaborately, impersonally—I realize why one observer describes her as "*so* smooth." She hides behind an expression that I begin to think of as The Mask, a commedia dell'arte public face that she rarely removes. After half an hour, it's clear I'm getting a variation of the same answer to every question. How does she really feel about Bob Scott? Has she ever felt it a burden following in her famous father's footsteps? What's she really like at home with her bubbly husband, senior PMA curator Joseph Rishel? "Wonderful," "Fantastic," "No one could replace Bob Scott" come the responses. Occasionally, she looks directly at me, though much of the time addresses a point somewhere over my right shoulder.

Ironically, for a woman so guarded and removed, physically d'Harnoncourt almost couldn't be more accessible, more *there*, availing herself of none of the usual masquerade that fashion provides: She wears not a lick of makeup, her clothes are of the sensible, good-quality variety, solid wools and silks, and her skirts are never above mid-calf. Only her jewelry—bold pieces in silver, and on one occasion a big pin that looked remarkably like a cockroach—hints at a sense of whimsy. Her wedding band is gossamer-thin; her eyes, cheekbones, and hands are wide and commanding.

After about a half hour of d'Harnoncourt's elegant parrying, we take a quick trot through the revamped European galleries, she trilling hellos to guards and elevator operators and shoving signs into place. I notice a Museum volunteer greeting visitors at the west entrance. Everything about the woman screams *Bryn Mawr*, her blond coif sprayed into submission, her legs barely supported by the highest of heels. She looks rather sweetly thrilled to be a part of it all; somehow, next to Anne d'Harnoncourt she is a mere shadow of a woman.

PICTURE Anne d'Harnoncourt sitting on a rock on the coast of Maine.

"Anne loves the sun—I can see her there just soaking it in," says Elizabeth Cropper, a professor of art history at Johns Hopkins University who's been one of d'Harnoncourt's closest friends since the late 1960s, when Anne first came to PMA as curatorial assistant in the painting department. "Her happiest times are when she's swimming in Maine or Martha's Vineyard, going to some flea market, picking out the one really neat thing there—and then probably giving it away."

Indeed, d'Harnoncourt is filled with such contradictions. She is beyond sophisticated, but a bit awkward; in her musical passions a lover of both Prokofiev and Miriam Makeba. She looks the part of a traditionalist (and that voice!), but her area of expertise is the work of Marcel Duchamp, the early-20th-century provocateur. She and Rishel give famously brilliant dinners at their Center City townhouse, but she often seems uncomfortable at large Museum receptions. She is extremely capable, but has never learned to drive a car.

One gets the sense that she is not concerned with the trivial. She is not the sort of person, for instance, you can imagine calling in sick on a Friday for a good shoe sale at Neiman's. She's careful, disciplined and—whether consciously or not—intimidating. When she occasionally does let down her guard a bit, to reveal quite charming details about her youth or personal likes and dislikes, she becomes the "incredibly generous spirit" with "an amazing ability to relate to people" described by her most intimate friends. And yet they are traits that, for some reason, many are still waiting to see.

"She's the kind of person you can meet 30 times and she still doesn't remember your name," says one local cultural-community leader. "Bob Scott not only remembers your name, he remembers and asks about your family and your kids and everything else."

Even so, the trade-offs between d'Harnoncourt and her gregarious predecessor don't worry the Museum's top patrons. After all, while Bob Scott schmoozed locally, d'Harnoncourt has moved globally, establishing a high-profile friendship with Marcel Duchamp's widow that resulted in a major gift of archival materials to the Museum; thanks to her, Cy Twombly personally planned the installation of his 10-part painting "Fifty Days at Iliam" at the PMA. She is esteemed by curators around the world—critical in the 1990s museum scene of traveling blockbusters and loans for shows like Cézanne. Board members mention again and again that she is a product of the best schools, brought up around such modern-art royalty as Mark Rothko and Philip Johnson. So what if she can be a bit, well ...

"She's liked, but she's standoffish," is how one former staffer describes the view of d'Harnoncourt from inside the Museum's walls. "There's a little bit of fear, a wariness of her—I always have the feeling she's not quite upfront, that you never know exactly what she's thinking.

"I think she's really pathologically shy, but it's something she's learned to hide. I always thought it was because she grew up in the shadow of her father."

LITERALLY. René d'Harnoncourt stood 6'6", a giant of a man with a distinguished family, a brilliant mind and all the qualities of a natural leader.

"This guy, the Chevalier, was granted the right to build a fortified house. It's still there, right on the Maginot Line," confided d'Harnoncourt pere over lunch to a *New Yorker* writer in 1960; he was speaking of his ancestor, chevalier Jean de la Fontaine. "My daughter Anne, who's now 16, found it when my wife and I took her abroad in 1957 to meet some of her European relatives. She met 53 of them ... It was very *gemütlich.*"

René d'Harnoncourt was born in 1901 in Vienna and spent his childhood summers playing at his family's "little place," a 94-room castle in Moravia; but by 1924, his family had lost its estates to the new Czechoslovak government and he was left with his degree in chemistry from the University of Vienna and several 15th-century woodcuts that he sold to finance passage to Mexico City. (The U.S. quota for immigrants was full.) He arrived broke, worked briefly in advertising and retail, then began advising wealthy expatriates on collecting art and antiques and started organizing art exhibitions.

During the 1920s, d'Harnoncourt orchestrated shows in Mexico of such painters as Diego Rivera; in 1930 he organized a landmark show of Mexican art at the Metropolitan Museum of Art. He married Sarah Carr, a Chicago-bred fashion editor at Marshall Field's department store, in 1933; in 1943, the year Anne arrived "to their surprise and I think delight," she laughs, he went to work at the Museum of Modern Art.

Very much an only child, Anne grew up in a rambling Central Park West apartment filled with thousands of books and works by Calder, Lipchitz, and Baziotes; she socialized with the children of Mark Rothko. She remembers her childhood as magical, and when she speaks of it, The Mask slips.

"I could tell which room my parents were in by the way the floor creaked," she says over lunchtime salmon between meetings in the Museum's restaurant. "We did our trick-or-treating running up and down the stairs of the building and punching the doorbells of the particularly irascible old ladies," she remembers with an appealingly loud, braying laugh.

Of MoMA, she says, "It was just where my father worked—I never dreamed I'd work in a museum someday. Although my most vivid memories are of works of art."

At the upper-crust Brearley School, Anne loved acting and writing; the family traveled to Europe during summers. On their only trip to Philadelphia, Anne promptly contracted a case of measles.

Even as a child, she confounded expectations. "I would *not* have said I was too hot at sports," she hoots. "Everyone thought because I was tall I should be terrific at things like basketball. I took up *fencing* instead.

"I got pretty tall pretty fast. My father was 6'6", my mother was 6', so at home I was normal," she elaborates. "The only time it was fairly depressing was when I went to dancing school and all the boys were half my height. Otherwise, it's been great—I can peer over people's heads in crowds." She lets out her characteristic laugh. "It's not always easy to find the right length of skirt, but that's another story."

At Radcliffe, Anne studied French, English, and German literature and history, and spent a summer teaching English in a community center in Dar es Salaam, Tanzania. ("I don't know how much they learned, but I certainly got a lot out of it.") It wasn't until her last year at college that she realized she was "dying to learn more about art and the history of art," she says, polishing off her salmon with great efficiency. In 1965, she went to London's Courtauld Institute, specializing in 19th- and 20th-century art and finding herself enchanted by everything from the English Renaissance to cubism; she returned in 1967 and "tumbled around the country knocking on doors" of museums in Boston, Chicago, Cleveland, and Philadelphia.

She raves about her first extended stint in Philadelphia as a curatorial assistant from 1967 to 1969: "I was enormously impressed by the sense of big-city amenities and lots of history and how amazingly easy it is to get into the country. And you could get into New York in an hour and a half!" D'Harnoncourt spent her weeks cloistered in the Philadelphia Museum's enormous collections; weekends, she traveled to New York galleries and to see her parents. She shared a Fitler Square apartment with her close friend Kippy Stroud, who later founded the Fabric Workshop; she was welcome at Henry McIlhenny's and all the best houses in town. Educated and gracious as she was, though, she was shy, lacking her father's breezy, facile charm.

René d'Harnoncourt died in a car crash in the summer of 1968, the same year he retired as director of MoMA. Those who know her well say that Anne was very close to her father and, at 24, devastated. "He never really got to do some of the things he had planned," she says simply, The Mask adjusting back into place. "I often wish I could ask him things about situations that arise here."

The next year, Anne left the East Coast and took a job at the Art Institute of Chicago to work in the renowned 20th-century-art department. In the adjoining painting department worked a young assistant curator from the University of Chicago, Joe Rishel: a demonstrative character and dapper dresser given to black-velvet sports coats. When the pair began dating, colleagues were delighted, if surprised; nevertheless, two months before d'Harnoncourt's return to Philadelphia as curator of 20th-century art, they married.

WE DIDN'T exactly hang out in each other's offices," says an amused Bob Scott about d'Harnoncourt. "We're friends, but our working relationship was not based on friendship."

For 14 years, d'Harnoncourt and Scott worked "40 feet from each other," says the retiring president. He was finance, administration, marketing, the schmoozer of funders; she handled all things artistic. When they moved into leadership positions together in 1982, she after her star turn through the 20th-century department, he after serving as unpaid president for 2 years, the institution's endowment, at $21 million, was one of the country's lowest for a major museum; by 1995, it topped $100 million. They oversaw a $64 million capital campaign and an ambitious reinstallation of the tattered European galleries. Along the way, there were frictions, of course, but, in general, close observers describe it as a good working relationship.

So what of the recent intrigue, of d'Harnoncourt's supposed role in shoving her longtime colleague out? Actually, as insiders point out, people were questioning his future at the Museum as far back as 1991, when concerns surfaced about his drinking (a problem that, he told *Philadelphia* magazine last year, "just sort of crept up") and the board received an anonymous letter detailing a litany of mostly petty staff complaints against him. Gallantly, Scott sought treatment.

A couple of years later, the city's fiscal crisis brought more hassles as Scott took on Rendell and Cohen over Museum funding and convened a special cost-saving task force that, among other possible measures, looked at folding the $140,000-a-year director and president jobs into one. "He basically told the group," recalls one board member, "that he was ready to go anyway."

And d'Harnoncourt was emerging as more than a curator. With the encouragement of Scott, she became more involved in the business side of PMA, and applied herself to the fine art of soliciting large checks over a canapé and a cocktail. She assumed a bigger role in dealings with Rendell and Cohen, presumably as a way for Museum-city relations to make a fresh start. Other museums naturally took notice. In the early 1990s, the National Gallery in Washington came calling; in early 1994, MoMA. The timing of Scott's adieux was the only real issue that remained. When the Lord Study came out, with its implicit accolades for Scott and d'Harnoncourt, a wearier-than-ever Scott had his opportunity to go out a winner.

"There was that understanding," confirms board member M. Todd Cooke, referring to possible promises made to ensure d'Harnoncourt's rejection of MoMA. As to how explicitly she expressed presidential aspirations to the Philadelphia Museum board, Cooke says, "She made it clear in that graceful way Anne makes anything clear."

WE HAD some Italians staying with us last weekend," Joe Rishel confides to me one morning at the Museum, "and we walked them over to the Pennsylvania Academy of Fine Arts—which is one of the *most* beautiful spaces to see art anywhere—and then we went to the Convention Center to see the Judy Pfaff, and then what I did was buy a bunch of little tiny birds at Reading Terminal and mango sorbet and a good dry chocolate cake. And then we put these little birds, with *lots* of rosemary, under the grill, and stuck the birds on top of polenta and had a chicory salad—really fresh and delicious."

Twenty years after Rishel and Anne came to Philadelphia, Rishel—well-fed and even more vivacious than in his youth—has secured his own reputation as one of the country's leading experts in his field and as one of Philadelphia's best hosts. "I don't let her cook often," says Rishel of his spouse, "although she's *not bad.*"

Their genteel Center City house is filled with pieces from the d'Harnoncourt apartment in New York and works by some of their favorite Philadelphia and Chicago artists. They have no children, no dogs, but travel together whenever their busy schedules permit—Rishel is frequently on the road for Museum business, especially while putting together the Cézanne show. On vacations, they've stayed with friends in the south of France or driven through Austria. They also report that they "mooch off" friends in West Chop, Martha's Vineyard.

"We do talk about art constantly," says Rishel cheerfully in his hard-to-place, vaguely British accent (he's actually from upstate New York, the son of a farmer/superintendent of roads). "And then like many people, we come home sometimes and turn on the television and plop down."

IT IS A Tuesday-morning curatorial meeting at the Art Museum, and a handsome, dressed-to-kill man in hip black boots is tossing silk scarves on the executive conference table to howls of delight from the largely female, very vocal staff. The scarves are rich made-in-Italy silk in art-modern patterns taken from Museum textiles; there are neckties, too, which Joe Rishel snatches up and immediately winds around his collar. D'Harnoncourt is positively girlish as she drapes an $85 navy scarf around her own shoulders, trilling "These are wonderful!", sounding exactly like Julia Child exclaiming over a really good lamb chop.

The man in the black boots, Stuart Gerstein, the Museum's new director of wholesale and retail operations (d'Harnoncourt hired him away from the Guggenheim last year), has plans to remodel the Museum store with a separate entrance and expand PMA publishing efforts to books that people will actually buy; he has even whipped up Brancusi tchotchkes like notepads and jewelry to tie in with last fall's exhibit. For Cézanne, you can buy everything from a child-friendly CD-ROM to a "Cézanne" All-Star Game baseball.

This is the new, more practical Philadelphia Museum, one where shows like Barnes and Cézanne attract record attendance and new supporters. Tourists now rank the Museum as a destination second only to the Liberty Bell, and their full wallets—museum-goers being upscale consumers—contribute tens of millions to the region in restaurants, hotels, and shopping. As for Philadelphians themselves, the Museum has become a Fun Thing on Wednesday nights, a cool place to shop for gifts, a meeting place for brunch or cappuccino and a quick spin through the galleries. Better yet, we are not so intimidated by the place.

"It's not always easy to find out what people want," d'Harnoncourt mulls. "The job of a museum like ours, a big comprehensive museum, is to give people the chance to look at and understand a lot of different kinds of art. We all could spend our lives doing nothing but 19th-century French painting shows, all of which would be popular, although we'd sort of run out of artists after a while.

"In the case, alas, of Brancusi, you can have a show that is very beautiful and potentially very popular which doesn't catch the imagination of a sponsor. You balance out the schedule as much as you can—supporting other exhibitions that just cry to be done. If Chicago, the Museum of Modern Art, if Los Angeles, if all of us didn't do shows of 20th-century artists, contemporary artists because we couldn't find a sponsor, how would the next generation ever know?"

WHEN Anne d'Harnoncourt talks about art, she drops The Mask completely.

It is my last meeting with her, on a freezing April evening at the Philadelphia Antiques Show; she blows in a bit late, alone, clutching a well-stuffed canvas tote bag and an armload of files. She strides through the vast West Philadelphia armory, admiring heavy silver Navajo belts and a French trompe l'oeil watercolor, and, though her hair is tumbling out of its knot and her collar is askew, looks quite comfortable amid the crowd, a colorless, well-groomed herd browsing over mahogany gaming tables. Tonight she is the woman of humor and charm her friends describe, the most attractive figure in the room.

We sit down at a little white-clothed table and talk about Duchamp.

D'Harnoncourt met Marcel Duchamp once, just before his death in 1968. She had gone to see him in New York to interview him about PMA benefactors Louise and Walter Arensberg. Later, d'Harnoncourt became close to his widow, Alexina "Teenie" Duchamp, an American-born woman whose first husband was the art dealer Pierre Matisse, son of painter Henri. Thanks to her relationship with Anne, Teenie joined the Museum's board and gave the PMA invaluable archival materials.

Duchamp made art that was avantgarde in the extreme. Magnificent abstract works such as the PMA's "Nude Descending a Staircase" (1912) had come so easily to Duchamp that, bored, he stopped painting them and began making pieces designed to rock our worlds. The best collection of his work anywhere is at our Museum in the Duchamp Gallery, including "The Large Glass" and "*Etant Donné*" a surprising peep show through a plain door.

Those who get Duchamp adore him. And talking about Duchamp's most inaccessible pieces—art she knows perhaps better than anyone else's on the planet—d'Harnoncourt is wonderful to listen to.

"He was on an adventure, a very intellectual adventure," she says, intent, her hair a bit wild. "What's so fascinating about him is his question of what art can be. A lot of people think of him as a very sexual artist; a lot of people think of him as a very intellectual artist. There are just about as many approaches to him as there are people approaching him."

"Duchamp always said that art is about what you bring to it," adds d'Harnoncourt, smiling. "The viewer completes the work."

With that, she graciously bids me goodnight and begins wandering the booths of antiques, greeting acquaintances, looking very much the Museum president. She appears to be enjoying herself.

JUDY WICKS

White Dog Cafe owner/social activist; 56; West Philadelphia

It's taken me most of my life not to feel I'm inferior because I'm a girl.

When I moved here in 1970 to start the Free People's Store [now Urban Outfitters], it was largely because there were no stores at all for students. Now University City is abuzz with shops, restaurants, and active community groups and cultural institutions. It is a wonderful place to live and do business.

In fifth grade, I chose my future husband. It was Dick Hayne [the future founder of Urban Outfitters and Anthropologie]. He was a good baseball player, and because I was a girl, I wasn't allowed to play. I crossed off "Judy Wicks" and wrote across my tablet: "Mrs. Richard Hayne. Mrs. Richard Hayne. Mrs. Richard Hayne." After we graduated from college, that's who I married. I left the marriage because I realized that I wanted to find out whatever happened to Judy Wicks, who I crossed off my tablet.

I wasn't really into the whole counter culture thing.

Ira Einhorn was a regular at La Terrasse, and I was the general manager at the time. I remember having dinner with him one night after Holly Maddux disappeared, but before she was really considered to be missing by other people. And I said, "Ira, I haven't seen Holly lately." And he said, "Oh, she went to the store and she just didn't come back." I said: "Well, aren't you worried?" He said: "Oh no, you know how flighty Holly is," and I thought that was kind of weird, but I figured, he's just being nonchalant because he really loves her.

My children were two and four when I started the White Dog Cafe. So I really didn't spend much time actually mothering them.

When I turned 50, I bought a cabin in the Poconos, which changed my life. Turning 50 was like being 10 again—playing in the woods, swimming in the lake, being close to nature and really regaining a sense of freedom from the childbearing years when having a mate and raising a family were priorities.

I've never had an occasion to work with Mayor Street. Perhaps that says something in itself in that he has never reached out to me, but then again, I have been focusing on national work lately—the local-living economy movement—and haven't approached him.

People should be angry about what's happening to this country. Our country's being destroyed. It's amazing to me that people aren't more angry.

I don't cook at home. I don't even cook. I eat at the cafe, basically every night.

The White Dog is the first business in Pennsylvania to get 100 percent of its electricity from wind. The windmills are along the Turnpike in Somerset. The cost is 15 percent higher.

We pay a living wage at the White Dog, rather than the minimum wage. In Philadelphia, that's around $8.25, somewhere around there.

It's Philadelphians who are my customers, it's Philadelphia where I live, and I want my money to go to work for Philadelphians. So I put all of my savings into a local investment fund.

Ben Cohen [of Ben & Jerry's ice cream] and I were romantically involved about 10 years ago, but he lives in Vermont, and I live here. We remain great friends.

My favorite Ben & Jerry's flavor? Coconut Almond Fudge Chip.

The older I get, the more I'm used to having everything my own way. I think: Would I want a man in my bed, in my bedroom, again, sharing my closet, sharing everything, having his alarm go off when I want to sleep in? What for?

Usually, when you have one guy, they don't want you to go to Guatemala for a week with someone else. And then you're just stuck with the one person all the time. And that just seems so boring to me.

By Larry Platt
November 1997

ROBERTS RULES

upelo, Mississippi, 1963: It starts with shoe-shine kits. Ralph Roberts, Julian Brodsky, and Dan Aaron, three Philadelphia entrepreneurs, buy a batch of shoe-shine kits as closeouts from Hickocks Department Store and start knocking on doors. The pitch opens with the free gift—Ralph has the kit in folks' hands before they know they're being offered something—and then comes the kicker:

"By the way, we'd like to talk to you about cable TV."

There is silence or puzzled stares or clever retorts such as "Cable what?"

And they explain. We're wiring the town, this proud birthplace of Elvis, they say. Because of our wires, you can get five channels—including the networks—instead of just one. And the best part is that this new world of entertainment and news and, yes, community can be yours—all for $5 a month.

They knock on the doors, lug the wires across lawns and down side streets. And they sign up 85 percent of the town.

REDMOND, Seattle, 1997: It's cocktail hour, and Bill Gates has lightened up. Just hours before, Brian Roberts and the rest the Cable Labs delegation—a research and development consortium of the cable industry—had caught the ire of Microsoft's legendary founder and the richest man in the world.

Not that the men with Roberts weren't substantial business personalities in their own right. There was TCI's John Malone, the longtime face of the cable industry; Time Warner's Joe Collins; U.S. West's Bill Schleyer, Cox Communications' Jim Robins and Rogers Cablevision's Ted Rogers. But two hours ago they were face to face with an unhappy Gates.

Gates' frustration lay in the apparent slowness of the cable industry's building its "broadband pipe." Put simply, that means the combination fiber-optic and coaxial cables the industry is committed getting into the American home—the much-hyped "information superhighway." Why does Gates care? Because that pipe will change how we watch television; more data than ever will find its way to your TV, either in the form of the Internet, 200-plus cable channels or interactive video. And it will need an operating system. Microsoft Software, in other words.

Roberts and the others pointed out that in fact, they are rapidly building the pipe. Roberts' Comcast, for instance, is reinvesting over $600 million of its annual cash flow this year and next.

Then Gates unveiled his bottom-line complaint. Cable's Internet-access program, @Home, has a Netscape navigational system—Microsoft's archrival. Roberts and Malone, investors and moving forces behind @Home, assured Gates they were committed to "open architecture"—free competition among all software makers: Microsoft, Netscape, Java, Oracle. Gates seemed mollified.

Now it's cocktail hour at an exclusive Seattle restaurant, and Gates is smiling. Just before dinner, Roberts seizes on the shift in mood. "You know, Bill, if you really want to accelerate the building of the broadband pipe, you should buy 10 percent of everyone in this room. Buy 10 percent of the cable industry."

Everyone laughs, but Roberts doesn't let the joke die. He looks at his Cable Labs partners. "John, you in? How about you, Joe?" he asks, down the line.

"Hey, whatever you say, Brian," they chime in, sheepishly.

At dinner, Roberts finds himself sitting with Gates, Malone, and Collins. Gates begins regaling the group with plans for his vacation, which begins in the morning, when he and ex-partner Paul Allen will depart for the Amazon.

But Brian Roberts, at 38 the youngest executive in the room and renowned as the most enthusiastic, is still fixating on his "joke." Every time Gates pauses for a bite of salmon, Roberts jumps in: "So, Bill, what about my idea?"

As Gates continues to hold forth on the adventures awaiting him in the jungle, he occasionally leans toward Roberts and begins a new conversational thread. "Brian, Microsoft has a cash position of $10 billion, so how much would something like you're talking about cost?" he asks one time. Roberts, quickly calculating, responds, "about $5 billion."

Gates goes back to the others, all looking at Roberts wide-eyed. Moments later, Gates leans over again. "Is there a regulatory limit on what I can do?"

"Yes, but if you own less than 5 percent of a company, it's probably not deemed an attributable interest."

This goes on throughout dinner. Afterward, Roberts' colleagues mercilessly tease him. In the morning, he calls his father, Ralph. "You'll never believe what I did, Dad," he says. "What do you think? Did I do wrong?"

Ralph Roberts bursts out laughing. "Hell no. Sounds like you did just fine."

The next day, back in Comcast's offices at 15th and Market, one of Gates' lieutenants calls. Gates, taking a respite from marveling at pink dolphins, has e-mailed from the Amazon with instructions to call Roberts and begin talking about an investment in cable.

Thirty-odd days later, Microsoft makes its largest-ever investment in another company—$1 billion—all in Comcast. What does Microsoft get? No seat on Comcast's board. No guarantee that Microsoft products will be used on Comcast systems. Instead, it gets a sizable investment in a company (not to mention its president) that is fast coming out of TCI's (and Malone's) dark shadow. The deal changes the future of cable, solidifying its place as the 21st century's provider of everything from the Internet to shopping to movies on demand, all on your TV. And it caps a year that has made Brian Roberts the leading man in this new Communicopian Age, as big or bigger than Malone, Murdoch, and Turner.

Tupelo never felt so far away.

THE STORY of Comcast's ascent is, in fact, many stories. There's the rise of the son, the gangly, boyish, seemingly unassuming Brian, the only businessman on the planet to have persuaded the likes of Gates, Malone, and Michael Eisner to take minority positions in deals. But it's also the story of modern American business: Comcast's metamorphosis from a rural mom-and-pop cable-TV operation into the nation's fourth-largest operator and a major national player is no less than the story of the American century itself.

Most important, it is a story about vision, the vision of the son who knows his history. After all, had the CEOs of the thriving railroads early in this century recognized that they were in the *transportation*—as opposed to the *train*—business, our airlines today would be called the Pennsylvanian, the Santa Fe and the Atchison-Topeka. Brian Roberts, who took over as president in 1990 at all of 32, was determined not to fall prey to similar myopia.

"What they've done under Brian is to broaden out," says Gerry Lenfest, whose Lenfest Communications and Suburban Cable have 1.2 million area subscribers—more than triple Comcast's local base—and who now finds himself with viewers his old friend Ralph wants. "See, I'm in the cable business. Under Brian, Comcast has become a diversified communications company."

The branching out began eight years ago, with a decision to get into cellular phones. That foray wasn't so unfamiliar. It entailed a massive investment (over $1 billion) and the establishment of customer-service operations—precisely what's involved in starting up cable operations. Then Brian lured Barry Diller to West Chester to run QVC. When Diller's bid for Paramount Studios failed and he turned his attention to CBS—a deal that would have relegated Comcast to minority status in QVC—the Robertses stunned Diller with a dramatic tarmac confrontation at Teterboro airport: They were offering $2.2 billion to become majority owner of the home-shopping network, effectively scuttling Diller's deal.

Today, with Malone remaining as a minority investor, QVC is a cash cow for the Robertses, taking in some $2 billion a year.

In the last couple of years, however, the deal-making has kicked into overdrive, as the younger Roberts has assumed more control. There's the 66 percent ownership of the 76ers, Flyers, Phantoms, CoreStates Spectrum, and CoreStates Center that has yielded the new Comcast SportsNet channel and all sorts of synergistic possibilities. (A Jerry Stackhouse talk show? Lindros paraphernalia sold on QVC?) There's the formation of a Hollywood production arm, C3, run by Rich Frank, the former programming guru at Disney who oversaw the creation of *Home Improvement*. (Things have been slow-going for C3; its first syndicated program, a talk show starring former football great Terry Bradshaw, recently debuted.) There's last year's deal that landed 69 percent of the E! Entertainment Channel, a coup that fueled industry-wide buzz about this young upstart from Philly. And there's the 14 percent interest in @Home, which might be the most important of all, for what it signifies: that Comcast, especially now with Gates along for the ride, is uniquely positioned to shepherd in a new era of communications in your home, the melding of the computer and the TV, an amalgam of something profound with something popular.

WHEN Brian Roberts announces he's about to share one of his "macro conclusions," it means you're about to peek into his ever-strategizing mind. That's what Comcast staffers got the morning of Roberts' return from Redmond, even before Roberts knew about Gates' e-mail from the jungle.

The Cable Labs expedition had not simply been an exodus to Microsoft; Seattle had been the last stop after a whirlwind Silicon Valley tour. First, the group visited with Intel, the computer-chip maker, and its dynamic chairman, Andy Grove. In space suits, Roberts and the rest slipped into a lab to witness the latest in chip fabrication and were shown something called Intel's Entertainment PC—a computer using a new TV-compatible chip.

Then came a pilgrimage to a company called Navio, which is underwritten by a consortium of Japanese consumer-electronics companies and by Netscape. Navio, under the direction of engineering guru Dr. Wei Yen—developer of Sega and Nintendo 64—was also working on a plethora of futuristic applications for TV. Its primary goal was to come up with an alternative to WebTV, using Netscape software rather than Microsoft's. (Microsoft had recently paid more than $400 million for WebTV—a high-end television equipped with Internet access, thanks to a built-in phone modem, which is about 100 times slower than cable modems. Until its Comcast investment, it was the largest purchase in Microsoft history; in the subsequent year, only 100,000 WebTV units have been sold.) Not surprisingly, two weeks after Roberts' visit, Microsoft archrival Oracle formed an alliance with Netscape and purchased Navio.

But even before these clear battle lines had been drawn, Roberts saw the "macro" point, and stressed it to his staff. "Silicon Valley has been driving the information economy," he said. "But the inevitable is happening—PC sales are slowing. It just doesn't make sense for someone to invest another $2,000 for newer software enhancements. So the chip companies, the browser makers, the software companies, they're all focusing on the same thing: enhancing TV, taking it digital, and making it two-way. Once TV goes digital and the big pipe and the navigating systems are in place, the consumer can get the Internet and 200 channels at home on the TV."

But to do that, they'd need the broadband pipe-fiber-optic wires capable of carrying multitudes of data to neighborhood nodes, where cable's coaxial wires would then make the delivery into the house. (Over 99 percent of American homes have TVs—vs. 33 percent with computers—and 70 percent already have cable.) Roberts realized that, in virtually every other aspect of consumer electronics, the world had gone digital; yet, television—where Americans spend some 5 hours a day—was still utilizing antiquated analog technology.

The future was clear, Roberts preached. But the digitization of TV meant significantly increased channel capacity. In Roberts' view, cable could be in danger of making Bruce Springsteen a new media prophet: "57 Channels and Nothing's On." Not content to sit around and wait for his industry's golden asset—the pipe—to pay off, Roberts has systematically sought to establish a programming empire as well. Thus, the sports teams and SportsNet, QVC and, most of all, the acquisition of E! earlier this year.

Few stories illustrate Roberts' zeal better than his pursuit of the E! entertainment network. Comcast had been a minority (10 percent) owner, along with TCI's programming arm—Liberty Media—Cox Communications and Continental Cablevision (now U.S. West); Time Warner owned 45 percent and was the managing partner. The original deal had been structured as a buy/sell, meaning that on an agreed-upon future date the minority owners tell Time-Warner that they're triggering an exit; Time-Warner then has to name its price, and each member of the group has 30 days to buy or sell back to Time-Warner at that price. It's a system that insures the managing partner will name a fair price, because it doesn't know whether it will be buyer or seller.

As it turned out, Comcast was ultimately the only company interested in buying the channel, which Time-Warner valued at $550 million. "We were big fans of [Doylestown native] Lee Masters, the CEO of E!" says Roberts. "He's a good friend, and he came out of MTV and has that iconish, hip, very definable sensibility. And the channel was already in 40 million homes. We hadn't seen a channel with that much distribution come up for sale since QVC."

Wall Street, however, tends to react skeptically when Comcast delves into programming. Though Comcast stock is healthy now, it's dipped with each foray into TV-land. (In the late 1980s and early 1990s, Comcast piled up several billion dollars in debt, a consequence of its meteoric rise; most analysts today give it a thumbs up.) But, contractually, Comcast had 30 days to change its mind. That's when Brian decided to take on a programming partner—someone to foot the bill for the acquisition.

An auction was held at a law firm in New York, and everyone came. For a week, Roberts shuttled between conference rooms, trying to pick a dance partner from among a veritable who's who in media: In one room, there was Rupert Murdoch; on another floor, NBC's Robert Wright; elsewhere, CBS' Michael Jordan. All wanted to do a deal, and all were impressed with Roberts' take on the future of E!: That, by rerunning old *Melrose Place* episodes and the like, it had gotten too general, too removed from its niche. As ESPN is sports and CNN is news, so, too, should E! be about the entertainment industry, he argued.

Finally, when Disney's Michael Eisner showed up, the deal began taking shape. Eisner hates auctions and does not readily accept minority-investing positions; in this deal (because of a standard "no-flip" provision in buy/sell contracts), Disney could get no more than 49 percent, and there could be no sale of its share for at least two years. Yet Eisner wrote a check for $322 million, and Comcast—without putting up a penny—took control.

"Watching Brian that week was amazing, because he's a master at this," says Tom Baxter, president of Comcast's cable division. "He's expert at playing guys off against one another."

"Actually, watching Eisner and Gates do business has been a wonderful learning experience for me," counters Roberts, sitting in a conference room with a view of the still boarded-up One Meridian building—a constant reminder, he says, of how temporary things can be. (It was the sprinkler system on Comcast's floors that kept the building from completely burning down.) "When entrepreneurial companies push things over the top, it's usually the power of one person to make something happen. Michael Eisner wanted that deal to happen."

Yet Roberts doesn't cull his management style from these adversaries. His style is in his genes. He has inherited his father's casual, nonhierarchical bent. When Dave Watson, 39-year-old president of Comcast Cellular, is asked to whom he reports, for instance, he laughs. "That's really not a Comcast-type question," he says, pointing out that brainstorming and decision-making happen constantly on an ad-hoc basis, in stark contrast to where he used to work, Bell Atlantic, where action takes a back seat to bureaucracy. It is a corporate culture singled out by writer Kevin Maney in his 1995 book, *Megamedia Shakeout: The Inside Story of the Leaders and the Losers in the Exploding Communications Industry*. Maney names Comcast one of five companies to work for in megamedia because "it wants employees to feel like partners or part of a family." Ralph says it's all because of Brian: "He's a young guy, and he attracts young, energetic people." But the son says it's about the dad: "Ralph is the true entrepreneur," he says. "Compared to him, I'm a company man."

LAST NIGHT, Brian Roberts was moved. It was at the opening party for Comcast SportsNet, and he was in a reflective mood. When it came time to speak, he talked about a dinner the night before at the Four Seasons for Wharton's Entrepreneurial Center, founded by Ed Snider, Roberts' partner in Comcast-Spectacor.

At that dinner, Penn's Judith Rodin, Mayor Rendell and Brian Roberts listened intently as Snider talked about philanthropy as a value instilled in him by his father, Sol, who had built his own grocery business. The night took on grand significance for the younger Roberts, given its timing sandwiched between the opening of QVC's $120 million StudioPark in West Chester and the launching of SportsNet, during a week when Ted Turner was on the cover of *Newsweek* boasting about his own charitable acts. (The Robertses have preferred to let their good deeds remain outside the spotlight.) "Yeah, I was thinking about what a big week we'd just had, and about what our family business and the Snider father-and-son story had in common," Brian says. "Ed's remarks about the importance of family and giving back seemed appropriate. But then, after the party, I had a quick bite with my wife, and then played squash and lost, 9–7, in the fifth. It was back to earth, real quick."

With the exception of his family, those are Roberts' twin passions: deal-making and squash. A nationally ranked player at Penn, he took up the game again after a 10-year hiatus, with characteristic single-mindedness, playing three to five nights a week after his kids went bed; he skipped last summer's annual Sun Valley gathering of mega-moguls to play in Israel's Maccabiah Games, where he was part of a silver medal 35-and-older team.

"Squash isn't the center of my life," he stresses. "But it gets me out of the office, and, for me, it's better than running on a treadmill, because I enjoy the competitive element."

As for the rest of his life, it's intensely private, and, attest friends and business associates, strikingly normal. When he agreed to co-chair Philadelphia 2000 with David L. Cohen, spearheading the city's push for a political convention, it was a rare embrace of the limelight. He lives in Chestnut Hill with his wife, Aileen, who is on the board of the Avenue of the Arts, and their children. He counts David Binswanger, of the real-estate Binswangers, among his friends. He is a member at Philadelphia Cricket Club.

"You'd never know from anything you see outwardly that Brian is as high up or as wealthy as he is," says Ken Bacon, Roberts' neighbor. (Roberts' 1996 compensation included a salary of $625,000, a bonus of $662,000 and some 300,000 shares of stock valued at close to $8 million.) Roberts sponsored Bacon for membership at Philadelphia Cricket, and Bacon became one of the club's first African-American members. "I mean, he's not flipping hot dogs on the front yard or anything like that, but he coaches soccer and is very down-to-earth."

The Robertses are genuine when they wax sentimental about family. Pains are taken to make corporate headquarters feel that close, too. Brian's office is adjacent to Ralph's, and both men casually stroll the hallways, chatting with "Comcasters"—Ralph's affectionate moniker for employees. In fact, a couple of years ago, I was in Brian's office when Suzanne Roberts walked in with a sculpture and began scouting locations for it. "Mom," Brian said, laughing, "I'm kinda in a meeting."

Since adolescence, Brian wanted to work side by side with his father. "I remember when he was in high school, I'd take him on negotiations for bank loans, and he'd sit in the corner, always listening," recalls Ralph. "I'd explain to him what was going on, and he'd just sit there, taking it all in by osmosis."

In high school and college, he worked summers at Comcast. (Around this time a youthful Brian reportedly found and was intrigued by one executive's collection of *Playboy* magazines.) Ralph put him to work: He climbed poles to install cable, went door-to-door, telemarketed. When he graduated from Wharton in 1981, he turned down offers from the likes of Goldman Sachs.

The Comcast family ethic, Roberts has spent weeks telling me, is why this shouldn't be a personal piece about him. "I have my own hang-ups about my privacy," he says, "but the more substantive thing is, Comcast is not about any one person. It's about a new leadership team that is working side by side with the founders. How unique. You don't see that."

True, but, as his father, his employees, his business adversaries, and a bevy of analysts agree, it is undeniable that Roberts' vision is leading the way. Still, he blanches at questions about his personal life, in part to protect his privacy, but also because, friends testify, like his father it's simply not in Brian's makeup to offer any outward displays of ego. He is either the healthiest mover-shaker around or incredibly repressed. Everyone—literally everyone—who knows him opts for the former.

But don't confuse the lack of ego or the feel-good family rhetoric for a dearth of passion. The Roberts' competitive fire is legendary. Last summer, on Long Beach Island, Roberts became obsessed with winning a miniature-golf tournament, which was hard to do when Arthur Makadon, Center City lawyer and political power broker, was around. Makadon *averaged* a score of 24 on 18 holes. Finally, one day in late summer, Roberts was ahead on the leader board when Makadon showed up. Roberts, whose round had concluded, followed his rival through the course, trying to jinx him. It came down to the last hole: Makadon needed a hole in one; he scored a 2. Roberts celebrated like a grade-school kid.

But he celebrated too soon. While he was out with Makadon, some guy named Izzy beat him by one stroke. The moral in Roberts' world? You can never stop worrying. And what could *he* have to worry about? "Try owing *billions* of dollars to banks—like six, seven billion," he says. "One of the great things about being an entrepreneur is you assume you could be out of business tomorrow. I worry about that every day."

BRIAN Roberts has been telling me I'm cynical about the future. But I can't help wondering if all this telecommunications hype isn't simply a triumph of marketing. Have the Robertses, the Gateses, the Murdochs convinced us that their products are more than some really cool luxuries, that they are, in fact, essential?

Five years ago, after all, it was going to be the telephone companies vs. the cablers (see "Wired!", *Philadelphia*, July 1993); then conventional wisdom had it that they were going to converge. It all turned out to be a smoke screen, all hype that an acquiescent press passed on, playing into elaborate corporate agendas: Both industries got what they wanted from the 1996 Telecommunications Act.

The Baby Bells got the go ahead to begin providing long distance, and cable got regulatory breathing room.

Have we now entered the second round of rhetoric? "Hype has a way of feeding on itself," Roberts responds. "We say good, Wall Street says great, writers say greatest, we say better than greatest, and we go around in an echo chamber. But a lot of hype about cable has come true. It was only 15 years ago that we had three channels of TV. Today we have 25 or 50 times as many choices. Sure, there's some programming I wish were better, and not everything is for everyone, which is why I support a ratings system. And, you're right, we can't always predict the next great application ahead of time—will it be sitting at home and getting elaborate statistics in the middle of a game, on demand? You say, 'Well, do I *need* that?' I understand that. I once had a Commodore 64 and threw it out because I couldn't figure out what to do with it. There was nothing to do with it. But a lot of people saw the power of what that might become and kept pursuing the dream."

We are in a Comcast conference room, and, as he talks, Roberts gets increasingly animated. His normally soft-spoken voice rises a few levels.

"The Internet is such a success because the consumer has the power to go anywhere they want and look at any data file with the push of a button, but that's just the first step," he says. "I'm convinced that the Internet as we know it now will someday be as outdated as the black rotary phone we grew up with. Maybe it's movies on demand, or video phone, or video conferencing. But it will be TV-quality video, and the consumer will have all the choices. I don't know precisely how it will work, but the broadband pipe will lead to the creation of applications that aren't even on the drawing board yet."

Roberts knows that business has always followed the lead of technology—and that man has then molded those advancements to fit societal needs. "I remember when I was in business school, I read about a small, obscure bank in Ohio. The CEO said, 'We're going to invest 5 percent of our earnings in R&D.' So you'd ask, Why would a bank invest in technology? Well, they invented ATM machines, and fundamentally changed the convenience of banking.

"The beauty of business is that it can never stop. A couple of years ago, I went to a self-serve gas station, and they'd just installed the pumps that you can operate by swiping your credit card. Now, who is sitting there thinking about gas stations? About how to make that experience better using new technology? At some point, someone sat in a room like this and came up with these ideas."

He pauses, takes a breath. "Look, I don't want people to get overhyped," he says, getting up, stretching his lanky frame. "This may take us 10 years. It won't happen overnight."

Then he fixes me with a hard, determined stare, the kind Diller or Gates or Eisner must have seen across the negotiating table. "But we're going to change the TV experience," he says, and then Brian Roberts is off, a handful of pink message slips in tow, headed for his office, where a spate of brainstorming phone calls cry out to be made, and barely hatched dreams wait to come true.

By Sabrina Rubin Erdely
October 1997

MURDER, HE SCULPTED

rank Bender is working late, as usual. He prefers the solitude the night brings, when the telephone is silent and the bill collectors stop coming. There are to be no distractions; tonight's task requires Bender's most grim concentration. His foot taps to the eerie gloom-rock of David Lynch's *Lost Highway* soundtrack, as he scribbles calculations on a legal pad. Then Bender turns his attention back to the human skull sitting unceremoniously on his desk.

"This young girl here," Bender yells over the rising swell of music, "she's about 23 years old. White. Her torso was found in a suitcase in Chester County. Her legs were in another township. That's about all we know." Bender falls silent as he measures her nasal cavity and makes a tiny pencil mark on either side. He is an impish, energetic man with a silver tooth and a white Vandyke that tapers to a sinister point beneath his chin. Blue tattoos from his Navy days peek out from the sleeves of his black T-shirt. Across Bender's cavernous studio/home—a converted meat market near the South Street Bridge—Frank's wife chews on an ear of corn at their kitchen table, all but oblivious to the thumping music and the grisly work under way.

It is in these late-night hours that Bender, a facial reconstructionist, exercises his uncanny ability: to visualize what a person looked like in life simply by studying her naked skull. He then constructs a mold and plaster bust of his vision, to be flashed on television and printed up on flyers, in the hopes of getting a positive ID. He has a success rate of 90 percent; when finally identified, the victims often resemble their plaster likenesses right down to the hairstyle.

Already Bender has filled this skull's eye sockets with balls of white clay and mounted it onto a pair of plaster shoulders. "I want her looking a little off to the side," Bender says, angling her clay neck to raise her chin slightly. "I don't know why yet." He gets to work smearing hunks of red clay over the bone. Although no leads have developed since this skull was found two years ago near Brandywine Creek, Bender is unfazed. He has worked on many such cases for state and local police, the U.S. Marshal Service, the FBI, Interpol, Scotland Yard and *America's Most Wanted*, including the pursuit of famed onetime Philadelphia guru and 16-year fugitive Ira Einhorn. However, perhaps Bender's proudest affiliation is with a group he helped found: the Vidocq Society, whose members help solve "cold," or old crimes. After keeping a low profile for the first six years of its existence, the Vidocq Society was discovered several months ago by Hollywood, and now a movie is in the works, for which Bender and two of his cronies received a seven-figure deal.

"The forensic team, we're the last ones to represent these people," Bender goes on, packing red clay around the skull's eyes, plugging up its nose. "There's nobody else left to stand up for them. So you have to give it your all." Much later in the process, after he has created a mold of this sculpted head, he will undo his handiwork, stripping the clay from the skull before returning it safely to the morgue. For now, however, the skull is Bender's canvas. He spreads clay over the exposed teeth, and suddenly it has become a rough-hewn face with pursed lips, staring at its sculptor with unseeing eyes. Bender stares back. The police delivered this head to him in an airtight bucket; he "defleshed" it himself, and has already felt compelled to paint a series of nightmarish watercolors for his own mental health. All around him, the plaster busts of past murder victims watch from their places on his shelves.

"I have to stop here," he says heavily, snapping off the desk lamp. "I have to be alone with her now."

MOST homicides are solved within 72 hours," explains Vidocq Society commissioner Bill Fleisher, swirling horseradish into a jar of cocktail sauce at Seafood Unlimited. "If not, the chances of solving them go down exponentially. The evidence gets old. People's memories change. Bad guys get farther away."

For those reasons, the mission of the Vidocq ("Vee-DOCK") Society is a formidable challenge. Named for 18th-century criminal-turned-master-detective Eugene Francois Vidocq, and begun as a social club for criminologists, forensic experts and other law-enforcement types, Vidocq has evolved into a prestigious think tank made up of some of the best minds around, who unite to help solve crimes that have baffled everyone else. Membership is a privilege: According to its quirky bylaws, only 82 people can join (82 being the number of years Monsieur

Vidocq lived). District Attorney Lynne Abraham is a member. Others include the FBI profiler who coined the term "serial killer," Interpol agents and the forensic dentist who testified in the Megan Kanka trial, as well as three people—the Montgomery County coroner, the polygraph expert *and* the defense attorney—currently involved in the murder case of Stefanie Rabinowitz. Every two months, all gather at the Downtown Club, where, over lunch, they come up with pro-bono advice for stumped investigators and bereaved families.

The group has consulted on more than a hundred cases since its inception, but only the toughest are formally presented at its luncheons. The Cleveland torso murders, for instance, in which 32 hobos were killed from the 1920s through the 1950s. Or the case of a Miami woman found with six bullets in her, whose death was curiously determined by police to have been a suicide. Or the suspicious 1987 death of a New Jersey man who Vidocq believed was actually alive and well in Puerto Rico. "All solvable crimes," says Fleisher, a rounded, easygoing guy with a graying beard and a head of jet-black hair. "They were just never solved." According to its commissioner, Vidocq has never *not* been able to provide some insight into a case. On about 30 occasions, Vidocq members have volunteered to actively join in investigations. Of those, two have resulted in convictions, and one ended in an innocent man's name being cleared.

Vidocq's quest is more crucial now than ever, since unsolved cases in the United States are at an all-time high—a consequence, suggests Fleisher, of rises in both the rates of stranger-on-stranger murders and the number of seriously disturbed individuals walking around. As murderers become increasingly random and deviant, Fleisher says, they exploit the limits of police departments that often fail to share information with one another until it's too late. "Lack of communication is law enforcement's downfall," reasons Fleisher. "Take Andrew Cunanan. You're trying to tell me he drove a red pickup truck down 95 from New Jersey to Florida and nobody spotted him?!"

Collaboration among all areas of law enforcement is a major emphasis of the Vidocq Society. Vidocq's trio of founding fathers exemplifies the group's range of expertise: polygraph analyst Fleisher, psychological profiler Richard Walter and Frank Bender. Of the three, Bender—part sculptor, part pathologist, part mystic—has attracted the most attention. He is featured in several true-crime books, and was the inspiration for a Nancy Drew mystery in which Nancy joins forces with the Vidocq Society and the Hardy boys. He's the one who originally sent Hollywood swooning earlier this year, with Danny DeVito's Jersey Films ultimately outbidding Disney, Warner and Paramount for the Vidocq Society story. And rumor has it that someone else was fascinated with Bender: Many are convinced that Chris Carter, creator of *The X-Files*, based the main character of his show *Millennium*, "Frank Black," on Frank Bender. Though Carter denies, through a spokesperson, any connection, the similarities between the two Franks—men who, using psychic-like insights into the minds of killers and victims; help solve crimes on behalf of underground societies—are eerily similar.

But for all the interest in what Bender does, no one knows quite how he does it. "Maybe he has messages beamed to him from outer space," cracks Fleisher. "Would you doubt it?" He laughs uproariously. "Frank works on instinct," he continues, serious now. "Maybe it's his artist's eye. Maybe it's his sixth sense. Whatever it is, it works. And that's all we care about."

ALL BENDER was looking for, really, was a cheap anatomy lesson. It was 1976, and as always, money was tight. Frank Bender had endured his share of hard knocks—a North Philly childhood, a stint in the Navy in lieu of college—only to be eking out a living for his wife and two daughters as a commercial photographer, which he hated, while yearning to focus on his pastels and sculptures. At 34, Bender had decided to use his VA benefits to take some night classes at the Pennsylvania Academy of Fine Arts. But no anatomy class was being offered. So when a friend at the Philadelphia Medical Examiner's Office invited Bender to the morgue for an anatomy lesson of sorts, Bender jumped at the chance.

He peered under the white sheets while his friend read off the corpses' names, ages and manners of death, until they reached one unidentified woman. Bender's friend explained that hers was a hopeless case: She had been found near the airport two years earlier, too decomposed for anyone to tell what she looked like, her flesh nothing but a messy sludge of black rot oozing off her yellowing skeleton.

"I know what she looked like," Bender said immediately.

"How could you know?" his friend scoffed. But pathologist Dr. Halbert Fillinger overheard their conversation and asked Bender if he had any forensic experience. "I don't even know what that word means," Bender confessed. Even so, Fillinger encouraged him to reconstruct the woman. The resulting plaster bust was of a fleshy, thin-lipped face with a pointed nose. Photographs of the bust were printed on police flyers and distributed throughout the area; six months later, she was identified as a 62-year-old woman from Phoenix.

Everyone who came in contact with the case was blown away by the resemblance between Bender's bust and the actual victim. Bender wasn't. "I knew. I don't know how, I just did," he remembers now. "Certain psychics say that I'm psychic, but…" He waves a dismissive hand. "I just pay close attention to the forms of the skull, and what they're saying." Dr. Fillinger began commissioning Bender to do other reconstructions, and his success was astonishing. He would use forensics as a starting point, referring, for example, to the standard chart of average tissue thickness. But then, as he'd bury his marks with clay, a mental picture would emerge. "That's where the science ends and the art begins," says Bender. "I follow the flow of the face. Whether a face is beautiful or ugly, there's always a harmony. Like in music: You change a note, and it goes sour. So if the eyes and the nose work, you make the mouth to go with the eyes and the nose."

He was asked to lecture to law-enforcement organizations about his techniques, and impressed the U.S. Marshal Service enough to be invited on a manhunt for mob hit man Hans Vorhauer and Robert Nauss, ex-president of the Warlock biker gang, who had escaped together from Graterford Prison. Vorhauer was a master of disguises with a genius I.Q., clever enough to have built an armoire in Graterford's woodshop and sell it to accomplices on the outside—with him and Nauss hidden in it. Bender enlisted the help of Bill Fleisher, then a U.S. Customs agent; from the leads Fleisher supplied, Bender predicted—correctly, of course—that the brown-haired Vorhauer would bleach his hair blond and that the bearded, scruffy Nauss would be a clean-shaven, shorthaired suburbanite.

The marshals called on Bender again in their search for Alphonse Persico, the Colombo crime family underboss who had been on the lam for 12 years. Working from 14-year-old photos, Bender concocted a bust with an appearance radically different from what the FBI had been looking for. Four months later, Persico was nabbed, causing some awkwardness for Bender with the Bureau's forensic staff, but further adding to his reputation.

Then, a few years later, Bender's bust of an aged Ira Einhorn helped lead authorities to the Stockholm lair of the 1960s icon who'd been convicted in absentia of murdering girlfriend Holly Maddux and stuffing her remains in a trunk. Though they missed Einhorn by one day, the near-capture generated key breaks in the case that eventually led to his arrest in Champagne-Mouton, France, in June and an extradition hearing last month.

In 1987, Bender was contacted by a television producer who wanted to re-create the Vorhauer/Nauss case for the pilot episode of a show devoted to catching fugitives. *America's Most Wanted* was so pleased with Bender (because the show had little money to hire actors, Bender actually played the part of Vorhauer) that he was soon tapped to work on another segment, this one on fugitive John List. In 1971, List had vanished after killing his family in their Westfield, New Jersey, home. AMW wanted Bender to create a bust of what List might look like 18 years later. Working with profiler Richard Walter, Bender aged List's face, adding a pair of heavy, dark-rimmed glasses because "it would be part of his facade to make him look more intelligent than he really was," Bender explains. The bust was featured on AMW, and the FBI caught List 11 days later—wearing dark-framed glasses, naturally. *America's Most Wanted* ratings soared.

Bender was thrilled to be using his artistic skills for such a noble purpose, one that served justice and finally gave restless souls peace. But though his triumphs piled up, he continued to struggle financially. The plaster busts, each of which took a month to make, brought in only $1,200 to $1,700 apiece. In addition, the publicity generated by his unorthodox hobby had ended his career as a commercial photographer. With two kids to put through college, Bender tried his hand at a hodgepodge of odd jobs, from making bronze plaques for hospitals and schools to diving under tugboats in the Delaware to inspect them for damage. Never mind that Bender had no diving equipment; he would just put on a pair of coveralls and a face mask, hold his breath, and call upon his Navy training.

OF ALL THE connections Bender made through his law enforcement adventures, none were as important to him as his friends Bill Fleisher and Richard Walter. But until 1990, the wisecracking Philadelphia polygraph expert and the deadly serious Michigan prison psychologist had never met. That's when Walter found himself in Philadelphia for a couple of days, and Bender insisted the three of them get together over lunch. At Day By Day they batted around theories on the motivations of serial killers and the positioning of dead bodies. Before they knew it, the sky was growing dark. And they were struck by an idea.

"There's a relatively small group of people who are really in the know," says Walter. "The idea was to bring them all together, as a way to organize the casual information-sharing that goes on." The name "Sherlock Holmes Society" was floated, then nixed as being too cliche. Fleisher is the one who thought of Eugene Vidocq (the other two had never heard of him), and sent out exploratory letters to medical examiners, prosecutors, attorneys, detectives and special agents he knew. Almost all responded positively.

The cases presented at the Vidocq Society's first few meetings were simply meant as intellectual exercises. Fleisher would introduce the particulars of a murder case before the salad course, let members talk among themselves, then open the floor for discussion before the entree was served. By dessert, the group would be teasing out untried leads and overlooked clues. Not only was it fun, it was a great networking opportunity, and membership swelled. Before long, Vidocq had decided to use its collective skills to provide pro-bono advice. "A lot of departments can't afford experts, or don't know the right people, so their cases never get solved," Bender explains. "We became an organization that can give the police, for free, the best information there is."

Vidocq's most recent success was a tough case involving a young Philadelphian named Roger Scott Dunn, who moved to Lubbock, Texas, and disappeared shortly thereafter, in 1991. Despite evidence of foul play—a large, irregular shaped section of carpet in Dunn's apartment had been replaced, and the floor underneath was stained with his blood—Dunn was officially listed as "missing" until Vidocq got on the case. The investigators determined that the blood loss must have been staggering to soak clear through the carpet; splatter marks on the walls and ceiling were other telltale signs of a severed artery. Walter called friends at Scotland Yard, who confirmed the team's diagnosis. There was no way Dunn could have survived the crime scene. And incredibly, though his body has never been found, Dunn's girlfriend was convicted of his murder last May. Her alleged accomplice goes to trial next month.

But Vidocq cases don't always have such neat endings. After its experts offer advice, police and prosecutors sometimes choose not to follow it. For example, there was the 1991 shooting death of a Toms River, New Jersey, woman, ruled a suicide, which the Vidocq Society concluded was actually a murder. It even fingered the woman's boyfriend as the prime suspect. But after Vidocq issued its finding, the Ocean County prosecutor's office decided that the case was closed. "The buck stops with the prosecutor, because the prosecutor wants to get re-elected!" Frank Bender fumes. "It's all about politics. That's the reason why some crimes are solved and others aren't. That's the part you never see in movies."

If it's up to Bender, though, it will appear in movies. His own movie.

For years, Bender has had a kind of cult following in certain star circles. Robert De Niro is a fan, and when Bender gave a talk at De Niro's Manhattan screening room a few years back, he was approached by a friend of Michael Douglas who said Douglas was dying to play Bender in a movie. By early this year, New York agent Jody Hotchkiss was calling to tell Bender he'd be the perfect subject for a feature film. Bender couldn't believe his luck; he was teetering on the edge of bankruptcy. But he had an even better idea.

"You should come check out my friends at the Vidocq Society," Bender told Hotchkiss. "Now *there's* a movie."

Hotchkiss showed up at the February 1997 Vidocq meeting and was floored. When the next Vidocq luncheon rolled around in April, Bender arrived at the Downtown Club flanked by a baker's dozen of studio reps and producers. After the meeting, they all hustled back to Bender's house to start the bidding. Danny DeVito's Jersey Films bought Bender's, Fleisher's and Walter's life rights for seven figures.

"So the deal was made," Bender recounts happily. "We split the money between the three of us and Vidocq. So now the Vidocq Society has money. And I can pay my taxes back."

BACK IN Frank Bender's studio, the radio is tuned to an oldies station. "*Heat waaave,*" Bender absently sings along with Martha and the Vandellas as he sculpts a pair of crescent-shaped eyelids between his fingers. The dead woman's head is looking more and more lifelike every day. Over the course of two weeks, Bender has slowly given her a long, heart-shaped face, a tapered nose and prominent cheekbones. "That might change before I'm done. I might flatten those cheekbones out a little," he says, surveying his work critically. "I just have to let it happen naturally, till I exhaust myself. Then I regroup, and think it out again, and boom, it hits again."

It's late afternoon, rather early in the day for this sort of work, but Bender wants to get some time in before he and his wife meet the Fleishers for dinner at Opus 251 to officially celebrate their movie contract. He's trying to keep from becoming too absorbed in his work, and failing: A little change to her eye gives way to new insight into the ridge of her brow. "*Lou-ay Lou-aaay,*" he breathes along with the music. Quickly he fashions an ear; as he does, something catches his eye, and his hand shoots over to her nose and adds a smidgen onto its tip.

And then Bender leans back. He's through for the day. "I need to think things over. This is too important to rush," he declares. He fondly rests a hand on top of her head—a habit he's developed as he's gotten closer to her. "This is a lot of responsibility. I don't want to let anybody down by not doing my best." He gives her a rub. "Especially her."

Three weeks later, the plaster bust is complete. She has been transformed into a young woman with softly rounded features, a straight nose, slightly uneven brown eyes and short, dark hair. She has a distracted look about her, as if she is gazing at something in the distance. The person who killed her and sawed her in half is still on the loose, but that's out of Frank Bender's hands now. All he can do is wait. For the next few weeks or months or even years, Bender will see her face—his creation—on flyers handed out on sidewalks, taped up in store windows and tucked under windshield wipers in supermarket parking lots. He will see it displayed in shopping malls and on the evening news. And he will pray for someone to recognize her.

By Mark Cohen
February 1997

WHO'S AFRAID OF RICHARD GLANTON?

ehind the big, fancy desk, he's sitting up straight now, his thick upper arms tensing beneath his exquisitely tailored suit. The crooked grin that just a moment ago was lighting up this portion of the Center City sky has turned into something closer to a snarl. His voice, a high-pitched Southern twang, has gone from sweetness to a slap.

He's talking about racism in America. These days, Richard Glanton always seems to be talking about racism in America. As he speaks, some of the area's most voracious attorneys are racking up hundreds of thousands in legal fees and slaying scores of trees to support Glanton's talk about racism in America—especially that found in a well-heeled neighborhood on Philadelphia's Main Line. "My point," he says, connecting the big-picture dots, "is I'm just as American as anybody, and that if we can fight and die in battle in defense of America, at least we can be treated equally in our daily lives, even if it takes a little bit of extra effort on your part to treat us equally. You know," he pauses, gathering his thoughts, "Jefferson said that 'We are holding a wolf on the ground by its ears. And we know that justice demands that we turn him loose, but our self-preservation commands us to hold it. But we know we can't hold it forever.' And that's the same dilemma we have today."

"So you would be the wolf?"

"No," he smiles, "that was part of the fallacy in the analysis. Just because you want to enslave me doesn't mean that I'm a wolf." He breaks out in a belly laugh. "Jefferson was wrong in his characterization. I brought it up because this subliminal sort of wolf characterization is still out there." He laughs again, quieter now. "It is. Except that I'm not a wolf. I'm not going to bother anybody."

OUTSIDE, it's a brisk autumn morning, but on the second floor of the Lower Merion Township Administration Building, a zoning hearing is deep in the usual torpor. Arcane questions about budgets and head counts are followed by roundabout, somnambulant answers. Like so many Lower Merion zoning disputes, this has been a long one, having dragged on, in one form or another, for close to a year. The issue is whether the Barnes Foundation, under the leadership of its president, Richard Glanton, has changed from an "art education" facility with a minor gallery component into a "museum" that is drawing too many people to Latch's Lane and is in violation of its zoning requirements. One of Glanton's attorneys flips mechanically through a book on Cézanne; up front, Robert Ryan, the chairman of the zoning board presiding over the hearing, slumps in his chair, his hands poised contemplatively against his chin in a pose that almost conceals his closed eyes. Still, with Richard Glanton in the room, sleep and torpor are never entirely safe.

This is the same Richard Glanton, after all, whose civil trial on sexual-harassment charges four years ago titillated the city for weeks. He is the Richard Glanton whose 1991 threat to pawn some of the Barnes' impressionist masterpieces provoked a collective gasp from the international curator community; the Richard Glanton who has repeatedly squared off in court with the charitable and art-education groups that once were the Barnes' most loyal sources of support and who is now being sued by the city of Rome. Of course, he is also the Richard Glanton who breathed life into a kooky, cloistered institution, painstakingly restoring its 70-year-old Main Line estate with millions raised from a spectacular world tour of its paintings, though even there, he complains that he has failed to receive the recognition in Philadelphia that he has in other places. Or, as he puts it, "France has given me all these awards. Here—spit."

But, in a sense, all of that is mere prelude to Glanton's current donnybrook over race in Lower Merion Township. Whether the people who live and work here saw black when they first looked at Richard Glanton, they're definitely seeing red now. It all started as a zoning dispute. Glanton then filed a lawsuit claiming the township had violated the Barnes' civil rights—in essence that the zoning laws were being enforced against the foundation only because its leadership is black. Before long, some township commissioners had hired their own notoriously hardball attorney, Paul Rosen, to accuse Glanton of defamation for statements he'd made in the press. The people who live across the street from the Barnes, who were also sued, are still so angry at being accused of racism that, even though the judge has dismissed them from Glanton's case, they, too, are talking about hiring lawyers and exacting revenge. The blood-letting could go on for years.

Predictably, reaction to Glanton's suit splits along racial lines. While many white people see opportunism, J. Whyatt Mondesire, the newly elected head of the Philadelphia NAACP, praises the Barnes' president for raising important and long-neglected issues. Depending on your perspective, Richard Glanton, in launching this assault on the Main Line, has either committed his most reckless, coldly cynical act yet or finally ripped the cover off institutionalized racism in suburban America. Either way, he's playing with incendiary stuff.

Back at the zoning hearing, Glanton is testifying, assuring the torporous group that once a parking lot is installed, crowd control will improve. "But the quicker we can get past these, uh," he pauses before dropping his bomb, "Jim Crow hurdles..."

"Objection!" shouts the suddenly apoplectic township solicitor, Gilbert High. "I would like to object to that! 'Jim Crow hurdles' is an absolutely outrageous comment for this man to make. Absolutely outrageous."

"Down..." calls suddenly conscious chairman Ryan.

"It is—it is outrageous!"

"Down, Mister High!" Ryan commands again, rapping his gavel. "As for you," he turns to Glanton, "I ask you to please keep the testimony free of that kind of thing. This is not the place for that."

"Yes, Mister Chairman," Glanton politely responds, without completely wiping the smile from his face. "Of course, this is America."

IN A TOWN starved for real celebrity, Richard Glanton is getting close. Squeezing up the narrow streets in his giant black $90,000 Mercedes with the single digit "6" on the license plate (a perk he's retained from his days working in the governor's office—the governor always gets "1"), fanning the rumors that the Republicans will run him for mayor (or is it senator?), overwhelming a corner at the Palm with that great, booming laugh, the 50-year-old Glanton seems at times almost too big for his adopted city, a character more on the scale of New York or Los Angeles or a Tom Wolfe novel.

Remarkably, four years after enduring a lurid sexual-harassment trial, the Glanton persona just keeps growing. Four years after the local media were chronicling courtroom debates about the color of his chest hair and the ergonomic feasibilities of having sex in the front seat of a Mercedes, the married father of two is still making an estimated $450,000 a year as a partner at the politically prominent law firm of Reed Smith Shaw & McClay, and still in charge of one of the world's great art collections. He is also aspiring, in the waning moments of the 20th century, to be Philadelphia's walking conscience on race. "I'll tell you something," says one of his former partners, "if it were me in that courtroom and I'd endured those two years of agony, I don't know if I could do it. It takes the rare person not to go into hiding and into a state of depression after something like that."

Clearly, Glanton is a survivor. He grew up in Villa Rica, Georgia, a segregated, backwater-farming town where the odds against any person, let alone a black person, achieving legal superstardom were beyond long. But, aided by an early wave of affirmative action, Glanton was the second black student at West Georgia College and a member of the first University of Virginia Law School class with more than just a couple of black students. He was the first black at the Atlanta law firm where he worked right out of UVA and the first black on the legal staff of United Airlines in Chicago.

People who knew Glanton during those years remember him as charismatic and outgoing, popular not just with his fellow trailblazers. "A few of the militants in our class would tease him about being too friendly with white students," recalls one black UVA classmate, Jean Roane. "They'd say, 'Oh, you're just like one of them' or 'You Oreo.' They were looking for an argument, but Richard would smile and laugh as if it was water going off a duck's tail. I admired him for that."

His choice to be a Republican (a decision Glanton traces back to when he first registered to vote and the simple observation that "where I was from, the Democrats were segregationists") is recalled in a similar light, apparently striking some of his Great Society- and Nixon-era peers as a badge of his individuality and some as a calculated ploy to get ahead by standing out.

By 1978, Glanton was pushing paper as a staff attorney for Conrail and living with his wife, Scheryl, in Society Hill when he got his first real taste of the inner workings of power. Malcolm Lazin, a Republican neighbor of Glanton's who'd played a key role in the campaign for gubernatorial candidate Richard Thornburgh, recommended him for a job on the new governor's staff. ("I guess you can say," Lazin muses jokingly today, "I created the monster.") Glanton put in a quietly effective four years in Harrisburg, serving as Thornburgh's liaison with several agencies, including the Southeastern Pennsylvania Transportation Authority. Shortly before he left, though, he and his boss and colleagues had a falling out.

Glanton has explained his differences with the former governor by saying "Dick Thornburgh wants people around him to kiss his ass, and I don't kiss anybody's ass." But those close to Thornburgh say that what really happened was that Glanton got caught trying to engineer a little going-away present for himself. Prior to his departure, according to several Thornburgh insiders and then-SEPTA board chairman Lewis Gould Jr., Glanton told Gould he expected the SEPTA chair to send legal business to Glanton and Wolf, Block, Schorr, and Solis-Cohen, the law firm he was about to join. Gould balked ("I have never before or afterward had anyone else make that approach," he says), prompting Glanton to work behind the scenes to try to get a friend, former U.S. Attorney David Marston, elected chairman in Gould's place. (Marston, now a partner of Glanton's at Reed Smith, did not return phone calls.)

When Thornburgh found out about the scheme, these sources say, he quickly quashed it. Several months later, says one Thornburgh loyalist, "We began hearing from our sources in the political and business community in Philadelphia that Richard was spreading stories that we were racists."

The vendetta apparently didn't stop there. Six years later, Murray Dickman—who had been Thornburgh's secretary of administration in Harrisburg—was in Washington working for then-U.S. Attorney General Thornburgh when, Dickman says, he was told his former colleague was now spreading rumors that Dickman had a drug problem. Though another member of Thornburgh's staff did subsequently go to jail for drug use, there was never any evidence suggesting that Dickman was involved, and Dickman says he is convinced Glanton knew that. "After I heard it from two reporters, I hired a lawyer," Dickman says. "He took a couple of depositions and affidavits. Then he called Richard and said, 'This is what so-and-so says you told him and this is what so-and-so says. You know it's not true, so stop it, Richard.' And Richard said, 'Okay, I'll stop it.' Later that same day, my lawyer said Richard ran into him coming across the lobby of his building. Richard put his arm around him and was, like, 'Hey, how are you doing!' as if nothing had happened two, three hours before. When he told me about it later, my lawyer said, 'Murray, that was the strangest part of all.'"

AND THUS began a pattern. Glanton continued to ascend in conservative political and business circles; he continued to thrive in large, politically active law firms. And yet, for all his success in predominantly white arenas, he started to play the race card with alarming frequency. Since branding Thornburgh and his aides with the tag some 15 years ago, Glanton has accused enough people of racism to fill a gallery at the Barnes.

Glanton accused Kathleen Frederick of racism during her sexual-harassment suit against him. He accused state Deputy Attorney General Lawrence Barth of racism for reviewing possible conflicts of interest in the awarding of catalog rights for the Barnes tour. He accused former Barnes board member Cuyler Walker of racism for questioning items in the Barnes' budget and for objecting to the transfer of $1 million to minority-owned United Bank in violation of bylaws of Dr. Albert Barnes, the foundation's late founder. He accused another ex-board member, Charles Frank, of racism for opposing the use of endowment funds to publish a promotional brochure. And he accused Walker of racism when he and Frank backed ex-board member Shirley Jackson—instead of Glanton—for president (even though Jackson, too, is African-American). He accused Montgomery County Court Judge Stanley Ott of racism for ruling that the Barnes' re-opening party violated another provision in Dr. Barnes' will. He accused federal judge Anita Brody of racism for not recusing herself from his civil-rights case on the grounds that her daughter is active in Lower Merion politics. He accused opposing lawyers involved in two of his four pending legal matters of racism. He accused two *New York Times* reporters of racism—though on the whole he has said he finds the paper's coverage of him fair—and he has repeatedly dismissed the *Philadelphia Inquirer* as "racially motivated" or "a rag for attacking Americans of African descent" or "the kind of stuff you find from somebody who was Ku Klux Klan." During Glanton's three days of deposition testimony in the defamation case brought by some of Lower Merion's commissioners, he was asked whether there was ever a time he could think of when someone challenged him and he *didn't* counter with an accusation of racism. Glanton's response: "Not offhand."

So perhaps it was only a matter of time before the other shoe dropped on this magazine and this writer. After a pleasant two-and-a-half-hour interview in his office and several meaningful, and lively, phone exchanges about the Lower Merion racial controversy, the latest of which had occurred less than 24 hours earlier, a letter arrived over *Philadelphia Magazine*'s fax machine early one evening: "...Accordingly, I am hereby requesting that there be no further contact by Mark Cohen in his efforts to contact me or my family, and I am demanding that this invasion of privacy be ended now. ... Your conduct in this case has been exactly what I would expect from a publication which has a preoccupation with undermining, disparaging, and maligning the character of Americans of African descent."

While Glanton's race-card strategy continues to play differently in black and white communities, there are black people who see Glanton's accusations as more bluster than substance. "He does a great imitation of that Clarence Thomas thing, 'It's a high-tech lynching of an uppity black person,'" says Joe Tucker, an African-American trustee of Lincoln University, the small, historically black Chester County College that Albert Barnes entrusted with the stewardship of his foundation. "[Glanton] uses the race card to scare you white folks. Usually he doesn't even have to fully play it. He just shows it."

GLANTON'S Lower Merion race war began with a dispute about parking. In the summer of 1995, neighbors across the street from the Barnes on North Latch's Lane began to worry. As they saw in the news how lines stretched on for blocks at foreign stops of the Barnes tour, they began to have disturbing visions of what might happen to their quiet street of half-million-dollar homes when the paintings returned. The district's township commissioner, James Ettelson, spent months pursuing solutions with Glanton's people and assured the neighbors that everything would be fine.

Then the most popular parking plan fell through, and news of the plan's demise failed to spread among the neighbors. In early September, Glanton notified the township that he wanted to build an on-site parking lot in a part of the arboretum in back of the gallery and was told that approval would take at least until the spring of 1996. Several weeks later, less than a month before the Barnes' scheduled reopening, most neighbors learned for the first time in a tense meeting at the Merion Civic Association that not one of their concerns about traffic had been addressed.

The dispute broke open on a rainy, blustery November night in 1995. Latch's Lane was completely impassable as 600 black-tie guests descended for the Barnes Foundation's reopening gala. Across from the front gate, a bedraggled group of former Barnes art students held signs conveying their distaste for the glitzy affair and Glanton's leadership in general. FROM L.A. TO P.A., MONEY BUYS THE LAW, read one, drawing a connection between Glanton's legal victories and the then-recent O.J. verdict. Some of the neighbors came out in the rain to videotape the line of cars; one couple invited the protesters in to dry off.

The following week, during the public-comment portion of a Lower Merion town meeting, several neighbors lit into the commissioners. One of the most emotional neighbors, Robert Marmon, said of Glanton that "I now finally understand what a carpetbagger is." A few weeks later, the township issued a cease-and-desist order, which the Barnes immediately appealed to the zoning board, effectively starting the wheels of justice grinding. A month later, Glanton filed the civil-rights suit. By spring, the commissioners had hired Paul Rosen. (Full disclosure: Rosen's daughter works for *Philadelphia Magazine*, and the magazine frequently retains Glanton's law firm, Reed Smith, for legal work.)

Now, $800,000 in combined legal bills later, the parking squabble has turned into a racial Armageddon, one being fought in one of America's best-known suburbs. Bob Sugarman, a white civil-rights attorney to whom Glanton turned last May, has moved to amend the original suit to claim that Glanton's problems with the township are part of a larger pattern of historical racial discrimination that includes everything from a policy limiting blacks to the lowest-paying jobs on the township's payroll—"such as trash collection"—to "minimizing the creation of affordable, new or rehabilitated housing...available to African-Americans." There is even mention of an incident involving the long-deceased Dr. Barnes: when he proposed erecting a public statue to honor a well-known African-American composer and his neighbors insisted that it be located in the town's one black cemetery.

Glanton's battle, it turns out, is eerily reminiscent of his white forebear's. Dr. Barnes, the irascible millionaire inventor and manufacturer of the antiseptic Argyrol, loved to flout the racial conventions of the 1920s and 1930s. One of his favorite practices was to hold recitals by black musicians in the gallery. Piqued by a proposed housing development adjacent to his property, Barnes even threatened to move his art collection to New York and turn the entire estate into an institution for the study of black culture. When, just before his death, he rewrote his will to bequeath the eventual care of his collection to Lincoln University, it was probably as much a reflection of his fondness for black causes as it was a way to stick it to the Philadelphia art establishment and his neighborhood.

Today, in a small garret-like office that at one time was the living quarters of Barnes' maids, some of the fallout from those earlier fights spills from a dog-eared file: angry screeds from Dr. Barnes alleging "corruption" and "conspiracy" by township officials, an anonymous letter referring to Barnes as "a clap doctor" and "nigger lover," a cartoon from a local newspaper depicting him walking down a street in his bathrobe with a grotesque caricature of a black toddler by his side. As Laura Linton, the Barnes' development director, sits flipping through the file, she remarks at how struck she is by the similarities between the foundation's founder and its current president. "I asked Richard once when he was born to see if maybe it was the same day that Barnes died. It turned out I was off by a few years," she laughs, "but I'd had this theory that when Richard was born his body was inhabited by the ghost of Dr. Barnes."

IN AUGUST 1995, while the people who live on Latch's Lane were focused on parking, a construction crew at the Barnes was removing the limestone from the building's front steps so it could be cleaned and reinstalled in time for the November 11th reopening gala. As the workers took apart the steps, the limestone disintegrated in their hands.

Glanton instructed his project manager, Tom Massaro, to replace the stone with the same kind used by Dr. Barnes—from the same quarry. "No, Richard, I don't think you understand…" said Massaro, who figured it would take eight months to get any limestone, let alone the same limestone. But Glanton wouldn't discuss it. So at the height of the $12 million restoration project, Massaro flew to France, where he somehow got the original quarry reopened (it had been closed since 1946), spent a week nursing 211,000 pounds of limestone from quarry to stone-cutting village to a two-centuries-old barn high in the Alps, where it had to be polished by hand. "Every night I'd call, I'd say, 'Richard, we really need a back-up plan here.' But Richard's view was, like, 'Why are you calling?' Click."

Massaro saw to the remaining details; he had the stone crated, inspected and booked on four successive US Air flights. When Massaro walked off the plane in Philadelphia with the first shipment, "I was ecstatic," he says, "I couldn't believe it. Everyone except Richard said it couldn't be done. And this is what he said to me when he came to meet me: 'See, I told you it was not a problem. Just thank God the plane didn't crash. We would have lost the steps.'"

Actually, the entire Barnes revitalization effort has been a little like that. Today, with the Barnes a cornerstone of the region's tourism plans, the solution may seem obvious: a decaying building, the world's finest art collection that almost no one's ever seen, but a single clause in the dead founder's will stipulating that the paintings aren't supposed to travel. … No problem, we'll just break the will. It seems obvious now, but before Richard Glanton, no one had the stomach or creativity to try.

The whole seven-city tour was predicated on a giant leap of faith. Each of the host museums signed contracts conditional on the Barnes getting court permission to take the paintings on the road. Deadlines for booking airlines and arranging for security and promotional materials were bumped repeatedly by motions, postponements, and appeals until the deadlines could no longer be pushed and multimillion-dollar commitments had to be made based on the assumption that Glanton and his lawyer, Bruce Kauffman, would win their case. Which they did, by arguing that the clause in the will prohibiting travel should take a back seat to another clause requiring the preservation of the collection.

Then there were the fees Glanton squeezed out of the museums. As Irene Bizot, general administrator of France's Réunion des Musées Nationaux, recalls, "When he first mentioned money we were very puzzled." World-class museums don't usually pay to borrow artwork; they obtain it in exchange for pledges to lend out their own pieces. But the lack of precedence for what he was doing seemed to have a kind of liberating effect on Glanton. "He just said to the French," relates Laura Linton, " 'You pay me $2.5 million or you won't get the paintings.' Then he made the Japanese pay $4.5 million. When they asked, 'Why, if the French were only paying $2.5 million?', he said, 'Because you have more money.'"

Glanton also hawked the catalog rights to Alfred A. Knopf for $1 million, bagging an additional $800,000 donation from the S.I. Newhouse Foundation (S.I. Jr. owns Knopf) for Lincoln University. And when late offers from museums trailed in, Glanton went back into court for permission to make additional tour stops, all the while taking criticism from art purists from Merion to Milan. "People say anyone could have done what he did," says Linton, "but I don't think anyone else would have taken the personal grief."

Even Glanton's supporters concede, however, that the very arrogance—fine, we'll break the will—that allows him to achieve greatness also gets him into trouble. The picture that arises from the four major lawsuits and the zoning matter in which Glanton has been embroiled over the past four years is that of a man who if not completely out of control is close to it. At the Barnes, Glanton appears to be ruling almost by fiat. Twice in the past four years, his presidential term has expired and he has continued to serve for extended periods without official election by canceling the annual board meetings and failing to reschedule them. He has allowed the operating deficit to balloon to $249,700, a move seen by some as a ploy to pressure the court into granting him longer visiting hours and a higher admission charge.

The deficit has caused other members of the five-person board some consternation, but that hasn't seemed to bother Glanton. Board members' questions, whether about the magnitude of his entertainment, travel and other business expenses (in 1995 they topped $56,000) or the appropriateness of having his former secretary and her husband live rent-free at another estate owned by the Barnes, generally seem to get evaded or ignored. "It was almost impossible to pin him down," says former board member Cuyler Walker. "We'd try to talk to him about the deficit. We'd say, 'Richard, we just can't keep doing this indefinitely.' He'd say, 'right, you're right. I'll do that.' He sounded so charming that you'd want to believe him, even though the pattern taught you otherwise. Then six months would go by; pretty soon, years would go by, and nothing had been done about the deficit."

Though Glanton is fond of saying, "I'm not getting anything out of this, I don't get a single dollar in salary from the Barnes," the lawsuit filed by the city of Rome alleges that he might benefit in other ways. The essence of the case is that he breached a contract with Roman officials when he made the final stop of the tour Munich instead of Rome's Museo Capitolino. The complaint—brought by prominent Center City attorneys James Beasley and Michael Smerconish—accuses Glanton of using Rome to further "his personal law practice and...his active social life." It suggests that in return for the Barnes tour Glanton sought help in securing legal business for Reed Smith from a host of Italian concerns, including Alitalia airlines and Fiat.

In February 1995 Glanton made a third and final trip to Rome. During his stay, the suit claims, he signed a letter of agreement with Rome's mayor finalizing the deal; it also says the Italians put him up at the five-star Hotel Bernini Bristol and provided him with a car and chauffeur that—according to one plaintiff's deposition—he kept out late one night for a "date" with a married woman he'd met in Rome, thereby missing a dinner planned in his honor.

A month after Glanton's Roman holiday, the *Philadelphia Inquirer* reported that the exhibition would be going to Munich—not Rome. But Glanton, according to the suit, still led the Italians to believe they had a deal—dismissing the *Inquirer* article, according to his main Italian contact, Dr. Antonio Guizzetti, as "racially motivated" and "garbage." This, the suit claims, caused the Italians to continue their preparations for another several weeks "The president, Richard Glanton, this nice black American, came here for three days as our guest," one Italian cultural official, Gianni Borgna, told a Rome daily. "He visited the city. I suspect that for him it was only a happy vacation.... His is a ridiculous and grand gaffe." Glanton denies virtually all of Rome's allegations. He claims they never had an agreement and that he ultimately chose Munich because of concerns about security in Rome and because he had a better rapport with the Germans.

With four legal matters pending and teams of lawyers rooting through Glanton's life, it is clear that one price he will pay for continuing to wage war is further revelations about his personal life. There may even be more to come from the Frederick suit. Back then, the former associate claimed that when she stopped sleeping with Glanton, he blocked her career at Reed Smith; Glanton denied everything. He never slept with her, he never hindered her career. The jury didn't completely believe him, but its verdict was ambiguous. It found he'd committed harassment but assessed no financial damages. (It did find him liable for $125,000 for defaming Frederick at a news conference.) Then the verdict was appealed—which eventually led to a settlement that included Glanton's payment of an undisclosed sum and the vacating of the original verdict.

The jury, however, never got to see certain evidence that lawyers have learned more about in the course of research for the Lower Merion defamation case. Back in 1993, the judge refused to allow Frederick's legal team to introduce evidence of an alleged extramarital affair with a Reed Smith partner as well as a deposition from an associate describing a series of spurned sexual advances and reprisals. This third woman, who is now living in Chicago and just happens to be the niece of City Councilwoman Augusta Clark, declines to comment. "Whatever happened to my niece," says Clark, "she's gone on to bigger and better things. I'm not a big supporter of Richard Glanton, but if he falls, it won't be at my hands."

All this plus the Lower Merion controversy would seem enough to test even Glanton's survival skills. His law partners may continue to stand behind him.

("He is a very valuable member of the firm," says Michael Browne, managing partner of Reed Smith's Philadelphia office. "Most of the partners view his role at the Barnes as completely separate from his role here.") And Glanton may yet have a political future. ("I don't think he wants to run for mayor," says former mayor Wilson Goode, "though I can't think of anyone else who could energize the black community the way Richard could.") But some of his other bases of support appear to be eroding. There is a sense, for example, that his broadsides on the judiciary and the Philadelphia establishment may be starting to reflect poorly on Lincoln University, where there's a small but growing movement to rein in or even unseat the Barnes president. "Let's say a few of us are at least talking about it," says Joe Tucker.

And Deputy Attorney General Lawrence Barth (whose office is charged with enforcement of nonprofit organizations) confirms that he plans to look into allegations that Glanton has violated his fiduciary responsibilities, noncriminal behavior that could, however, result in his being removed as a trustee and financially penalized. Barth says that an issue of particular interest may be whether Glanton over-stepped his authority in even filing the Lower Merion civil-rights suit, which, combined with the defense of the subsequent defamation suit, already has cost the Barnes more than $200,000. In January 1996, Glanton sent a preliminary copy of the civil-rights suit to the three other active board members (Cuyler Walker's term was about to expire) with a note attached asking them for comment. Charles Frank, according to his deposition, read the proposed suit and wrote back that he didn't see where the Barnes had a case of racism. "It's a done deal," Glanton responded, according to Frank's testimony. "I have got three signatures, anyway." And then, even though any legal action requires unanimous, written board approval if no meeting has been called, the Barnes president responded with what would have to be considered classic Glanton behavior: He went ahead and filed suit anyway.

EARLY ONE Sunday afternoon, Toby Marmon is sitting with her husband in their den watching a video of tour buses parked across the street from their house on Latch's Lane and talking about what it feels like to be on the other end of a dispute with Richard Glanton. "I could be a piece of dried poo poo for all Mr. Glanton cares," says the small, dark-haired woman in a rapid New Jersey accent. "He's in a position of public trust and he's using public funds to stifle people's freedom of speech. Ten people stood up to complain at the public meeting the week after the opening party. You know how many people were there at a meeting after we got sued? Nobody."

In his lawsuit, Richard Glanton will try to prove that the Marmons and about a dozen other people like them are intent on ridding the neighborhood of tour buses and tourists only because an aggressive African-American man happens to be running the Barnes now. Largely Jewish, predominantly Democratic, the residents of Latch's Lane today are the kind of liberal, successful, well-educated people who have always assumed they were above charges of racism. A few of them marched as young adults in the Civil Rights Movement; Toby Marmon's father was a lawyer who represented the NAACP and black churches fighting discrimination in Essex County, New Jersey.

That Bob Marmon's use of the word *carpetbagger* has become a central piece of evidence in Richard Glanton's discrimination suit disturbs and riles Toby and him to no end. "When I grew up," says Bob, "Bobby Kennedy and Jack Kemp were both accused of being carpetbaggers when they switched jurisdictions to run for office." He turns to his wife, who is leaping from her chair to grab a dictionary off the shelf. "You should look it up in the dictionary!" she says. "'Carpetbagger' doesn't mean anything different than what it says in the dictionary!

"This whole thing makes me sick," she goes on. "I can't even go to the store to buy bread without hearing comments. There's a shop in Narberth where I go to buy challah for Shabbes, the guy says to me, 'Don't sell her any bread, because she's one of those nasty racists over there on Latch's Lane.' Ha! Ha! Ha! He thinks it's a big joke. But would you like it?"

Toby Marmon is sitting back down now. She looks as if she is about to cry. "It makes you take a good look at yourself. When I go to a store now and I'm in the check-out counter, I have to think, 'Am I treating this person any differently because of the color of his or her skin?' I never thought about it before. I treated everybody as a human. It's a terrible feeling. I can't sleep at night. Why should I question myself? I'm a nice person. I need Richard Glanton to make me think if I'm a racist or not?"

TO AFRICAN-AMERICANS, racism on the Main Line is not news. But Michael Brokenborough wants you to understand one thing: At first, he was as skeptical of Richard Glanton as the next person. When Glanton's attorney, Bob Sugarman, came to pay Brokenborough, the minister of a small black church in South Ardmore, Lower Merion Township's one tiny black neighborhood, a visit last spring, Brokenborough saw self-interest written all over the overture; indeed, up until that point, Glanton hadn't paid the slightest attention to South Ardmore. Still, when Sugarman approached the preacher for information that might help Glanton's civil-rights case, it didn't take him long to decide how to respond: He gave the man everything he had.

Other black leaders feel the same way. "Hey, I grew up on the Main Line," says former Philadelphia School Board Chairman Rotan Lee, who is a good friend of Glanton's. "I think some of the times Richard has pulled the race card have been a lot more Machiavellian than this one."

The NAACP's Mondesire says that in Lower Merion, black people can feel the racism in the air. About a year ago, he and Glanton and two other African-American associates took a construction tour of the Barnes. "Four black men are walking around in suits," says Mondesire, "and people stop to look at us. Then they just get back in their cars or houses. Nothing is said, no placards.

You just know. If you're 47 years old and have been a black man all your life, you just know."

Today, Brokenborough, the fit, soft-spoken minister in his mid-1940s, sits at his dining-room table, talking about some of the things he told Sugarman last spring. He talks about the ugly traffic stop of another South Ardmore minister by Lower Merion police two years ago; the persistent difficulties faced by minority students at Lower Merion High School; the unwanted development projects that have been dumped on South Ardmore over the years; and the invisible, well-oiled machine that always seems to spring into action when a similar project is proposed for a white neighborhood.

As Brokenborough talks, a clipped, angry tone creeps into his voice. "I sit on the board of a group trying to bring affordable housing to Lower Merion," he says, recounting a recent incident. "We bought some property in Bala Cynwyd that was going to be used for affordable housing. Then the neighborhood club of Bala Cynwyd protested, and with Joe Manko, the commissioner for that district, also putting pressure on our board, the board backed down. In our meetings, blacks and whites, we would discuss that the neighborhood club was just afraid that blacks were going to move down there, but then most people on the board didn't have the conviction to vote their conscience. They ducked it. See, there are some unspoken things that go on in this township. I think most people under-stand there is a kind of atmosphere that, we will let some blacks here, but don't get outrageous on us."

But does that have anything to do with the Barnes? A few days later, in a glass office tower a mile up City Avenue, Joe Manko grapples with what has been wrought by the unlikely alliance of Michael Brokenborough and Richard Glanton. A liberal Democrat and environmental lawyer who recently helped launch an unusual city/suburb cooperative venture—a City Avenue special-services district—with Philadelphia City Councilman Michael Nutter, Manko maintains that Brokenborough is glossing over some salient issues in the Bala Cynwyd dispute (for instance, the project started out and was ultimately approved as *elderly* affordable housing). Still, Manko's real argument, he says, isn't with the minister but with Glanton— with whom Manko was once law partners, some 15 years ago at Wolf Block.

"Are there people in my neighborhood who don't want blacks?" asks Manko. "I'm sure. I also have basketball courts in my district that some residents want me to take down because blacks come into the neighborhood to use them—I won't do that, because I think it's wrong. These are hot issues. But when Richard charges racism for his own self-serving interests—and in a situation that has nothing to do with race—it doesn't help any.

"Look, there are racists in every neighborhood. But *I* don't happen to be one of them. And what happens? I get hit with a lawsuit."

RICHARD GLANTON'S hometown is still just a tiny place. Some fast-food restaurants have risen out by the interstate and a few new subdivisions have been built for folks who don't mind the 40-minute drive to Atlanta, but downtown Villa Rica is still the same single strand of low-lying buildings it was when Glanton was growing up here in the 1950s; the freight trains still roar through twice each hour.

A mile and a half from downtown in a new housing development, just on the other side of the old "colored section" where most of Villa Rica's African-Americans still live, Norace Glanton is sitting in a kitchen talking about the fourth of her 11 children. Though in failing health now, Norace quickly warms to the subject of Richard Herbert Glanton. "I suppose he always did favor me," she says with a sly smile at one point.

There are still plenty of folks around Villa Rica who remember Richard Glanton, the local boy made so unbelievably good. There is a fastidious former high school English teacher who remembers how Richard "always was bold." There is an old friend who, during a break in his shift as a supervisor at the chicken-processing plant, the flecks of chicken guts still stuck to his coveralls and scrub cap, remembers how Richard was the only one in their circle of guys who had the courage to talk to white girls— "I think it was his way of showing 'I'm just as good as any man.'" There is an old farmhand who remembers how Richard's demanding mother tended to walk all over her simple, uncomplaining sharecropper husband Herbert—"He had to do what she said whether he wanted to or not."

There is also an elderly white woman, Evelyn Green, whose husband was once the Glanton family's landlord. Though she only vaguely remembers Richard, Green does recall the circumstances that led to the Glanton family's departure from the huge farm owned by Green's second husband, Frank: "The government kept raising the minimum wage and Frank had to give up farming. Besides," she adds, seemingly unaware of the condescension in her voice, "Mrs. Glanton also had some high-minded ideas and wanted to move into town."

That condescension today only hints at what life must have been like for poor black families in the middle part of this century. "It was the kind of town," says a childhood friend of Glanton's, Mattie Worthy, "where everybody knew everybody, white or black. Many of the black women worked in the white people's houses, so they'd know us as children; some of us wore their children's hand-me-down clothes. So long as your family was well-known and liked, no one caused you any problems." But, Worthy adds, "you knew your limits. When you walked into the drugstore to get your ice cream cone, you got it to go whether you wanted to or not.

"I tell my own daughter about what it was like and she can't believe it. She'll ask me, 'Mom, how could you put up with that?' It does kind of make you wonder why people acted the way they did. But it doesn't make you bitter, exactly. I don't think it did Richard, either. Or at least he didn't discuss it with me."

Over Thanksgiving, Worthy had a chance to spend some time with her old friend. While in Villa Rica visiting with his mother and siblings, Glanton stopped by Worthy's dress boutique on the main street to say hello and to warn her not to cooperate with a certain magazine article being prepared up in Philadelphia. "But I *already* talked to him," Worthy told Glanton, surprised. "I thought that's why you gave him my phone number." Glanton hit the roof, prattling on about how the article was part of a plot by his political enemies attempting to preempt a run by him for the U.S. Senate. "Wait a second," Worthy stopped him. "I don't know what this is about. But I'm sure I didn't tell him anything bad about you." Then she thought of something else. "C'mon," she said. "Take a drive with me to the old Green home-place. Did you know that place is for sale?"

"It is?"

"Yeah, and I want you to buy it and turn it into a bed-and-breakfast so I can manage it."

They hopped into Glanton's rental car and drove the mile and a half to the sprawling estate where Richard Glanton was born. With the tenant houses at the bottom rear of the property long gone, they spent their time wandering around the front yard of the spectacular white Victorian mansion at the top of the hill, gazing up at the same grand white portico and chimneys and the same towering oaks and sycamores that must have once loomed so large and oppressive for the young Glanton. "Oh, God, look at these trees!" he said. "I remember these!"

Sensing she had her friend in a weak moment, Worthy again pressed her case. "You should buy this place, Richard. That's the thing around here now, bed-and-breakfasts. Why don't you move back home?"

Glanton simply laughed, his sweet and friendly laugh: "Oh, no time soon."

ABOUT FOUR hours into Richard Glanton's last day of deposition testimony in the defamation suit, there is a telling exchange between Glanton and Paul Rosen, the commissioners' attorney. The two men are sitting about three feet apart, across a table in a drab, fluorescent-lighted conference room at the Montgomery County Courthouse. "What I'm asking you," Rosen says, "is it possible, Mr. Glanton, that the fact that you are who you are, not your origin, is responsible in some form for the way you are treated?"

Glanton straightens. "Well, I mean if you are saying that I should bend my back so people can stand on it, and shuffle and scratch my head…"

"That wasn't my question."

"That's what you're…"

Rosen tries another tack. Within a couple of minutes, he gets Glanton to agree that, of course, a white person could criticize him and be motivated by something other than racism. But then Rosen follows with a dry, "Do you ever give anybody the benefit of the doubt?" And from the moment Glanton responds, it's clear that they—Lower Merion, all of Richard Glanton's world—are right back where we started. "We're still fighting the Civil War in America," says Glanton. "And it hasn't ended, and I think that anybody who turns their eye to the venomous racism that is a daily part of the lives of black people really has to be educated. And so I'm not going to say that there is no racism. It is everywhere."

JUDITH RODIN

Departing Penn president, 59; West Philadelphia

If I was applying to Penn today, I wouldn't get in. Definitely not!

It's not easy to pack a house with 18 rooms. The number of closets! I just can't believe how much Penn stuff I've accumulated in 10 years. I must have 150 t-shirts, 20 caps, cups, mugs, everything.

Philly's biggest problem is that there's not enough collaboration. We have so many organizations all doing a piece of the same thing. And the sense of turf competition makes us get in one another's way.

I love the food at Susanna Foo. I often take out-of-towners there. Brasserie Perrier, too. And Pod.

Pat's or Geno's? Oh, I'm not enough of a cheesesteak connoisseur.

During a really stressful day, if I have a minute to clear my mind, I go to the Furness Building, next door. Actually, it's something I did as an undergraduate 40 years ago, when I felt stressed on campus. It's very quiet inside, and very beautiful and very contemplative. It makes me feel calm.

There are very few things in my life that have a beginning and an ending in a very narrow window of time. Cooking is one of them. So if my husband and I are here for a weekend, I'll cook. Like this Saturday night, I'm making chili.

When Alex was little, he used to tell people his mom's job was signing her name. Because that's all he'd see me doing, sitting at my desk, signing things.

Of all the Big 5 mascots, who would win in a fight? Oh, Ben Franklin! He'd use his brains to overcome the brawn.

My unhappiest time here was when the medical center was in such financial distress, and having to fire people. These are 1,800 people with families and lives. It makes you feel awful. But you have to do it sometimes.

I'll tell you another thing that I hate. I hate admissions time. Because I hate being called up, with people lobbying to get people in. I hate having that much control over people's lives. It isn't what I love about this job—I don't love the power.

Philly is not a self-promoting place. A lot of other cities will say better things about themselves, whether they believe it or not. And Philadelphians kind of let it all hang out. But if we badmouth ourselves, we're doing ourselves a disservice.

Oh yeah, I knew Ed Rendell as an undergrad. We were both in student government. He's still the same as he was then, totally rambunctious and out there. The difference? He was always a politician, but now he's a policy wonk. And he had more hair then, of course.

It's wonderful to get to the top. Particularly if you're a woman. Because now I can express the female side of myself more readily, without worrying that it'll seem like a weakness. Like today I was given an honor, and I cried. I never would have done that 10 years ago.

The students call me J.Ro.

Your family tells it like it is. They're not impressed by what you've accomplished. They really want you for who you are as a person. And that's very grounding.

Bono? I wanted a graduation speaker students would be excited about. And I wanted to go out with a bang.

Alex is coming to Penn Law this fall. Now that his mother's leaving, he can safely return.

Leaving here is bittersweet. It's hard to walk away from the best job you've ever had. But I need a deep breath. I definitely need some time off. So I'm going to move to New York for the year. I'm going to live with my husband for the first time since we were married. I'm writing two books. And I'm going to put my feet up. Play more tennis.

You have to know when to go. When you're in these kinds of jobs, you get a stack of chips when you come in. And you have to use those chips effectively to get things done. But when the stack is gone, you ought to leave. And I kind of feel that I've done it. The stack is gone.

By Stephen Rodrick
October 1997

THE TROUBLE WITH HARRY

t's a sultry summer evening, and the pulse of Philadelphia night life is flat-lining. By dusk on this Monday, most of the dwellers of America's fifth largest city have already tramped home. Jaywalkers on Broad Street pause in the middle of the city's most famous boulevard for aimless chitchat without fear of vehicular homicide. A valet stands idle, rhythmically tossing and catching a lone set of keys. It's no different inside the Palm, a sirloin and potato establishment popular with the folks who rule this town. But at 8 p.m. sharp, the mood goes from tepid to warm. Harry Jay Katz has arrived.

"Hey, Bubbie!" Katz shouts to one and all, leaving behind a trail of camaraderie and cologne. The hostess is smooched, the bartender back-slapped. The 56-year-old Katz sports a *Saturday Night Fever*-era black shirt. Three buttons are undone, exposing a plush rug of curly white hair. His retreating hairline divulges a sunburned pate. In the back, there are longish silver strands that flip upward like feathers. With his beakish nose and sharp eyes, Katz is the American bald eagle incarnate.

Curiously, his face is not among the caricatures on the restaurant's walls. "I overslept the day they were drawing," he says. But first things first. He buys a round of drinks for the party at the other end of the bar. They are a trio out of Mario Puzo's imagination: a heavily mascaraed, frizzy-haired beauty; a no-neck lawyer in a dark suit; and a man sporting white shoes, a bad toupee and a severe eyelid tic. "Those guys are *connected*," whispers Katz, pushing his putty-like nasal cartilage to the side with his right forefinger. "The least I can do is buy them a fucking drink."

Katz begins chain-smoking Camels. He brushes off the complaints of friend and cardiologist Dr. Ronald Pennock with a Borscht Belt "I die, when I die." Amidst all the merriment, Katz has forgotten to order himself a drink. He requests a martini fuelled by Ketel vodka. The bartender pours the ingredients into his trusty shaker. "Hey, make sure you shake it up by your ear," implores Katz. "Don't give it a pussy shake, give it a *shake*."

It's another night out on the town for Harry Jay Katz, Philadelphia's geriatric libertine. The guy who kibitzes with Schwarzenegger and Stallone. The Don Quixote dealmaker behind a bushel of ballyhooed failures, beginning with the never-opened Playboy Club of the 1970s and ending with last year's never-published book on what really happened to Jimmy Hoffa. A prankish sorcerer who magically insinuates himself into nearly every aspect of Philadelphia lore. Sure, everyone remembers that some woman drowned in his hot tub while under the influence of cocaine and antidepressants, but that was 2 years ago, and Katz is a man who lives in the hyperpresent. The games must go on.

Just now, a long-haired blonde walks by wearing CK ONE, a tight black dress and stiletto heels. Katz moves into action. He's flying solo tonight, and it makes him itchy. "You know, I had hair just like that," he calls to her. "Then it all fell out. What's your name?" The young lady looks at him quizzically, stutter-steps backward, pirouettes, and canters away. Harry, callous to the anguish of rejection from years as a singles warrior, shrugs, and gives his best Alfred E. Neuman "what, me worry?" smile. Still, a waiter friend gives Harry the raspberry.

"Hey, Harry," he says, "you're losing your touch. Three years ago, she would have been sucking your cock at the bar."

HE'S BEEN called a Gadfly with a multi-million-dollar trust fund. Zelig before Zelig. The ultimate dilettante. No one has squeezed more lines of type out of stillborn projects, a shuttered restaurant and roguish behavior than Harry Jay Katz. Today, politicians duck his calls. He reeks of two botched marriages and a black book flush with the names of women who would love to witness his slow castration.

Still, Katz remains an undeniable and unpredictable presence in Philadelphia. Foes grumble that he has never held a real job. They're wrong. *Being* Harry Jay Katz is a full-time job. You have to work at it. There are the choreographed late nights. The mornings spent calling columnists—primarily his friend Stu Bykofsky of the *Daily News*—to pass on a gossipy tidbit. Then there's his street rep as an incorrigible womanizer. That requires long hours of indefatigable maintenance.

The fruit of Katz's labor can be found by his toilet. Katz's celeb ties are on display in the tiny downstairs bathroom of his East Falls home. Above the throne is Maria and Arnold's framed wedding invitation. On the right wall is a large photo of Katz and his second wife, Andrea Diehl, at the wedding of Sylvester

Stallone and Brigitte Nielsen. To the left, there's a Polaroid of Sly with Girl Scout cookies bought from Katz's daughter Jessica. There are letters from George Bush, Bill Clinton, Gerald Ford, and Lyndon Johnson. (He's dined at the White House under three presidents.) Down to the right is an invitation to a fund-raiser the Katz family held for District Attorney Lynne Abraham. That's the image Katz has painstakingly created. The bon vivant. The last boulevardier. The man about town. Philly's connection to the stars.

But there's another image of Harry Jay Katz that no amount of self-promotion can burnish. It's an ominous picture of a playboy prince of darkness. Part of Katz's less-charming underbelly was exposed with the 1995 drowning of Valerie Sheridan in his hot tub, and the attempted suicide of Susan Delplanque the next day. More is revealed in court documents. In 1994, Katz was found liable of sexual harassment. In a separate 1996 case, he was accused by another woman of physical abuse and intimidation. Three women who know him say part of his problem is cocaine. In April, a Philadelphia Family Court judge ordered him to pay child support for a son he fathered out of wedlock. In an effort to evade paying for his sins, Katz, a man who continues to live in a mansion and dine at Philadelphia's most expensive bistros, declared bankruptcy in 1995. He claimed to be worth only $150. "He's failed at everything he ever tried," says one former friend. "He even failed at suicide."

But for Harry Jay Katz, the party goes on.

"HEY CUTIE, C'MON IN."

Harry Jay Katz greets me at the door of his East Falls home. It's 10 a.m. on a brutally hot Wednesday. Katz is clad in a white beach jacket and swimming trunks. In his left hand, a celery stick peeks out of the top of a plastic cup holding a Bloody Mary. He has already done the morning chores: calls to his mother Selma, brother Phil, and pals Bykofsky and Ron Pennock. Our meeting was scheduled to be a brief session, laying down ground rules, but Harry has other ideas. He loans me a swimsuit. I go upstairs to change. On the stairs is a life-size cutout of Wilson Goode wearing a RENDELL FOR MAYOR T-shirt. The bedrooms are pretty much as his kids left them years ago, with video arcade games and a vintage 1983 rock poster of The Police.

Past a cluttered kitchen, where there are BB guns and an Old South statuette of a grotesquely featured black man eating a watermelon, is a sprawling backyard that frequently attracts deer. Harry has installed a plastic doe standing under a Deer Crossing sign. "The real ones come over here and start humping the plastic one," Katz says, laughing. "The stupid shits." Near the plastic deer is Katz's whirlpool.

Soon, we're lounging poolside in the relentless sun. A cabana stocked with beer and Coke is nearby. All one hears are birds and the gentle trickle of water dripping off the pool's slide. Katz applies some lotion and begins speaking a bizarre hybrid of street lingo—he refers to black people as "nigs"—and baby talk:

"Hey, sweetie," he says into the phone, "your baby's making wee-wee. Call back in ten."

It's just a few days after Ira Einhorn's capture, and Katz has a lot to say on the subject. He thinks the CIA might have framed Einhorn and implies that he helped the hippie guru procure a passport to get out of the country. "Ira came over to see me the night before he allegedly left," says Katz. "He said, 'I have confidence being in front of a jury of my peers.' I said to him, 'Ira, you're a smelly, long-haired Jew wearing a dashiki with body odor, with sandaled feet that make you look like a member of MOVE, and you allegedly killed a blond Christian cheerleader? My sagacious counsel to you is, when you're in the can making license plates, make me HJK1.' With that, I never saw him again."

As the sun beats down, Katz switches from vodka to Heineken. At 1 o'clock, Katz has cheesesteaks delivered for lunch. Afterward, with the mercury close to 100 degrees, we move our discussion to the water. Katz dives in and gracefully swims a couple of laps, his long arms turning like paddle wheels. Winded, he takes a perch on the pool's steps.

As Katz reapplies suntan lotion, I bring up the name of Susan Delplanque (the widow of newscaster Jack Jones), who dated Katz in 1995. In fact, Delplanque had a date scheduled with Katz the night that Valerie Sheridan drowned in his hot tub. Katz broke it. The next day, Delplanque heard of Sheridan's death on the radio. Stunned, she drove to Harry's house. She was further devastated to find Harry in the company of yet another woman. Delplanque drove home, closed the garage door, and attempted suicide. Katz, thinking Delplanque was in a bad way, called her daughters, who saved her.

A few days later, Delplanque denied to the *Daily News* that Harry's actions had led to her suicide attempt, blaming it on the fourth anniversary of her husband's death. "That's B.S.," says Katz, sounding downright offended that someone else might get credit for triggering Delplanque's trauma. "I had a date with Susan planned for that evening. I blew Susan off because I preferred spending the evening with two women who were interested in all three of us."

Katz estimates that he has slept with more than 4,000 women. In particular, he remembers 24 hours in Russia.

"Three on one, four on one, I love bisexual women," he says, squinting into the setting sun. "It gives me a wonderful intermezzo, so the pressure's off for a little while. The most ever was in St. Petersburg 2 years ago. Over the course of 24 hours, I had 15 women in my suite—not bad for an old guy, right?"

HARRY JAY KATZ'S paternal grandfather was the kosher-chicken king of New York City. In the 1920s, he also owned Jewish theaters that featured Al Jolson and Eddie Cantor. Then the crash came. The theaters and poultry business were gone. Despondent about his losses, Katz committed suicide. He left a lucrative insurance policy, however, that paid his son, Lawrence, about $1 million.

Seventeen at the time, Lawrence played around a bit. He bought a schooner and sailed to Tahiti. He tried polo. After attending New York University, where he played basketball, Lawrence married Selma Green, from the Bronx. Once he finished law school at St. John's University, he entered business. On Christmas Day 1940, the second of three children, Harry Jay, was born.

In 1948, Lawrence Katz bought the Fidelity Machine Company, which developed equipment to mass produce hosiery. Back then, Jews were discriminated against in the market, and Katz initially had a difficult time. Then in 1951, he connected with an 80-year-old inventor, Walter Larkin, who thought he was close to inventing a machine that could mass-produce seamless stockings. Larkin told Katz that he thought better when he was driving, so Katz bought the man a car. Somewhere around Arizona, Larkin called and said he had figured it out. Katz told him to fly back. Soon, Fidelity Machine Company was mass-producing the revolutionary machines. For 5 years Katz sold the machinery only to Jews.

In 1955, the Katz family, now consisting of Harry, Philip, and sister Terry, moved to Melrose Park. Five years later, Lawrence sold Fidelity and began an early retirement of traveling and tending to his world-class stables. Eventually, he would purchase Camden's MacAndrews and Forbes, a mass processor of licorice, which would much later become Ron Perelman's holding company.

Despite the family wealth, Harry Jay Katz spent his youth working odd jobs. Besides one as janitor, there were stints as a pinsetter at the Jersey shore, and as a caddie. After graduating from Pennington Prep, he attended Penn State, where his image was formed. Nicknamed the Great Katzby, he tooled around State College in his Mercedes and on an Indian Chief motorcycle. He had his own house and threw lavish parties. However, the high life ended soon after he dropped out of college. After a brief stint in the Army, Katz, 23, married Julia Mae Levin in 1964. In 1965, Susan was born, followed by David the next year. As the 1960s exploded around him, Katz enjoyed married life and worked as an investment banker.

Things changed in 1967, when he found himself on his way to Chicago for a meeting with Hugh Hefner to discuss investment opportunities. He stayed at the Playboy Mansion. "Cleavage and spiked heels changed my life," Katz says today. "Boink! Back in those days, who had sex? If you got dry-humped, it was a blessing. All of a sudden, I am with all these magnificent women. That's when my marriage started to go."

FIVE OF Harry Jay Katz's favorite stories about, who else, Harry Jay Katz. Warning: He insists that they are not apocryphal, but don't bank on it.

1. Katz met Maria Shriver when she was interning at KYW back in 1977. They dated for a while and remained friendly. Independently, Harry got to know Arnold Schwarzenegger. During the early 1980s, while Arnold was making his transition from Mr. Olympia to the Terminator, Schwarzenegger stopped in Philadelphia to visit Harry's ailing father. On the drive over, a man in a Volkswagen

cut Katz off. When Katz returned the favor, the man yelled "Jew motherfucker" at Katz. At the next light, Arnold got out of the car and twisted the other guy's door off the hinges. "I cannot remember this incident," says Schwarzenegger.

"Arnold's a product of his environment," says Katz. "His father was a member of the Brownshirts, a Gestapo member. And Arnold is 50 or 51 now, so Arnold had to be peripherally involved with the Young Nazis' corps. Everyone had to. I had a little bit of difficulty with that, but we talked at length and got over it." This is obviously wrong: "My father was not in the Brownshirts," says Schwarzenegger, who has won a libel suit on this very point. "I was born in 1947, so there was no Nazi party. It was all outlawed in Austria. It is true Harry Jay Katz and my wife have been friends. We still consider him a friend. He has a great sense of humor, but we haven't seen him in a very long time."

2. In 1974, Harry Jay Katz encountered porn star Linda Lovelace trying to go legit in the years after *Deep Throat*. "Linda was in town with a show called *Pajama Tops* at the then-Locust Street Theatre," recalls Katz. "She needed a hundred G's, she owned the show, and they were out of money. She came to me at the Erlanger [a club Katz owned at the time], and I said, I'll raise you the hundred thousand. I said, I'll get you 10 guys, each of whom will give $10,000, but you gotta suck their cock, each one of them. My part of the deal is I go first, and I get the freebie. The finder's fee. Each of the guys got their blow job and gave their check. I knew Sunday they were padlocking the theater and throwing her the fuck out, and it didn't matter whether they gave $200,000. So Linda left town on Monday morning, and everybody stopped payment on their checks. And that took care of Linda." (Ms. Lovelace could not be found for comment.)

3. In 1972, Katz turned his attention to writing of a sort. *The Drummer*, an alternative weekly in the vein of the *Village Voice*, hired him to write a weekly column, the "Katz Meow," for $10 a piece. The columns, always a mixture of fact and fantasy, were due on Sunday, and Katz would rise at 4:30 a.m. that day to crank them out. He went too far in 1978, when he wrote a piece satirizing a feminist conference in Mexico City. He wrote that he and Elsa Goss, an *Inquirer* columnist, went down to the conference and sat at a table with Gloria Steinem and Bella Abzug. He suggested that Goss was fondling him under the table, that they later took a "delicious siesta" together, and visited bars featuring nude male dancers.

Goss filed a libel suit. At the April 1979 trial, she also testified that in 1975, an unknown person had marched in front of her residence with a sign reading "Harry Jay Katz Loves Fucking Elsa Goss." Katz took the stand and stated that he was an unemployed man who relied on his parents to pay his bills. He also brought in, as an expert witness, now famous *Rolling Stone* satirist P.J. O'Rourke, who testified that Katz was operating within the boundaries of satire. The jury didn't agree. Goss won a $130,000 judgment. Three months later, *The Drummer* folded. "Everyone knows I made the stuff up," says Katz. "I couldn't believe anyone took it so seriously."

4. In 1974, Katz dabbled in professional sports, buying the fledgling World Football League's Philadelphia Bell. When asked by Howard Cosell on *Wide World of Sports* why someone who didn't know how many players were on a team would buy one, Katz answered succinctly: "cheerleaders." The league publicly said that he had paid $1 million for the franchise. In fact, Katz got it for a dollar so that the WFL would have a team in the fourth-largest television market. One of the people who didn't know that Katz got the Bell for free was his buddy Jack Kelly, Grace's brother. After a few months, Kelly bought the Bell from Katz for $750,000. "Kelly wanted to buy the team," remember Katz with a smile. "I said, 'Hey, I had a really good year, and you guys can pay $750,000. I'll take the loss.' He [and his partners] ended up losing millions."

5. Katz tells me of a woman from Boston he used to date. She started spending the weekend at his pad. He bought her clothes from Saks. Later, he found out something unusual. "Turns out she's a witch," he says. "But a white witch, a good witch." Katz and the witch dated a while. One weekend, they flew down to Haiti. They piled into a car and drove into the country, where a ceremony was beginning. "A girl, maybe 14 or 15, is being led out in a white sheet," remembers Katz. "And there's all this chanting. Then a priest slits her throat, swear to God. That night I had the best sex of my life: I was like a dreadlocked Jew motherfucker savage."

KATZ RETURNED from Chicago and his time with Hugh Hefner breathing a new idea: He wanted to open a Playboy Club in Philly. Ever confident, he rented 20,000 square feet in a building across from the Bellevue-Stratford. He made the newspapers by disclosing he had shown nude photos of prospective Bunnies to his wife.

The stodgy Philadelphia fathers were not amused. Mayor James Tate and the police department loathed the idea of a Playboy Club within spitting distance of City Hall, and Katz hit another stumbling block. Playboy Clubs required their members to charge all meals and drinks to their Playboy credit cards. Unfortunately, an archaic—and widely flouted—law prevented the buying of liquor on credit in Pennsylvania. Over the next 2 years, Katz lobbied Harrisburg to change the law, eventually succeeding. By then, however, he was $200,000 in the hole and enthusiasm had faded. The club never opened.

At the same time, Katz's marriage disintegrated. Julie and Harry separated in 1970. To this day, Katz says Julie remains the love of his life. Nonetheless, the former Mrs. Katz had to file for bankruptcy in 1974, citing $71,550 in debts. In court documents, she testified that Katz verbally agreed to continue paying her credit card bills while they were separated. According to Julie, Katz stopped paying her bills in 1972, leaving her $16,550 in debt to department stores, other retailers and Continental Bank. Julie also asserted that some of the debt was from personal items Harry had charged to their joint account. Strangely, Julie's largest creditors were Selma and Lawrence Katz, Harry's parents. The couple had borrowed $55,000 from the Katzes, and Julie had signed a promissory note for the loan. "The only way I can explain it is that all transactions amongst the family were Harry's," testified Julie. "Harry's and my life still were at a point where every now and then they would have to give us money to see us through. And at that particular point, we owed about $55,000. And they gave us the money, but they made us sign a note for it." Katz says his parents never expected the money back.

Even in 1974, the judicial system was sympathetic to the plight of women who had dealings with Katz. When a creditor's lawyer objected to a delay in proceedings because Julie was away in Europe, Judge Emil Goldhaber said, "Won't you agree that anybody who was married to Harry J. Katz, and is free of that bond, has a right to go away for a while?"

Katz had taken the Playboy debacle and his divorce hard. Coming back from New York one evening in 1970, he asked John Wallace, his chauffeur and long-time friend, to pull his limo into a Howard Johnson's on the Jersey side of the Lincoln Tunnel. He got a glass of milk and took 83 sleeping pills. A few minutes later, Katz was comatose in the back seat. Wallace made the drive from Newark to Philadelphia in 40 minutes. He carried his buddy into the emergency room, where Katz lay in a coma for five days. "The Playboy thing was a debilitating failure," Katz says today. "I was drinking too much, and I was unhappy about the breakup with my wife. In those days, I also had a mistress and broke up with her because I was cheating on her. I was just a piece of shit."

Though not close to his son, Lawrence Katz had observed enough to know Harry could run through money with the best of them. This became evident in the 1970s, when Harry defaulted on his Pine Street house because of his Playboy problems. His father bought it back at the sheriff's sale. This wouldn't be the last time Lawrence Katz would apply financial tough love. In his will, Katz, who died in 1983, gave Harry's siblings, Terry and Philip, an outright gift of $100,000 each. Harry's $100,000 was put into a trust that would pay him interest quarterly.

It's not entirely clear that Harry appreciated the favor. "I worked for my father when he had the machine company," he says. "I was the janitor for two summers. Close as I got was I cleaned his bathroom. He never said, 'I love you.' Never to the day he died."

DESPITE THE ATTEMPTED SUICIDE and the Playboy failure, Katz had arrived. Building on the contacts he had made as the young impresario behind the stillborn club, Katz began cultivating friendships among Philadelphia's social upper crust. On Halloween 1972, he held a costume party at Old Fort Mifflin for 1,200 of his friends, including Arlen Specter. Harry arrived in black tie and jacket but no shirt.

Katz kept the momentum going by opening the Erlanger Theatre at 21st and Market. Featuring performances by the likes of Bette Midler, it flourished for 5 years before closing. It was there that he claims to have bamboozled Linda

Lovelace. Katz went on with second wife Andrea Diehl to start *Electricity*, a weekly paper, and the National News Bureau, a wire service for college papers. Katz's mini-media empire was most notable for employing nonwriter types like trumpet-lover Roxanne Pulitzer and congressional-wife-turned-*Playboy*-centerfold Rita Jenrette as journalists.

The News Bureau still exists, but only as a way for Katz to get free vacations. According to Judi Tafuto, an ex-girlfriend, Katz persuades unsuspecting PR people that the NNB is a viable news organization. The flacks in turn provide him free lodging and transportation in the hopes of winning positive publicity. On a recent Caribbean junket, Katz introduced Tafuto, a waitress by trade, as the bureau's lifestyles editor.

In 1987, Katz opened Hesch's, his vision of a "Jew joint," on Chancellor Street. It proved to be popular with the over-35 set for a while. Its quintessential Katz moment came that July. The restaurant was being picketed by Restaurant Employees Union Local 301. One day, Katz placed a sign on the door saying the eatery would be closed because of air-conditioning problems. The picketers went home. Later that day, Katz took the sign down and hosted a congressional delegation led by representative Tom Foglietta, a staunch union supporter. Foglietta, a longtime Katz friend, was furious. The restaurant closed 2 years later.

These days, Katz still does deals, but they are quixotic at best. His latest, a proposed book on the real story behind Jimmy Hoffa's death, appeared promising, and Katz even held a press conference on it last year. Today, Katz says the story is "too hot" to handle. He also claims that fallout from his personal life has left him "dead" in Philadelphia. But one of his best friends thinks the answer is much simpler. "I don't think the Val Sheridan thing is the reason," says Ron Pennock. "You have to question what deals do people know he's been successful at? Has he had a Bookbinder for 25 years? What has he run successfully?"

ON A JUNE NIGHT, Harry and I have a drink at Tony Clark's bar. Katz alternatively puffs on a Camel and swishes vodka around in his mouth like mouthwash. In front of us, a raven-haired barmaid ascends a ladder to pull a bottle off a top shelf. Katz gives me a nudge: "Hey, look at that ass."

He makes a request of the barmaid: "Could you climb back up there? I could watch you climb all night."

Our service deteriorates.

We jaywalk across Broad and pile into his Lincoln Town Car, owned by his brother but seemingly always in Harry's possession. It's about 10 p.m., and the Lincoln creeps down South Street. Katz is on the prowl. After we pass a pubescent girl wearing a halter top and cut-offs, Katz lets out a sigh. "Not so long ago, I had a girl at my house and we were about to make love," he remembers. "I could have sworn she told me that she was 20, but it turned out she was 17. I said, 'Could you excuse me for a minute?' I called my lawyer, and he told me I was in the clear."

We head into Jim's Steaks at 4th and South. On the wall is a picture of him from his days as a columnist for the *Drummer*. A man in Bermuda shorts sees the picture and approaches: "Hey, you're Katz from the photo."

Harry and the man start talking. Turns out he's a tourist from California here with his wife and two boys. Katz insists on giving them a tour of the city. Soon, Harry, four Californians, and I are bounding through Old City in the Lincoln.

Katz tells the Californians about the private fire departments of Colonial days. As he narrates, a burly guy walks by on the street. Harry rolls down the window: "Hey, you want to arm wrestle for big money?" The man does not reply.

We finally drop the family at Dave and Buster's. Like a magician, Katz combs through his wallet and finds game cards for the two kids. Their parents thank Katz. Everyone exchanges phone numbers.

"Next time you're in town, you guys will stay with me," promises Katz.

Next stop is Paradigm, a trendy bar on Chestnut Street primarily known for having bathroom doors that fog up. Katz knows a waitress here, but she's not too happy to see Harry. She hangs out at the other end of the bar, ignoring him.

Katz, meanwhile, starts hitting on Pam the bartender. A drop-dead-gorgeous brunette, she's having no part of the shtick. "Man, you're the worst fucking bartender in America," coos Katz. Pam smiles sarcastically. So Katz resorts to one of his primary ploys, a war of attrition. He peppers Pam with a nonstop barrage of bad jokes, puppy-dog eyes and outright begging. The sheer persistence eventually wears down Pam to a point where fury is replaced by bemusement. "Won't you give me your number?" pleads Katz. "I bet you live in Rittenhouse Square. Can I try and guess it?" Pam says no, but does take Katz's card. Harry beams a smile of triumph. (The next day, Harry calls Paradigm, impersonates me and asks for Pam's phone number for a story on bartenders. He gets the number.)

Eventually, the waitress comes over. It quickly gets ugly. "I was reading in the paper about Ira Einhorn, Harry," she says. "You used the same pick-up lines he used: 'When you sleep with me, and you will, it will be the best night of your life.' You are the biggest liar I've ever met."

Harry replies loudly: "That's not what you were saying when I was fucking you up the ass."

She stares at him, her eyes brimming with contempt. She starts taking off jewelry. "Here's your watch back. When are you going to pay me the $1200 you owe me?"

While they were dating, it seems Katz charged car repairs on her credit card. He's paying the minimum each month. Katz repeats his mantra: "That's not what you were saying when I was fucking you up the ass."

Eventually, she leaves, and Katz sighs in relief. "I'm glad I got the watch back," he says. "It belonged to Valerie Sheridan."

ON FRIDAY, March 3, 1995, Katz, Valerie Sheridan, and a second woman had a few drinks at Katz's place, and then went to Manayunk for appetizers. After some barhopping, the trio returned to Katz's house. Sheridan eventually headed outside in a robe. A half-hour later, Katz and his companion discovered Sheridan in the whirlpool. By the time paramedics arrived, rigor mortis had begun. The next day, Susan Delplanque attempted suicide.

Katz's reaction to the tragedy received as much attention as the actual accident. News of the Sheridan drowning didn't become public for a number of days. When Katz confided his predicament to Stu Bykofsky, the *Daily News* columnist urged Katz to lie low and hope nobody would notice. But word got out. Katz described Sheridan to the media this way: "We were soulmates. She had the same bullshit, and she could work a room beautifully.... She loved the hot tub. She was a woman of the water ..." He summed up the Sheridan/Delplanque affair this way: "What a fucking weekend!"

Two weeks later, toxicology reports on Sheridan came back positive for drugs. Katz told the *Inquirer* she had a cocaine problem. He was cleared of wrongdoing, but the fallout continued. "Certain alleged friends dumped me like a hot potato," says Katz. "People like Steven Korman from the Korman Corporation. He was my best friend and usher at my first wedding. Then there's Stephen Klein [of the Klein Company] who I went to Penn State with."

There was also a prominent split with District Attorney Lynne Abraham. The Katz family had been a patron of Abraham's political career from the beginning, holding a number of fund-raisers for her. The morning after Sheridan's death, Katz called Abraham for advice. Her husband, Frank Ford, answered the phone. Though Abraham and Katz never spoke, the D.A. personally observed Sheridan's autopsy.

These days, Abraham no longer returns Katz's phone calls, but they both attend Hanukkah and Passover dinners at the home of Katz's mother, Selma. "I say hi," says Katz. "At Hanukkah, Lynne was at my mother's house, and I had gotten a photographer to take pictures. Lynne was standing by the bar, so I put my arm around her and said, 'Why not take a picture of me and Lynne?', which we had always done. The photographer developed the proofs, [but] I was missing the two shots of Lynne and myself. He was told by Lynne not to develop them. [Abraham declined comment.] Finally, he brings the proofs over. I blow them up to 5 by 7, and send one to Lynne at work and one to her house with a note saying 'I know you would want this for your wall.' She didn't mention it next time I saw her. Fuck her."

VALERIE SHERIDAN'S death and Susan Delplanque's suicide attempt were neither the first nor the last controversies involving Harry Jay Katz and his revolving harem. Katz has recently faced three more crises involving former lovers. In July 1995, just four months after Sheridan's death, Katz fathered a child with a woman named Susan Arnold. After taking blood tests that confirmed his paternity, Katz was brought into Philadelphia Family Court on April 9th to determine child support. Judi Tafuto, his girlfriend at the time, went along.

"Harry didn't bring a lawyer," says Tafuto. "He was rehearsing lines on the way down. He gives me a sheet of paper, which is totally bullshit, about how she [Arnold] used to be a drug dealer. There was this little boy, an absolutely beautiful child who looked just like him. Harry started screaming 'Get that fucking kid out of here! I don't want to see that kid!' He started swearing at her lawyer, 'Fuck you, we went to school together! Fuck you, you piece of shit!'"

When asked about the child now, Katz immediately begins to impugn the child's mother, alleging multiple examples of illegal behavior. "I went to her lawyer, David Grunfeld," says Katz. "David's a Jew, he knows me, and I said, 'David, I have written out all these things about her, the DUIs, being a Jew hater and a drug dealer.' He says, 'Harry, this is Pennsylvania [a tough state for fathers]. Keep your fly zipped up.'" Harry sighs. "I think it is really unfair there are no rights for the father."

Katz, who insists that Arnold had agreed from the beginning that she would raise the child on her own, was ordered to pay $350 a month, along with $50 a month in arrears until the child turns 18. His problem with Arnold, however, pales compared to his wrangling with former fiancée Susan Croge. Katz and Croge became engaged in December 1994—approximately two months after he impregnated Arnold. Their impending nuptials were announced to the public by Bykofsky. But within a few months, the relationship was over.

The gory details became public in 1996. Katz, citing more than $500,000 in debt, filed for personal bankruptcy in November 1995. Remarkably, he claimed assets of $150 in cash, roughly the cost of one Katz night out, and $100 in used clothing. In retrospect, he probably didn't help himself by using Lawrence Mazer, a disbarred lawyer who is now deceased, to prepare his bankruptcy application.

At the time, Katz told Bykofsky and the *Daily News*, "These are all business and corporate debts, no individuals have been screwed." That wasn't exactly the case. Among his creditors were ex-fiancée Susan Croge and Lucinda Roney, who was once operations manager of Katz's restaurant.

According to court documents, Roney came to work at Hesch's in March 1987. Soon, they began a sexual relationship. That July, Roney ended their relationship after finding out Katz was sleeping with another employee. Katz, she alleges, continued to proposition her and humiliate her in front of other workers. In August, she was fired. Almost immediately, she filed suit. In December 1994, Judge Russell Nigro entered a judgment against Katz for $65,000 after Katz repeatedly missed legal deadlines to respond to Roney's complaint.

Croge is part of the Katz bankruptcy because she's suing him for $50,000 in defamation and damages, a claim that is still pending. She also filed suit to have his bankruptcy request denied so that her claim would not be swept away. That led to the public release of details of their breakup. According to court papers filed by Croge, she claims that in January 1995, "The defendant [Katz], after abusing cocaine and alcohol, grabbed the plaintiff by her hair, squeezed her throat and threatened to 'blow [her] head off and kill' her with one of his many guns." Croge moved out the next day. The brief goes on to claim that Katz began harassing Croge, her friends and relatives, threatening dire consequences if she pursued legal action. Both Katz and Croge sought restraining orders against one another. Katz denies the charges. Bykofsky—riding to the rescue once again—pointed out in his column that his buddy owned nothing more powerful than the BB guns in his kitchen.

After weeks of haggling, it was agreed that Croge, with a police escort, would pick up her belongings on March 24, 1995, just three weeks after Valerie Sheridan's death. Katz put them on his porch, attaching a ribald addendum to each box: nude photos he had taken of Croge.

Katz warns me against placing faith in the testimony of "scorned women." As much as Katz talks of scorned women, however, it is Harry who turns shrewish when an infatuation goes sour, throwing bombs and insinuating criminal behavior. For Croge, he gives me two typed pages of her alleged shortcomings. This isn't an isolated incident. What follows are examples of what he has to say about various former flames:

"She's a junkie … She's a drug dealer who supplied the Grateful Dead … She was all coked up and had her brain banged out by a bunch of guys and this was on her honeymoon … She asked me to have her ex-husband killed… We picked up a heroin junkie at Circa and she took her home and made love to her in the car… She forced me to have sex with her fat cousin…"

Of course, even if some of these accusations happen to be true, they mostly demonstrate that Katz appeals to an unusual strain of women. Katz himself blames his lady problems on his inability to perform due diligence. "I hate to use the term fatal attraction," he says, "but I see someone or see a piece of art that makes my heart sing, I know if you get too close, it's not the same. Goose pimples are important to me—not so much an erection, but goose pimples. I want my heart to sing, be it for an hour, a weekend or a meaningful relationship that ends in the morning."

In court, Croge alleged that Katz had fraudulently obtained credit cards in her name. Among the evidence submitted was a credit report listing American Express and other credit cards requested to be sent to Katz's address a full four months after she had moved out. Furthermore, Croge presented copies of two credit-card applications from June and July 1995 listing Harry Jay Katz's address. (This wasn't the first time Katz was accused of credit card fraud by a loved one. In his 1994 divorce proceedings from Andrea Diehl, it was alleged that Katz forged Diehl's signature to credit cards and accrued an estimated $125,000 in debt—all of which was found to be Katz's responsibility. Katz, who served five days in jail for missing a child-support deadline, insists they were joint credit cards and denies any forgery or fraud. A delicious irony: Diehl now lives in Vermont and runs a counseling practice with Katz's first wife, Julia.)

When asked about the Croge credit-card applications under oath, Katz took the Fifth. But because Croge was contesting his bankruptcy claim, Katz's finances were thrown open. Among the interesting things found was that in the seven months after Katz's claim of bankruptcy, $61,000 was deposited to a corporate account that he had access to. That account was not listed on his bankruptcy report. In his testimony, Katz claimed it was not his account, but that of his children. When pressed, Katz admitted that he was the sole signatory on the account, that family members deposited money into it, and that he paid his bills from it. In fact, court documents show that from 1988 to 1997, Katz deposited nearly $1 million into the account, including $182,000 since his 1995 bankruptcy claim.

Although it is hard to pinpoint where exactly Katz gets his money, it seems Harry's mother serves as his maternal MAC machine. During his bankruptcy trial and in pretrial depositions, big-spender Katz painted himself as a penniless 56-year-old depending on the kindness of his elderly mommy. When asked by Croge's lawyer how it worked, Katz described their phone calls: "Hi, Mom. It's Harry. I've got a bunch of stuff here that needs to be taken care of. Is it possible to take care of it, please?"

Croge testified Katz made lavish claims to her: that he had $3 million to $4 million in the bank and that his family owned 10 percent of the land in New Hope. (Katz's brother, Philip, lives on a sprawling family estate there.) She also alleged that Katz's home held a signed Picasso, antique furniture and cases of wine. In his defense, Katz maintained that his house and all of his furniture were owned by other members of his family. This doesn't square with a notarized letter sent by Katz to Chestnut Hill Bank in January 1986. Hoping to obtain a loan to open Hesch's, Katz claimed a net worth of $1 million. In a subsequent letter to that bank, Katz upped his net worth to $3 million to $5 million. He listed the East Falls home as his own, with a value of $550,000. Katz also maintained he held a one-third interest in the family's New Hope property. Katz now says he inadvertently included his home in the letter.

Federal Bankruptcy Judge David Scholl didn't agree with Katz's poverty plea. He dismissed his bankruptcy claim, stating that Katz "systematically, consistently, unrepentantly, and therefore knowingly, failed to schedule assets or list creditors for the express purpose of avoiding further investigation of his affairs, which constitutes fraud." He also chastised Katz for attempting to introduce alleged sordid details of Croge's past into court. Christine Shubert, the bankruptcy trustee of Katz's claim, appointed lawyer Edmund John to investigate whether any other assets are available to satisfy Katz's creditors. So far, Katz's home has been searched for valuables and his mother has been asked to give a deposition. According to court documents filed on September 9th, John alleges that Katz currently holds a 12.5 percent interest in the family's New Hope property valued at $15 million in 1990, making Katz's share $1.875 million.

When asked about Judge Scholl's proceedings, Katz is succinct. "This little fucking guy," says Katz. "This Howdy-Doody-looking guy, this Jew-hating motherfucker—I knew from the get-go I was fucked."

SOMEHOW, DESPITE all of his well-documented troubles with women, Harry Jay Katz never seems to lack for a date. His house is filled with friends, new and old. To most of them, he is just an old softy who calls his mother every day and is a victim of his insatiable need for attention. "I have called Harry my bad-weather friend," says Ron Pennock, who has known Katz since 1970. "I could depend on Harry being by my side more than any person I know. He's always at a funeral consoling a family."

The bad-boy image, whether sought or not, has obscured Katz's generosity. The grease monkeys from his favorite gas station often come over and use the pool. During his Hesch's days, he comped many a meal. One day, while I'm at Katz's house, a man nicknamed Chap calls to see if Katz has any yardwork for him. While Katz goes to freshen his vodka, Chap tells me how Katz employed him at Hesch's and paid for his drug rehab.

To his son, David, Dad's life is performance art. "He's an entertainer on a social level," says David. "He has his shtick, the way he interacts with people. You always hear these ridiculous Harry Jay Katz stories, but people want to spend time with him."

Frank Stallone, a dear friend of Harry's, thinks Katz is a victim of changing times. "When Harry was coming up, Philadelphia was a more exciting and thriving town," says Stallone. "He's kept the same exuberance, but his friends have settled down, and the city has become a lot less interesting than it was in the Rizzo days."

Stallone is right that Philadelphia isn't the towel-snapping place it once was. But the country's attitude toward women has evolved. Almost everyone has adapted. Except Harry. To him, there's a simple explanation for why women continue to find him attractive: old-fashioned chivalry. "The best ticket is to be honest and be a gentleman," advises Katz. "I stand when a lady's in the room. I open car doors. I light cigarettes. I don't let them buy me a drink. I think looking them in the eye and not lying to them really works."

"He comes off very charming," says Paulette Fallon, a 1995 *Penthouse* centerfold who was pursued by Katz. "You open up to him, he gets you to a certain point, and he finds a very vulnerable spot where you're needy, gets a finger in there. Soon, he has his whole self in there. He uses you, and then you owe him."

Like Croge, Fallon claims cocaine abuse is at the root of Katz's problems. She says he has a black shaving kit in which he keeps his stash. Another ex-girlfriend claims to have witnessed Katz doing a line at 10:30 in the morning. Katz swears he's only done cocaine once in the past year. "It would kill me," he says. "I have a bad heart, I've been treated for hypertension. Vodka is my drug of choice." Later, he clarifies a bit. "People have done cocaine in my house. People have had cocaine delivered here, but I don't do it."

Katz doesn't seem surprised by his ex-girlfriends' venom. "When I stop dating someone, I stop dating someone," says Katz. "When I'm done, I'm done. I don't think it is possible [to be friends]. You show me a heterosexual male who's friendly with an attractive heterosexual female."

He pauses and arches his eyebrows.

"Or a bisexual female."

IT'S THE FOURTH OF JULY at Harry Jay Katz's house. On the refrigerator, spelled with kiddy magnetic letters, are the words WELCOME CHRISTINA. Christina is a new guest *chez* Katz. A 19-year-old with dark eyes and baby fat, Christina had been working as a nanny for the family of former Rendell chief of staff David Cohen. Then fate intervened. A couple of weeks earlier, according to Katz, he rescued her from some "greaseballs" at a bar in Manayunk. The two became friendly. Eventually, Katz, impersonating a friend of Christina's family, called Cohen's wife to tell her that Christina was quitting because she was homesick. After a trip to her hometown of Geneva, New York, to pick up her poodle, Christina has returned.

The poodle is already causing trouble. This morning, Harry stepped in a pile of dog excrement in the hall. Later, the poodle will drop another pile. "If that dog shits one more time, you both go," says Katz.

The day is spent by the pool. Visitors include Harry's brother. A mountainous man, perhaps 6'10" tall, 300 pounds, Phil keeps an eye on Harry and begs him to show some discretion. When Christina repeatedly tosses her poodle into the pool, Harry quips: "You better stop, or we're going to have another Val Sheridan on our hands." Phil's eyes bulge.

"What? What did I say?" asks Katz.

Also present is John Wallace, Harry's friend who took him to the emergency room after his suicide attempt. Another bear of a man, Wallace stands 6'9" and weighs in at 250 pounds. Best friends for 30 years, they tell war stories ranging from attending a civil-rights rally to Wallace's recent stay in the New Jersey penal system for running what Katz calls the "biggest chop-shop in the Northeast." Over the course of the afternoon, Katz repeatedly calls Wallace, who is black, "Big Nig."

The gang heads over to Mel's International in Bala Cynwyd for dinner. Dressed in black, hair slicked back, his sunburned nose red as a maraschino cherry, Katz orders for Christina. He scolds her for putting her elbows on the table. Everyone is in good spirits, and the liquor flows freely. But in a moment, the goodwill disappears. Wallace mentions a mobster friend that he and Katz have had some dealings within the past, and Katz lashes out at his old pal. "You stupid nig motherfucker," blares Katz, brandishing his cigarette wildly. His face flushes blood red. "After all I've done for you, you stupid motherfucker."

Restaurant patrons hold their forks and stare. Christina eyes her feet and looks very small. Wallace, who seems to have endured this treatment before, stares at his buddy coolly. After imploring from the waiter, Wallace and Katz move to the bar where Katz, sweat beading up on his forehead, repeatedly pokes Wallace in the chest with his finger. Eventually, Wallace leaves.

The rest of the dinner party drifts away. Harry, Christina, and I head off to Manayunk's bars. The Lincoln trawls down Main Street at five mph so Katz can get a good look into the bars we're passing. Much to Katz's chagrin, Christina pops the radio on a rock station. Nirvana merges into David Bowie's "Modern Love."

Katz valet-parks the car. He spies a shapely woman through a bar's windows. We go in so Katz can get a look at her face. Like an art dealer, he finds a suitable vantage point to appraise the object of his desire. No sale. Disappointed, he turns on his heels and leaves.

Back at home, Christina heads off to bed. Katz pours some vodka, and we sit on his porch. He wants to make sure I have one thing clear. "I'd give this all up to have the right woman," he insists, his eyes glassy and blood-shot. "Just to come home and hear someone say, 'Hi honey,' and to smell soup cooking in the kitchen."

We sit in silence. The rumble of faraway fireworks sounds like the advancing of troops. Then, the doorbell rings. In a minute, Katz returns with a thirtyish blonde we'll call Stacy. "Fucking Stacy from Pittsburgh. She's driven all this way to see Harry," says Katz.

When she goes off to the bathroom, Katz confides that he's been sleeping with Stacy on and off since she was a teenager. After she returns, I head down to the whirlpool that claimed Valerie Sheridan so the two lovebirds can be alone. Despite the water's heat, I shiver. After a few minutes, I head back up and say goodnight. Inside, Christina grabs my arm. "Harry hired a hooker, didn't he?"

I tell Christina that, as far as I know, Stacy is not a prostitute. Christina nods, her lip quivering, and heads back into her room.

From my bedroom window, I can see Harry trying to pull the cover over the whirlpool. He pulls, almost falls in, and pulls again. After a minute, he gives the cover a tug, and it falls into place. Katz lets out a childish laugh, slapping his hands, congratulating himself on a job well done.

In the next room, Christina cries herself to sleep.

By Buzz Bissinger
November 1998

RICHARD SPRAGUE KNOWS EVERYTHING

 am riding into the maw of Norristown, and I am feeling the palpitations of intimidation.

Part of that may have to do with the drive itself. The deeper you go into downtown Norristown, the more you begin to consider the hidden quaintness of Camden. But much of it has to do with the object of my journalistic desire—the ultimate keeper of the secrets.

I have never met him, but his reputation is that of a tidal wave composed of nails and rusty razors, and as I edge closer to where he is, the Montgomery County courthouse, I can just imagine the sheer force of him crashing into me—relentless, reducing me to babbles and humiliating half-sentences and apologies for being that lowest form of vermin.

A reporter.

I want to spend time with him and interview him, to shake loose not just his secrets but, more intriguing, the secret of him. For all that has been written about him over the past 30 years, nothing has really been written about him at all. I know from a book he was born in Baltimore. I know he served on a submarine in World War II. I know he went to Temple and then Penn Law School, where his academic performance was mediocre. I know he had two marriages that ended in divorce. (So did I; maybe that can be our common ground.) I know he has two children to whom, by all accounts, he is devoted. I know he lives in a baronial home in Haverford that undulates over several acres of perfect green sea. I know he has dinner parties to which the best and the brightest and the most powerfully connected of the city are invited, and I know that when children of guests come along, he goes out and rents videos for them to watch in his splendid theater room so they won't be bored. I know he plays tennis with Jim Beasley, one of the city's most tenacious plaintiff's lawyers, and I can only imagine the suits that have been threatened over a foot fault.

But these are all just little here-and-there strands, and I have no real expectation of tying them together into any greater whole. Instead, I just hope to escape with all my limbs intact.

Even his name, Dick Sprague, sends chills through me—no waste, no pleasing vowels off the tongue.

Sprague.

As in plague.

Not vague.

I know about others who took him on and somehow thought they could outlast him or outsmart him or outdo him—murder defendants, congressmen, clever lawyers bulging at the seams with their own courtroom testosterone, bosses, reporters determined to expose him. And I know what happened to all of them—how they were reduced to absolute dust. For this story, for everybody who was willing to talk, at least half a dozen people did not want to be quoted by name or wouldn't even come to the phone.

He is 73 now, and there are some who say he has mellowed a little bit, enjoys life in a way he never did when he was younger. There are some who wonder if he has slipped a notch from the ranks of the great ones because of age, because his hunger, his "overriding tenacity," as one lawyer described it, has lost its voraciousness. But in my mind, at least, the aura of him has not lessened at all. I still see him as the most powerful man in the city, not simply a remarkable lawyer to the rich and powerful but the consummate collector of confidences, the man who knows everything, because everyone, at one time or another, has come to him for advice. Who among the city's elite, whether out of respect or legal acumen or maybe sheer fear, hasn't been influenced by him in some way?

Perhaps there is more illusion than fact in that reputation, but that still doesn't diminish him. "I think that's one of the lures he has, that he has millions of secrets," says Arthur Makadon, a lawyer who has been a confidant of the politically powerful in his own right and worked under Sprague in the district attorney's office in the early 1970s. "I don't think he has any more than I have, but it doesn't matter. Dick sits there, and [people] give him credit for knowing all this. He must laugh his ass off."

Makadon may be right. But there is one thing I can never visualize, no matter how hard I harness my creative powers.

Dick Sprague laughing his ass off.

———

I PARK the car on some squalid Norristown side street where a man hobbles down the sidewalk on a cane, mumbling to himself. I head toward the steps of the courthouse, but then I turn into a convenience store and buy a pack of cigarettes, the ultimate sign of disintegration and cowardly delay.

There is so much I want to ask him about, even if I know my questions will go unanswered. I want to ask him about the time, relatively early in his career as a homicide prosecutor, that he obtained a first-degree murder conviction against a husband for the killing of his wife, even though certain physical evidence, such as the victim's body, was never found. I want to ask him about his prosecution for murder of a 14-year-old boy whose own father had gone to the electric chair. I want to ask him about his role as special prosecutor in the execution-style killings of United Mine Workers Union reform leader Jock Yablonski and his wife and daughter in a tiny town in southwestern Pennsylvania in 1969.

I want to ask him why he ended his career in the district attorney's office in 1974, after 17 years, the way he did—not by going quietly, but by being fired after publicly accusing his boss, Emmett Fitzpatrick, of lying. I want to ask him about his wild ride as chief counsel to the House Select Committee on Assassinations, where in six months he appeared to alienate more politicians than Bill Clinton.

I want to ask him about his relationship with Frank Rizzo when Rizzo was mayor and with Arlen Specter when Specter was district attorney and with Ed Rendell when Rendell was an up-and-coming assistant district attorney. I want to know what it has been like to represent a spectrum of clients that includes John du Pont, State Senator Vince Fumo, deposed union king Earl Stout, Pennsylvania Supreme Court Justice Rolf Larsen, Larry King's former wife Julie (two Sprague investigators served the talk-show host with divorce papers on the Metroliner), one of the police officers accused of beating Delbert Orr Africa during the 1978 shoot-out with MOVE, and former City Council president George X. Schwartz after he was accused of taking a bribe during the FBI's Abscam probe.

I smoke my cigarette, and I think of his face.

I have seen it only in a photograph. It appeared in the newspaper roughly a decade ago, and I have always remembered it, or at least I believe I have, given the way in which memory is little more than a psychological tool. Actually, it isn't the face I remember as much as the expression—rigidly humorless, devoid of a single touch of softness, utterly miserable-looking, to be honest.

I think about turning around and just going home.

But I also know he has a middle name: Aurel. There is something pretty about that name. It rolls around the tongue in a kindly and melodious way, without bark or bite.

It suggests something to me altogether different, dimensions and hues to this man that go far beneath the surface of instantaneous impression.

Those who have encountered him over the years confirm that. They describe a man of myriad complexity in whom all the pieces, much to the journalist's regret, don't combine into one sweet little package with a bow on top. One calls him "bleak." Another calls him "charming." One, when asked about his personality, says, "He doesn't have one." One, when asked about his personality, calls him a Renaissance man capable of discussing any subject with wit and grace. One notes his love in his early years, when he was with the district attorney's office, of putting defendants on death row. Several note his love, in his later years, of music and opera, his subscription to the Metropolitan Opera and trips at Christmas to Vienna.

He is a man who spent so much of his life in the grit of the D.A.'s office, obtaining murder convictions with machine-like precision. (Legend has it he tried 66 homicide cases and obtained first-degree verdicts in 65 of them.) Given that, it seems somehow likely that he came from a lowbrow background—father a meatpacker, mother a housewife with forearms the size of bowling pins, a child whose idea of fun was to go into the backyard and pour boiling water on ants. And yet his mother and father were a psychologist and a psychiatrist, respectively. His mother, Marian Barsel Sprague, born in Palestine and the daughter of a rabbi, became renowned for her work with children. His father, George S. Sprague, a Quaker who never used profanity, was an internationally known adult psychoanalyst. The talk around the dinner table at home was not of murder and mayhem but of politics and world affairs.

"You look at his background," says Makadon. "He's the son of two psychiatrists, yet on any level you're dealing with him, he's not involved with psychiatric babble. He has none of the affectations of that. He can synthesize very complicated subjects and make them come out very simply. He has all kinds of relationships with all kinds of different people…. The juxtaposition of all these things is just very weird to me."

If there is any kind of universal agreement about Dick Sprague, it has to do with the fire that burns inside him. He is a man, unlike most men, utterly and completely convinced of the correctness of whatever he does regardless of what others think, refusing to even momentarily yield to the self-doubt that privately eats away and tortures the average soul. While others sweat at night in clammy sheets over the choices they have made, Dick Sprague has sweet dreams. "I don't sleep during the week before a case," says a lawyer who has known Sprague for more than 30 years. "Dick once told me, his head hits the pillow, he's asleep. I don't think anything bothers him because he has this enormous ego strength. I've never met anyone with more enormous ego strength than Dick. There is no doubt. There is no anxiety, no hint of anxiety. He thinks everyone he has punished deserves it. He doesn't have a bad conscience about anything he's ever done…. There is an enormous force that he obeys that is very spiritual in a sense, and I don't know what it is."

Or as former U.S. Attorney Michael Baylson says of Dick Sprague, "He is a complete advocate. That's really what guides him. In a way he's very complex, and in a way he's very simple."

Baylson also tells an instructive story about him. It has to do with the Metropolitan Opera in New York, where Sprague has a center box. Sprague has also been a substantial donor to the Met, in the $10,000-a-year category, according to

Baylson. His name was right there in the program. Then, says Baylson, an usher who had gotten to know Sprague told him that he was being unfairly treated by the opera management. The issue might have had to with scheduling. Baylson isn't quite sure, but he is certain of how Sprague reacted to the usher's plight. Sprague said he'd keep the center box seats but would take away the donation.

NOT EVERYONE agrees with his advocacy all the time. In the early 1970s, Sprague personally handled the prosecution of then-*Philadelphia Bulletin* reporter Greg Walter for violating the state's wiretapping laws by taping phone interviews without getting the consent of the other parties. Makadon was in the district attorney's office then, and he felt what Walter had done was "such a minor offense" that it wasn't worth pursuing. But according to Makadon, Sprague "strongly disagreed." There apparently was something about what Walter had done that got caught in Sprague's warp, and he had the ultimate last word anyway. In 1973, as a reporter for the *Inquirer*, Walter coauthored a story that questioned whether Sprague had quashed a murder investigation as a favor for a friend, former state police commissioner Rocco P. Urella, Sr.

Sprague responded almost immediately with a libel suit, claiming the story was motivated by a vendetta against him by Walter because of the wiretapping case. In 1990, a jury awarded Sprague $34 million, then the largest-ever libel verdict involving the news media, after finding that the paper had acted with actual malice. The award was reduced to $24 million. And then, in 1996, 23 years to the day after the story had been published, the *Inquirer*, despite repeated claims that the story had been merited, settled the case for an undisclosed sum.

Sprague's tenure as the chief counsel to the House Select Committee on Assassinations can also be construed as an example of utter faith in himself regardless of decorum or the slightest whiff of political sensitivity. His refusal to play along with the politicians he was working for might have satisfied the righteous side of him, but it also created self-defeating havoc. Because he alienated so many so quickly, nothing got done.

He was named to the post in October 1976, ostensibly to head up a new congressional examination of the killings of President Kennedy and Dr. Martin Luther King Jr. According to various accounts, he was determined to examine the assassinations in the same manner he had handled his homicide investigations—exhaustively, with nothing left to speculation.

It was an approach that clearly did not sit well with various members of Congress, who were ambivalent about reopening the investigations anyway. They only became more skittish when Sprague asked for a budget of $13 million for a 2-year investigation.

There was further concern, according to the *New York Times*, when it was discovered that the select committee planned to secretly record the remarks of potential witnesses with hidden body transmitters and then submit the responses to psychological stress evaluation. (Perhaps Sprague was thinking of hiring

Greg Walter as a consultant.) Such a tactic, the chairman of the House Judiciary Subcommittee on Civil and Constitutional Rights said, would be "wrong, immoral, and very likely illegal."

In February 1977, the head of the House Select Committee, Henry B. Gonzalez of Texas, tried to have Sprague dismissed. When that didn't work, Gonzalez himself resigned, calling Sprague "an unconscionable scoundrel" who had run up "unjustifiable salaries, unjustified employees and reckless, inexplicable financial obligations."

Sprague himself held on for another month before resigning at the end of March 1977, when as many 40 members of the House indicated that they would not vote to continue the existence of the committee as long as Sprague was there. Those on the committee said they accepted Sprague's resignation "with regret" and further asserted that there had been absolutely no basis to the allegations raised by Gonzalez.

Roughly two weeks later, Sprague himself held a final press conference. Refusing to yield an inch, he criticized certain members of Congress for their "political expediency" and "push to titillate the public." It seemed a Spraguian pronouncement to the core, a final middle finger to the politicians who had dared to question the style in which he operated.

But more than two decades later, Sprague could claim a certain measure of vindication. In his press conference, he urged that both the Kennedy and King assassinations be fully pursued. What he said that day about the Kennedy killing in terms of new leads was hardly revelatory. But based on an interview with James Earl Ray, Sprague said he believed that Ray had not acted alone in the King assassination.

Last year, the family of the slain civil rights leader made headlines when they urged the reopening of the investigation into his killing. The source of their conviction that the case had never been properly resolved?

James Earl Ray.

"In his own way, Dick has contempt for all the right people," says Makadon. "I admire him for that." Makadon remembers an incident back when they were both working for the district attorney. He was with Sprague in his office, and they had to speak to then-D.A. Arlen Specter. So Sprague called Specter's secretary and was told the district attorney was at a meeting with U.S. Senator Hugh Scott over at the federal office building. Sprague immediately telephoned Scott's office and told a secretary that he needed to speak to Specter. She explained that Specter was busy at the moment talking with Senator Scott, to which Sprague responded: "I want to talk to the district attorney right now. Please interrupt him."

As Makadon recalls the story some 25 years later, the force and intent of what Dick Sprague was trying to do is still abundantly clear, as is the message he wanted to get across:

"Who the fuck is Senator Scott?"

I MARCH UP the courthouse steps. I peer into Courtroom H, where Dick Sprague is defending eight Pennsylvania counties in a tax appeal involving Walter Annenberg, in which hundreds of millions of dollars in state tax collection money are on the line because of the possible precedent that could be set.

The courtroom is empty, which gives me a sense of relief and reprieve. But then I walk outside, and there he is, right beyond the doors, talking with someone. He is smaller than I thought he would be—a physical reality in which I find great comfort. The face, which I expected to be even harder with age, actually seems softened, and I find myself transfixed by his hair, a coif of gray that falls in a creative flourish to his collar. It gives him an interesting touch of character and idiosyncrasy that I find totally unexpected.

I take a deep breath....

And like a scared schoolgirl, I walk back down the steps.

I begin to rehearse what I am going to say. Should I be acquiescent and deferential? Should I set aside my intimidation and forge right in? As far as I know, journalists still have a right to ask questions.

Attorney George Parry stood up to Sprague once, in a different context. Parry was with the district attorney's office and was prosecuting the three Philadelphia police officers who had been accused of beating Delbert Orr Africa during the 1978 shoot-out between police and members of MOVE. Sprague was a defense attorney in the case, and the relationship between him and Parry was not one of mutual love.

It was Parry's sense that Sprague was trying to bully him as a kind of trial tactic, attempting to gain an extra edge. During a break, Parry went into the robing room of the judge hearing the case to get a drink from the watercooler. Sprague followed. He told Parry not to go in there again. He wondered if Parry might try to have an ex parte conversation with the judge about the case in Sprague's absence.

Parry defied Sprague. He drank from the watercooler in the judge's robing room again. Sprague followed him once more and said, "I thought I told you not to come back here." Parry walked toward Sprague with his fist clenched and said to him, "You don't tell me what to do. You got that?"

"If you don't stand up to him, he'll keep rolling over you," says Parry, and after that moment, there was no more dirty dancing around the watercooler, and there were no more tests of Parry's legal manhood. "He tried his case, and I tried mine," says Parry.

And even if Parry did not find the experience of trying a case against Dick Sprague particularly pleasant, he did find it instructive—the hypnotic way Sprague mesmerized the jury by convincing them, without histrionics, that what he was telling them was the most important thing in the world, the way he seized control of the courtroom as a matter of territorial right, the way in which he challenged the smallest detail.

"I learned a lot from him in that case," says Parry. "The good parts, I've tried to adopt as a lawyer."

MAYBE THAT'S what I should do: approach Dick Sprague with fists balled and clenched, float like a butterfly and sting like a bee, threaten to pummel him unless he talks to me.

But then I think of his role as special prosecutor in the killings of Jock Yablonski, his wife, Margaret, and their daughter Charlotte in the stone house in Clarksville. I think of the way he turned one accomplice against another without promising deals, without promising anything, as if nothing—not even the possibility of the electric chair—was more cruel and tormenting than not giving Dick Sprague what he wanted. "In a funny way, he seduced them," says the lawyer who has known him for more than 30 years—as if, in an odd and eerie way, they had "some feeling of comfort that they were confessing to God."

That attorney recalls, "He didn't give them an inch. He established almost a parent-child relationship [with them], and then they opened up and told him. In a funny way, he absolved them and then killed them."

I think of the way he tried the case, peeling it back like an "onion," as Jock Yablonski's son Kenneth, a lawyer, puts it today. Bit by bit, with each exposed layer, he moved closer and closer to the president of the United Mine Workers, Tony Boyle.

I think of how relentlessly methodical Sprague was—going after the three killers who crept into the house that December night while the Yablonkis were asleep in their beds, then moving his way up into the corrupt union to those at the very top who had ordered the assassinations. I think of the names of the men who were drawn into the vortex of Sprague's fire, names as simple and dark as the mines from which those men were drawn—Prater, Pass, Huddleston, Boyle.

I think of how Dick Sprague was spit at during one of the trials, a stream of saliva hitting his face, and how he calmly took a handkerchief from his pocket and wiped it away. I think of how a witness in one of the cases, sitting in a federal holding tank in Maryland, turned to a fellow witness in protective custody and said that Dick Sprague was the toughest son of a bitch he had ever run across. I think of how, when the first-degree murder conviction of Boyle was reversed on procedural grounds, Sprague simply went out and convicted Boyle of first-degree murder all over again.

I think of the stone house in which the Yablonskis died, and I imagine Dick Sprague going through it for the first time, soaking up every clue, retracing the choreography of the killers so he knew their movements even better than they did. I imagine him, without expression, crouching down in Charlotte's room to examine the stain of blood on the carpet. I imagine him going into the adjoining room, crouching down to see the graze of a bullet hole in the floor near the bed where Jock and Margaret slept until the peace of that farmhouse night was shattered by the sound of two shots into the skull of their daughter.

"The smell in this house. You could never get rid of the smell, no matter what we did," says James Luzier, who has lived there for roughly 25 years. "My dad scrubbed it. But for 3 or 4 years, you could never get rid of the dead smell."

I wonder how much Dick Sprague even noticed the smell. Not because of callousness or disregard, but because it just got in the way.

Shortly before the first trial began at the county courthouse in Washington, Sprague had Ken Yablonski come to the headquarters he had set up at the local Holiday Inn. It was Ken who had discovered the bodies of his parents and sister the Monday after New Year's in 1970, who had realized that something must be wrong when his dad didn't show up for the swearing-in of the sheriff and the county controller and the jury commissioner and the recorder of deeds. Over and over, as Ken had driven from his home in Washington to Clarksville, he tried to tell himself that maybe, just maybe, Jock and Margaret and Charlotte had gone away for the New Year's weekend, gotten a little breather from the bitter legal challenge his dad had been waging against Tony Boyle for the presidency of the United Mine Workers.

It was Ken who pulled up to the stone house, where his sister Charlotte's car sat with its tires flattened and the mailbox ran thick with accumulated mail. It was he who opened the door and found the dog running around inside, he who proceeded into the kitchen, then the living room, and then up the simple stairs into the bedrooms.

At the Holiday Inn, Dick Sprague placed a manila envelope in front of Ken Yablonski. Inside were 8×10 glossies of the murder scene.

"I know you remember," Dick Sprague said to him. "I want you to refresh how horrible it was."

Ken Yablonski, then 35, didn't want to look at those pictures. He didn't want to relive what had happened, see it all one more time. But he also knew Dick Sprague wasn't approaching him as he would a bereaved relative. Sprague was preparing him to be a witness in front of a jury. "He didn't want me to look at the pictures for the hell of it," says Ken today. "He had a reason."

And however hard it was, Ken Yablonski looked again. He did what Dick Sprague told him to, just like everyone else.

I WALK back up the steps of the courthouse. I move toward him, and I can tell he sees me coming even though he is talking to someone. I tap him gently on the shoulder and introduce myself and hand him a copy of a letter I sent to his office stating my desire to spend time with him.

I wait for that moment when his mouth will open, like that of Beelzebub, revealing snakes and rotted teeth and bellows of fire.

I brace myself.

He looks at me....

And he is gentle.

He talks to me....

And there isn't a trace of antagonism.

He says his office has already made him aware that I am interested in talking to him. He doesn't say yes to what I am seeking, but he doesn't say no. I ask him about the case he is trying, and he patiently explains it to me. It has to do with the state's controversial personal property tax on shares of stock in out-of-state corporations. If the stakes are high, with more than $200 million in potential tax collection on the line, it is also the type of case, from a journalist's point of view, that makes a father changing diapers at midnight seem riveting by comparison. Sprague acknowledges that, and I interpret it almost as a kind of lament, as if he wants me to see him in full-bore action, not in the plodding swim of some tax appeal in which almost all the talking is done by academic experts who know more about millage than is humanly decent.

I watch him in court anyway, and I feel buoyed by the possibility of setting a tiny foothold in the core of this man, loosening a sliver of him. I congratulate myself on my charm, on how I approached him just the right way. I feel empowered by what propels the journalist, the knowledge that everyone, everyone, at some point in their lives, wants an ear to whisper into.

I return to the Montgomery County courthouse the next day. I hear more tax drone, and during a break in the proceedings, Sprague motions to me to go outside into the hallway. It is an abrupt gesture, and I obey, like a well-trained witness.

He has read my letter, he tells me. He is aware of my work and acknowledges that I have a reputation for being fair, he tells me.

But the answer is no. There will be no access. There will be no interview.

His manner is almost avuncular. No venom. No spitballs of rage. No fish eye of contempt. I am disappointed, my journalistic vanity wounded, since I really would have made a wonderful priest. I think of all he could have told me, a career unlike any other, a life unlike any other.

But as I look at him, I feel something about Dick Sprague that I didn't think I could ever possibly muster. Not anger at being deprived. Not animosity. But a sense of admiration.

A man with secrets to tell. So many secrets.

And no compulsion to let them go.

By Christopher McDougall
August 1999

SHUT UP, YOU WIMPS, AND PULL

ined up on the Princeton dock like a platoon of grunts, a dozen freshman rowers are sweating under a simple question from probably the most pissed-off guy they've ever met. "You're all geniuses, arncha?" Coach Mike Teti is taunting them. "Smart kids. I'm just a dumb guy from Philly. I *cheated* my way through school. So how come you don't know what *commitment* means?"

Silence. They smell a trap.

One rower takes a stab at it: "Commitment means trying to do your very best."

"Try? You're just going to *try*?" Teti snarls. In quieter moments, his thick Italian brows and melancholy smile give him the look of a brooding rooftop saxophonist. But when he's steamed, they twist into a Yanomamo war mask. "*Try* means you can fail." He growls from one corner of his mouth like an old-time cigar-chomping fight manager, though he's only 42. "So you're *committed* to the possibility of failure? Next!"

"It means *do* your best," the next rower astutely replies.

"Yeah, you *losers* are always whining about 'your best,'" Teti sneers. And so it goes, each response triggering a blistering appraisal of the rowers' cushy home lives and preppy parents and obvious unworthiness for the warrior's sport of rowing since—Christ!—they don't even know the meaning of *commitment*. Even Teti's younger brother, Paul, a Princeton frosh who was raised in the same cramped row-home by the trolley tracks as Mike, gets scorched for being too pampered.

To these freshmen rowers, with their powerful Princeton vocabularies, this is just locker-room semantics. But for Mike Teti, a working-class kid from Upper Darby who bulled his way to the top of this upper-crust sport, *commitment* is a word that vibrates with meaning. He made it the mantra for a team of underdog Americans who stunned the rowing world in Germany last year, and it's sure to be shouted at a key moment this coming August 29th in Canada, when Teti leads the Americans back to the World Championships for the third time in his tenure as National Rowing Team coach.

By this point, on the other hand, the Princeton frosh are starting to loathe it. Finally, Teti gets to the last guy in line.

"Mike, commitment is like ham and eggs," the rower says. "The chicken is pretty much just along for the ride. But the pig—that pig is committed."

Silence. The war mask softens to a smile. Maybe these Princeton kids aren't such numbnuts after all. "We thought Mike was gonna kiss him," says Tom Herschmiller, the Princeton senior and Canadian National Team rower who's telling the story. At first, he and the other frosh oars were just relieved the ordeal was over. But the more they thought about it, the more ominous it seemed. "We realized," Herschmiller says, "that Mike seriously expected that level of dedication."

"HI," Mike Teti had greeted the throng of aspiring Princeton rowers that fall of 1996. "I'm the asshole you've all been hearing about." Two hundred heavy-weights showed up for tryouts; within months, all but a dozen of them had quit. But those who remained would become part of Teti's legacy. When he arrived at Princeton, the freshman crew hadn't won a championship in nearly a century. When he left after 8 years, the frosh had bagged five intercollegiate titles, never finishing worse than third.

There is a good reason why Teti made a perfect freshman coach: Almost nobody, it was thought, could endure him for more than a year. In a sport demanding physical power and puritanical dedication, Mike Teti has two herniated disks and a devotion to sex, cable TV, and pizza. Rowing is a silent, solitary discipline, but Teti is a yakker, a roving high-pressure system who stirs up constant tumult. In a gentleman's sport, his language is, well…"Truly remarkable," says Dr. Fritz Hagerman, sports physiologist for the U.S. Olympic crew team. "He curses so much, it's hard to believe the sentences hold together."

And when the top rowers of his generation were polishing their technique at Ivy League and West Coast universities, Teti was rowing for a rowdy second-rate Philly team that won as many fistfights as races. When he wasn't pulling an oar, he was stocking shoes at Florsheim's or pumping gas. Ask about the Best Day of His Life, and instead of the 1984 Olympic Games, you'll hear about three honeys and a hot tub.

What's he think of classic crew texts like David Halberstam's *The Amateurs* and Stephen Kiesling's *The Shell Game*? "It makes me want to vomit. Bunch of whining millionaire weirdos."

His tips for after-practice relaxation? "Eat a lot of food, have a lot of sex." Sex, in fact, is the only excuse Teti accepts for rowers arriving late to practice—and the tardy oarsman better have a hot story to share.

THAT THIS former gas station attendant would become an Olympic medalist is not even the most remarkable chapter in the Mike Teti story. More astonishing is that he would be named, in 1997, head coach of the U.S. National Rowing Team. For decades, American rowers had been coached by the best European talent, medal-winning masters schooled in biophysics and race strategy. But after going more than 30 years without winning the showcase Olympic event—the men's eight—American rowing needed a jolt. So Teti, the roughneck nicknamed "Darth Vader" by his Princeton frosh, was given a shot at overhauling the team and leading the charge on the 2000 Sydney Olympics.

As soon as he had the keys in his hand, Teti threw open the National Team to black sheep like himself: raw, hungry outsiders who could revive this gentrified sport. He issued an open challenge to every American rower: Finish 2000 meters on a Concept II rowing machine in under 6:04, and you, sir, are invited to try out at the National Team Camp in Princeton. Last summer, a guy from California made the score, drove cross-country, and slept in the back of his pickup truck for a week while Teti gave him his shot. (Way overmatched, he eventually dropped out.) Soon, Teti had recruited a rowing Marine, a forest-fire smoke jumper, and two absolute phenoms from Minnesota and Ohio State, schools that are way off the rowing radar.

ON A MISTY lake in the French Alps, just six months after being named coach, Teti gets to see his Great Democratic Rowing Theory put to the test as five gold-colored torpedoes and one somber dark shell charge away from the stake boats at the start of the 1997 World Rowing Championships. The awesome Germans are flying, the massive Romanians are charging hard...and the dark-horse Americans, in their appropriately black boat, are fighting to stay out of last.

Rather than wait blindly at the finish line for the boats to appear, Teti watches the race on a lakeside TV monitor. A quarter of the way into the 2000-meter race, the Americans are lagging the field, and the BBC race commentator is already making polite apologies. "This is a new outfit for the Americans after their disappointing fifth-place finish in last year's Olympics," he's saying. "They seem to have struggled off the start...."

"Yeah!" Teti is huffing at every stroke. It's hard to say which is bugging him more, that BBC accent or his own creeping doubts. Maybe he should have heeded the gibes of the Polish rowing guru after a dismal preliminary race: "Mike-el, your five-man is so short in de vater," Kris Korzeniowski, perhaps the best rowing coach in the world, had said. "Ve all are laffing about it."

Flourishing a stopwatch, Teti had shot back, "I used to be Roman Catholic, Kris, but you know what? I got me a new religion—this watch. I do whatever it tells me, and it says we're three seconds faster with that guy in the boat. I ain't changing *shit*."

"Vell…Ve'll see vat hoppens."

THERE ARE students at Yale and Harvard whose ancestors have pulled oars for five generations. But the first time "crew" was mentioned in Hank and Mary Teti's Upper Darby home was the day Michael came home from Monsignor Bonner High School in 1973 with a permission slip. A chunky boy who'd hit 200 pounds in eighth grade, he wanted to toughen up for football, so he'd spent the winter of his junior year working out in the gym with the Bonner rowers. That spring, he decided to see what it was like to actually go on the water.

"You could tell from the start this kid was something special," says Chuck Crawford, then coach of the Bonner novices; a few years later, Crawford would turn a dying program at St. Joseph's Prep into a national dynasty. Few coaches have a better eye for rowing talent than this amiable Arby's owner, and in Mike Teti he saw championship stuff: "He just loved it. Whenever he was in the boat, he just hauled on it."

Novice crew meant long afternoons in a crappy wooden shell, but Mike stuck it out. Fat was melting off his body, and his limbs were thickening. The one time he considered quitting, Crawford let him row varsity, so he could feel the glory of a well-manned boat skimming over the water. "It was amazing!" Teti gushed to his mom that night. "I think we rowed to Harrisburg!"

To the uninitiated, rowing looks like slave-galley drudgery, but a well-executed stroke is exhilarating. Your body compresses to a squat, your back and arms stretch out to place the oar, the blade locks into the water, and you explode. If all eight rowers nail it just right, the boat springs forward like a pole-vaulter on takeoff.

Still, that doesn't explain why a teenager would devote himself to one of the world's most grueling and least watched sports. "Michael kids us that no one ever cared about his rowing," his mother, Mary, recalls one afternoon in the living room of the Teti home near the 69th Street terminal. "And he's right." With 10 kids, one car, and a husband who migrated from construction jobs to cab-driving to auto sales, Mary's only real concerns were that Mike stay out of trouble and take care of his own rides. "He'd come home from school, work at my cousin's Florsheim's at 69th Street, then hitch down to the river and row," she says. On the water, her son was, for the first time, a standout. Once, a Bonner crew member fell overboard during a race, but Teti kept screaming: "We can win! We can win!"

Two months after he first touched an oar, Mike made the junior varsity boat that won the Catholic League championships. The next year, as a senior, he made varsity and won the Catholics again—something that hasn't happened since Teti graduated in 1974.

Even though he was little more than a tyro, Mike's potential was so apparent that he was named to the Junior World Championship team that would race that summer in Germany. "The fucking greatest two weeks of my life," Teti sighs. He drank beer with Communists, chased girls, and got an intoxicating look at the upper reaches of the sport. "When I got back, I swore I'd do whatever the fuck it took to get to the Olympics."

AS THE FIVE yellow boats bear down on the halfway point, it's make-or-break time. The Americans are trailing badly, and coxswain Pete (Chip) Cipollone knows he's got to bring his black boat into contact now, or the race is over. His oarsmen are already cranking at 39 strokes a minute, so he tells them to keep the cadence steady—don't sprint!—but pour on the power.

"Romania is trying to hold on. The world-champion Germans are a few seats back," the announcer informs the viewing public. The American boat is starting to move; by the halfway mark, it has rejoined the pack. Cheers rise as the sculls come into view from the finish line, but Teti remains inside the viewing tent, glued to the TV.

He always hated coaches who created teams in their own images, but the truth is that his face is all over this boat. Chip, the coxswain, is an Upper Darby guy whose dad coaches at Bonner. In seat seven is Garrett Miller, a pudgeball from LaSalle High who became a powerhouse at Penn. Another Philly rower, big Bob Kaehler, is in the three seat, the "engine room." In front of him at four is Mike Wherley, the awkward recruit Korzeniowski mocked.

Teti studies their faces on the screen. Did they drain the tank in that big mid-race move? Bob Cummins and Chris Ahrens, his stroke, are heads down and deeply focused. That's good—it means they're not exhausted, looking around desperately. And Christ, look at Garrett! He's about to rip a frigging rib out of the boat. They're still in this. They'd better be, he thinks, since plenty of other coaches would like—or have been fired from—his job.

Suddenly, there's shouting from the TV monitor. "This American crew, new, untested, is flying like the wind!" the sportscaster is hollering. "Five hundred meters to go, and this is a whole new race!" Excited murmurs fill the tent. Teti knows exactly what his guys are up to: They've just taken their Commitment.

At practice, he gathers his rowers and quizzes each one about what he holds most dear: a person he'd die for, a moment he'll never forget. Teti pushes deeper, makes it personal. (*Could you bear to lose her?...Did you cry when it happened?*) So when Cippolone calls a Commitment, each stroke is a test of devotion: You say she's important to you? Show me now.

There is pandemonium in the stands. Germany, Romania, Australia, and the United States are sprinting neck-and-neck for the finish—the cruelest possible scenario, as only three boats will medal. It's the point in a race where your lungs are starving, your muscles scorched. You fantasize about slipping overboard. You pray something on the boat breaks.

The camera cuts to the finish line. For seconds, there's nothing but calm water on the screen...then a black bow pops into view. Teti leaps into the arms of his old mentor, Gavin White, as younger brother Paul comes tearing into the tent and dives into the scrum. Soon, the tent is aboil. "Some old woman was screaming underneath us," White recalls. "I don't think international rowing has ever seen that kind of hysteria."

SOMEHOW, Philly rowers found a way to bring the badass attitude of street hoops to the world's most regimented sport. "They act like they've got this chip on their shoulder," says Dr. Hagerman, 30 years a crew expert. "It's this attitude, like everyone's out to screw them, so they better come out charging."

Maybe the 'tude comes from the fact that rowing, like halfball, was once *our* sport. Back in the 1800s, Philly was the rowing capital of America. (It still is, with 4,000 Philadelphians taking to the water each day.) The Schuylkill Navy was the first rowing association in America, and at the turn of the century, working stiffs from East Falls and Fishtown were among the fastest scullers in the country. When crew became an Olympic sport in 1908, a Vesper boat won the first gold medal.

But gradually the leisure class took over, a lesson Philly bricklayer John B. "Jack" Kelly would bitterly learn. The most famous oarsman of the 1920s and 1930s, Kelly won gold medals in the Antwerp and Paris Olympics. But he was barred from England's Royal Henley Regatta because he was a manual laborer. His son, John Kelly Jr., would win Henley twice, in 1947 and 1949, avenging the insult to his father and giving Philly rowers a sense of righteousness. Kelly *père*'s statue, at the finish line of the Schuylkill racecourse, gives a lasting up-yours to rowing snobbery.

The working-man's torch was picked up by guys like Gus Ignus, "The Hammer," a craggy Fishtown bartender. The Hammer was a respected rowing teacher, but most stories about him involve beer, cigarettes, and fists. "He was the baddest mutha on Boathouse Row," says Mike Porterfield, an assistant National Team coach. The Hammer punched out two National Team coaches, one for borrowing his launch and the other—Kris Korzeniowski, in fact—for being Polish. He was known to taunt opponents by tossing panties into their boats, shouting, "Ya forgot yer underwear!"

Even respectable Penn turned out notorious rowers. Theta Xi, Penn's rowing frat, was infamous for launching refrigerators off its house roof and staging an annual grossout contest, the crown one year going to an oarsman who strolled around campus in shoes full of excrement. After two decades of campus complaints, Theta Xi was finally closed in the early 1990s.

"Pulling a Philly job" has become a recognized phrase in rowing vernacular. For example, in 1983, Princeton's undefeated varsity eight was looking for an easy win before the Eastern Sprints. They invited Temple, then a second-rate squad, to their private lake for a friendly scrimmage. The boats lined up—and suddenly, the Owls were rowing away, leaving Princeton in their wake. False start? No flag went up, so the Owls kept charging. Princeton fought back and eventually recovered the lost water. In the final 50 strokes, Temple shot across the finish line to win. Exhausted, but overjoyed to have beaten one of the country's best teams, the Temple rowers were still cheering when Princeton coach Larry Gluckman came roaring over in his launch. "That's typical Philly bullshit!" he shouted.

"Let's turn them around and race it again," offered Temple coach Gavin White, but Gluckman was pointing to the bridge out of town like a county sheriff: "Get your boats and get the hell off our lake!"

As they were loading the boat trailer, two owls sidled over to their assistant coach and offered to beat up the Princeton coach. A tempting prospect, but one the assistant coach—Mike Teti—decided to turn down.

IN 1980, White had invited Teti to coach the Temple freshman crew, ignoring the advice of nearly everyone on Boathouse Row. "Mike had a reputation for being opinionated and egotistical," the easygoing White recalls. But White had noticed something while Temple was training in Vesper Boat Club: When his guys were on the rowing machines, Teti would sometimes interrupt his own workouts to go whisper something in a rower's ear. "In every case, the kid started rowing better," says White. "*Immediately.*"

At the same time, Teti was working hard to improve his own bladesmanship. After four medal-less years at St. Joe's University, he'd begun selling insurance by day, still rowing at dawn and dusk. His mother urged him to hang it up and get married, but Mike, locked in a fantasy of Olympic glory, mulishly kept hitting the weights in a tiny Upper Darby gym and rowing laps from the Art Museum to East Falls and back. In foul weather, his family would hear his rowing machine zinging for hours in the basement.

It paid off. By the early 1980s, he'd grown into one of the most formidable racers in the country, a river warrior the Vesper rowers called "God"—partly for his fantastic conditioning, partly for his attitude. ("And when God rested on the seventh day," the Vesper joke went, "Mike took over.") But elite-team coaches weren't sure what to make of him: Teti was one tough bastard, true, but his technique was dodgy, and his rowing-machine scores were unimpressive. Besides, unlike the Ivy Leaguers, he had a fantastically foul mouth and would go toe-to-toe with any coach who pissed him off.

In 1984, Korzeniowski's first year as National Team coach, he tried to get rid of Teti by subjecting him to row-off after row-off. Faced with such obvious prejudice, most athletes would either quit or silently row their asses off and hope to change the coach's mind. Not Teti. He hurled his oar to the dock one morning and challenged Korzeniowski to bring it on. "If you're waiting for one of those guys to beat me, it'll never fucking happen," Teti stormed. "For one reason—I'm better!" Rejection only got him juiced, a lesson he'd learned from his day job. "Selling insurance, I got told to fuck off 10 times a day," he explains. "It just means you're closer to the next sale." (For the record, Teti now says he has a "good relationship" with Korzeniowski.)

SO WHAT was it like to row with a wild man like Mike Teti? "Awesome," says world champion and Olympic oarsman John Pescatore, who shared both small and large boats with Teti. "He's a lotta, lotta fun, and an unbelievable motivator." Pescatore was just out of college when he teamed up in an elite four with Teti, 10 years his senior. Mike not only ran the practices but provided mock commentary in a weird European accent from the back of the boat. "We'd be cranking along at full pressure, and we'd hear, 'Ze Boolgarians are movink, but ze Americains are cummink strong! *Here cum ze Americains!*'" says Pescatore. "God, it got us so fired up."

Something happened, though, when Mr. Bubbly put a stopwatch around his neck and started coaching. He turned into Darth Vader.

"A lot of guys talked about hitting him," recalls former Temple rower Tom Kowalik. "He was ruthless. He'd go up to a guy's face and say, 'You know what? You stink.'" Coach White arrived at practice one day to find Teti's jayvees in the midst of "wall leans," a notoriously painful drill where you brace against the wall like you're sitting on an invisible chair. The rowers were grimacing in agony, their legs shaking.

"How long you gonna keep them at it?" White asked.

"Till they drop," Teti replied.

"He wanted them to feel that nothing could be harder than his practices," says White. "He would torture them, abuse them with cutting comments." Rowers were soon dropping off the team, but those who stayed felt invincible. Kowalik has to agree. "For years, we were finishing 12th and thinking we were hot. After Mike arrived, the varsity finished second and the jayvee finished third, and the guys were in tears. They were the first medals Temple had won in 10 years, and we were crushed we didn't win."

It was a lesson Teti was learning in his own pursuit of Olympic gold: Eight guys make the boat, and the rest, no matter how hard they've trained, disappear. Three teams ascend the podium, and the rest vanish. "The great thing about our sport is, there's no mystery," he'd lecture. "I could train 10 times as hard as Michael Jordan and never beat him. But in rowing, there's only one question: Are you willing to do the work?"

"I look at the guys I work with now on the stock market trading floor, and Mike is so *real* in comparison," says elite rower Kay Worthington, a double gold medalist for Canada and Teti's girlfriend of 15 years. "He's all about what you do, not what you say."

Over the years, Teti made National Team boats, was cut, suffered injuries, came back. The rowers he grew up with retired one by one, but Teti, still coaching at Temple and selling insurance, kept banging at it. He almost made the 1984 Olympic eight, but ended up as a spare. In 1985, rowing stroke for the U.S. eight, he won his first World Championship medal, a bronze. Two years later, he made the boat with Pescatore that won World Championship gold. Then, in 1988, after millions of miles rowed and 10 years of sweating in the basement, Teti was chosen for the Olympic eight.

White received a long personal letter from his assistant coach that spring, postmarked from the Olympic training center, with instructions to read it to his rowers just before the championships. By then, Temple had blossomed into one of the top 10 teams in America. "I'm so proud of you guys, and I wish I could be there to cheer for you," the letter began. By the end, most of the Temple rowers were covering their eyes with their hands. "All these big, strong guys crying," White says. "They just adored him."

That summer, Mike's older brother John worked to pay for Paul's airfare, and two of Mike's sisters took bank loans so that the Tetis, as a family, could watch Mike hoist the bronze medal over his head in Seoul.

DAY HAS barely broken on the Princeton docks, where the U.S. national team has been training. Rowers are lounging around and chatting. At 6:40 on the dot, they begin throwing 12-foot oars over their shoulders and carrying them to the water's edge. At 6:44, a minute before practice is scheduled to start, a black-clad figure with dark wraparound shades appears on the dock with a blue binder, where he records every workout and test score for every rower he's ever coached. "Amazing how quiet it gets when he opens the Book," says assistant coach John Parker.

Without looking up from the Book, Teti calls off names, dividing the rowers into boats, and heads for his launch. Instead of putting his best rowers in one boat, like most coaches, Teti has picked two even crews and ordered the coxswains to stay side by side the entire practice. "I want them looking over at each other," he confides, "so they realize just who the guy is who's trying to take their seat."

It's a spectacular morning, gold light glowing on the placid lake, but Teti is oblivious. He's pissed about the "idiot" who called him last night with some stupid question, and the goddamn rain, and grumblegrumblegrumble. He's soon ripping into one of the coxswains for not keeping the two boats even. Even though it's a low-pressure drill, the rowers can't help trying to pull ahead of one another. "It's pretty fucking simple," Teti barks, "but you went to an Ivy League school, so you can't understand that. Too fucking smart to figure that out, right?

It's baffling how anyone can be that worked up by seven in the morning—until a pattern emerges, all woven around Teti's "dumbness." Teti says it himself, all the time: "I'm a lot dumber than most of you guys." He's almost proud of his combined 850 on the SAT.

Just the way Cyrano needs to hear "big nose" to be at his fighting best, Teti needs to think he's being rejected. It worked when he was challenged by Korzeniowski, it worked when he was rebuffed as an insurance salesman, and now he's trying to make it work for the U.S. Olympic team. That's why, unlike other coaches, he makes everything deeply personal, both for himself and his rowers. Last summer at the World Championships, his brother Paul was stroking a lightweight four that had a poor heat. Mike pulled him aside. "How can you tell our mother about this?" he snarled. "She went through seven hours of labor, and you row like that?" "Mike's very passionate," explains Paul, his brother's leading apologist. "He operates on a very personal level."

At those same World Championships, in Germany, Teti got the kick he needed just before the first heat. After the Americans' miraculous upset win at the 1997 Worlds in France, few people seriously expected them to repeat. Only two teams had ever won consecutive championships—Germany, with three straight, and New Zealand, with two. Realistically, it was a long shot. But even though Teti knew the odds, he became enraged when he saw a European magazine article listing the Americans as a "dark horse at best." How *dare* they? So Teti ordered Cipollone not to count out the strokes of the Commitment, but to scream, over and over, "AMERICANS CAN'T REPEAT....AMERICANS CAN'T REPEAT...."

Once again, the final came down to a furious sprint. The Americans pulled ahead with 20 strokes to go, but the Germans came blazing back, sending up a roar from the hometown crowd that drowned out Cipollone's commands. The Germans were moving fast, and the Americans outstroked them by inches. After the race, the head of the German Rowing Federation approached Teti. "We are not finished yet," he growled.

"Neither are we," Teti snarled right back.

Which is why, back in the United States, he began recruiting Marines and forest-fire smoke jumpers and Midwestern nobodies, in addition to the familiar stars from the familiar rowing powerhouses. They're all gathered here at the National Team camp in Princeton, living in an on-campus Catholic mission, borrowed apartments and cheap hotels, some 50 rowers competing for eight seats in the championship boat.

Teti's pushing them hard, but he's pushing himself even harder. To this day, he can hold his own on long rowing-machine tests with just about anyone on the team, and they know it. No American eight-man crew has ever achieved the grand slam of rowing: three World Championships, followed by Olympic gold. So it's not surprising to learn that for some rowers, just having Mike Teti as a coach is too much.

"Who needs the abuse?" questions Kurt Braunder, a 1996 National Team rower. Along with several other independent rowers, Brauder is training at Penn AC Boat Club in hopes of defeating one of Teti's smaller boats, the pair or the four, and taking a spot at the Worlds. "Mike Teti will probably end up the most successful National Team coach this country has ever seen...but what purpose does it serve to rip into guys? Why can't they just pull you aside and say, 'Hey, if you don't measure up, you're out'?"

American rowing has certainly boomed, Brauder acknowledges. "Even I've gotten stronger—I hated his stupid insistence on erg scores, till I realized I was working harder and getting better." A high work standard is one thing, but when it comes to the Darth Vader act, Brauder is dismissive: "That's just Mike's ego at work."

Back on the Princeton water, the two National Team eights are soaring, side by side. They're supposed to be holding it at three-quarters pressure, but the force of the rowers' strokes is nearly lifting the boats off the water. Teti is serene, relaxed and quiet for the first time this morning...until he's told about the criticism.

The tribal war mask reappears. He looks like he's about to spit. Then he shakes his head. "Yeah," he says. "Everybody hates me till the first race."

TERRY GROSS

Host of *Fresh Air*, author of the new book *All I Did Was Ask*, 53; Society Hill

In high school I filled out a career questionnaire. Under what I'd like to be, I wrote "lyricist." Under what I thought I'd be, I wrote "secretary."

I don't look like what listeners expect. They expect someone taller. I'm five feet tall—when I'm standing straight.

Before I found radio, I felt this kind of hole in my life. I envied all the people who had something that they loved.

My first real job was teaching eighth-grade English in Buffalo's toughest inner-city school. I was fired before Christmas. I didn't have a clue how to be an authority figure. I dressed like I wished my teachers had dressed—I'd wear purple corduroy jeans and work boots to school. Things just got more and more out of control. A few students even told their parents that I was a heroin addict—they knew that because I always wore long sleeves to cover my track marks.

I'm often on adversarial terms with my body. I'm not a physically strong person, and I'm a physical coward. I always feel like my body is rebelling.

Deep down, I'm still pretty shy. We did an onstage event at the Sundance Film Festival, and after a luncheon, Robert Redford invited me to his office. So the first thing I said to him as we're walking was, "Do you think it's going to snow?"

Through my whole adult life, I've never known what it was like to come home and not work. I work at home every night except Friday and Saturday.

The story of your life is one of the most precious things you can have.

My parents were very private. We were always told what things could be public and what things couldn't.

I showed my parents an article in a magazine that said I was really hard to get to know. My mother said, "You told them too much!"

I've given up on the idea of writing lyrics.

I look at my interview with [rock star] Gene Simmons as one of the high points of the show. You don't hear many guests telling public radio hosts that if they want to welcome them with open arms, they also have to welcome them with open legs.

I think Howard Stern has some of the gifts that Lenny Bruce had. He has the soul of an old man, and the body of a heavy-metal fan. And the juxtaposition of the two is kind of hilarious.

My husband Francis [Davis] won a Pew fellowship in the arts, so we went to the reception with my mother-in-law. One of the wives of the Fellows goes up to my mother-in-law and says to her, pointing at me, "Look over there—that's Terry Gross. Did you know she's a lesbian?"

I find it really entertaining that people think I'm gay. However listeners want to imagine me is great.

I never felt the urge to be a mother.

I like the scale of Philadelphia—there's so many nice places to walk around. You know, I like Manhattan, but when you walk there, you are walking at the same pace that the crowd is walking. You cannot walk any faster or any slower than the crowd.

I've lived here since 1975, so I certainly feel like it's my home. But truthfully, I don't get to do very much. I mean, the real truth is, I'm reading or going to movies.

I wish there were more jazz clubs in Philadelphia; I wish I could go hear the music I want to hear on a Saturday night.

Take away my microphone, take away the studio and just put me in a room with people, and I'm much more uncomfortable. I have a lot of deep insecurities that are never gonna go away.

I probably would have gotten a lot more sleep over the years if I had known that until this point, until today, nothing unmanageable has happened in my life. But that doesn't guarantee me anything about tonight.

PART 3

_2000 – 2004_

By Christopher McDougall
September 2000

SECOND COMING

early every house on the block is still dark at this miserable hour of a wet spring morning when Mayor John Street comes double-timing down the steps of his North Philadelphia rowhome, coatless in the fine, needling rain. Street's face is stony, but his body jitters with energy as he rams a Hefty bag into a trash can and speedwalks down the driveway.

"Okay, 'Bush," he orders his driver by way of greeting. "Office."

Marion Winbush slides open the side door of an all-black van that from the outside could pass for the A-Team command vehicle; inside, with its deep crimson upholstery and dim yellow lighting, it feels more like a hearse.

Breaking news is chattering on KYW radio as Street enters the van—but not for long. "Put this in, 'Bush," the mayor says, shoving a cassette toward the driver. Gospel music floods the vehicle. Contented, the Mayor nestles into his seat, tossing aside fresh copies of the *Inquirer* and *Daily News*. "I listen to very little radio," he says. "I've got a few gospel tapes, so at least I can control that part of my environment."

He begins to hum along with the a cappella tenors as the world outside changes from tidy to tragic. Within a few blocks, the neat brick homes of Street's Yorktown neighborhood have given way to the dying Richard Allen housing projects on 12th Street.

Through the windshield, the downtown high-rises look massive and impenetrable, a far-off kingdom framed by this foreground of boarded-up apartments and abandoned corner shops. Suddenly, Street is tapping urgently against the tinted windows.

"See there?" the Mayor exclaims, still tapping, as ecstatic as the gospel singers' voices. "That's where the new stadium is going to be." He's pointing to 12th and Callowhill, an *Eraserhead* zone of tar-stained train trestles, high-voltage conductors, dead warehouses, a pocket or two of rehabbed housing and a strip joint that explicitly prohibits weapons.

This is a most interesting comment, given that his tour of *all* the possible stadium sites is not scheduled to begin until that afternoon. Even more surprising is the reasoning he gives. "A stadium will pop development from here all the way up to Temple," he exults, still staring dreamily through the window. Not south from the stadium toward Center City, as he will later promise, but the other way—toward his own neighborhood.

This scene will nag at me during the following months, as Street "inspects" rival sites and begins hectoring the city on live TV to back his choice even though he has no financing, no building plans, and no agreement with the Phillies. There was something oddly familiar about the way he spoke—about his behavior and his view of the city. This fall, he'll ask City Council to approve nearly $2 billion in projects that will primarily benefit North Philadelphia. And as he talks about these staggering expenditures, it hits me: Frank Rizzo is back.

THE MORE STREET talks policy, the more he sounds like he's channeling the Bambino, the dominant figure in town when young John was just learning the back-room game. Like Rizzo, Street has been paid by taxpayers nearly all his adult life, never working more than a brief stint in a for-profit business since his days inside Milton's hot-dog cart. Among Rizzo and Street's shared traits: a deep allegiance to a single neighborhood, a stubborn romance with the past, a feeling of personal victimization, and a suspicion of elites and outsiders. Rizzo scorned intellectuals and liberals the same way Street sneers at the Rittenhouse class. (He refers to them in our conversations as "the 'smart' people, over where you live.")

Unlike Rendell, who hails from New York and believes that without a thriving nucleus there is no city, Street is strictly Rizzo-like in the way he sees Philadelphia as his own neighborhood, extended outward. When the Mayor launched his car-towing campaign, he led the tow-truck parade straight to North 23rd Street—in the heart of his old councilmanic district. And there's no explanation for rehabbing Richard Allen other than sentimental allegiance.

Even from the early days, Street gleaned from Rizzo that bluster wins big in Philly. Rizzo's legacy included an out-of-control patronage machine, a massive tax hike and a budget-busting union contract, but he got a downtown statue and a 9th Street mural. Street has never won better press than when he was blowing the most smoke: Both the *Inquirer* and *Daily News* toasted the "boldness" of the stadium proposal, when it's still no more than a whim.

IT WAS THE same with the endlessly trumpeted car-towing campaign.

"You're here because of the abandoned cars, aren't you?" Street spokesman Ray Jones asked as we waited in the drizzle that April morning outside the Mayor's house.

"Not exactly."

It was baffling how convinced Street's staff was that one month of towing cars was an abiding national—or even local—issue. Actually, I was there at the behest of *George* magazine, which wanted a profile of Street timed for the GOP convention.

That profile would touch off a minor firestorm. It quoted the Mayor making a crack that "all you white guys look alike" and threatening "a very ugly response" to "disrupters" who got out of hand at the convention—a phrase that immediately linked Street, nationwide, to Philadelphia's latest adventure in full-contact policing. While the comments were embarrassing, it's doubtful any locals were surprised.

Voices in the Mayor's office complained (anonymously) to local media that the *George* article only told part of the story, and they're right. The real news for Philadelphians isn't these familiar Street flare-ups, but what's happening on the second floor of City Hall since Rendell's desk was moved out to make room for John Street's treadmill. Ultimately, Street won't be remembered for what bubbles from his mouth, but for what's boiling in his mind—for whatever master plan he has to reinvent a city that even Ed Rendell left office thinking was still on course for financial disaster.

Rendell found us a temporary fix in tourism and hospitality, a goal-line stand based on the same logic as nudie bars: If we can't produce anything, at least we can show off our goodies. But no number of busboys and chambermaids can save the tax base. So now it falls to Street to solve the fatal urban algebra of high taxes + crime = fewer residents = higher taxes + even more crime.

Rudy Giuliani, in the same boat, managed a Manhattan makeover by using Disney dollars to turn Times Square into a family attraction. Chicago's Richard Daley, realizing that inferior schools were driving away his tax base, made education his top priority. Stephen Goldsmith of Indianapolis lowered taxes by privatizing city services. So far, Street has been tight-lipped about his own big idea. But his behavior, examined up close, speaks volumes.

WELL BEFORE 7 A.M., the Mayor-mobile hops the curb and drives across the sidewalk to the front door of City Hall. Street pops out and, ignoring the elevator, bounds up the stairs two at a time. On the second floor, he peeks back to see how far he's outdistanced his aides, then vanishes into his office. It's massive—Street appropriated Rendell's cabinet room as his personal office.

They're peculiar digs for a 21st-century chief executive: There's no computer, nor even the customary muted TV tuned to CNN—just a big tape box playing gospel on a bookshelf. The desk is surprisingly neat, with small stacks of papers, an autographed basketball, and two books: *The Age of Spiritual Machines* (by Ray Kurzweil) and *Engines of Creation* (by Eric Drexler), texts on the highly speculative field of nanotechnology, which envisions a future when scientists can manipulate DNA through microchips and download brain waves onto computers.

"What did you think of those?" Street asks Shawn Fordham, his chief of staff's assistant and also the Mayor's nephew by marriage, as he gestures to the books.

"They just blew me away," Fordham replies, shaking his head in wonder. "That's some mind-blowing stuff."

Though Street has conducted several online chats, he never touches the keyboard himself; he dictates to a surrogate typist. Arthritis prevents him from hitting the keys, claims spokeswoman Barbara Grant.

Lots of people lack expertise in new technology. But it's unfortunate that one of them is our mayor. New York City has seen its Internet job pool double in the past 3 years; today, more than $4 billion in Internet income is generated in the Big Apple. Philly's e-market, meanwhile, has barely budged. At a recent local e-commerce conference, the sense was that Street wasn't committed. "It would have been nice if he came with one concrete thing that he could talk to this sophisticated audience about," Ellen Thompson, founder of Know It All, Inc., complained to the *Daily News*.

Much the way his desk is host to wild-eyed books about technology but no actual technology, Street seems gripped by ideas whose currency expired in the 1970s, back when computers were things of the future and government was about Big Construction—about pouring oceans of concrete into housing projects, stadiums, waterfront districts, a Liberty Bell plaza, a new Chestnut Street ... the very things Philadelphia is now tearing up.

Like Rizzo, Street comes across better in person than on camera, and he tries—a bit too hard—to make the most of his available face-time. His daily agenda looks like the starting schedule of a track meet: There's a new activity every hour, often with no time allotted for transportation and, occasionally, with multiple events scheduled simultaneously.

This leads to TV news cameras waiting in one part of town while the Mayor turns up in another, and to repeated, chaotic scenes of Street squirting out a side door of his office and down the stairs as aides scurry behind, alerting one another with calls of "Mayor's on the move! Mayor's on the move!"

On this April day, in fact, chief of staff Stephanie Franklin-Suber was careful to be waiting right next to the Mayor's front door 10 minutes before we were supposed to meet him for lunch.

Contrary to her fire-breathing image, Franklin-Suber operated in a state of constant anxiety, looking more like a nervous office assistant than the Mayor's second-in-command. She spent a good part of her day by Street's side, pad and pen in hand, and was obsessively quick to dive on the sword when anything went wrong. When slides were beamed out of sequence during a transition-team presentation, Franklin-Suber immediately piped up, "That's my job, to make sure those things are done right."

She also became the fall gal in the Street administration's early media disasters. Showing a Tarantino-esque taste for bloodletting, Franklin-Suber axed media director Ken Snyder while he was being married in an emergency ceremony at his father-in-law's deathbed. She then sent police to forcibly evict aviation director Alfred Testa, while Street kept himself out of the fray.

Despite, or because of, such take-a-bullet obedience, Franklin-Suber became a regular target of Street's practical jokes. Earlier that morning, Street and I were chatting in his office when Franklin-Suber called, wondering where I was. "He left. I told him I don't have time to be playing around with some guy asking a bunch of questions," he improvised. "So he got into a snit and left. *You* go find him if you want to." He hung up, grinning. Moments later, Franklin-Suber burst through the door, super-charged for damage control. When she caught sight of me, she froze. Then she giggled in embarrassment and backed out the door.

"He's a prankster. I'm so gullible," she told me later, as we waited in the hall. Fearing that she might come across as disloyal, she tittered and shook her curly bangs. Then her cell phone bleeped. The Mayor, it seemed, had somehow escaped out the back door and was already en route to the Palm. Franklin-Suber looked stunned. "No, we *cannot* just catch a cab!" she argued. This time, there were no titters or shaken curls.

It was no surprise when she quit three months later. The breaking point was the furniture scandal: Just when the Mayor was telling city workers the budget was so tight that he couldn't pay any more, the Associated Press revealed that Franklin-Suber had ordered $60,000 worth of custom-made, solid-cherry office furniture.

In announcing her resignation, Franklin-Suber sounded much like her boss when he railed against the city for being too conservative and cynical to get behind his unfunded, unplanned and unwanted-by-the-Phillies ballpark site. It wasn't her fault, Franklin-Suber complained; it was everyone else's. "It is still, in the year 2000, difficult for society in general to be comfortable with a woman in such a high position," she said.

The true cause of her problems, as she well knew, was in the office around the corner. At the critical moment, when a vote of confidence would have made the matter disappear, Street instead declared that it looked "inappropriate" to him, too—never mentioning that his own office renovations cost almost a third more than hers.

BUT THERE'S a vibrant, stirring side of Street that occasionally breaks through, like the Nordic sun. At an early-morning cabinet meeting, the Mayor is on a tear, and his staff is feeding off his excitement.

"The old folks come with tears in their eyes, because they can't live like that anymore," Street says, face furrowed into the familiar glower. "The police can't do anything, because it's jamming up 911!"

"Maybe—" begins managing director Joe Martz, but the Mayor is too hot to stop.

"We need a way to control public nuisances. It's people with big, ugly speakers in their cars. It's people with barking dogs," Street says. All around the table, his staff is scribbling down ideas. "We need a solution! If we get this blight stuff underway, we have to do this as well."

"For the crime initiative, we talked about 'Take Back the Streets,'" chips in city solicitor Ken Trujillo. "How about 'Take Back the Neighborhoods'?"

"Good," says Street. "The issue here is personal responsibility. Good."

"Once we get the 40,000 cars towed, we can enforce guys who repair cars in the street," offers Martz.

Street, who loves any mention of the dead-car campaign, beams. "Great! And we can set up a hot line, so people can call and ask to have, like, a refrigerator hauled away. We don't want to make criminals out of people, force them into being illegal dumpers—we have to give them a proper solution first."

"You know, the Actors Theater could do plays for kids about cleaning up," muses Joyce Wilkerson, the secretary of strategic planning who will later replace Franklin-Suber.

The meeting continues for another half hour at this breakneck, brainstorming pace. As it wraps up, the staff is still chattering animatedly. Trujillo and Martz, in shirtsleeves, look like they're ready to go haul some abandoned fridges themselves.

But their energy may partly be due to a release of tension, because the meeting got off to a sticky start when Street asked to be briefed on plans for GOP convention security. After mentioning his own activist past, Street soon began making heavy-handed comments about handling "idiots," which Trujillo, at least, found troubling.

"Barbara Grant, myself, and others here have been on the front line of demonstrations in the past, so this is real important to us," Trujillo said. "We're concerned about setting the right tone."

"I agree, I agree," Street said. "But we're not letting disrupters take over our city." As he continued talking, his rhetoric wobbled between allegiance to his bullhorn-toting days and veiled threats to pull the nightstick from his waistband. "There was a time when no one cared for my opinion—"

"Took you a long, long time to open those bronze gates," chimed in Augusta Clark, the 67-year-old former councilwoman Street hired as a $135,000-a-year adviser. "Had to start leaping over them."

"But they have no right to intimidate Philadelphia citizens," Street interjected, swinging back the other way. It was only when the conversation shifted to a solid, feel-good issue that the tension eased.

A good number of seats were vacant around the conference-room table, revealing a troubling pattern to Street's hiring. By April, he'd filled all the social-services posts, and had also added four new positions to the mayoral staff and increased cabinet salaries by an average of 40 percent. He'd hired a friend's firm to do his head-hunting (the same firm the city had previously paid $20,000 to conduct a nationwide search for an antiviolence director and, shazam!, found Street's wife), and paid a chubby church pal $80,000 a year to be the city's first "Health and Fitness Czar" (whose valuable work, of course, we benefit from every day).

However, he was slower to hire directors of commerce, budget or planning—suggesting that while spending money was a priority, controlling it could wait.

"I don't see how the hell he's going to make it through his first term without going broke," says one of Rendell's former top aides. "It's funny—I always thought Street would be good with the budget and lousy with the PR, but he's well on his way to blowing both of them."

Of course, Street's open wallet shouldn't be all that surprising. Asked during the campaign if he'd deal in political favors, Street shrugged and said, "the people who support me in the general election have a greater chance of getting business from my administration." As for political hires: "That's just patronage. It has always been that way—and it will always be that way, at least as far as I can tell."

Mayor Rizzo couldn't have put it any better himself.

MANY PEOPLE thought Street would never be more than a loudmouth district councilman," the Mayor says as we head north to cut the ribbon on a new computer center at Creighton School, in Northeast Philly. "Then they look around, and he's City Council president. Look around again, and he's on the second floor"—home of the Mayor's office.

For a man who's lived the American dream, rising from dirt farm to law school to City Council by age 36, the Mayor dwells considerably on the slights he's suffered along the way. A high-school teacher, Street says, told him he'd never make the grade in college, and a law-school dean predicted he'd flunk out. "I let him have it, though," Street says. "He was pushing all kinds of buttons under the desk, calling security. People think the only place I was ever carried out of was City Council, but it was already a tradition by then."

The conversation shifts, naturally, to his current image problem. Street laughs it off, yet he keeps picking at the topic like a scab. "People don't understand me. I told one woman, 'The person you think I am doesn't exist. The media has to have a shorthand for everyone.'" This is a man, remember, who used to tape every negative thing ever written about him on a wall in his office. "The Wall of Shame," he called it—"till I decided to run for Mayor, and all my little media gurus said, 'You gotta take it down.'"

One reason for his ailing popularity becomes apparent as the Mayormobile pulls up at Creighton. We're already late; several hundred children have been squirming in auditorium seats for nearly an hour. Just as we arrive, Street's cell phone rings. "Hey!" he greets the caller happily, then waves us out of the van. Inside the auditorium, a desperate teacher is sweating in front of a microphone. "Okay, the Mayor must be putting his galoshes on...." The Mayor doesn't appear for another 10 minutes.

Watching him in action has been like following Napoleon across Europe: Everywhere he goes, Street stirs up battles. Senator Vince Fumo has gone from grudging rival to full-blown enemy. Governor Ridge had to be miffed by Street's strong-arm play over school funding. Chinatown is considering filing a race-discrimination lawsuit over the stadium site. And if things weren't prickly enough with city workers, Street tried to help unseat blue-collar union boss Pete Matthews before negotiations began. "If this union wasn't united before, it is now—against John Street," Matthews declared.

Over at City Council, Street's former colleagues are becoming increasingly miffed over his love of secrecy. The Mayor cut a school financing deal with the Governor but didn't tell Council until after the handshake. When Street made his unusual televised appeal for his 12th and Callowhill stadium site, Council President Anna Verna didn't even bother coming back from the Shore. "I had a feeling it wasn't going to be much of anything," she groused to the *Daily News*.

Besides cracks in allies' solidarity, flaws in Street's math are appearing. The state oversight board reviewed his first budget and basically called it dreamy-eyed, noting, "The uncertainty surrounding the City's financial leadership generates increased concern as to the seeming capricious nature of the planning process." Millions in cuts are promised, with no specifics given. A $7 billion economic stimulus program has no performance standard to monitor whether it's working. Besides the $1.3 billion—and rising—stadium project, he wants to spend $250 million to battle blight, and $150 million to convert the Richard Allen projects into commercial housing. Basic accounting says you spend when you're flush and hold off when you're not, but Street is doing the opposite.

"The City's proposal," the report marvels, "is simply counter-intuitive."

STREET SEEMS sleepy and disinterested during our last talk. He answers questions laconically while eating fruit, flipping the gospel tape in his office cassette player, and as he often does to fight a yawn, mopping his hand around his face.

But suddenly he leans forward intently, shaking his head in scorn. "You want the vision thing? I'll give you the vision thing." And so, finally, he begins sketching his notion of what Philadelphia will look like once John Street has come and gone.

We've been discussing Rendell's big footprints. Al Gore called Fast Eddie "America's Mayor" because in Rendell, he'd finally found a local leader who *got* it: The days of big government spending were over, and the full-frontal seduction of private enterprise had begun. But while Rendell managed to make eensie cuts in the wage tax and ink deals with Home Depot, Wal-Mart and Kvaerner, he never succeeded in reforming Philly's business-choking tax and licensing codes.

That's the job Street has inherited. Philadelphia has a gold mine within reach: the booming suburban tech community known as "Philicon Valley." Internet jocks are natural urbanites, college grads with a taste for Starbucks, films and mega-music stores, and the support talent they need—the lawyers, bookkeepers and business consultants—is located in the city. But the vast majority of start-ups head straight to the 'burbs, thanks in part to the far more welcoming tax structure.

Street, though, is convinced the bait to attract businesses is a boss new ballpark—as if Amazon's presence in Seattle has anything to do with the Mariners. "E-commerce entrepreneurs want a 24-hour city," Street says. "They don't want Berks County; they want to be near stadiums, concerts."

Mystified by his reasoning, I ask what studies he's read. Many agree that while stadiums are pleasant ornaments, they aren't economic engines. "Megaprojects have not ignited powerful downtown revivals," says Joel Kotkin, of Pepperdine's Institute for Public Policy. "Baltimore and Cleveland remain among the most poverty-stricken urban centers in the country; their downtowns are home to virtually no new industries and only a sprinkling of new residents."

That's when Street gets fired up.

"I'm telling you, people from North Philadelphia will come flocking to a 12th Street stadium," he says, his eyes dancing. "They'll come walking with their strollers, like they do on the Fourth of July—" Then Street catches himself. "I mean the *real* North Philadelphia," he says, "not—" He gestures toward the Art Museum area, the kind of yuppified neighborhood that Rizzo would have hated.

"Not over there," Street concludes.

By Maximillian Potter
April 2000

NIGHT MOVES

id you see that?" Night asks. It's awards season in the movie business, and M. Night Shyamalan, local Hollywood golden boy, is a finalist for everything. His breakthrough *The Sixth Sense,* now one of the highest grossing films in history, is up for six Oscars and every other cinematic honor. But as Night sits in his musty, drywalled Civic Center office—his HQ 2 years ago during the filming of *Sense,* and home again for his follow-up *Unbreakable,* which is about to begin shooting—he isn't talking movies. He's discussing a slam dunk, the one Toronto's Vince Carter nailed during the NBA All-Star competition, in one superhuman motion announcing himself as the future.

"Carter was *amazing*," Night says. "He took a bounce pass, put the ball under his legs, and did a crazy reverse jam. The stands went nuts." Wearing jeans and a black hipster shirt with a wrinkled collar, Night is rocking in a leather chair behind a cherrywood desk. The sunlight pouring in from the window behind him makes the Indian-American's light-brown skin glow. A wide white smile connects his cymbal-size ears, and his brown eyes flicker an electricity so pronounced that I expect to hear them crackle.

The real drama of Carter's dunk came when he returned to earth. There was still one more round in the competition, which was then his to win or lose. Though basketball has long been Night's other passion—his pickup playing not long ago sent him to the hospital for reconstructive knee surgery—he will never know what it's like to dunk Carter-style. But he can easily imagine what the player was going through. *Sixth Sense* was actually the second movie written and directed by the Conshohocken native. *Unbreakable* is Night's third dunk.

"Carter didn't stand back going, *My God, the entire world is here to see the big star of the slam dunk contest,*" Night says. "He went out and jammed again." He went out and jammed much more conservatively, however—enough to win on points, but not trying to compete with what he had just done.

I ask Night if he sees the similarity.

"My situation is *sooo* precarious." His grin says: *Just maybe that's why I'm telling you this story.* He leans back slightly in his chair and with both hands quickly adjusts his necklace, a thin black leather choker with a silver canister-like charm. "This success is only for now. Whatever I do on the next movie will decide what happens."

Because of the success of *Sense*—just released on DVD—Night will always be able to make movies for a living. "That," he says, "is a load off of my shoulders." But he is savvy enough to recognize that if *Unbreakable* tanks, he might be considered a one-hit wonder. That would not only be bad for Night. It would be bad for Philadelphia.

WHEN I first met M. Night Shyamalan (pronounced SHAH-ma-lan) for lunch two and a half years ago at the New Deck Tavern on Penn's campus, he was a notch above nobody. He was coming off a miserable directorial debut, *Wide Awake*, and preparing to go into production on *Sense*, a movie that was clearly, in the Hollywood vernacular, not on anyone's radar. I had just left my Los Angeles-based staff-writing job with *Premiere* magazine to work in my hometown. We talked shop: He wanted to know how he could get into the pages of entertainment magazines, and asked what I may have heard about Bruce Willis, the first real star Night would ever direct. I satiated my jones for studio dish by asking about his industry dealings.

Since then, we've periodically hooked up over burgers, usually in Conshohocken, near his home, which is only minutes from the office of his Blinding Edge Pictures. (The Civic Center location is his office only during production.) Obviously, much has changed for Night. *The Sixth Sense* has grossed more than $600 million worldwide. (He now picks up the lunch tabs.) In addition, he cowrote *Stuart Little* and made uncredited script contributions to *She's All That*—both top moneymakers for their respective studios, Columbia/TriStar and Miramax, last year. For writing and directing *Unbreakable*, the 29-year-old is being paid $10 million and a percentage of the profit from ticket sales—the kind of back-end deal reserved for the Hollywood A-plus list.

When I visited him before *Sense* went into production, I listened to his dream of someday having his own postproduction facility not far from his home, so he wouldn't have to go to L.A. or New York to edit his flicks. Figuring he was naively delusional, I informed him Spielberg was one of the very few directors with that kind of setup. Today, there's little doubt that Night will have his own facility. He has met with Will Smith's brother, Harry, about a partnership on the Smiths' development planned for the Avenue of the Arts. And he is also investigating the possibility of leasing more space in his suburban office complex in Conshohocken and setting up there. Seems he, too, is not crazy about Philadelphia's wage tax.

Now, he is an unrestricted free agent calling his own shots. Night recently rejected an offer from Disney that would have paid him an astonishing eight-figure fee, up front, for first and second dibs on all of his projects. He felt such a housekeeping deal was too restrictive.

In the time I've known Night, he has more than fulfilled the prediction he made in his Episcopal Academy High School yearbook that he would conquer Hollywood. But it hasn't been the fairy tale he sometimes makes it out to be, and he hasn't done it entirely his way. Though his success is based on his talent, ambition, and business acumen, he has also endured a series of Pyrrhic victories. A studio forced him to fire a friend and ultimately undermined his directorial debut. On *The Sixth Sense*, he had to overhaul the film's critical last scene and was forced to leave what he considered the best writing he'd ever done on the cutting-room floor.

IN *THE SIXTH SENSE*, Night cast himself as an emergency-room doctor. The cameo was a loving poke at his parents, who had urged him to go to medical school instead of film school. His mom and dad are both doctors, and they wanted Night and his older sister to be physicians, too. But M. (for Manoj, pronounced MAH-no-sh) Night Shyamalan began making movies almost as soon as he could walk.

His parents came to the United States from India in the late 1960s. His father, Nelliate, chose Philadelphia because of the city's rich American history and excellent hospitals. Though his sister attended medical school before finding her calling as a computer consultant, Manoj never contemplated such noncinematic distractions. At age 10, he picked up his father's 8mm camera and began documenting family events at their Penn Valley home. Once Manoj hit his teens, his father bought him a videocassette recorder, and he started writing, directing, and starring in his own productions. He imitated the plots of the *Friday the 13th* installments and got creative with camerawork to shoot James Bond-like spy movies. For one flick, Manoj talked a friend into hanging from the window of his moving car to film the spinning wheels. A Lower Merion cop pulled them over, and the director talked his way out of the ticket.

The summer he turned 16, Manoj spent a few weeks attending a filmmaking program at New York's School of Visual Arts. The course was for college and graduate students only, but he lied about his age on his application and shacked up with an uncle. His parents supported the adventure, hoping it would be the end of his movie hobby.

Just before his senior year at Episcopal Academy, Manoj informed his parents he was applying to NYU's film school. Had he announced he was going to medical school, he knew, his parents would have called everyone and bragged. At his news, though, they didn't call anybody.

Then he changed his name. The idea came when he was applying for American citizenship at age 18. (His parents had traveled back to India specifically so Night could be born in their homeland.) While filling out the paperwork, he saw the opportunity to reinvent himself in the space left for his middle name. He was Indian-American, but he had always felt a spiritual kinship with American Indians. He liked the "simplicity and purity of their beliefs: mother earth, the ground, the stars; there is no negative." "Night," he recalls, "just felt right."

For his senior yearbook picture, Night submitted a mock *Time* magazine cover portrait, with the headline NYU GRAD TAKES HOLLYWOOD BY STORM. Some of his friends may have found his plans and his new name laughable. But that yearbook picture was one of the things his wife, Bhavna, found appealing about him when they met during his freshman year at NYU.

As he was finishing his studies there, Night made a film called *Praying With Anger*, about a young American's spiritual journey to India. The $750,000 picture, funded partly by his parents, was named Debut Film of the Year in 1993 by the American Film Institute, and it enabled the 21-year-old to land an agent. A year later, his first script, *Labor of Love*, about a man's love for his dead wife, sold to 20th Century Fox for $750,000. He wanted to direct the film, but the studio refused, instead giving it to Wolfgang Petersen of *Das Boot* and, more recently, *Air Force One* fame. (*Labor* has not made it into production.)

Thinking he needed a better agent, Night shifted to Peter Benedek at the powerful United Talent Agency. When Night finished his next script, *Wide Awake*, about a young boy's search for God in the wake of his grandfather's death, Benedek sold it to Miramax, which also hired the screenwriter to direct. Night would come to see that day as one of the best and worst of his life.

Night was ecstatic that Miramax had bought *Wide Awake*. The New York-based company, founded by Bob and Harvey Weinstein, had a reputation for discovering and bankrolling the hottest young filmmakers—Quentin Tarantino, Kevin Smith. But Night soon realized why Miramax also has a reputation for being too hands-on and suffocating.

The trouble began when Miramax ordered Night to fire a close friend and work partner, the Indian director of photography who had shot his award-winning student film. Miramax declined to comment for this story, but according to numerous people who worked on *Wide Awake*, after studio executives saw the first few dailies from the production, they demanded that Night get a new D.P.

"Regardless of the things [the D.P.] did wrong or right," Night says, "it was the thing I had laid all of my rep on. I said, I'm gonna bring the new talent in visuals over from India to the U.S.... They lost complete faith in me after that and tried to take over. That killed my relationship with Miramax. Killed it."

Wide Awake made a pitiful $250,000 in the month it was in theatres. Even more heartbreaking to Night, the critics hated it. Stephen Holden of the *New York*

Times considered the film overly sentimental and self-indulgent: "*Wide Awake* imagines it's a seriocomic 'coming of age' film radiating waves of healing sweetness and light. But beneath its suffocating, smug sentimentality, you have to look hard to uncover a single moment of truth and genuine feeling." The flop rocked Night's confidence. He slipped into a second-guessing slump, obsessing: How could he have made a film with intelligence and care, yet have that somehow escape everybody? He decided not to direct for a while. His plan was to disappear until the few people who actually saw *Wide Awake* forgot about it.

He concentrated on screenwriting. First, he cowrote *Stuart Little*—a screen adaptation of E.B. White's novel about a mouse adopted by a human family. It was because of his draft that the studio decided to green-light the film—a boost his ego badly needed. He finished off his commitment to Miramax by taking a pass at the *She's All That* screenplay, an ugly-duckling-turned-Cinderella comedy. And finally, he finished *The Sixth Sense*.

In the aftermath of *Wide Awake*, Night concluded the film failed because it had been too religious, and, as he says, "Those kinds of movies are the last thing people want to see." Though the mystic deities of his parents' Hinduism, the Trinity he studied in Catholic grade school and the Native American gods he admired continued to rattle around in his head like chain-wielding ghosts, Night struggled to keep the spirit world of *The Sixth Sense* a suspenseful subtext. This time, he was much more conscious of what a studio would need to market his story about Cole, a young boy haunted by ghosts, and Malcolm Crowe, the child psychiatrist who helps him.

By fall 1997, he was ready to come back. "I won't take less than $1.5 million," he told Benedek when he gave him the *Sense* script to sell. Night also insisted on *directing* the film—and directing it in Philadelphia. If the agent thought Night was crazy, he kept his opinion to himself.

On September 7th, Benedek sent the draft to a few high-profile producers, giving them 24 hours to make offers. Night and his wife were in L.A. at the time. He was changing their baby's diaper when he got the call informing him that New Line had bid first, at $1.5 million. He immediately rejected the bid and went on with the baby's changing, thinking that if one studio would offer so much so quickly, better bids would probably come. A half hour later, Disney offered $2 million. Pass. Disney then came back with $3 million and agreed—no strings attached—to all of Night's demands. The bidding war lasted only six hours.

After a director produces a flop, the Town usually waits until he or she has gone through several bottles of Xanax before offering a chance at redemption. First-time directors who bomb, however, may as well look for work as video-store clerks. So how did a 20-something with one good student film and a low-budget dud on his resume get the Almighty Mouse House to give him everything he wanted?

"I totally understand the power of what's on the page," Night explains. "In *The Sixth Sense*, they saw that I understand storytelling and characters. They gained a certain confidence with that, and they said, Oh, he already directed two movies, maybe this is the moment. If I was just a director, I would have never gotten material [like *Sense*]. I would have been doing *Home Alone* V, and maybe 10 years from now, I'd make a decent movie like *My Cousin Vinny* and then escalate slowly."

Joe Roth, the former chairman of Walt Disney Studios who green-lit the *Sense* deal, agrees. "I had seen *Wide Awake*," he says. "We acquired *Sixth* based on the script. It was his gift as a screenwriter. I had a feeling that this was somebody who was going to be around for a long time. I've only felt that way a few times before, like with a 26-year-old Chris Columbus [*Home Alone*] or John Hughes [*The Breakfast Club*]."

Even before he had put pen to paper on *Sense*, Night was telling people the script would sell for more than $2 million and Willis would star. Amazingly, Willis did fall in love with the story, but he had reservations about working with Night as a director. "It went all the way to the point," says Roth, "where someone [on Willis's side] said, 'There is no way Bruce will work with this director.' At that point, it would have been insane of me to say that I was as confident in Night as a director as I was of him as a screenwriter. But I was confident in him, period. All I may have said to Bruce's people is, 'Well, you're gonna miss out.'"

It didn't hurt that Willis owed Roth three pictures. About a year earlier, the temperamental actor had fired a director, a producer and a cinematographer from *Broadway Brawler*, a multimillion-dollar production that eventually collapsed under the weight of his demands. Roth cleaned up the mess, paying some $17 million to make everyone go away. In exchange, he got a three-picture commitment from Willis. *Sense* fulfilled one-third of the payback.

ON SEPTEMBER 25, 1998, Night was wrapping up the first week of production on the movie that would make his career and break his heart. The pressure was immense.

"You've got to understand," says Frank Marshall, one of *Sense*'s producers, who has worked on blockbusters like *E.T.* and *Raiders of the Lost Ark*. "Night was 28 years old, standing out there with Tak Fujimoto [probably the best cinematographer in the world], 200 extras, on a Disney picture, and we had just shot an emotional scene that wasn't easy on anyone."

That afternoon, fall was enveloping Boathouse Row; vibrant oranges, reds, and yellows were everywhere. It was a perfect setting for the wedding speech the crew had just shot. In the scene, Willis's Malcolm Crowe is a new bridegroom professing his love for his wife. He is slightly tipsy, slipping into a *Cat in the Hat* speech pattern. Standing on a boathouse deck, framed by the sun-reflecting Schuylkill River, Willis uttered the lines Night treasured most in his script, ending with, "Anna, I am in love, in love I am."

Night had demanded several takes. But he thought that the payoff was worth it. Then a production assistant wearing a walkie-talkie headset and an expression of urgency ran up and said, "Bruce would like to see you in his trailer." According to Marshall, the young director started "shaking in his boots." Perhaps, Night worried,

Willis didn't share his sunny perspective on the day's shoot. He turned to Marshall for advice. "You're the director," Marshall said. "Just go down and talk to him."

When Night stepped into the star's trailer, Willis hugged the awestruck director and said, "I just want to tell you that you are doing a helluva job. This week has been one of the best acting experiences of my life. This is going to be a great film." That moment, according to Marshall, was a turning point for Night and for the production. But it wasn't *the* turning point.

Thirty-nine days after cameras started rolling, the picture wrapped. Disney began test-screening four months later. The results were almost as scary as the dead people who inhabit *The Sixth Sense*. As scripted, the audience and Crowe together learn why he has difficulty connecting with his wife yet is able to help Cole: Crowe himself is deceased. But the screening audiences didn't get it. Or, if they did, they didn't like it.

In Night's original version of the film—the director's cut—the revelation is as follows: The camera begins with a two-shot of Crowe finding his wife, Anna, asleep in a living room chair. Camera pans to Anna, who in her sleep asks her husband, "Why did you leave me?" She then drops her husband's wedding ring. Camera pans back to where Crowe was standing moments ago, revealing that he is gone, and their home, which has been dark and cold throughout the movie, is now bright and warm. Camera pans to and squeezes in on the television playing a videotape of Crowe's wedding-day speech, ending with Night's precious Dr. Suess-like lines. Fade to black.

The problem editorially was twofold, according to *Sense*'s Oscar-nominated editor and second-unit director, Andrew Mondshein: "One: When is the actual moment of revelation? When does the audience realize he is dead? And two: Once viewers realized he was dead, they were taking themselves out of the movie by going back to figure out how, if he was dead throughout the film, he was able to do the things he did."

More upsetting for Night, the screening scorecards indicated audiences didn't like the wedding speech he felt was "beautiful poetry." "The feeling was the movie ended on too sad of a note for a guy who can't be with his wife anymore," he recalls. "Which isn't what you're supposed to feel. You're supposed to feel that they're better off." As far as Night is concerned, emotional scenes like those final critical moments in *The Sixth Sense* are tricky "because that's when you say to the audience: Are you with me? Are you absolutely with me? Are you perfectly in sync with me? If they're not with you, they're just watching you flail away." According to the audience, he was flailing: "It was sad, man, really sad." Shell-shocked and no doubt experiencing a bit of *Wide Awake* déjà-vu, Night took a few days off. Then he started modifying his masterpiece.

In the editing room, Night added a voiceover. After the sleep-talking Anna asks Crowe why he left her, young patient Cole is heard saying, "Sometimes they don't even know they're dead." He cut back to a horrified Willis, then slipped in a brief spate of flashbacks, allowing the audience time to absorb the realization and test it against the previous two hours' worth of story. Finally, once Night resigned himself to cutting the wedding scene, he added a scene after the flash-backs in which Willis and his wife have time to say goodbye.

"The idea that Crowe was a ghost and reveals it at the end was always Night's brilliant creation," Mondshein says. The challenge, Night explains, was how to "tweak things so that the ending honored the two hours previous. How can you make that moment a surprise?"

Still believing in the power of his original ending, Night included the director's cut on the *Sixth Sense* DVD, just released by Buena Vista Home Entertainment.

The plot of Night's latest film, *Unbreakable*, is top secret, though I did manage to get a draft of the script. Willis plays David Dunne, a Philadelphia security guard who catches a train after a New York job interview and becomes the sole survivor of a massive rail wreck. Samuel L. Jackson plays Elijah Price, a comic-book junkie who helps Dunne understand why he survived; Robin Wright Penn is Dunne's wife, Megan. Once again, the final moments of the film contain a plot-rocking rev-elation. A Night insider worries that the structure is too similar to *Sixth Sense*, that Night may be going to the well once too often. The box office will tell.

"Each film is about where I was in my life," Night says. "*Praying with Anger* was about finding identity. *Wide Awake*, a search for faith. *Sixth Sense* is about manag-ing a career and a family. *Unbreakable* is, what is your potential?"

IT IS A Friday afternoon, two weeks after *Sixth Sense* received its six Oscar nom-inations, including Best Picture, Best Director, and Best Original Screenplay, and Night's potential has never seemed so limitless. I ask him, "Are *you* unbreakable?"

"*That* is the question," he says.

The walls of his office are covered with storyboards, hundreds of tiny pencil illustrations of *Unbreakable* scenes. For me, they are a tease. In one, Dunne is wear-ing a poncho and fighting a monster of a man; in another, a child points a gun at him. For Night, the storyboards are a constant reminder that the final draft of his script is due at Disney in one week.

At the moment, however, Night is brain-storming a different project. "How about something with midgets? A midget love story?" he asks the handful of us gathered in his office for a photo shoot. The photographer proposed that Night act as though he is pitching his next big hit, and the director, knowing how important authenticity is to the camera, has jumped into his role, talking and scribbling furi-ously. "Think of all the money we would save," Night's assistant and trusted friend Jose Rodriguez fires back. "We'd cut our budget in half. Food services, half; ward-robe, half." Night met Jose, a soft-spoken, freckle-faced 36-year-old, in a karate class 5 years ago. *Wide Awake* was then about to start production, and Night needed an assistant, a confidant who could help him karate-chop Hollywood. Jose left his job as a customer service supervisor with Bell Atlantic Business Systems, and the two have been inseparable ever since.

I mention to Night that a colleague recently sold an *Esquire* story about dwarfs in love to Hollywood for a potential movie. "You're behind the curve," I tell him.

He laughs and without pause begins developing another "concept," the entertaining star of his own show. The photo shoot he regarded as a nuisance in his hectic schedule has become a welcomed distraction. Across the top of a yellow legal pad, he jots, "All work and no play…" Then, "Journal entry #1: We've been trapped on this planet for two weeks now. Journal entry #2: The natives are very friendly. They have asked us over for a ceremonial meal tonight. Journal entry #3: They're savages. They want to eat me."

The impromptu script outline could be a glimpse into how Night feels about his calendar packed with ceremonial dinners as Hollywood sinks its teeth into him. His phones ring incessantly; every so often, Jose pops in to make a report: Versace, Hugo Boss, and Zegna are calling, wanting to provide his Academy Award wardrobe. Tom Hanks and "S.S."—that's Steven Spielberg—have called, "again," to schedule meetings with him. Oh, and there's that offer from Bill Mechanic. The chairman and CEO of Twentieth Century Fox called to tell Night that if he wants to direct *Labor of Love*, it's all his.

"Journal Entry #4: They've eaten my left leg and my right index finger. As long as they don't take my elbows." Night is concerned the media will devour his privacy. Make a hit movie, and the press can't get enough of you. As I've been talking with Night, an *Esquire* writer is trailing him around the country; in the coming weeks, *Entertainment Weekly* and the *New York Times* will cover him in the pre-Oscar hoopla. For now, the attention is, he says, "definitely cool. But I know inevitably it could be bad. What if I make a bad movie?"

Or what if those aspects of his life he wants to keep private should appear in print? Night is extremely protective of his family; fan mail that so much as mentions his children's names worries him. "It's not necessary to know certain things about me," he says. "I'm a storyteller."

I can't help but think of what Roth told me days ago: "He definitely wants it all. He wants his privacy, and he wants his fame. Is he naive about that? Probably."

Promptly at 6 P.M., with elbows and privacy intact—for now—Night picks up his shoulder bag, adjusts the thin leather choker with the silver charm, and tells his assistant he'll take care of the loose ends in the morning. He hops into his green Land Rover, headed for what he considers his most important appointment of the day—dinner at home with the in-laws. He already called to let his wife know he'd be a little late.

As Night merges with the Schuylkill traffic just west of 30th Street Station, my cab is behind his Rover, and I see him once again finger his necklace, almost as though making sure it's still there. Before we said goodbye, I asked him about the charm. He lowered his head and smiled, and with his hand covering the silver piece explained: "It is a gift." His father brought the necklace back from a priest in India after the release of *The Sixth Sense*. The silver charm is actually a tiny repository; inside are scrolls with Sanskrit sayings about keeping up your guard, staying grounded—and not dwelling on your last slam dunk.

By Larry Platt
August 2001

VERNON THE BARBARIAN

hey're shimmying into the Tweeter Center arena now, 5,000 strong, drinks in hand, silver New Year's hats emblazoned with WOW! atop their heads, while the piped-in music blares custom-made lyrics to the tune of Lou Bega's "Mambo No. 5":

A little bit of Monica on the phone
Helping out a customer who's at home
A little bit of David at his desk
Making every customer feel their best...
A little bit of Commerce Bank here and now
Is just enough to make you feel that WOW!

They wear their team color, red, as they boogie in and are met by a dancing red C, or, more accurately, a Ritalin-deprived guy in a giant red C costume. Some of them bump and grind with the big red C; others launch copious amounts of Silly String all over their colleagues; still others punch a huge beach ball. One group comes in carrying a sign reading SHORE RULES #1! The contingent from North Jersey enters chanting: "*We want the cup! We want the cup!*"

These are bankers. "That's where you're wrong," says their leader, red-jacketed Commerce Bank founder and CEO Vernon Hill II, his voice barely audible above the din. "They're not bankers. They're *retailers*. And my job is to convince them we're on a mission from God."

These are Commerce Bank's annual WOW! Awards—the South Jersey bank's version of the Academy Awards. It's a night of open bar, elaborate spreads of food, a giant WOW ice sculpture, and, inside the arena, a raucous awards ceremony complete with spotlights and bad jokes from presenters. Tonight, instead of Oscars, winners of categories like "Best Part-Time Teller" will take home red C statuettes, and one of the company's divisions—either North Jersey or Central Jersey or the Shore or Commerce Insurance—will win the award for having Commerce's most spirited employees.

Vernon Hill is introduced as "that Master WOW-er himself, our chairman," and rousing applause drowns out his name. You expect the cheering throng to start waving lighters as Hill stiffly takes the stage. In truth, though, there is little that is WOW about him; he's a slender, bespectacled man of 55 with thinning, matted hair and a slight stutter. He has a gruff—some say rude—demeanor; he answers his phone by barking "You called me" into the receiver. A self-described "doer," he's the kind of boss who's more inclined to shoot off orders than offer pats on the back. As tonight's ceremony wears on, he'll grow increasingly impatient during each winner's jubilant, spotlighted walk down the aisle. When Cleo Morrison wins for Best Retail Support, Hill bellows into the microphone: "If you're not here in one minute, I take the award back!" When Boots Zurbano, winner of Best Full-Time Teller, isn't quite quick enough to the stage, Hill barks, "C'mon, folks! It's getting dark outside! Let's go!"

And yet they cheer, for he is their leader. He boldly announces his latest stratagem: "Most of you know that each year, we go and save another part of America that's not served by Commerce," he says, in a clipped cadence that serves to fire up his audience. "And Manhattan is our next stop, and the poor underbanked, overcharged people of Manhattan need to be saved by Commerce!"

The audience jumps up with a roar, stomping and screaming, a spontaneous eruption reminiscent of the frenzy on the floor of political conventions after a killer applause line. Hill, who likes to call himself banking's Genghis Khan and who hands out to visitors at his office a book titled *Leadership Secrets of Attila the Hun*, breaks into a wicked, thin-lipped smile as he looks down upon his flock. He's basking in the adulation, but he's also surveying his troops.

THE DIFFERENCE between Vernon Hill and the rest of us, he will tell you, is that he wakes up and decides to do things. One day last year, Hill woke up and decided to build a mansion—"Villa Collina"—in Moorestown that is, at 45,854 square feet, bigger than Bill Gates's home, and almost the size of the White House; it features a marble fountain in the foyer, a two-story atrium-windowed living room, an exercise room bigger than most health clubs, 14 built-in televisions (some wall-sized), 94 doors, and 131 windows. It is under construction now, and it will be a reality this fall because he made it one.

One day 15 years ago, Hill woke up after suffering a lengthy tee-time delay at Atlantic City's prestigious Seaview Country Club and decided to build his own state-of-the-art golf course. Seven years and $15 million later, he produced Galloway National Golf Club in Galloway Township, which is consistently ranked among the nation's best courses. It is also one of the key perks Hill uses to entice prominent business leaders to bring their deposits to Commerce.

One day 28 years ago, Vernon Hill, then 27, woke up and decided to start a bank. It has succeeded beyond anyone's expectations—including his own. In a struggling industry known for widespread consolidation (quick, what is it to-day—CoreStates, First Union or Wachovia?), Cherry Hill-based Commerce is the nation's fastest-growing bank: 30 new branches and 1,500 new employees each year, earnings up by 16 percent (seven percentage points ahead of the industry average), and a stock that has risen a remarkable 278 percent over the past 5 years (more than double the industry average). At a time when few of this region's companies go national—least of all banks—Hill has devised a model that he hopes will take the country by storm. "Commerce is like the Mongolian horde coming across the plains, threatening the Roman Empire," says Brock Vandervliet, the Lehman Brothers analyst who first dubbed Hill "Genghis Khan." "In this case, the Roman Empire is the larger, established banks that still don't fully recognize the threat posed by Commerce."

The vision heralded by Vandervliet starts with the figure Hill is proudest of: his bank's stockpile of deposits, driven mainly by consumer checking and savings accounts—the retail side of banking. Between 1995 and last year, Commerce doubled those assets to $5.6 billion. In the past year, that figure has jumped to $9 billion. Hill's goal—which most analysts consider attainable—is to reach $25 billion within the next 5 years.

It all starts with a simple yet revolutionary idea. Most banks subscribe to something called the 80/20 rule, the theory that 80 percent of their revenue is generated by the top 20 percent of their customer base. So they saddle nonrevenue customers with fees or inattentive service, focusing on the commercial side, viewing their retail operation—the branches—as a necessary evil and the first to be crunched come cost-cutting time. Hill, who also owns 41 Burger Kings, primarily in Montgomery and Bucks counties, has radically deviated from the conventional wisdom, applying fast-food retail theories to the staid world of banking. He knew from the fast-food world that it's the fries and Cokes that are truly profitable, while hamburgers are a break-even proposition. Applying the 80/20 rule at BK would mean mistreating anyone who orders just a burger. "It's ridiculous on its face," he says, leaning in closely to share a guarded secret over lunch at TGI Friday's (a chain, of course). "The truth is, bankers aren't very smart. The ones that have followed the 80/20 rule have had the worst results. You don't have to look any further than First Union, where they've been hemorrhaging customers because of inattentive service." ("It's common to attack us for what was happening over 2 years ago," says First Union spokesman Don Vecchiarello. "Since then, our service scores have increased in every quarter, and our customer complaints to federal regulatory agencies are down 500 percent.")

Hill has been called America's McBanker. The red C logo is his version of McDonald's golden arches, an easily identified extension of the brand. Six years ago, inspired by McDonald's Hamburger University and Disney's Disney U., he invested more than $20 million—while other banks were cutting back on employee-training programs—to start Commerce University, which has its main campus less than a mile from Commerce's Cherry Hill headquarters. It's an indoctrination program masquerading as employee training, where the curriculum teaches the customer-service culture of Commerce while deprogramming incoming branch managers who have worked for other banks. In a class called "Traditions," students practice their phone greetings while peers grade them on their cheerfulness. The university dean is Debi Jacovelli, who started at Commerce as a clerk 20 years ago, after working at a McDonald's drive-thru while she was in college. Hill liked her zest for Commerce culture, and when he asked her to head up the university, she agreed, she says, "for the good of the Order," sounding every bit the cult member she proudly claims to be. "That's a phrase you hear a lot of around here," she adds.

"I think when people deal in the retail business, often the product is secondary," Hill says. "Have you ever flown Southwest Airlines? It's owned by Herb Kelleher, who is from Haddon Heights. Here's a guy with the lowest-cost carrier, in the crappiest planes, with no food, yet he's created this culture about how great this experience is. He's turned a low-price experience into a fun experience. Or Starbucks. These guys are getting $7 for a cup of coffee. Yet they've got 'em waiting in line."

Hill's outrageous and radical notion is that people will do business with a bank if they *like* coming to it. Commerce calls itself "America's most convenient bank," and everything is tailored toward pleasing the seven million customers who use the bank's 150 branches each month. Commerce offers legitimately free checking (First Union has about 10 different checking accounts with differing fees), free money orders, and Hill's no-float rule, whereby deposits clear instantaneously. "Every check in America can clear in one day," Hill says. "When a bank tells you it'll take three business days to clear, it's a bullshit gimmick to make money." All Commerce branches share the same retail-like hours: weekday teller service from 7:30 a.m. to 8 p.m., plus hours on Saturdays and Sundays. Competing banks thought Hill was crazy—why take on such burdensome overhead? "You don't have to think about what time a Home Depot, a McDonald's or a Starbucks is open," Hill says. "They're open. You just go. My theory was, if you advertise that you're open on Sunday, the consumer will automatically believe you're open all the time. That message is more important than the savings. It says, 'We're always there for you.'"

While other banks try to cost-cut their way to prosperity, Hill spends and spends and spends. He throws a three-day Christmas bash—a carnival, really—for customers, employees, and their families. He gives away Commerce's next battleground.

Slackman briefs Hill on his latest intelligence operations. He has been "shopping the competition"—walking into Chase and Citibank branches and gauging the quality of customer service by asking for, say, a small business loan application. He regales Hill with tales of the dumbfounded looks he receives, of flustered customer service reps scurrying off to find the manager, unsure where the form is or if it even exists. He tells Hill of the Chase branch right near their forthcoming 6th Avenue site where there is nowhere to sit while you open an account and where he stood for 20 minutes before someone reluctantly asked if he could be helped. "I'm too lucky," responds Hill, gazing out the window. It's only four o'clock on a weekday, but as he cruises past a Chase branch, Hill notices that it's closed. "This is the city that never sleeps," he says. "Except for the banks."

Slackman points out an HSBC branch—Hong Kong Shanghai Bank—and observes, "Ninety-seven percent of their customers don't know it's a Hong Kong bank. They try and keep that a secret." Hill mulls this over. "How about this for an ad?" he says finally. "'Do You Really Want Your Money Going to Red China?'"

They ponder the in-your-face idea. A longtime admirer of Commerce's renegade style, Slackman, at 53, jumped over from New York's Atlantic Bank last March, after concluding that the Commerce way can't be copied; since it's all about culture, an existing bank would have to start from scratch to do it right. (This is why Hill won't acquire other banks; it would taint his pool of true believers.) "Would an ad like that work here, on the Upper West Side?" Slackman asks.

"Oh, right," Hill says. "The liberals up here would *want* their money going to Red China."

Both men point excitedly each time they see a woman pushing a baby carriage. They call the Upper East and West sides "vertical suburbia," viewing the residents as kin to their customers in the South Jersey 'burbs and along the Main Line. Hill instructs the driver to stop at various locations he's considering and snaps photos with a digital camera he retrieves from the trunk, so he'll remember each site.

"Site selection is an art, not a science," Hill says, clicking away at an Upper East Side corner property. One of his side businesses is Mt. Laurel's Site Development, Inc., a company he started in the late 1960s, before founding the bank. Site Development handles the all-important first step for any retail operation: For a fee, it finds a site and works out all the related zoning and traffic issues. Way back in 1969, Hill's first client was McDonald's; he'd drive Ray Kroc around South Jersey in search of locations. Today, Site Development has a staff of 19 and acts as a broker for most of Commerce's branches, so Hill is in the unusual position of profiting as a Commerce contractor, in addition to his CEO role. (Last year, Site Development, Inc., was paid $1.1 million by Commerce.) Hill argues that this allows him to make sure the all-important site selection process is done right.

Even before those car rides with Ray Kroc, Hill had an affinity for fast-food retail. He still recalls his excitement 45 years ago, when he was a 10-year-old growing up in Northern Virginia and his father took him to McDonald's for the first time. Other kids were enthralled by the big arches, the clown mascot, the junk food. Not Vernon: "I can still remember wondering, how the hell can you make money selling hamburgers for 15 cents apiece?" he says. "I mean, I just couldn't get over that. Still can't, really."

His father, Vernon Hill Sr., was a successful real estate broker with 14 offices who had this advice for his son: "Never work for anybody but yourself." In the mid-1960s, Hill attended early morning classes at Wharton and then worked from 11 a.m. to 6 p.m. at Haddon Township's First People's Bank, a local bank started by Bill Rohrer in 1959. Rohrer was a Chevy dealer, and Hill watched as his boss's car-dealer mentality informed his running of the bank. First People's stayed open late, and focused on gathering deposits. Meantime, as much of South Jersey began to morph into strip malls, Rohrer had Hill make loans to franchises such as 7-Eleven, Wawa and, of course, McDonald's.

It was this experience that led directly to Hill's creation of Commerce Bank. "A lot of us knew Vernon from being involved in real estate at that time," recalls 70-year-old Morton Kerr, chairman of the board of Markeim-Chalmers, Inc., a real estate firm, and one of the original Commerce board members. "He was a 26-year-old kid who called about 15 of us to a meeting in his office on Haddon Avenue in Haddonfield. I'll never forget it. He said, 'We're going to start a bank.' And he said we'd each have to put up between $250,000 and $500,000. This was 1973—who had that kind of money? But he'd arranged for all of us to borrow it. If you could put up $100,000, he got us loans for $400,000. Only seven of us didn't get up and walk out, but we still thought he was crazy. We thought it would be a half-assed thing, but what the hell? We were young, and it would be glamorous to say we owned a bank."

Hill put up about 10 percent of the $1.5 million he raised. Commerce was born in a one-room office, with nine employees, on Route 70 in Marlton. If you had invested $10,000 with Hill back then, it would be worth $2 million today. An original flyer of $100,000 would now yield $20 million. "Did we think this would happen?" asks Kerr, sounding as if, all these years later, he still can't quite believe it. "Are you kidding me?"

"**WAIT A** minute," says Vernon Hill, interrupting an employee during one of his monthly senior staff meetings. He has just spotted someone who works for him taking notes—with a CoreStates pen. "Can I see that pen?"

All eyes are fixed on the pen as it passes to him; all eyes stay glued to the CEO as he methodically disassembles the pen and, holding its parts, stands and walks to the corner of the conference room, where he deposits them in a trash can. Without saying a word, he sits down again and reaches into his breast pocket, removing a Commerce pen and holding it out to the aide next to him, who dutifully passes it down to the red-faced employee. "That guy, uh, is no longer with us," says Glenn Holck, president of Commerce's Pennsylvania operation, chuckling as he recounts the incident.

When Holck was at CoreStates, he sat in meetings every day. To Hill, meetings are where you talk about the work you're going to do instead of actually doing it. So senior staff meetings at Commerce are limited to the third Wednesday of every month, and the agenda is always the same: Each market—Holck, representing Pennsylvania, is one—reports on its performance in three areas: deposits, fees, and loans.

The reports are easy because Hill has invested in a state-of-the-art computer system that allows every Commerce employee to hit a key and check how each branch is doing every single day in all three areas, then compare that performance to its month-end goals. "At CoreStates, if somebody asked how your business was doing, you'd say 'Okay,' and no one—including you—knew if that was true," says Holck. "Here, everybody knows. And they know Mr. Hill is checking the numbers."

He's also checking the e-mail updates that every manager is required to send him every Monday by noon. Holck once made the mistake of skipping a Monday; the following Monday, just hours after he'd sent the update, his phone rang. As usual, Hill offered no greeting. "Perhaps I should just pay you for every other week," he said—before hanging up.

Good soldiers like Holck insist that Hill's hectoring is simply a form of mentoring. But it is certainly the stuff of legend at Commerce. Hill still conducts the year-end job reviews of his senior managers—an appointment few anticipate eagerly. "How'd your department do this year?" he'll ask. If the answer gets past two sentences, he'll bark: "*Too many words*! Let's try again: How'd you do?"

"You have to learn how to talk to Mr. Hill," says Commerce University dean Debi Jacovelli. "I have a tendency to ramble, so he'll blurt out, 'Will you just shut up and listen?' It's forced me to get to the point much quicker."

Like Attila, Hill is known to leave bodies in his wake, particularly on the loan side, where his lenders either sink or swim. Loan officers who fail to meet agreed-upon goals—say, $20 million in new business—tend to disappear mysteriously, like dissidents in Third World republics. There's even an office catchphrase for the phenomenon: DDTB, as in Don't Drag The Bodies. "If you're talking about someone who is behind plan, all you have to say is 'DDTB,' and it's understood what's happening," says Holck. "You don't need to say anything else."

Commerce loyalists like Holck and Jacovelli characterize Hill's style as eccentric and quirky, but others see his warrior mentality as representative of something darker. He is a man who demands that his branch managers smile constantly and that his drive-in tellers hand out doggie biscuits to customers with canines in the car, but he rarely practices what he preaches. He walks the halls grunting greetings to staffers—if he says hello at all. Even on the Galloway golf course, where Hill is an 11 handicap, his demeanor hardly smacks of the common touch: No one is allowed to play the hole behind him or the three holes ahead of him.

More important, Hill doesn't seem to have the same zeal for customer service when it comes to making loans. He personally approves every loan in excess of

$5 million, which has resulted in some embarrassing last-minute about-faces for Commerce. One businessman received a call from the bank saying it couldn't meet the terms proffered by its own term sheet—because, the businessman presumed, Hill had crunched the numbers and changed his mind. Another businessman says he discovered at closing that Commerce's interest rate had suddenly changed, and fees had been added: "It's a classic bait and switch," he fumed. (A former Commerce loan officer and fan of Hill's confirms that these weren't isolated incidents—that Hill's last-minute dictums often force his people to go back to borrowers and rework agreed-upon terms.) "Most CEOs of a bank our size don't get involved in loan approval," says Hill, making no apology. "But I've got a good bullshit detector. If a deal doesn't smell right, I step in—often late in the process."

As Hill's ostentatious home, "Villa Collina," nears completion—all he'll say about it is, "That's my wife's project"—some critics take issue with his compensation. Last year, he earned roughly $1.2 million in salary, bonus and perks, and exercised $856,858 in stock options; he holds some $33 million in unexercised options. Then there are the fees taken in by his Site Development Corporation, and the $3.6 million for branch and office decorating and design that was paid to Interarch, the Mt. Laurel interior design and architectural firm owned by Shirley Hill, Vernon's wife. When word spreads that Mrs. Hill is on her way to the Cherry Hill headquarters, employees routinely rush to pull up the window shades in their offices, knowing of her fondness for natural sunlight. Hill laughingly boasts that when he assigned Shirley the job of designing Commerce's Philadelphia offices, on Market Street, he "gave her an unlimited budget—and she exceeded it."

Vernon Hill makes no bones about the fact that he is well paid—or that he loves to spend. In that sense, he's the antithesis of once-hyped Albert Dunlap, the cost-cutting CEO who dismantled Scott Paper here before selling it and moving on to Sunbeam. "What a horse's ass," Hill says of Dunlap, whom he sees as someone who tears down, in contrast to his own pro-growth agenda. Thus far, there have been few if any complaints from the board or anyone else about Hill's spending—presumably because the bank has been doing so spectacularly well. Might that change if the stock drops? Possibly. But it seems unlikely, unless, as his competitors are hoping, the invasion of New York turns out to be Hill's Waterloo. He is guarding against that possibility by launching a measured rollout, beginning with the two branches next month. "There's an unstoppable nature to the Commerce strategy," says Lehman analyst Vandervliet. "They won't take no for an answer. They are going to have their way with the market."

VERNON HILL is in the back seat of the car, checking his e-mail on a handheld BlackBerry, the portable personal organizer that makes the PalmPilot seem Jurassic. Hill, of course, has provided BlackBerrys to everyone in his company who needs one. "You know what's giving me agita now? It's not the New York rents," David Slackman says from the front passenger seat, looking back at his boss. "And

I'm not worried about growing the deposits. My issue is getting good branch managers. A lot of the people I'm meeting, they're fat, dumb, and happy."

"Of course," Hill says. "At a lot of these 100-year-old New York branches, you can just retire while you continue working, and nobody bothers you. We're better off gambling with the second or third level down, taking an assistant manager as a branch manager."

"But that's what I'm saying," Slackman says. "A lot of the assistant managers are terrible here. I talked to a 60-year-old career assistant manager at Citibank—"

"What does he make?"

"Sixty thousand dollars. And he says, Oh, I'm too old to leave and head up a branch, I'm going to retire soon." Slackman shakes his head. "He's not looking to be challenged. I left that meeting and turned to whomever I was with and said, That guy's a loser. Scratch him from the list."

Vernon Hill breaks into that wide, thin-lipped smile. "Hey, what do the kids say?" he asks as he raises his right hand, clenched in a fist but for his L-shaped index finger and thumb, and puts it to his forehead: "Loooserrrr!"

Slackman laughs, and now he joins in, putting his L to his forehead and moaning, "Loooserrrr!"

As Vernon Hill sees it, the world is divided into winners and losers. And like his role models Attila and Genghis, he is determined to be in the first group, and to throw a whole lot of people—in this case, sleek-suited, genteel bankers—into the other. As the car arrives at the heliport pad, Vernon Hill is checking Commerce stock on the BlackBerry, but he's still chortling like a mischievous teen, laughing and coughing out "Loooserrrr" again and again.

SMARTY JONES

Thoroughbred, 3, Bensalem

The better horse won. I can live with that. Props to Birdstone. Some people say he was doping, of course, but that's just speculation. Nice horse.

Philadelphia needs to get over the whole "symbol of civic pride" thing. Newsflash: I'm a horse.

Listen. Seabiscuit still couldn't carry my jock.

You know he was gay, right?

No, my grandfather wasn't Jewish. Who told you that?

Hay I like. Grass never did much for me.

To us, it's just taking a leak, you understand?

The first time Jay-Z called, I hung up on him. He was all, "You the shiz-nit." But it's cool. We're in the studio now, laying down final tracks. It's off the chain.

Do I know pain? You ever have a goddamn plate nailed onto your foot?

This is what it's like: You're rounding the bend at Pimlico, and the blinders are flipping and flapping but you can still see a little silver, and up ahead the finish line's coming at you. You're in the *zone*, man. There's, like, a hundred cc's of pharmaceutical-grade shit running through your veins, and … um, I don't think I'm supposed to talk about this.

I knew about the drinking. What he does after he dismounts isn't my affair. He never rode me drunk, I'll tell you that.

I can't prove Seabiscuit was gay, but look how he trotted.

That Ricky Martin stuff is a load of crap. We're just friends.

People are always like, "What's with horse names?" Well, guess what: To a horse, human names sound silly.

My father's name was on the money. Elusive Quality. He ran like the wind and never really said much.

When my mom was a filly, she was a piece of ass. The studs all wanted to get with her. So then she hooks up with my dad, and everyone's like, "She could have done better." Well, um, somebody who won the Derby *and* the Preakness thinks she did just fine.

We say "hung like a black guy."

My owner sells cars for a living. Can you imagine having to do that your whole life?

Don't tell Smarty Jones you've always loved him. Smarty Jones knows you never heard of him before he made the cover of *Sports Illustrated*. But that's okay. Smarty can handle it.

Most of the time the fans are great. I only get pissed if someone comes up to me when I'm trying to eat. That's just tiresome. It's like, hello-o? Manners?

Those quotes about Asians were taken out of context. I've got nothing against them. Nice people. But Don Rickles had a point. They do burn a lot of shirts.

I don't go in for any of that Great Paddock in the Sky nonsense.

When it's over, it's over. Jell-O. Glue. Short ribs. It's all the same to me.

I suppose it's possible Seabiscuit was only a metrosexual. But Secretariat: He was a little light in his horseshoes, if you catch my meaning. That's not even up for debate. Everyone knows that.

By Benjamin Wallace
June 2001

THE PRODIGY AND THE PLAYMATE

an and hungerless from fatigue and mono, Mark Yagalla picks at his lunch and tells some more lies. The woman sitting across from him is old enough to be his mother. She has entrusted this mild-mannered young investment manager with most of her life's savings—$4 million—so he certainly can't tell her about the pressure, the debts, the insomnia he can't escape.

Instead, as the trusted boy and the trusting woman sit through lunch at an Italian restaurant in Edison, New Jersey, he unspools yard after yard of fabrications about how much money he's making for her and the 109 other investors who've enlisted his services. He talks about his shaky health. And then, inevitably, he starts in on the subject closest to his heart—his girlfriend—which is appropriate, since she's what Mark Yagalla has been spending Mrs. Kalko's money on.

It is for Sandy Bentley, the beautiful and semi-famous concubine of Hugh Hefner, that Yagalla has been writing checks and financing vacations and buying furs and jewelry and cars and houses. He talks about marrying her. He daydreams aloud about bringing her to his 10th high-school reunion and parading her in front of all the classmates who used to make fun of him.

214 PART THREE

And then, as if on cue, Sandy calls his cell phone. Yagalla cradles the Nokia and breaks the news that he has mono. They'll have to cancel their planned weekend in a $6500-a-night bungalow at the Westin Hapuna Beach Prince Hotel on Hawaii's Big Island. He listens quietly. "We'll get out of this," he tells Sandy. And he asks her to come to Delaware to take care of him. Martha Kalko, watching from across the table, sees the look of disappointment cross his face.

"She's taking you for a ride, Mark," she says. But by now, Martha Kalko is more concerned that she has entrusted this kid with millions of dollars. *We'll get out of this*, Yagalla had said to his girlfriend.

Get out of what? Kalko wonders.

MARK YAGALLA'S audacious joyride has brought him light-years from Weatherly, Pennsylvania, a close-knit rural community northeast of Allentown where he grew up on the grounds of a 2,000-acre tree nursery owned by cousins. His father drove a truck for the nursery, and Mark, as a kid, spent his summers there, making $4.25 an hour. He was shearing hemlocks in 95-degree heat when it first occurred to him there had to be a better way to make money.

When he was 12 or so, he saw the movie *Wall Street*, and it wrought a powerful change in him. He started spending his free time reading the *Wall Street Journal*, ordering financial statements from corporations, and journeying to the public library to read S&P reports. His heroes were Ron Perelman and Carl Icahn and Michael Milken. At 15, Mark decided he was ready for Wall Street. Frustrated by the age requirement for becoming a stockbroker, he convinced his mother to give him a chunk of his saved earnings, half of which he promptly lost.

Determined to try again, he convinced one of his cousins, Francis Dolinsky, to give him $5,000 to invest, with the agreement that they'd split any profits. This time, Mark took care not to rush. He read voraciously, at last settling on Dell, with its custom configuration of computers and impressive young founder. He sank the whole $5,000 into the stock. This was in 1994, just before tech stocks took off. Dell went vertical.

Dolinsky gave Mark more money, which he put into tech issues like Microsoft and Intel. These, too, only went up. Mark bought a Corvette, and then a Chevy Blazer. Word began to spread about this kid over in Weatherly. He was an investing prodigy—and a classic high-school nerd. He hit five-foot-three, then stopped growing. He wore button-downs, khakis and glasses, and carried a bag phone, the clunky predecessor to the cell. The other kids called him "Urkel."

Mark bandaged his wounds with defiance. The more he was called Urkel, the more nerdily he dressed. On prom night, he stayed home—if he couldn't go with a trophy girl, he preferred not to go at all. Instead, he spent the day manically trading stocks, and made almost $23,000. Something calcified in him that day, some belief about what he could and couldn't do. Making a lot of money became his near-exclusive preoccupation. His parents were simple people who didn't know quite what to make of their unusual son. He had big plans, many of them cribbed from videos he'd watch over and over, movies about hookers and unscrupulous businessmen, like *Indecent Proposal, Other People's Money* and, especially, *Pretty Woman*. That *Pretty Woman* was a fairy tale was lost on him. He seemed to possess a Disney-manufactured filter that transformed *every* story into a fairy tale. Even when he watched morality plays like *Wall Street*, what he took away was the glamorous premise, not the unhappy ending. Years later, he would say he might have watched too many movies as a kid.

His class rank slipped from first to second, but when he graduated, Mark had $125,000 in the bank.

HE SPENT much of the next year at Wharton, day-trading out of a one-bedroom apartment at 36th and Powelton, riding Dell skyward and taking huge profits investing in tech stocks and trading S&P 500 futures. With a knack for flipping failure into success, he started calling himself "the Teflon Kid." A year and a half out of high school, he was worth $1 million. He was a player, but he told no one of the accomplishment—which had merely awakened a thirst for much more money.

Yagalla spent another semester at Wharton, where he felt socially isolated. Then he dropped out to concentrate on investing full-time. He continued his margin investing in Nasdaq stocks, and began branching into other business ventures. While still in high school, he'd registered Apex Investments as a business name, and he now submitted filings with the Securities and Exchange Commission to establish it as a hedge fund. He also started another fund, Ashbury Capital, with the enthusiastic support of Delaware orthodontist Ron Collins and his wife, Lorraine. The Collinses, who'd met Yagalla through a mutual market-playing friend and written out a check the same day, were now something like surrogate parents to him. At their suggestion, he moved to Wilmington, buying a McMansion close to Winterthur for $1 million and leasing an office in a nearby strip center.

The first investors in Apex were people from Weatherly and Wilmington, like the Collinses and their friends, who knew the Mark Yagalla story and were impressed by the earnest, polite kid with the unbelievable returns. At the age of 20, he could already boast of more than 5 years of investing experience.

The Ashbury Capital offering documents billed the fund as a tech-heavy venture that would engage in several risky practices, among them shorting, margin investing, big bets on a single stock, and trading in derivatives. Yagalla was to receive one-fifth of all profits as well as an annual fee of one percent of assets. By March 1999, Ashbury had 15 investors. The hedge fund's offering statement listed $1 billion in assets as its goal.

ON A Thursday afternoon that summer, a chestnut-haired, gypsy-eyed, silicone-bosomed young woman named Tishara Lee Cousino, who had been *Playboy*'s Miss May 1999, reclined on a gently rocking bed and looked expectantly at Mark Yagalla, whom she'd just met. They were in the Florida Keys, aboard a 125-foot yacht Yagalla had leased for the weekend. "Do you want to do anything with me?" she asked.

Yagalla had come a long way from the night of his high-school prom, when he'd stayed home distraught over his inability to get a date. Since then, he'd been with more than a hundred women, but he'd paid for all of them, one way or another. Beginning with a high-school experience with a call girl at a nursery convention in Chicago, he had become a compulsive procurer of high-priced "escorts," taking them on yachts and vacations and generally living the life of a playboy. After he made his first million, business became just numbers to him, a rigorous tedium of sitting before a computer screen and holding the hands of anxious clients. But he remained socially undeveloped, without hobbies to distract him or the self-assuredness to enter a bar alone, and he sought to combat his loneliness by purchasing companionship.

After a while, though he enjoyed the transactional efficiency of renting prostitutes, he felt bored by them and sufficiently confident to go after a woman who wasn't a sure thing. He started going to New York and making the strip-club rounds with $10,000 in his pocket. While other lonely men paid 20 bucks a lap dance, the 20-year-old CEO of Apex Investments would peel off a Benjamin.

He churned through strippers as if sheer numbers could fill the hole in him. But again he grew bored, and this time he turned to the Internet. It was there that he stumbled on Nici's Girls, a website that was just then taking the online escort business to a new level. Men willing to pay a $5000 "admission fee" could gain entry to Nici's "Millionaires Club," billed simply and mysteriously as a harem of unnamed porn stars, Penthouse Pets, and Playboy Playmates. That was enough for Yagalla. He called Nici, who was herself just 21, and said he was young and had a lot of money. She matched him with a pin-up girl who came to his home and flew with him to Puerto Rico. The four days only cost him $28,000 plus airfare.

Soon, Yagalla was flying two new Nici's girls a week to his house in Wilmington, laying out $10,000 to $20,000 for the pleasure of their company and the only sort of love he knew. He relished the jittery feeling of driving to the Philadelphia Airport to pick up a girl. Eventually, he started flying to LA to rendezvous with Nici's "specials," including porn megastar Jenna Jameson.

Nici was fast becoming the new Heidi Fleiss, LA's reigning madam, and Yagalla, as a preferred (and relentless) customer, ended up befriending her and learning her real name: Michelle Braun. She had grown up ordinary, discovered certain talents, and gotten sidetracked, not unlike Yagalla. Both were aggressive and in their early 1920s, and they shared an interest in talking about Nici's clients and how screwed-up Nici's girls were.

Eventually, Yagalla asked Nici to set him up with Playmates. She had a connection at Playboy, so all Yagalla had to do was page through the magazine and, when he saw a girl he liked, call Nici. She'd obtain a phone number or e-mail address for the girl and make the pitch. The women she set Yagalla up with included two Playmates of the Year in addition to Tishara Cousino, whom Nici priced at $40,000 for an introductory weekend.

Yagalla had been searching for a trophy to cast in a real-life enactment of *Pretty Woman*, and he viewed Tishara as the best candidate yet for something he'd developed called "The Program." Mark would supply a woman with a car, a place to live, a credit card, and an allowance set according to her needs and market value. In return, she would be his "beck-and-call girl."

When Tishara lay down in the ship's berth that first weekend in the Florida Keys and offered herself to Yagalla, he said no. In thrall to a romantic fantasy, he was put off by her bluntness. He said he only wanted her when she wanted him. That Saturday, he bought Tishara a black Mercedes SL 500. When she said she was unhappy with where she was living in Las Vegas, he offered to buy her a house. She ended up going for a place that cost $450,000. Mark thought this was a bit much, but he wasn't good at saying no. He wanted his girlfriend to have whatever she desired.

THIS WAS 1999, the year when a lot of people were under the impression that a dot-com-fueled Nasdaq could defy gravity. Being 22 wasn't just acceptable; it was desirable. And Yagalla—affable, earnest, clearly bright—lacked just enough polish to avoid seeming slick. Investors fearful of missing out on the gold rush were scrambling into his funds. A Weatherly couple, Tom and Marion Huf, would ultimately invest more than $3 million with him.

He'd send them monthly statements from the "Apex Investments Aggressive Growth Fund," detailing precisely what he'd done with their money. He was big on tech and Internet stocks. Initially he divvied the Hufs' money up among AOL, Dell, Microsoft, Yahoo!, and EMC. Then he pulled out of EMC and moved into eBay, Amazon and CMGI, among others. Over time, the Apex statements became less detailed. By the fall of 1999, Yagalla was reporting to the Hufs that their portfolio had leaped more than 50 percent in one month. In November alone, a statement showed their account soaring from $2.15 million to $3.47 million.

From the start, Ashbury's monthly statements disclosed nothing more than the net change in an investor's account, but they were just as bullish as the Apex reports. An investor who gave Yagalla $20,000 on July 1, 1999, would have shown assets of $34,730 by the end of the year. As for Yagalla, he would later report that his personal income for 1999 was $6 million.

MARK Yagalla was cruising through Las Vegas in a limousine, sitting between Tishara Cousino and Sandy Bentley, when he began to get the picture. This was the last weekend of August. A few days earlier, Tishara had called him on three-way with fellow Playboy model Sandy on the line, and they had all agreed to go to tonight's Cher concert at the MGM. Yagalla knew that Sandy was one half of the busty, platinum-blond Bentley twins, who were themselves one half of Hugh

Hefner's current quartet of official girlfriends. Suddenly, Mark Yagalla, who not 4 years earlier had answered to the name Urkel, was asking: "Won't Hefner mind?"

"He wishes," Sandy replied.

Now, as the threesome headed toward Crazy Horse Too, a strip club where Sandy used to dance, things began to make sense. At dinner before the show, Sandy, in a red cocktail dress, had patted the banquette next to her, beckoning for Yagalla to sit there. And in the limo now, postconcert, Sandy said she wished he was her boyfriend, too. Yagalla viewed a girlfriend of Hugh Hefner's as the ultimate trophy, and he rose to the challenge: He *could* be her boyfriend, too, he said. "We'll be a happy family," Tishara said. At Crazy Horse, Yagalla reveled in the moment. He had Tishara on one knee, Sandy on the other. They took turns kissing him. When the club's silicone-bolstered talent wondered aloud what his secret was, he replied honestly: "I'm fucking loaded."

The next morning, Yagalla bought Sandy a Mercedes SL 500 for $97,000. Then the two of them joined Tishara for lunch at the Venetian, where Yagalla laid out his most outlandish version of the Program yet. He would give both women Platinum American Express cards and pay them each monthly allowances of $20,000 to $25,000. Tishara already had her car and house; Sandy had the car and would get a house. Yagalla wanted to make it so they would have a lot to lose by leaving him. Tishara suggested they all get HIV tests. (Though she declined to be interviewed, Cousino denies that she met Yagalla through a madam and that he put her on a "program.")

Sandy began house-hunting by looking at properties in the $300,000 range. Nothing she saw was quite right, though, and the price escalated until she fixed on a home in one of the most exclusive developments in Las Vegas—Spanish Trails, a gated golf-course community southwest of the Strip.

The house Sandy wanted was a 6,700-square-foot two-story Italian villa with a pool. Yagalla paid $1.7 million for it. Sandy, unlike Tishara, didn't push to have the house put in her name, which pleased Yagalla. Sandy even said she was eager to visit him in Delaware. There was just one hitch: She refused to fly commercial.

The next weekend, she arrived in Philadelphia on a chartered Challenger jet. Yagalla picked her up in his red Ferrari, and they drove to Manayunk to have dinner at Kansas City Prime. Then they went back to Yagalla's house in Wilmington, where they were amazed to discover that they had the same taste. Sandy loved the decor and decided to use the same interior designer for her house in Vegas. Then she and Yagalla watched *Pretty Woman* on DVD.

POSSESSIONS meant nothing to Sandy, she told Mark; at the end of prior relationships, she'd FedExed back any gifts she'd received. In the first few months Yagalla and Sandy dated, he gave her, in addition to the house and Mercedes, a red Ferrari F1355 Spyder, a Range Rover, a black Cadillac Escalade SUV to drive when she was visiting Mandy in LA, a pair of fur coats from Bloomingdale's, two Rolexes, a platinum-and-diamond bracelet from Fred Leighton in Vegas, and $190,000 worth of jewelry from Venetzia in Vegas. On a December trip to New York, he bought her two more Bloomingdale's furs—a shaved mink and a monogrammed chinchilla. Each time Yagalla unveiled a new gift, Sandy would light up, drawing her hands together and clapping with glee. Yagalla wanted his girlfriend to live a life without limits. "She's used to billionaires," he explained to a friend. "Millionaires are nothing to her."

Going out on the town with Sandy was a narcissist's fantasy. Yagalla had million-dollar lines of credit at several casinos on the Strip, and he loved walking into a high-roller room with two bodyguards and his girlfriend, who'd be shimmering in diamonds and platinum. When Yagalla arrived at the baccarat pit, the croupier would say, "Mr. Y's here," and slide a million in chips in front of him.

Yagalla believed that Sandy's love was genuine. She wrote him little notes, signing them "Princess" and calling him "sweet pea," "doe-doe," "honey-bunny" and "my little weirdo." Nevertheless they made an odd couple. Yagalla now wore Brioni shirts and $3,500 suits from Barneys and shoes by Bruno Magli. He had a year-round tan, courtesy of a tanning bed at his house. He no longer wore glasses, thanks to Lasik surgery, and Sandy tweezed his eyebrows to sleekness. But he remained short and a bit flabby, with a persistent Eastern Pennsylvania twang and an earnest manner straight out of Weatherly. He didn't smoke or drink much or do drugs or even dance, and he liked to go to sleep early. At clubs, he'd sit yawning at the table while the girls were out on the dance floor.

Sandy, close to five-foot-nine, had hair extensions and breast implants (the latter paid for by a pre-Hefner boyfriend, slain Vegas mobster Herbert "Fat Herbie" Blitzstein), and ambitions centered on fame and fun and wealth. One night at Rum Jungle, a savage-tropics-themed club at the Mandalay, Sandy was gyrating on the table with her eyes closed. Back in their upstairs suite, after she and Yagalla had sex, Sandy wandered out of the bedroom. A while later, security called to tell Yagalla there was a naked woman outside his door. Sandy had gotten lost. (Through her lawyer, Sandy Bentley declined to be interviewed.)

Yagalla's friends—or what passed for them: his employees, clients, and business associates—almost to a person frowned on his dating her. Sandy was using him for his money, they told him over and over.

PHOTOGRAPHS Sandy Bentley kept from those heady first months of the relationship preserve some of its flavor. For instance, the pictures from the Bahamas, where Yagalla took her that December, show a group of young, lithe, beautiful, sun-baked bodies intertwined. There's Sandy and her twin Mandy, who met Yagalla for the first time on that trip, and Dave Osokow, an LA club promoter and aspiring actor who was Mandy's real boyfriend. And then, standing off to one side or lurking awkwardly in back, there's Yagalla, who was paying for everyone else.

As Sandy was Princess, Mandy called herself "Superstar." "Su-pa-stah, Su-pa-stah," she'd say in a breathless staccato. The girls used gangsta slang and called each other "nig." Stabs were made at including Yagalla, with Osokow calling him "little brother" and Hefner girlfriend Jessica Paisley telling him he was "one cool nig," but the only way he knew to relate to them was with money. At the Atlantis hotel in Nassau, he excused himself from the dinner table one night, then returned and surprised Sandy with a $100,000 necklace she'd admired in a store that day. He even bought a $3,500 diamond-and-gold bracelet so Dave Osokow would be able to give something to Mandy.

Yagalla wanted to settle down and have kids, and he and Sandy were already talking marriage. (To mollify Tishara, he bought her a new house for $850,000— even though they never did have sex.) On the way back from the Bahamas, he took Sandy blindfolded into a New Jersey car dealership and presented her with a white Bentley Azure convertible he'd just bought for $310,000. On a piece of stationery, at the dealership, Sandy wrote out possible names for herself: *S. Yagalla. S. Bentley-Yagalla.*

That Christmas, Yagalla gave Sandy $600,000 worth of jewelry, including a custom-made ruby-and-diamond necklace patterned after the one in *Pretty Woman.*

SANDY'S duties as an official Hefner girlfriend required her to spend Christmas and New Year's at the Playboy Mansion, and Yagalla, feeling used, briefly broke up with her. But his business dealings, happily, were going better than ever. At the beginning of 2000, he got a powerful new marketing tool for recruiting investors. Up to this point, he'd had to rely on clients who'd done well with him to back up his claims of astronomical returns. Now he obtained an audited financial statement, prepared by the accounting firm of Ernst & Young, attesting to the financial success of Ashbury Capital in 1999. His gain for the year, the statement declared, was a remarkable 62 percent.

Yagalla had begun to broaden his investor base. Perry Scarfo, a Porsche-driving Wilmington hairdresser who did Lorraine Collins's hair, had succumbed to the siren song in November, ultimately investing $750,000. One source of new referrals was Rita Johnson, a Florida madam whose little black book contained the names of many wealthy men. These investors were a different breed from Yagalla's Weatherly and Wilmington believers. Eddy Louis, for instance, was an absurdly tan French-accented former squash champion who lived in Palm Beach, drove a Bentley, and had recently been left a widower by a wife several decades his senior. Louis had a private investigator look into Yagalla's background; the investigator turned up nothing, and Louis gave Yagalla $2 million to invest.

Yagalla, in turn, gave Rita Johnson a Jaguar to compensate her for her referrals. He needed all the investors he could get. He was a millionaire who was growing dangerously accustomed to living like a billionaire.

In January, he began leasing a Gulfstream. When Sandy wasn't attending classes at UNLV or parties at the Playboy Mansion, she was overseeing the $1.3

million remodeling of her $1.7 million house, using Albert's Interiors, of Chester County. She was especially taken with the idea of creating a room to display her collection of Barbie dolls.

YAGALLA and Sandy were vacationing in Cancun in March when they spotted the paparazzi. On this trip, Sandy's posse included Mandy, Mandy's ex-boyfriend Mike, and future Playmate of the Year Brande Roderick, who brought along Chicago Bears quarterback Cade McNown. Each of the girls had to call Hefner daily to check in, and they were constantly worrying that "the old man," as they called him, was going to find out they were with other men. Sandy was already stressed about her upcoming *Playboy* pictorial, for which Hefner had agreed to pay her and Mandy $100,000 each—$80,000 more than the going rate. When cameramen with telephoto lenses appeared out of nowhere in Cancun and began shooting the group, the girls freaked. "April Fools!" said Yagalla, who had hired them.

Sandy was unamused, and when they got home, she and Yagalla broke up again. They were still estranged in April, when Hefner and the twins flew across the country to promote the May cover of *Playboy*, barnstorming from *The Daily Show* to *Late Night with Conan O'Brien*. Flanked by the twins in matching hot-pink cowboy hats, Hefner swaggeringly maintained the facade of a relationship, gushing about the power of Viagra. (The heterosexual icon, Sandy had told Yagalla, had trouble finding satisfaction through intercourse; instead, he liked the girls to pleasure each other while he masturbated and watched gay porn.) In New York, though, Sandy slipped away to meet Yagalla at the Four Seasons, and they had make-up sex.

For Sandy's 22nd birthday, on May 18th, Yagalla planned to pay Ricky Martin $1 million to sing at the birthday party, but logistics scotched the idea. Instead he gave her a $500,000 ring and then dropped another $225,000 on her at Fred Leighton jewelers. That night, they had dinner at Sandy's favorite restaurant in Vegas, Morton's steak house. When they returned to the Mandalay hotel, the elevator took them to the top floor. The doors parted, and Sandy saw a trail of rose petals leading to the Presidential Suite. Inside, the trail continued into the bedroom and up the steps to the bed, where rose petals had been arranged into a giant heart.

No one would have guessed that Yagalla was facing a small cash crunch that month. Writing to investors in March, he'd touted "the information technology age" and listed Ashbury's "top 20 holdings." They ranged from CMGI to Yahoo! to Red Hat to AOL. But in April, he took an unexpected tax hit, and in May, he bounced $500,000 in checks to American Express. He scaled back some, terminating his Gulfstream lease. His investors remained blithely unaware of his financial difficulties. Hairdresser Perry Scarfo constantly questioned Yagalla about Ashbury, often stopping by the Wilmington office unannounced just to see what was going on. Yagalla had sent him statements sporadically until Scarfo insisted he receive monthly reports. When Yagalla complained, Scarfo told him, "Get used to it." But in the spring of 2000, Scarfo had no inkling that anything was seriously wrong.

In a May 1st letter to Ashbury investors, Yagalla wrote that because of the Nasdaq's recent decline, he was shifting the portfolio out of speculative stocks and into blue chips. While he remained bullish on information technology, he noted that consumer spending was slowing: "Taking on that extra monthly payment, or spending on luxuries doesn't seem so feasible at this time." He was in no way referring to himself.

THE REMODELING expenses on Sandy's house at Spanish Trails were staggering. She was also making plans to buy an apartment in Chicago. And she told Yagalla she wouldn't move anywhere on the East Coast other than Manhattan, so Yagalla put a million down on a $10 million condo on Fifth Avenue.

He was planning to ask Sandy to marry him in Paris, over Christmas. Through connections, he was going to have the Eiffel Tower shut down, so only he and Sandy would be at the top when he proposed. Sandy said they'd have the biggest wedding New York had ever seen. But they were still having problems. In the Vegas house, while Sandy displayed only a single photo of Yagalla—a small framed shot squirreled away in the library—she scattered upwards of 50 pictures of herself and her sister. Sandy even put up a *Playboy* poster of herself in the Barbie room. Yagalla would joke, "You and I are in love with the same person."

Sandy often canceled weekends at the last minute, or would come to his hotel room and leave after an hour, saying she was tired. She resisted journeying to Delaware, and she refused to attend the Republican convention in Philadelphia with Yagalla, who had made Ashbury Capital the second biggest Republican donor in Delaware, sandwiched between MBNA and DuPont. Yagalla's friends, meanwhile, continued to view his girlfriend as an unalloyed gold digger. "She cut me off from Mark," Eddy Louis would say later, "because the more I talked to him, the more she had to fuck him."

By August, a full six weeks had passed in which Yagalla hadn't seen Sandy. She'd begun to press him to put the house in her name, and to stop her nagging, he sent her a fake deed. She'd had a miscarriage, and she blamed him for the pregnancy, because Yagalla, like Richard Gere in *Pretty Woman*, eschewed condoms. To cheer himself up, Yagalla went to buy a black 2000 Ferrari 456 GTS for $232,000. He was at the dealership in New Jersey when Sandy called to patch things up. "I just bought you a make-up present," he told her.

While Yagalla's expenses mounted, the stock market was tanking. Yagalla, however, continued to mail investors monthly statements showing gains in their holdings. "We have invested in stocks that have explosive growth potential and aren't too heavily tied to the slowing growth of the economy," he wrote in a June 30th letter to Ashbury clients. The stocks he named included telecom infrastructure plays like Redback Networks, Sycamore Networks and Juniper Networks. An August 1st letter to Ashbury investors boasted of "huge appreciations in some of [the fund's] core holdings." Calling the stock market overheated, Yagalla reported that he'd limited the fund's exposure by paring its market positions, taking profits, and shorting some stocks. As of the end of July, he was claiming a 50 percent return for the year.

And he continued to recruit investors. In a July meeting at neurosurgeon Charles Kalko's Jersey office, Yagalla came on strong, deriding the Kalkos' portfolio manager for "making peanuts" and boasting that his own fund had returned more than 80 percent the previous year. The Kalkos made an initial investment of $300,000; a few days later, Yagalla called to say they'd already doubled their money. When they asked for a detailed breakdown, he told them his rapid style of moving in and out of stocks made such statements useless. The Kalkos gave him another $3.7 million.

Yagalla was on the verge of taking Ashbury to a whole other level. Besides having a luxurious office constructed at 450 Park Avenue in Manhattan, he was beginning to attract pedigreed employees like Jack Regan, a Harvard-educated market strategist for Josephthal & Co. The Ashbury promotional brochure now even listed as a "senior adviser" Joseph DiMartino, the venerable chairman of the Dreyfus family of mutual funds. DiMartino, who'd met Yagalla through a mutual friend at Salomon Smith Barney, had tentatively agreed to lend his name and advice to Ashbury in return for an office, his secretary's salary, and a $20,000 monthly stipend. With investors, too, Yagalla had made A-list inroads, getting $1 million from Mel Sembler, finance chairman of the RNC.

A September 1st letter to Ashbury investors continued the theme of the "information revolution," but Yagalla now sounded a moderating note: "The days of the individual investor buying stocks blindly and making money are gone.... Our strategy has faired [sic] well during the markets' topsy-turvy ride this year, and we think it will serve us well going into 2001."

But the truth was, Yagalla hadn't traded a share of stock in three months.

ABOUT SANDY, at least, he was feeling more confident. By September, she seemed focused on marriage and was planning to move to New York, where she hoped to attend grad school. She intended to become a couples therapist. And she promised Yagalla she would officially sever her relationship with Hefner, who denied a tabloid report that he'd just thrown the twins out of the mansion, suggesting that the only waves being made in the Grotto's legendary hot tubs were the result of his girls' jealousy. "Do we sometimes have disagreements about me being with other women?" Hefner said. "Yes, we do."

But financially, Yagalla was far less sure of himself—the first time in his life when money, not the girl, was giving him trouble. The market's decline and the constant need to bankroll Sandy had left his investment funds in precarious shape, and he was starting to feel the heat. Some of his investors were beginning to sense that something was wrong. On a Friday in August, when Dr. Kalko was out of the country, Yagalla had pressed Martha Kalko to invest more money, personally delivering her in his chauffeured limousine to Summit Bank so she could wire another $1.5 million to his fund without delay. The pushiness troubled her, as did Yagalla's flash; he bragged about the $500,000 Chopard watch he'd bought Sandy, and talked about his Swiss Bank account. Kalko and her husband decided to begin withdrawing their money.

And investor Perry Scarfo, invited to join Yagalla in his box at FedEx Field for a Monday night Redskins-Cowboys game, didn't like the people with whom his host had surrounded himself, slick-looking guys in Armani suits who hung all over Mandy Bentley and lit up Cuban cigars even though Scarfo and his wife had their 19-month-old daughter with them.

Worse still, Yagalla started bouncing checks, including ones to Eddy Louis and the Collins family. As the pressure mounted, he began to avoid his office. For a few weeks, he was bedridden with mono. Late in September, he threw a Hail Mary, buying more than $7.1 million in stock in Intelliworxx, a software maker, and Travel-Now.com, two companies he'd been involved with at the venture-capital stage. He bought the stock through a margin account with the investment bank Lehman Brothers. On Friday, September 29th, three days after he had promised to wire the funds to Lehman, he showed up at its offices with a personal check for $4.5 million. On Monday, Lehman discovered he didn't have the money to cover that check. The next day, Yagalla again came to Lehman's offices, this time bearing a check for $1.3 million. It didn't clear, either.

As Yagalla dodged more and more of his clients, he began to feel the most intense pressure from his old supporters, the Collins family. When he confided in them about his problems, he'd later tell friends, they turned around and demanded he return their money—or they'd go to the SEC. In the first week of October, Yagalla managed to return $2.7 million to them. With other funds they'd withdrawn since April, they pulled out a total of $6.2 million. Still, the Collinses—according to allegations filed by a court-appointed receiver—continued to reassure at least one other skittish investor that Yagalla was past any troubles he might have had and that the investor needn't worry about his money. (The Collinses declined to be interviewed but have denied these allegations.)

But by this point, Ashbury Capital was a standard-issue Ponzi scheme. To appease the Collinses, Yagalla had turned over to them newly raised money from investors, including another $1 million he got from his cousin, Bill Dolinsky.

WHEN Yagalla's check to Eddy Louis bounced and Louis started making noise about it, Yagalla admitted to him that he'd gotten a margin call and was scraping for cash. He and a friend then picked up Louis in the Gulfstream and headed for Vegas.

It was late on a Wednesday night when they arrived, and Yagalla checked them into a suite at the Aladdin, then headed over to Sandy's house at Spanish Trails and crawled into bed with her. He told her he was in serious trouble. "As long as it's just fines," she said. Yagalla wondered if he should run. He had his passport, the private jet, the bank account in Switzerland. But the Teflon Kid still thought he could pull this one out.

Desperate to raise cash, he got Sandy to sign over the Ferraris and had them loaded onto a truck bound for Florida, where he thought he could get at least half a million for them. He had decided to take care of the Lehman problem by bankrupting Ashbury Capital. He was also trying to sell the helicopter, a limo company and the jewelry. During lulls between business meetings and talks with Sandy, he worked his way up and down the Strip, playing baccarat and blackjack. He'd have three $15,000 hands on the baize at the same time. But there was no way he was going to game back the $40 million he'd squandered—much of it on Sandy and the Program. At four different casinos, he lost another $800,000.

Running out of options, Yagalla had some frank phone conversations with Kenny Luppo, his right hand at Ashbury in New York. "Were all the statements phony?" Luppo asked.

"Ah, last year was not," Yagalla responded. "This year was the problem."

"So they were all phony this year?" Luppo asked.

"No," Yagalla said, "it's been within the last three or four months."

He still believed, at this point, that there was a way out of the mess he'd created. "I'm gonna make this right," he said, "if I have to go to every single client myself, look them in the eye, and show them what I did and work out a plan to make it right."

Near the end of the conversation, Yagalla turned wistful. "It's a shame all this happened, because I really think six months from now we're goin' to be rockin' and rollin' with big money.... I never wanted to hurt anybody. ... I just got myself in a jam ...I made a lot of mistakes."

He'd just made another one: Luppo had become an FBI informant and was taping their calls. Five days later, at the U.S. Courthouse in Wilmington, Yagalla was arrested and charged with mail fraud.

─────────

SITTING behind the wheel of his BMW 750IL, invisible behind its tinted windows, Mark Yagalla glances anxiously at the dashboard clock. His hair is gelled back, and he wears a double-breasted suit, a French blue shirt with his monogram on the cuff, and a Chopard watch. It's almost nine o'clock in the evening, six months after his arrest, and Yagalla is speeding along a country road in the Brandywine Valley.

He's tan, and so lean that his very expensive clothing, once form-fitting, bags around his truncated frame like a gangster's zoot suit. He looks as though he just returned from a month at Canyon Ranch. But it's his tanning bed that supplies the bronzed sheen, his home gym and new protein-shake diet that have shrunk his waist from a 34 to a 28, and his twice-monthly psychotherapy appointments that have restored some of his perspective.

He hasn't been doing much traveling, not since the government took away his passport, placed an electronic monitoring ring around his ankle, and put him under house arrest. He is allowed out of the house, but he has a 9 p.m. curfew. Tonight, he makes it home in time, easing the only car he has left into the three-car garage. And he won't have the BMW much longer; in a few weeks, the court-appointed receiver whose job it is to round up and sell anything of value that Yagalla has left in order to return money to his bilked investors is sending someone to collect it—along with his computer and Mont Blanc pen and cuff links and watches. The house has been sold; the new owners take possession this month.

The criminal case against Yagalla is in limbo while the receiver works to determine what fraction of the investors' losses can be recouped. Yagalla may be better off with no wristwatch. Time snails along as it is when you're awaiting a court's judgment. Yagalla is free of the intense pressures that preceded his arrest, but they have been replaced by a crushing boredom. Sometimes, now, he calls his old investors and tells them he wants to make things right, even if it takes him his whole life. Some of them, even those who lost millions with him, feel sorry for him, feel Sandy Bentley was the real con artist. These are the people who'll take his calls. Many won't. His cousin, Bill Dolinsky, told him never to call again, throwing the phone down so hard it broke. Even Yagalla's little brother, David, won't talk to him.

Some of the investors have been utterly devastated by their losses. Lorraine Fusco, an elderly woman in Scarsdale, New York, had to sell her house and move into a government-subsidized nursing home. Yagalla has cried a few times, thinking about what happened to her. He has suggested to a couple of lawyers that they file class-action suits against Ernst & Young, the accounting firm that gave Ashbury its audit. (A firm spokesperson says Ernst & Young stands by its audit.)

Sandy stayed loyal to Yagalla until she learned the government was going to take away all the things he gave her. Then she stopped calling him. The last time he saw her was at her deposition in New York, in December. The last time they spoke was in February, when she was forced out of her house in Vegas. She did call then, to say it was the worst day of her life. Now, Yagalla watches the Bentleys from afar. He watches Sandy refuse to give up her claim to some of the gifts she received. He watches as Tishara Cousino, too, is made to surrender assets.

He used to feel sorry for the women, but now he blames them for his predicament. Nici kept on e-mailing him about the latest "HOT!" girl in her stable, until in April he finally told her he wanted nothing more to do with her "harem of whores." Now, alone in his house, Yagalla is trying to become a person, to learn the social skills money made unnecessary. When the Sixers play the Pacers, he forces himself to watch; he's trying to develop interests.

A *Wall Street* poster still hangs in his house, but now Mark has new goals; he recently saw *The Family Man* and was moved by Nicholas Cage's performance as a man who lives for power and success, only to regret everything he missed. Yagalla busies himself studying books on mergers and acquisitions, reading the *Wall Street Journal*, and talking to people about businesses he'd like to start. The Teflon Kid has been readmitted to Wharton. He was planning to start last month and move into the dorms at Penn. He hopes to be finished with college by the time his criminal sentence is handed down. The most time he'll have to serve is five years. If the sentence begins soon, he just might be out in time to attend his 10th high-school reunion and show his old classmates what he's become.

By Elizabeth Gold
March 2001

SOUL REVIVER

rowing up at 30th and Poplar in the late 1980s, it was hard to escape the songs of Kenny Gamble and Leon Huff, the fathers of the Sound of Philadelphia (TSOP). Over the back fence of my family's tiny concrete yard, on warm days, we could hear those songs on WDAS loud and clear: "Back Stabbers" by the O'Jays; "Wake Up Everybody" by Harold Melvin and the Blue Notes (featuring Teddy Pendergrass); and, on Mother's Day, the Intruders crooning "I'll Always Love My Mama," over and over again. Sometimes it was great to hear them—they were a reminder of Philly's musical history and a testament to the Sound of Philadelphia's enduring appeal some 20 years after it first conquered the charts. Sometimes it was depressing, yet another indication that Philly's musical greatness lay in the past.

"The Sound of Philadelphia" was both a song title—it was the theme for *Soul Train*—and an idea. Musically, TSOP was sophisticated soul for grown-ups, combining gospel vocals, a funked-up rhythm section, and smooth-as-silk strings and horns. The lyrics expressed old-fashioned values that came straight from the black South ("Family Reunion"). Even as urban blacks grew poorer and the hopes of the civil rights movement faded, Gamble and Huff urged their listeners to embrace the positive side of black power ("Let's Clean Up the Ghetto") and chronicled real life ("Bad Luck"). In the wake of race riots and assassinations, Gamble and Huff's songs insisted that people could work together across their differences. They were idealistic without being too corny, because they told true stories.

Gamble and Huff's ride lasted just over a decade. In 1982, Teddy Pendergrass crashed his Rolls-Royce on Lincoln Drive and became a paraplegic. Soon afterward, Gamble and Huff lost their 10-year-old deal with CBS Records.

MANY OF the people who had been part of TSOP wondered what Kenny Gamble would do after the Sound was over. There were rumors that he was buying up property around his old neighborhood at Broad and Catharine, that he had big plans to turn the decrepit area into a center for Philadelphia's black community. It was hard to tell, however, if any of the rumors had substance. Maybe Gamble was just holed up; maybe he had given up on the city that had inspired him so much.

It took me a while to work up the nerve to approach such a legend. I was born in 1974, just as the Sound of Philadelphia really started to get big. My father, Larry Gold, a Jewish hippie from Kensington who had gone to the Curtis Institute of Music, played cello in MFSB, the house band of Gamble's Philadelphia International Records, and also wrote TSOP string and horn arrangements. For the past few years, I've been researching and writing a book about the Sound of Philadelphia. But when I finally interview Gamble, we wind up talking less about the music he made in the 1970s than the community work he's doing right now.

I expected we would meet at 309 South Broad, the offices he shared with Leon Huff and fellow hitmaker Thom Bell in the heyday of TSOP, since I knew he still had an assistant and other staff there. Instead, he asked me to come to the main office of Universal Companies, the "community development corporation" he founded in 1993.

Universal's headquarters is at the corner of 15th and Catharine, right next to the mosque that Gamble has attended for many years. The day I visit, Gamble is waiting at the front door. Inside, the decor is utilitarian: burgundy carpeting, some awards and prints on the walls, a receptionist's desk and several phones. The office women are wearing headscarves and long-sleeved shirts—proper Muslim *hajab* that reveals nothing but their faces and hands (though on a later visit I notice one leafing through a J. Crew catalog).

Gamble's appearance at age 57 is just as mythic as I expect—more so, actually, because I didn't know he would be so physically imposing: tall, with a broad-shouldered, hefty body. In old pictures he looks slighter, and he used to dress more casually. Now, with his below-the-chin beard and black-framed glasses, natty blue suit and high black felt hat, he could be central casting's vision of a rhythm-and-blues mogul turned Muslim community activist and philanthropist.

It is easy to see the changes Gamble's revitalization project has made. Outside the office, the streets are clean, and crosswalks are marked with fresh paint. Little kids from the Universal Institute Charter School across the street are lined up to go back in from recess; the mosque and a barbershop indicate that there is life and business on the block.

Universal intends to put more than $42 million into restoring the area, from federal, city and private resources. Abdur-Rahim Islam, Universal's CEO and president, has had a long career in finance and real estate development. He and Gamble first put their heads together in 1993, when they formed Universal Community Homes. In cooperation with Pennrose Properties and the Philadelphia Housing Authority, Universal has built Universal Courts I and II, two developments in the 15th and Christian area, and is developing the 247-unit Martin Luther King Plaza, which will be finished in December 2002. In addition, Universal and Pennrose are rebuilding the Schuylkill Falls houses, which will provide homes for 300 families in East Falls by 2004.

Among the other major programs under the organization's umbrella are the charter school and various companies that provide job training, employment opportunities and small-business support. Last September, Universal purchased the Royal Theater, a landmark and onetime cultural center at 15th and South that has been closed since 1970. "The Royal Theater is an anchor for that whole area," Gamble told the *Inquirer* after the purchase. "We're looking at South Street as an expression of African-American culture."

Islam says plans for the Royal go beyond redevelopment of the theater itself. "We want to transform the adjacent blocks to create an entire district for African-American culture, with restaurants, entertainment, and stores," he explains.

Gamble leads me to Universal's conference room, and we sit across from each other at a long table. After exchanging pleasantries (he asks after my father and wonders if I, too, play an instrument; I confess that I don't), we get down to business. As we speak, he doodles key words on a sheet of paper lying on the table in front of him.

I've heard the "Kenny Gamble Story" a zillion times—from newspaper articles and CD reissue liner notes, from musicians who had been Gamble's employees and protégés, but most of all from my father, who, as I was growing up, would periodically take out a bunch of his Philly Soul records and give me a little teach-in. I wasn't more than seven the first time he did this, playing for me the O'Jays' "Family Reunion" and "For the Love of Money." As the last strains of lead singer Eddie Levert's hoarse gospel shouts faded, my dad said, "Honey, you see how important this music is? Kenny Gamble grew up poor right here in Philadelphia, and he made music for the people of his community, to help them and give them hope. He had a real vision and achieved it."

As I got older, I wondered how Gamble accomplished what he did. I saw what my father went through every day, trying to score a hit record and becoming more and more frustrated. It seemed commercial musical success required that some sort of alchemical process take place, and that even if it had happened in Philadelphia before, it never would again—there was no room for further success here. As I sit across from Kenny Gamble at his conference table, I'm reminded of this. I have always thought of him as someone whose best days are firmly in the past. Surely the work he's doing now can't be as strong or passionate as the music was.

"Philadelphia is the city of firsts," Gamble tells me, his voice warmer and not quite as stentorian as I'd anticipated. "We had the first hospital, first fire-engine company, first just about everything. My dream is for Philadelphia to be the first city in America that gets rid of urban blight." I'm used to the grand statements of Gamble's songs, but even so, this sounds pretty sweeping. Sure, a few blocks of a neighborhood have been cleaned up, but eliminating urban blight in Philadelphia altogether?

"You're either a believer or you're not a believer," he says. "You believe in people and life and love and all these beautiful things, or you're the kind of person who sits around and throws rocks at things." He pauses and smiles, adding, "Which is a very uncomfortable life, I would think."

OF COURSE, Gamble never would have made it out of South Philly in the first place if he hadn't believed he could do exactly what nobody expected of a young black kid from a ghetto in a segregated city—i.e., make it out. By the mid-1970s, Gamble lived in a big house in Gladwyne. Years later, he reversed this most obvious sign of his material success. In 1990, he and his wife, Faatimah, moved right back to his old block at 15th and Catharine. It was time, Gamble had decided, to rescue his old neighborhood from the devastation of the previous two decades.

"What was this area like when you were growing up?" I ask.

"It was pretty much a neighborhood like most African-American neighborhoods, where you had mainly families that were renting in small apartments," he says. I expect him to tell me more about the buildings, about singing in street-corner doo-wop groups on hot summer nights, about the kind of food he ate for Sunday dinner. Instead, he begins to talk politics: "There was really no concentration on economics in the community. Most of the businesses were owned by people who didn't even live around here. When I was going to school, there was no mention at all of Africa or African life before slavery, and there was really no mention of slavery in the context of what it meant. It was just sort of taught to us as a matter of fact that this was part of what happened, and then we moved on. They didn't really explain all of the consequences. When you look at the African-American communities in America today, there's a direct legacy of slavery." He pauses for a moment, watching himself write SLAVERY in curly letters on his sheet of paper, then continues: "And so to answer your question, how was the community when I grew up—we had a lot of fun. We did a lot of great things, and I had a really loving family."

Gamble was always entranced by music. He loved "Benny Goodman, Glenn Miller—the big bands," he tells me. "In fact, *The Glenn Miller Story*, that's my favorite movie. When it comes on now, I try to catch it. It's a great story. It's almost like the story of what we did, how we got together and became successful."

When Kenny Gamble and Leon Huff started Philadelphia International Records in 1970, they had been a part of the Philly music scene for several years, going from singing in street-corner doo-wop groups to working with artists signed to Cameo-Parkway Records, home of the Twist and the Mashed Potato as well as many other 1960s dance hits. Philly was a good place to be in the music biz in the 1950s and 1960s. It was the home of *American Bandstand*, and the busy local recording scene included such artists as Fabian and Chubby Checker. Whether you were a songwriter, a session musician or a backup singer, there were plenty of gigs. In 1964, *Bandstand* moved to LA. Many of Philly's little independent record labels folded, but not all of the writers and musicians and music people moved to California or New York. Many of them stuck around, looking for work.

Two of these musicians were Gamble and Huff. They had met in 1960 ("It was just destiny," Gamble tells me), when they were both working in the Shubert Building at 250 South Broad Street. They put together a group, the Romeos, that also included Gamble's high-school friend Thom Bell—who later became one of the all-time greatest writers and producers of pop soul songs—as well as future MFSB rhythm section member Roland Chambers.

People who heard the Romeos back in the day say they were one of the great soul combos of all time. This band was the foundation of what would later become MFSB. The Romeos "gave us an opportunity to fill up this rhythm section and to be experimental," Gamble says.

It was only natural for him and Huff to get into producing. "To me, the producer basically was the person who was the coordinator," Gamble says. He told Huff, "We can be producers. All we have to do is figure out the business aspect, and we can go on from there." This was a fairly ambitious thought for a young black guy to be having at the time. Berry Gordy had founded Motown Records in Detroit in 1960, and Memphis's Stax Records had been run by Al Bell, an African-American, since 1968. But for the most part, blacks in the recording world were singers and musicians, not the people who ran the show. That didn't stop Gamble. "We started to produce our own products," he tells me, "and many of them turned out very well, like 'Expressway to Your Heart,' 'Cowboys to Girls.' All those great songs."

Gamble and Huff tried to succeed independently for a few years, but though they produced hits for Jerry Butler, the Intruders and Wilson Pickett, they weren't satisfied—they wanted to sign artists to contracts with their own logo printed at the top. Then, in 1970, they signed a historic deal with Clive Davis at Columbia Records, making them pioneers—black producers hooked up with a major label. In Davis's memoir, *Clive: Inside the Record Business*, he writes, "Not long after the signing, Gamble and Huff exploded. Within nine months, they had sold 10 million single records."

Kenny Gamble and Leon Huff had made it. They now had national distribution and the muscle of a major label behind their work, but they had given up their independence. It was during those first Columbia years that the pair produced their most political music, including the O'Jays' "For the Love of Money" and Harold Melvin and the Blue Notes' "Wake Up Everybody," as well as album tracks that delved deeper into the American black experience. (The O'Jays' "Ship Ahoy" was a pre-*Roots* story about the Middle Passage told from the point of view of African captives in a slave ship's hold, complete with the creaking of the ship's wooden sides and the lashing of whips; in "Am I Black Enough for You," Billy Paul asked his listeners to keep pushing for racial equality. This was when they wrote the first songs of what would later be called disco: the Blue Notes' "Bad Luck," and "Love Train," by the O'Jays.

"It was then that I really started to respect Gamble's ears," recalls Jack Faith, a string and horn arranger and flautist who played in MFSB. "He had a tremendous knack for what should appear on a record and what had to be cut."

During the 1970s, Gamble and Huff wrote and produced 16 number-one R&B hits—and the Sound, as a whole, was even stronger. Thom Bell was scoring hits with the Spinners; rhythm-section guys were branching off and producing their own acts, like the Trammps; and everyone from David Bowie to the Village People came to record at Sigma Sound, the studio at 12th and Race streets where most of the Philly Sound's hits were recorded.

Gamble had taken Motown's Berry Gordy as his model. "There was a format you could follow for how to write songs and produce records," he says. "I said to myself, 'Wow, if those guys could do it at Motown, a group of black guys in Detroit ...'" The Motown Sound, however, was never as socially conscious as the Sound of Philadelphia. (Gordy famously had to be convinced to release Marvin Gaye's seminal album *What's Going On*—he thought it wasn't commercial enough.) The slogan that Gamble coined to go with his new company, Philadelphia International Records, said it all: "There's a Message in the Music." He wrote, and encouraged his stable of writers to write, songs that would speak to the generation of blacks who had so recently seen the hopes of the civil rights movement dashed as urban poverty and discrimination persevered.

"I used to go to the office at Broad and Spruce every day, and I would see my old neighborhood, devastated," Gamble tells me. "All the jobs were gone. The world seemed like it needed some cleansing." The artists signed to Philly International and MFSB gave him an excellent forum for expressing his ideas. "It was a perfect combination," he says. "I think the record business is very political, and we really had to fight for everything we wanted to do. I think not only CBS, but everybody, the artists, sort of wondered why we had to write these songs. Some artists would say, 'Well, we don't want to do no more message songs.' And I'd say, 'Well, I can't record you.'" He tempers this by adding, "We did have great relationships. That's why we called it the Gamble, Huff and Bell family—the first time anybody in the music business did that."

TSOP wasn't an angry sound, like Sly & the Family Stone; it didn't act out surreal sci-fi allegories as a commentary on society's ills, like Parliament/Funkadelic; and it wasn't a one-man show, like Stevie Wonder. Gamble's philosophy accentuated the positive: Nothing ever got too weird, the beat stayed consistently smooth, and it was always a community effort.

"Philadelphia at that time was going through some tremendous changes," Gamble tells me. He describes the infamous strip-search in 1970 of Philadelphia's Black Panthers by Frank Rizzo's cops, and the general decline in income and standards of living. There were personal changes for Gamble as well. In the mid-1970s, after a long spiritual search, he converted from being a Jehovah's Witness (the church in which he was raised) to Islam, which he has practiced ever since.

His first attempt at community activism came in 1977, when he released *Let's Clean Up the Ghetto*, a compilation album featuring the whole Philadelphia International Records "family." He and Huff tried to get then-mayor Rizzo's cooperation for a citywide project to go along with the record, but their meeting didn't go so well.

"I guess they didn't really want to work with us," says Gamble. "I think Frank Rizzo wanted to work with us, but it was one of his aides who told him at the meeting, 'You can't get involved in this program, because it would be admitting that the city's dirty.'" He pauses, raising his eyebrows. "It was the first time I was ever in City Hall, and we had the president of CBS Records here. We were going to put together CBS, Philly International, and do something really nice with the city." He describes how he walked Rizzo across the room and over to a window: "There were bags, dust, and dirt flying around—it was a windy day. I told him, 'The city is dirty. There's no way the sanitation department can do this by themselves. You need to get the people involved.' He said, 'Oh Kenny, I'm sorry, I can't really do it.'" The message was clear: Write more hit records, but don't try to change anything for real.

In the 1980s, TSOP's popularity began to wane. People were sick of churchy message music and burned out on disco, and were looking to the beats, scratches and rhymes done by kids in the South Bronx as the next wave in black music. The Sound of Philadelphia was becoming passé—and then Teddy Pendergrass crashed his Rolls.

I remember the night of the accident. I was 7 years old when the phone rang one night, late. I remember my father's stricken voice saying to my mother, "Vick, Teddy was in a car accident."

I knew who Teddy Pendergrass was from one of the platinum records that hung on the wall leading upstairs in our house. It was for *Teddy*, the singer's third solo release, for which my dad had done some string arrangements. Platinum records meant money. I knew that if Teddy had been in an accident, there might not be any more platinum records. And there weren't, at least not for a while.

But even during the lean years, I heard Philly Soul just about everywhere I went: the Stylistics' "Betcha By Golly, Wow" (a Thom Bell-produced group) over the radio in a restaurant in New Orleans during Jazz Festival week, when everything else I heard was either Professor Longhair or Aaron Neville; in a bar in my New York neighborhood, where the only song that roused the uptown crowd to do anything but stare into their drinks was "Don't Leave Me This Way," by Harold Melvin and the Blue Notes; and, most memorably, on a little seashore road in Italy in the middle of winter, when a transistor radio blared McFadden and Whitehead's "Ain't No Stoppin' Us Now."

Every now and then, one of those "Where are they now?" pieces would appear in the *Inquirer* or the *Daily News*, and Gamble would reminisce about the good old days and say that he was working with some hot new artists and insist that TSOP would rise again, but it never did. Those articles never mentioned that he was busily buying up property in his old neighborhood at 15th and Catharine. By 1993, he owned a hundred buildings in the immediate area. He was ready, finally, to make his next move.

A FEW WEEKS after my interview with Kenny Gamble, I take a tour of Universal's projects and properties. My guide, Mu'min Islam, is the 19-year-old son of Universal's president and CEO, Abdur-Rahim Islam. As he shows me building after building full of computer labs, job-training centers, friendly counselors, and eager schoolchildren, I feel I'm being let in on a very well-kept secret. Everything I see is new, from the computers that still have protective wrapping around their cords to the fresh grout between the bricks on the newly built Universal Courts II houses.

"Just as the theaters along Broad Street have energized the area around them, the Royal should give energy to South Street," says Midge McCauley, who heads the urban projects arm of Kravco, owner of the King of Prussia mall. "Anywhere you have entertainment venues, food follows, and then retail. It's a beginning point."

"Soon, we're going to have a grocery store," Islam tells me. "And in a few years, a commercial center." He shows me where everything will go, walking around and around the neighborhood. "What we try to do is address the needs of the community, to give them what they ask for," he explains, and I think of the title of one of Gamble's songs: "Give the People What They Want."

"I'm just proud that we had an opportunity to share in and raise the consciousness in the industry," Gamble says. He's taking the same business sense and consciousness to urban redevelopment, showing the same willingness to work within the system (he spoke at the Republican convention this summer), but not caving to anyone. His home is a modest rowhouse, right next to the United Muslim Movement Masjid, where he does his best to pray five times a day.

ALL GREAT songs tell a story, with a fairly set structure: the beginning, or setup; the chorus, where the listener becomes familiar with what the song is trying to say; the bridge, where things get contemplative and a little unsure; another chorus; then the last verse and maybe a final repeat of the chorus. That's where most songs end, having come full circle. The great Philly Soul songs have an added component. After the final chorus, the singer or singers vamp, sometimes for almost the length of the track itself. This has always been, for me, the best part of the song. On "Bad Luck," the vamp is when Teddy Pendergrass starts blasting, "They've cut down on smoking, we have to cut down on dreamin'. … The only thing that I got that I can hold on is my God, huh, my God. …" Eddie Levert ends "You Got Your Hooks in Me," my favorite O'Jays song, practically speaking in tongues, repeating, "I'm caught like a fish, babe, caught like a fish. …" The music fades with him still singing.

So, in the Philly Soul tradition, here is the vamp to this story: I am hanging out at the Studio, a recording facility my dad opened with a sort of "If you build it, they will come" attitude about 5 years ago. It turned out to be a good bet. All of a sudden, the city is hot again for soul music, and the Roots, a hip-hop collective with a family vibe and a politically aware outlook (sound familiar?), are largely responsible. They've brought the music back home.

There are rows of gold and platinum records on the Studio walls. The bottom two look old—their frames are scratched up, and their labels have begun to fade. They are the two I grew up with: McFadden and Whitehead's *Ain't No Stoppin' Us Now*, and *Teddy*, by Teddy Pendergrass. Surrounding those are many more, all from the past 4 years: Brandy and Monica's "The Boy Is Mine"; Eric Benet's album *A Day in the Life; Like Water for Chocolate*, by the rapper Common; and, most significantly, *Things Fall Apart*, the Roots' third album, the one that has made them stars. There are platinum discs and Grammy-winner plaques for their single "You Got Me," a track for which my dad did the string arrangements and reunited the old MFSB strings for the first time in a long time.

Billboard magazine has just arrived, and my father is beside himself, jumping up and down, because five songs on the Billboard R&B Hot 100 chart—by R. Kelly, Erykah Badu, Musiq, Bilal, and Jill Scott—were either recorded in Philly or have some Philly connection.

James Poyser, the 33-year-old keyboardist and producer who's behind Erykah Badu's records, as well as Jill Scott and the upcoming Next Big Thing, Jaguar, can trace a more direct line from Gamble and Huff to his work. He used to have his offices at 309 South Broad, in Gamble and Huff's building. "I could go in and speak to Gamble about different things. He told me that every song has to take a journey. It might not be to Australia, it might only be to Broad Street, but it has to go somewhere," Poyser says, adding, "I see that people who worked with Gamble are still so in awe of him. He's obviously a man of great power." When asked how he would describe today's new "Sound of Philadelphia," Poyser says, "It's not all that bling-bling stuff," referring to the materialistic culture that so much current hip-hop and R&B glorifies. "It's a lot more conscious, more educational."

"I wouldn't say Gamble and Huff influenced me directly," says Richard Nichols, the Roots' manager and self-described "chief spiritual officer," a 42-year-old African-American who grew up in the midst of TSOP. "I had weird taste when I was a teenager. Gamble and Huff didn't feel youthful or sound cutting-edge to me then." He thinks for a moment, then adds, "They did have an influence on the town. It was like having a team that was winning."

It's a familiar plot: Local boy makes good, leaving home to seek his fortune, and finds in the end that his ultimate spiritual fulfillment lies right back where he started. The twist in the story is Kenny Gamble's consistent blend of ambition and humility. When he named his fledgling record company "Philadelphia International," he says, he was "just getting started, [but] thinking about the whole world." The name of his Universal Companies—and his Universal Institute Charter School—likewise imply a vision that extends far beyond South Broad Street. The songs of the Sound of Philadelphia succeeded because they never tried to please anyone but the folks who were living at 15th and Christian, shopping for shoes on Germantown Avenue, waiting for the bus at Broad and Lehigh. Yet those songs made (and still make) people dance, all over the world. Gamble's current work is no different: He's aiming to change the world, one rundown, hometown city block at a time.

By Robert Huber
October 2003

JULIUS ERVING DOESN'T WANT TO BE A HERO ANYMORE

A tap on my passenger window.

Huh? What?

Oh! Julius. I pop my seat upright—I've dozed off, waiting for him outside the Airport Marriott. Somebody with him, a woman. What time is it?

Christ, almost 2 a.m.

Julius gets in next to me, she gets in back, behind him. "There's a change of plans," Erving says.

He doesn't introduce us, I turn to say hello: young, lovely, a dusting of color like cinnamon.

"Let's drive back to the Academy House"—where he has a condo, where I picked him up at noon to start a day of driving him all over attending to the task of being Julius Erving. "We're going to meet a car there."

We head into town. I brought him to the Marriott—what? Three hours ago. He said he was getting a little room service, wanted to change clothes, that he'd be down in 40 minutes. We were going to a party on Delaware Avenue, the follow-up to a basketball exhibition in West Philly in memory of his drug-troubled son Cory, who died 3 years ago down in Orlando when he drove his car into a retaining pond.

Now the woman leans forward to talk to Julius—53 years old, a grandfather, his hair gone mostly white—on the far side of his headrest. Not for privacy, just to get close, to be near, to argue playfully about nothing, Julius volleying with a sporty mind-fuck—"You know I'm right because I said what you thought I said when you said ..."

His mood has shifted, gotten lighter. Driving to the Marriott, he asked me, "Do you think I should coach the Sixers?" A startling question—not because it was actually on his plate, given that the team hadn't even contacted him, but because Julius Erving was wondering out loud what to do with his life. He was leaving the Orlando Magic, a mutual decision after 6 years of an increasingly nebulous PR vice presidency. He does not know what he's going to do next, or, for that matter, where he's going to live.

When we get to the Academy House, he goes in to get something, leaving me alone with her.

"How long have you known Julius?" I wonder.

"I don't know Julius at all," she says quickly. Her name is Freddie. Freddie works in promotions down in Florida.

Julius returns with a bag. As a long black limo sidles silently next to us, I wonder aloud if he ever bothers sleeping.

"Sleep? I can do that at home"—presumably, for now, Orlando, his condo near the Magic arena.

Julius and Freddie are going to pick up Jenn in South Philly. She's another young, lovely, light-skinned black woman, a wannabe actress who, in fact, occupied Freddie's spot in the backseat for the better part of this day of gallivanting around town.

One thing hasn't changed from his playing days: Julius likes to keep moving. It's after two on a summer night, as the stretch slips off down Locust. After they get Jenn, it's on to Atlantic City. Julius keeps another condo there.

HE WAS THE one who was above all this, who would never go there. Julius Erving, the Doctor, arrived in town just when the NBA needed a big image lift, mid-1970s, a shining light in the coke-addled, pampered, arrogant, sexcrazed brotherhood of pro ball—the best brother, pure playground but responsible and winning, and better in *this* way too: dignified, a family man, smart, a stand-up guy in his careful baritone, a dream for white suburbia. For God's sake, he *lived* in white suburbia, not all gated-up but comfortably, and he used to joke that he was white—off the court.

Imagine the 76ers winning the championship now, a Broad Street parade, Allen Iverson saying a few words. Think he'd look over the sea of Sixer-jersey-clad kids and ask them why they weren't in school, as Julius did two decades ago? In his three-story-high mural on a rowhouse south of Temple U, Erving's in full flight but not dunking a basketball: He's dressed in a shiny gold suit, with glasses, gray-flecked hair, a serious message from Wilson Goode to North Philly. A big investor in Coke here, his finger in a myriad of other business ventures. Crossover indeed—the best of us and them, all rolled up into one guy.

And if anything, we need to believe in him more than ever, this summer and fall of Kobe, as the feeling grows that just maybe there are no star athletes, or for that matter klieg-light heroes of any stripe, whose performing personae hold up in private. It's gotten so wearying and sad, the *And you too?* feeling that big-time stardom is, inevitably, a morass of privilege and ego run horribly, selfishly amok.

Not Julius, no, never. But there it was, early this year: Turquoise is divorcing him after 29 years. What's more—hardly a ripple in the media—there was another kid outside the marriage.

Another kid? *Julius?*

You remember the first one: the tennis player, Alexandra. Pushing deep into Wimbledon in 1999 from out of nowhere, and suddenly her mother Samantha the ex-sportswriter who'd been openly hinting for years that the mystery father was athletic royalty, baiting the press to figure it out—well, Samantha got her wish. A phone call to California had produced a birth certificate. Alexandra Stevenson's father was Julius Winfield Erving II. At first, for a moment, he denied it, one of the few really bad moves he's ever made, publicly. But then he quickly caved to the obvious (God, how she looked like him, the long, sad face and those long, smooth strides…), admitted that he'd had an affair back in the late 1970s, with this hot-button white freelancer, one of the first female reporters to push her way into local locker rooms.

And then he explained how he handled it from day one, taking responsibility, supporting Alexandra in a nice life from afar—Samantha had bolted for home, California, when she was pregnant, and raised the kid out there. Handled amicably, no legal stuff, Turquoise had known about this child all along, and hadn't Samantha done a great job and he respected that, and now this was, in fact, a relief for him, for his family, that it was public. And of course you knew the affair and the kid were a mistake but, *just like that,* here he was, slipping into stride with himself: Dr. J took it on, seamlessly, the right way. Of course he did.

And then Cory. 3 years ago, the family down in Orlando now, after Julius took the front-office job with the Magic. Their baby, 19, with a drug problem, who'd been in and out of rehab for 6 years, who'd been busted with his older brother Cheo 2 years earlier burglarizing a car, a crack pipe on them (the charges were later dropped), went missing for 40 days. And there was Julius on *Larry King* pleading for information, pleading, right into the camera, for Cory to come home. Was he holed up in a crackhouse in Altamonte Springs? Was he already dead? You wondered—a bad private thought here—how it could be that he had two sons with drug problems: because Julius wasn't paying attention? Because the kids were spoiled, left to do whatever? But the look on his face there on *Larry King*, a father's worst horror, a guy who was always so careful and private especially about his family begging on national TV in a last-gasp possibility for his son's life. Then the subsequent news that yes, he was dead, he'd run his car into a pond a mile from their house, taking a shortcut home, there was some coke in his system but not enough to short-circuit his driving, it was just an accident, a kid battling his way in and out of drug troubles racing back with a loaf of bread for a barbecue later that afternoon. Not a blemish on Julius Erving's reputation but a tragedy.

So there was some bad trouble, yet the deal on him held.

But now this. Julius and Turk had been like royalty in Philly, running with Albert and Doris Taxin, Bennett and Judie Weinstock, Leonard Tose and whoever he was married to. Everyone touched by how beautifully, smartly, richly they conducted themselves. Now she'd booted him, filed, and there it was in the divorce papers: Julius claiming to be worth $10 million. (Sounds awfully low.) Turquoise spending $1,150 a month on "grooming" (is that possible?), her cable shut off because he's not paying her bills—the sublimely embarrassing clawing and scratching of a big-stakes divorce. Something else is in that file: another kid, 5-year-old Jules, with somebody named Doris Madden who sometimes calls herself Pearl. And the divorce papers allude to yet another woman Turquoise says Julius is supporting, one with a son who lives in Hollywood, Florida.

Julius?

What's more, when he quit the Orlando Magic early last summer, it was clear that management was ready for him to go—his mentoring and PR duties were never very well-defined or fruitful, especially in light of his personal turmoil. So Julius was leaving basketball.

All this puts everything in doubt. You feel, in fact, like you've been kicked in the stomach. You try to take the high road that somebody's marriage and sex life are none of your business—what's the point of taking an athlete's life apart?—but that misses the point. The possibility that you've been duped, that he showed off as one thing all these years, that he banked on the image, used what you were only too willing to believe but it's bullshit—you want to know. Is it?

"FREDDIE?"

She looks up sheepishly, smiling, over granny shades. Freddie, indeed, a month later, here in the pro shop at Julius's golf club just south of Orlando, a place so posh a guard in a booth has to nod you in; at last, off of Florida's ubiquitous sun-pounded strip into lush equatorial flora—moneyed Florida.

Freddie is trying on clothes for Julius. One number, brown shorts with overlying flaps to look like a skirt, Julius thinks might be too tight for golf. He hands her a golf ball. When she puts it in her pocket it protrudes absurdly, like a misplaced erection.

"Too tight, you need room to swing," Julius says, mimicking his own. "Sexy, though."

After she settles for a couple of trim tops, we head out in golf carts to the practice range. When you're sitting next to him, Julius doesn't seem tall—cut high, Larry Brown calls it, all legs, though he's 30 pounds over his greyhound playing weight of 216. And those hands. He lights a fat cigar with hands so long they appear blessed with an extra down-looping segment mid-digit, longer than any other player he ever measured against, what gave him control to wave the ball around like a pom-pom before finger-rolling or slamming it home. Freddie is going to hit balls while he watches and talks.

A long time ago, it was Isaac Hayes who taught Julius something important about how to conduct himself, though inadvertently. Julius loved Isaac Hayes, but once, when Hayes was giving a press conference in full Black Moses regalia, with the chains, the *look*, it didn't sit right with Julius. He was 20 years old, still at UMass, at the very beginning of his own phenomenon. He decided that off the court, he had to be himself—not Dr. J, but Julius Erving.

As he starts talking basketball, I think about how he came off over the years: the well-spoken intonator of careful sound bites, smart but a little boring. Yet the day I spent with him running around Philly, he surprised me, what a regular guy he is, relaxed, a little goofy, much younger-seeming than 53: As we were leaving Temple U hospital, where he got a knuckle replacement on his middle finger checked out, the elevator got peculiar, and when it opened, unbidden, a second time with nobody to get on or off, Julius looked down from his six-foot-six-and-a-half vantage to beckon: "Casper. How are you, Casper? Come on in, Casper." Back in my car, his cell plugged into my lighter, he was an almost nonstop Barry White baritone of "Wassup, dawg. Yeah, I'm in Philly, just checkin' in. Uh-huh. I'll call you later, cuz." And "Lambchops, how are you, Lambchops?" Or sonorous business with Val—his longtime around-the-clock secretary: "We should really move that board meeting to Wednesday afternoon." A busy guy, and a guy at ease with anybody; Lambchops turned out to be Doris Taxin, the widow of Albert, the owner of Bookbinder's who died of brain cancer in 1993—she put on a charity golf tournament that afternoon at Valley Green in his name. Julius, an old buddy of Albert's, spent a couple hours teamed up with three old stiff-swinging white guys, could only putt for them because of his bad finger, but interrupted his cell calls to champion every tiny parabola of an iron, high-fived dropped putts, was not so much doing the I'm-your-buddy star thing as, clearly, *enjoying* himself.

So I wonder, now, if he had to hold himself back when he was still playing, giving us just a small part of himself in the guise of responsible spokesman.

"A lot of stereotypes of black athletes used to bother me when I was growing up. So I wanted to rectify some of that. I was influenced by Jackie Robinson, Joe Louis, the things happening to Arthur Ashe. Bill Russell. Anytime they were interviewed, they took it seriously, they weren't laughing and joking and shucking and jiving. They wouldn't let people put words in their mouth. I saw microphones being shoved in front of certain guys who couldn't articulate the Queen's English very well—they spoke Ebonics. Or guys dismissed interviews as light and frivolous..."

"WHOA!" Julius interrupts himself to admire one of Freddie's shots. She looks over at us, we wait for the next one—ground ball, though the swing is pretty. Julius takes a pull from his cigar.

"When I got a platform, a stage, I didn't need to get up there to be Mr. Bojangles. It was important to me to be Julius Erving, not Dr. J. On the court I could don the cape and fly and soar and play, but when I stepped off I needed to be a person, a person that commanded a certain type of respect."

I remember. I bought it. But then I tell him my reaction to Jules, the second kid outside his marriage, how it hit me like a punch in the gut. How can I merge the guy he was just talking about with that one?

"I've removed myself from having to answer to the general public on certain issues," Julius intones, "and that would be one of them." For 16 years of playing, he carried the mantle of being somebody, of representing something, a heavy burden he placed on himself. "After it's done, it's done. How that relates to my children, whether it's children within my marriage or out of my marriage, are things I have to deal with, be accountable for, not the public. Not you."

It feels like a too-convenient line in the sand. The million dollars a year the Orlando Magic threw at him in 1997 to be a public face on a troubled team—that long-standing persona as a dignified, respectable family man sure came in handy there.

But Julius is dug in, patiently waiting, as he stares out at the driving range, to move off this. He works his cigar. We'll talk about his background, then: He was raised by his mother in an integrated project on Long Island; his parents separated when he was three, and he wasn't close to his father. "Being successful beyond my own expectations—I attribute a lot of that to the strength I got from my mom. She buried two husbands and a son and a daughter, she lost a set of twins back in the 1940s. I look at her and don't see her spirit broken, don't see her faith deterred. I know that much of what I have gone through is pale in comparison to what she has gone through"—the story you've heard a million times, the sweet overview of troubled waters that avoids them.

Freddie, who has quickly grown hot hitting balls and taken a golf-cart run through sprinklers, now glistens right next to us, listening, but I can't help it:

"Did you feel disappointed in yourself when you had Jules?"

"Why are we going back to that?"

"Because I'm still curious about it."

"*Why*? You think your readers are curious about it?"

"I don't know, but I'm going back to it because I feel like you danced around an answer."

"Answer my question. Do you think your readers are interested in it?"

"I think they're curious like I am, how it meshes with who they think or believe you are."

"My answer is, let them think what they want to think."

Julius wants to keep his heroes—Lincoln, Kennedy, Cosby—heroic. He doesn't go searching for chinks in the armor. The personal stuff is beside the point. "Do you," Julius Erving wants to know, "disrespect Thomas Jefferson?"

Not necessarily. But the private side, the real side, of someone important to us, a hero—yeah, we need to know. Who they really are is more important than their simple myth.

TURQUOISE finally decided she was not having it anymore. The women, the lying: "I kept those babies to myself all these years. But now I've got nothing to hide anymore. I've been hiding for years about Julius's babies."

She decides to get it off her chest, early one summer evening, in a private hallway of her apartment house on Locust—Philly is home again, where her kids live—what being married to Julius Erving is all about. It took an enormous toll, worrying, constantly, that the truth would get out. She did not tell her own mother, or her children, or anyone—although her mother knew that things weren't right, that Turk was on edge, that she was much too thin. Her marriage, though, that was her business. But that's behind her now, and she looks different: a slightly plump 53-year-old woman with cropped hair tucked behind her ears. She's happy with her weight. She's happy with who she is—because she's not lying anymore.

And she knows that maybe it is not smart to talk, to let this out, but she can't help herself, she's been silent about this for three decades: From day one, Julius was cheating on her. From the beginning she's been lying about those babies, protecting him, forever. She's not doing it anymore.

The beginning was 1972 in nothing Richmond, where he was playing for the Virginia Squires, his first pro team; she already had a son, Cheo, with Freddie Summers, who'd been one of the first black quarterbacks in the ACC at Wake Forest. After that marriage broke up, she came home to Winston-Salem, was visiting her brother in Richmond, went to a game and then a party afterward and there was Julius—case closed.

Blind love, girlish love—even though she already had a baby. She and Julius were only 22. They married a year later, Julius adopted Cheo, within 3 years they had J and Jazmin. When Turquoise would find out about another woman, she'd confront him—Turquoise doesn't take anything lying down—and he'd stop seeing her. One thing about Julius, he didn't throw it in her face, he was careful. But then Turk, who was always around, even with three little kids she'd go to practically every home game as he played, now for the Nets on Long Island, would find out about a new Julius bedmate. She'd make a scene, but swallow it. Being Mrs. Julius Erving—no matter what, no matter how many women, he was still the center for her; he and their kids were everything. "I would have—" Turquoise blanches at her own crudeness because she is a lady but this is the truth, and one thing she'll never do is protect Julius again, so she has to tell this truth too: "I would have eaten his shit."

She did know about Alexandra all along, as Julius claimed. Or almost all along, and it's not quite as Turquoise-is-cool-with-it as he made it sound when he came clean publicly.

In May of 1981, Julius playing in Philly now, they were back home on Long Island after the Sixers had washed out of the playoffs against Boston; Turquoise was pregnant with Cory, due that month. When Turk came home one day after being out, her housekeeper told her there's this girl who keeps calling for Julius, and she said don't tell you who it is: Samantha Stevenson. Now, that was odd—Samantha, a sportswriter, was her friend, in fact Turk was the only Sixer wife who would talk to Samantha, the only one who didn't feel threatened by her taking notes next to their half-naked husbands. Samantha had even ghost-written an article for Turquoise that ran in the *New York Times*, where Turk complained that the Ervings' reception in Philadelphia certainly could have been warmer, which ruffled feathers, naturally, in the team's front office—really the problem was that Turk's words had been twisted, made harder. Samantha had assured her that *she* didn't do that, it was some editor out of her control. Anyway, Turquoise hadn't seen Samantha for months, she hadn't been around, but now, when Samantha called back again, Turk got on an extension as Julius answered the phone, and silently listened in: Samantha was in California, there was this baby, and Turk didn't waste any time demanding to be brought up to speed as they talked about how to handle it: *What the fuck is going on here? What the fuck you doin' callin' my husband?*

Even with that, the truth in her ear, Julius denied it. At first. That was the hardest thing—the lying. It was almost a game. He would tell her anything, always working an angle with her. Tell her she had it wrong, she was crazy. It drove her mad. She'd fight him but cave; when Julius stormed out for a few days, she'd be worried sick: Where was he? Was he safe? He'd be holed up in some hotel, playing golf, maybe Vegas. Later, the condo he bought in A.C., or the Islands.

She was always anxious, so thin, not only battling Julius but having to play both mother and father to their kids—mid-1980s, they'd finally moved from Long Island, buying a mansion in Villanova, but to the boys the suburbs were milk-toast: *So you're the Doctor's kids.* As soon as they were old enough, could get out from under Turk, they hit the streets in Philly. Reality, not this fame bullshit. Cheo and later Cory got caught up in drinking, weed, coke. Turk *was not having it*, her babies were not going this way. But what could she do? Rehab, and then back out on the streets. Craving their father, she's sure now, that was the deal. Needing their father. Eventually they sent Cory to John Lucas, the player and coach who'd been an addict and had a treatment center down in Houston. The boy's drug problems weren't so bad, really—Lucas saw the challenge as helping 15-year-old Cory become Cory, whoever that might be. A tougher nut when your dad is so good and so famous and so busy. The one thing that Julius was totally dedicated to, that Turquoise gives him credit for even in the storm of trying to crawl out, now, from under *Mrs. Julius Erving*: He was always ready to perform.

She admires that still. The problem, though, is how everything centered right there. It was all about him, that's the way it had to be. All of them at the beck and call of Dr. J.

She thought it might get better, when he retired. But it was worse, he was around less. Chasing business or fooling around. They lived parallel lives even when he was in Villanova, Julius always hitting the sack at three or four in the morning, Turk up at six with her kids. She liked Philly, had found a network of lunch friends—Doris Taxin, Joanne Keenan, Riki Wagman, women who schooled her in moneyed class. She was friends, too, with singer Teddy Pendergrass—Teddy's seats were right next to hers at Sixers games—and somehow that became a big rumor about Turquoise: a partyer, in the car with Teddy and the transvestite the night of his accident in 1985, the wreck that broke his neck and paralyzed him. Turquoise, in fact, was not in the car; she was home in bed with Julius. Julius and Turk were among the first at the hospital early that morning to see him. Teddy himself told her what happened.

He was at the game that night with a woman, went out to a club afterward and ditched her for another. They left, heading for Teddy's place, him driving. Weaving Wissahickon Drive, he put his hand up her dress, and at the moment of getting the genital news—a man!—lost control of his car.

Really, Turquoise has always liked to stay home, with her children. Julius liked to be out. And it was the same once the kids were old enough to start living on their own.

Then, Orlando. He called her one day 6 years ago from Chicago announcing a new life—"I'm signing tomorrow with the Magic. They'll send a plane for you to go to the press conference." So she moved south with him.

Turquoise and Cory—still in and out of rehab, trying to get a grip—hated Orlando. Their lives thickened with public trouble. Cheo and Cory were busted with a crack pipe, charged with breaking into a car. The Alexandra story broke, while Cheo was in jail in Orange County on a drug-related conviction; Julius visited him the next day to explain the deal, but too late: Cheo had already been in a fistfight with another inmate who clued him in to his half-sister by running his mouth about how good she looked, and what I'd like to do with that, and how long she been playin' tennis, anyway? And then they lost Cory. What made it worse, even harder to take, was that he seemed to be doing better, was starting to find himself.

And Turquoise found out about Julius's young son Jules—though she got hit sideways with this one, too. An acquaintance had told her, innocently enough, about seeing Julius with his grandson. Little Cory, J's kid? That wasn't possible— J and Cory were up in Philly, and Julius barely saw them even when he went north. Turk went to Julius's Magic office, asked him point-blank: What little boy you spending time with down here?

"We'll talk about it later."

That night he admitted it: another woman, another child. But his attitude was, as always, that she could take it or leave it; this was the deal, take it or leave it. Julius was banking on Turquoise folding, letting him off the hook. As always.

By this point, she'd been trying to come to terms with herself, who the hell she was in this marriage, for years. Her therapists had been telling her that one day she'd wake up, decide that she loved herself more than she loved Julius—as trite, and as monumental, as that. And then he'd have nothing on her. She could tell him to get the hell out of her house and mean it. And all he could do was stop paying her bills, play hide-and-seek with his fortune. That was the only thing he had on her.

BUT WHO a guy really is depends, of course, on where you look, who you ask. And with Julius Erving, there are a lot of stories, a thousand moments, like this one.

Back in 1978, Fran Blinebury was 24, a new writer for the *Philadelphia Journal*, covering the Sixers. At training camp that fall at Franklin & Marshall, he got on the hotel elevator, and just as the doors were closing, a hand—an incredible hand, the longest fingers—parted them. Oh no, what was he going to say to—?

"Hi, I'm Julius Erving. You're the new writer, aren't you? Listen, if you need anything, need any help, let me know. Just ask me."

Last January, Blinebury, now working for the *Houston Chronicle*, was in town covering the NFC championship game. The evening before it, as he was walking through the downtown Marriott lobby: "Hey! Fran!" He peered across the room, searching. "Over here. Get over here!" Blinebury went to a group of guys. "You weren't going to stop and say hello?" Julius Erving laughed.

You can't fake this stuff, not over the long haul. Erving and Blinebury opened wallets, shared pictures of their grandchildren. It's high-fiving the old-fart golfers at the Taxin golf outing, sitting placidly in your lawn chair at the West Philly b-ball exhibit in Cory Erving's memory to sign autographs in your ornate script—not "Dr. J" but "Julius Winfield Erving II"—leaning lower to explain to the wide-eyed tiniest in Iverson jerseys that, you know, maybe sports isn't something you should count on because you could break a leg, so make sure you study. Julius Erving is a nice guy. He tries to do the right thing.

And as I press him, at his golf club south of Orlando, Freddie still taking it all in, on the greater meaning of mistakes he's made, Julius Erving suggests, with plaintive resignation, that we're all in the same boat: "Everything that happens in life isn't based on logic and reasoning and planning. I have to look at it as God's plan for me, and I'm dealing with it." Though he also comes up with what I'm doing wrong: "You should ask me if I love myself. I do love myself. I love all my sons, I love all my daughters."

Another opening! "So does that mean, then, that you have a relationship with Jules?"

"Bah-ob," Julius Erving complains in a weary singsong, "you're being a pain in the ass."

But I can't leave it alone. Julius Erving wants to have it both ways—the hero who is also a good man. Remarkably, pushed and pushed, he doesn't get angry, and he lands, finally, on a proud tidy-up note: "I've had two children out of wedlock, but I can walk down the street holding my head up high. There are 10,000 other children that I've been the catalyst for in all that I've done."

He did give so much. You could see it, watching him play, the playground gift in ordered service to his team, and maybe you could even feel, watching him, what his Sixers teammates leap now to verify, why they're so enamored with him still: calling team meetings, always sitting in the middle of the team bus to relate to the dudes in back or coaches up front, a guy who would offer a rookie a meal at home with Turk or have him call his very own agent, a guy who had Darryl Dawkins buying a dictionary to understand these great big words he used. The world's greatest teammate.

The problem is, we want it both ways too, so we imagine even more. We merge him, the part we can't see, with the talent, make it all one thing, create what writers covering the team the Doctor's first year in the NBA called Hurricane Julius. Taking the road by storm, as we watch, as we fawn.

It happens over and over, says John Lucas: "We think *he's* the one, and then we're let down. Now Dr. J the person has emerged, and we're still looking for that superstar in life, but he's just a man. He's Julius Erving. A man trying to grow up."

Still?

"It's true for all of us who play sports," Lucas says. "We miss childhood because we're working so hard, out there every day playing our sport. Athletes don't grow up into adults—after playing, they grow up."

Which would make Julius a 16-year-old. That's how Turquoise sees him: wanting more—more money, a better car, another girl. Still.

Another question for the Doctor:

"Think you'll get married again someday?"

Julius and Freddie don't even bother not to have eye contact as he answers: "There's a good possibility of that."

"You think you'll have more children?" Julius takes a puff of cigar. "That would be—no."

But what will he do? Julius doesn't know. His next venture might very well be gaming—he's looking into buying a casino. Longtime Erving acolytes like Pat Williams, who as general manager of the Sixers three decades ago bought him from the Nets, react to this idea with wide-eyed say-it-ain't-so disappointment: Gambling, so tacky, all about cold cash, is beneath Dr. J. But he's talking to Steve Wynn and others in the industry, performing due diligence. There's a lot of money in gambling, and after his divorce, Julius Erving might very well need it.

And this is the other fallout of Hurricane Julius, what happens to our heroes: an outsize life that splits, finally, at the seams. That June night, at the exhibit of street ball in West Philly, a couple dozen local dunksters performing for him, for the guy who spawned, more than anyone, playground ball as art—all Julius could manage was a tepid shoulder bob to the DJ's record-scratching funk. He barely acknowledged the fly girls getting close, checking in. Turquoise has it right. He looks lost.

The problems have piled up now. The word is out; people know about these other kids he's had, what he's done to his marriage. He's been thrown out of his house; he's not even talking to Turquoise. The Magic don't want him anymore. Alexandra is under her mother's wing, and there's no contact. He doesn't know where he's going to live, or what he'll be doing. Oh, he's trying, he's stoic: *That's my fate, not my plan.* But now, alley-oop and a jam, again and again and again and again, he keeps seeing Cory, his dead son, the son who got his athletic genes, a six-four kid who could put his elbows inside the rim. He'd never done anything with the talent; but he was beginning to, he was playing ball and getting his life together, he would be 22 now, these kids' age. *That should be Cory flying and jamming. Just like I did.* But Cory's gone. And Julius Erving just wants to leave the beautiful game that he, more than anyone, gave us, to get away, to be done with it. To start over.

PATTI LABELLE

Singer, diva; 60; Wynnewood

I hate that word, "diva." It was great to be a diva back in the day, before all these little divettes came along.

I've always been a Philadelphian, and I'm going to be a Philadelphian for the rest of my life. I have a home in the Bahamas, but I never visit. Philadelphia is calming for me. There are fewer temptations here than in New York or Vegas.

The Philadelphia personality is very honest, very direct. We don't pretend we love anyone unless we do.

My mother was a great homemaker. My father was a great father, but he wasn't such a great husband. I watched them fight, and I would think to myself, "Why doesn't one of them just leave?"

I remember learning to fry scrapple from my mother—I got a big burn on my neck. I can cover it up with makeup, though.

I went to 9th Street to shop with my mother every Saturday. Chubby Checker was working in Henry Colt's poultry shop when I met him—his name was Ernest Evans. He was probably 9 or 10 then. He didn't know if he was going to be a singer yet, and I didn't know that I was going to be one, either.

I had no idea what I was telling people to do. None of us knew what "Voulez-vous coucher avec moi" meant. I just loved the sound of it. I heard that song and said, "This is going to be a big hit!" Then afterwards, we got a lot of comments from nuns and people like that. Well, I just said, some of my best friends are hookers, that's how they make their living, and they don't come up onstage and take the mike out of my mouth, so I'm not going to take anything away from them.

When the girls did the song for the movie [*Moulin Rouge*] 26 years later, and gave it another life—I thought that was wonderful.

I had a big surprise party for my 60th birthday. It was at Denise Rich's in New York City. My three sisters all died before they turned 44, so naturally I thought I'd die young, too. Now I just celebrate. They'd love the fact that I'm still going on. I'm still here. I have diabetes. I'm menopausal. But I can handle that.

I never get angry at God. I've seen so many other people's losses—why shouldn't I have to go through what everybody else does?

We need to learn to deal with death. It's a fact. We all come to this planet, live here for a while, and then leave.

My divorce didn't come about through my being abused or fighting. I just fell out of love, and I think my husband did, too. But we went on for 32 years. I didn't know how to do it differently. I was thinking about my son, who thought he had this Ozzie and Harriet family.

Philadelphians are no fatter than anyone in any other city—and believe me, I've seen other cities. There's a lot of fat on those butts.

I think this city did help me become an overachiever, because Philadelphians are so critical. I have to represent, or they might beat me up. Philadelphia don't play.

I get a lot of love from white people, but I feel they could care less if I wasn't Patti LaBelle. I'll go out to the clubs or to boutiques with my friends and everything is fine, but it isn't fine if my friends go by themselves.

White people think they're so tricky, they think I don't see it, but I do.

We need to speak out when we haven't been treated right. If the food in a restaurant isn't good, you send the plate back, right?

If you don't speak out for what you believe in, then you *should* be treated badly. I speak out on anything I see that's even a little suspect. I'll address you on that.

I don't keep anything in. I let it all hang out.

By Sasha Issenberg
April 2004

BOO-BOOS IN PARADISE

A few years ago, journalist David Brooks wrote a celebrated article for the *Atlantic Monthly*, "One Nation, Slightly Divisible," in which he examined the country's cultural split in the aftermath of the 2000 election, contrasting the red states that went for Bush and the blue ones for Gore. To see the vast nation whose condition he diagnosed, Brooks compared two counties: Maryland's Montgomery (Blue), where he himself lives, and Pennsylvania's Franklin (a Red county in a Blue state). "I went to Franklin County because I wanted to get a sense of how deep the divide really is," Brooks wrote of his leisurely northward drive to see the other America across "the Meatloaf Line; from here on there will be a lot fewer sun-dried-tomato concoctions on restaurant menus and a lot more meatloaf platters." Franklin County was a place where "no blue *New York Times* delivery bags dot driveways on Sunday mornings ... [where] people don't complain that Woody Allen isn't as funny as he used to be, because they never thought he was funny," he wrote. "In Red America churches are everywhere. In Blue America Thai restaurants are everywhere. In Red America they have QVC, the Pro Bowlers Tour, and hunting. In Blue America we have NPR, Doris Kearns Goodwin, and socially conscious investing."

Brooks, an agile and engaging writer, was doing what he does best, bringing sweeping social movements to life by zeroing in on what Tom Wolfe called "status detail," those telling symbols—the Weber Grill, the open-toed sandals with advanced polymer soles—that immediately fix a person in place, time, and class. Through his articles, a best-selling book, and now a twice-a-week column in what is arguably journalism's most prized locale, the *New York Times* op-ed page, Brooks has become a must-read, charming us into seeing events in the news through his worldview.

There's just one problem: Many of his generalizations are false. According to Amazon.com sales data, one of Goodwin's strongest markets has been deep-Red McAllen, Texas. That's probably not, however, QVC country. "I would guess our audience would skew toward Blue areas of the country," says Doug Rose, the network's vice president of merchandising and brand development. "Generally our audience is female suburban baby boomers, and our business skews toward affluent areas." Rose's standard PowerPoint presentation of the QVC brand includes a map of one zip code—Beverly Hills, 90210—covered in little red dots that each represent one QVC customer address, to debunk "the myth that they're all little old ladies in trailer parks eating bonbons all day."

"Everything that people in my neighborhood do without motors, the people in Red America do with motors," Brooks wrote. "When it comes to yard work, they have rider mowers; we have illegal aliens." Actually, six of the top 10 states in terms of illegal-alien population are Red.

"We in the coastal metro Blue areas read more books," Brooks asserted. A 2003 University of Wisconsin-Whitewater study of America's most literate cities doesn't necessarily agree. Among the study's criteria was the presence of bookstores and libraries; 20 of the 30 most literate cities were in Red states.

"Very few of us," Brooks wrote of his fellow Blue Americans, "could name even five NASCAR drivers, although stock-car races are the best-attended sporting events in the country." He might want to take his name-recognition test to the streets of the 2002 NASCAR Winston Cup Series's highest-rated television markets—three of the top five were in Blue states. (Philadelphia was fifth nationally.)

Brooks could be dismissed as little more than a snarky punch-line artist, except that he postures as a public intellectual—and has been received as one.

IT'S HARD, in fact, to think of many American thinkers more influential at this moment than Brooks. His 2000 book *Bobos in Paradise* heralded the rise of a new upper class that mixed 1960s-style liberalism with 1980s-style conspicuous consumption; celebrated by reviewers, it quickly became a best-seller. Brooks wrote that his hometown, Wayne, was emblematic of the "Upscale Suburban Hippiedom" that was the natural habitat of these "bourgeois bohemians." Like "yuppie" and "metrosexual," Brooks's "bobo" entered the language as a successful coinage of pop sociology. It shows up in magazine articles and casual conversations, and the book itself is footnoted in dozens of books on American society and consumer culture, and cited in a college history textbook.

On the publication of *Bobos, New York Times* critic Walter Goodman lumped Brooks with William H. Whyte Jr., author of *The Organization Man*, and David Riesman, who wrote *The Lonely Crowd*, as a practitioner of "sociological journalism." (In the introduction to *Bobos*, Brooks invoked Whyte—plus Jane Jacobs and John Kenneth Galbraith—as predecessors.) In 2001, the New School for Social Research, in Manhattan, held a panel discussion in which real-life scholars pondered the bobo. When, in 2001, Richard Posner ranked the 100 highest-profile public intellectuals, Brooks came in 85th, just behind Marshall McLuhan at 82nd, and ahead of Garry Wills, Isaiah Berlin and Margaret Mead.

Following the success of *Bobos*, Brooks—who was then writing for the *Atlantic Monthly* and *Newsweek* and appearing on PBS and NPR—was offered the *Times* column, formalizing his position as the in-house conservative pundit of liberal America. In his column, Brooks writes mostly about affairs of state, but with the same approach—a cultural analysis grounded in social observation— that made *Bobos* such a success. This summer, *Bobos* will get a sibling when Brooks publishes *On Paradise Drive: How We Live Now (And Always Have) in the Future Tense.*

Brooks is operating in a long tradition of public intellectualism. Like William Whyte, another child of Philadelphia's western suburbs fascinated with the interplay of money and manners among his contemporaries, Brooks is a journalist who works on sociological turf. But Whyte, who was an editor for *Fortune* in the 1950s, observed how people lived, inferred trends, considered what they meant, and then came up with grand conclusions about the direction of the country. When, in 1954, he wanted to find out which consumers were trend-setters, he went into Overbrook Park and surveyed 4,948 homes—all inhabited by real people. Brooks, by way of contrast, draws caricatures. Whether out of sloppiness or laziness, the examples he conjures to illustrate well-founded premises are often unfounded, undermining the very points he's trying to make.

IN JANUARY, I made my own trip to Franklin County, 175 miles southwest of Philadelphia, with a simple goal: I wanted to see where David Brooks comes up with this stuff. One of the first places I passed was Greencastle Coffee Roasters, which has more than 200 kinds of coffee, and a well-stocked South Asian grocery in the back with a product range hard to find in some large coastal cities: 20-pound bags of jasmine rice, cans of Thai fermented mustard greens, a freezer with lemongrass stalks and kaffir-lime leaves. The owner, Charles Rake, told me that there was, until a few years back, a Thai restaurant in Chambersburg, run by a woman who now does catering. "She's the best Thai cook I know on Planet Earth," Rake said. "And I've been to Thailand."

I stopped at Blockbuster, where the DVD of *Annie Hall* was checked out. I went to the counter to see how Scott, the clerk, thought it compared to Allen's other work. "It's funny," said Scott. "What's the funny one? Yeah, *Annie Hall*, that's the one where he dates everyone—it's funny."

"In Montgomery County we have Saks Fifth Avenue, Cartier, Anthropologie, Brooks Brothers. In Franklin County they have Dollar General and Value City, along with a plethora of secondhand stores," Brooks wrote. In fact, while Franklin has 14 stores with the word "dollar" in their name—plus one Value City—Montgomery County, Maryland, has 34, including one that's within walking distance of an Anthropologie in Rockville.

As I made my journey, it became increasingly hard to believe that Brooks ever left his home. "On my journeys to Franklin County, I set a goal: I was going to spend $20 on a restaurant meal. But although I ordered the most expensive thing on the menu—steak au jus, 'slippery beef pot pie,' or whatever—I always failed. I began asking people to direct me to the most expensive places in town. They would send me to Red Lobster or Applebee's," he wrote. "I'd scan the menu and realize that I'd been beaten once again. I went through great vats of chipped beef and 'seafood delight' trying to drop $20. I waded through enough surf-and-turfs and enough creamed corn to last a lifetime. I could not do it."

Taking Brooks's cue, I lunched at the Chambersburg Red Lobster and quickly realized that he could not have waded through much surf-and-turf at all. The "Steak and Lobster" combination with grilled center-cut New York strip is the most expensive thing on the menu. It costs $28.75. "Most of our checks are over $20," said Becka, my waitress. "There are a lot of ways to spend over $20."

The easiest way to spend more than $20 on a meal in Franklin County is to visit the Mercersburg Inn, which boasts "turn-of-the-century elegance." I had a $50 prix-fixe dinner, with an entree of veal medallions, served with a lump-crab and artichoke tower, wild-rice pilaf and a sage-caper-cream sauce. Afterward, I asked the inn's proprietors, Walt and Sandy Filkowski, if they had seen Brooks's article. They laughed. After it was published in the *Atlantic*, the nearby Mercersburg Academy boarding school invited Brooks as part of its speaker series. He spent the night at the inn. "For breakfast I made a goat-cheese-and-sun-dried-tomato tart," Sandy said. "He said he just wanted scrambled eggs."

I LOOKED at another of Brooks's more celebrated articles, an August 2002 piece in the conservative magazine the *Weekly Standard* in which he discerned a new American archetype he dubbed "Patio Man." Patio Man, in Brooks's description, "walks into a Home Depot or Lowe's or one of the other mega hardware complexes and his eyes are glistening with a faraway missionary zeal, like one of those old prophets gazing into the promised land. His lips are parted and twitching slightly." Patio Man, Brooks wrote, lives in one of the new Sprinkler Cities, "the fast-growing suburbs mostly in the South and West that are the homes of the new-style American dream."

Brooks illuminated Patio Man's world with vivid portraiture, telling details, and clever observations about American culture. ("All major choices of consumer durables these days ultimately come down to which model has the most impressive cup holders.") Brooks's suggestion that Patio Man's brethren would become the basis of a coming Republican majority found many friends. *Slate* identified him as a "new sociological icon." The *New York Times Magazine* 2002 "Year in Ideas" issue cited Patio Man in its encapsulation of "Post-Soccer-Mom Nomenclature."

Unfortunately, as with the Red/Blue article, many of the knowing references Brooks deftly invoked to bring Patio Man to life were entirely manufactured. He describes the ladies of Sprinkler City as "trim Jennifer Aniston women [who] wear capris and sleeveless tops and look great owing to their many hours of sweat and exercise at Spa Lady." That chain of women's gyms has three locations—all in New Jersey, far from any Sprinkler City. "The roads," Brooks writes, "have been given names like Innovation Boulevard and Entrepreneur Avenue." There are no Entrepreneur Avenues anywhere in the country, according to the business-directory database Reference USA, and only two Innovation Boulevards—in non-Sprinkler cities Fort Wayne, Indiana, and State College, Pennsylvania. There is also an Innovation Boulevard in Saskatoon, Saskatchewan.

The basic premises of Brooks's articles aren't necessarily wrong. His Red/Blue article was anchored in the research of political analyst Michael Barone, who in a June 2001 article in *National Journal* delineated a country split evenly in two: "One is observant, tradition-minded, moralistic. The other is unobservant, litigation-minded, relativistic." Brooks's Patio Man article was a pop translation of a February 2002 paper by University of Michigan demographer William H. Frey, who wrote that 2000 Census figures showed growth of "the New Sunbelt."

Brooks, however, does more than popularize inaccessible academic work; he distorts it. Barone relies on election returns and public-opinion data as the basis for his research; Frey looks to the census. But Brooks takes their findings and, regardless of origin, applies to them what one might call the Brooks Consumer Taste Fallacy, which suggests that people are best understood by where they shop and what they buy. So Brooks takes Barone's vote-counting in a two-sided election and says the country is split between Anthropologie and Dollar General. Then he takes Frey's demographic studies and says Sprinkler Cities are marked by their Home Depots. At this point, Frey was already working on a paper called "Three Americas," which argued for a tripartite model for understanding the nation: the Melting Pot (populous, immigrant-heavy states like New Jersey, Texas, Illinois); the Heartland (rural, without much population growth); and the New Sunbelt. If one really believes that the New Sunbelt and its Sprinkler Cities mark a culturally distinct region (as Brooks does), Frey suggests, one can't also believe that the country is rather evenly split into two culturally distinct factions (as Brooks does).

There are salient cultural divides in the United States—and, in fact, different values and practices among residents of Montgomery and Franklin counties—but consumer life is the place where they are most rapidly converging. In this regard, Brooks would have been better off relying on the newest generation of elitist truism—tongue-in-cheek laments about the proliferation of ubiquitous chain espresso bars and bookstores. Last fall, Pottery Barn opened stores in Huntsville, Alabama, and Franklin, Tennessee, and the *New York Times* has introduced home delivery in Colorado Springs. It likely won't be long before Franklin County gets both; yoga classes have already arrived.

Most of Brooks's own ideas are clichés borrowed from popular culture. His Franklin County dispatch included a riff on the differences between "indoor guys" and "outdoor guys," a divide handled with more nuance by the characters on *Home Improvement*. Outdoor guys have "wraparound NASCAR sunglasses, maybe a NAPA auto parts cap, and a haircut in a short wedge up front but flowing down over their shoulders in the back—a cut that is known as the mullet," Brooks writes, before getting to their "thing against sleeves," their well-ventilated armpit hair, and the way ripped sleeves hang over BAD TO THE BONE tattoos. This is a clever homage to the fieldwork of comic/sociologist Jeff Foxworthy, whose 1989 study *You Might Be a Redneck If...* included: "You own more than three shirts with the sleeves cut off."

I CALLED Brooks to see if I was misreading his work. I told him about my trip to Franklin County, and the ease with which I was able to spend $20 on a meal. He laughed. "I didn't see it when I was there, but it's true, you can get a nice meal at the Mercersburg Inn," he said. I said it was just as easy at Red Lobster. "That was partially to make a point that if Red Lobster is your upper end..." he replied, his voice trailing away. "That was partially tongue-in-cheek, but I did have several mini-dinners there, and I never topped $20."

I went through some of the other instances where he made declarations that appeared insupportable. He accused me of being "too pedantic," of "taking all of this too literally," of "taking a joke and distorting it." "That's totally unethical," he said.

Satire has its purpose, but assuming it's on the mark, Brooks should be able to adduce real-world examples that are *true*. I asked him how I was supposed to tell what was comedy and what was sociology. "Generally, I rely on intelligent readers to know—and I think that at the *Atlantic Monthly*, every intelligent reader can tell what the difference is," he replied. "I tried to describe the mainstream of Montgomery County and the mainstream of Franklin County. They're both diverse places, and any generalization is going to have exceptions. But I was trying to capture the difference between the two places," he said. "You've obviously come at this from a perspective. I don't think if you went to the two places you wouldn't detect a cultural difference."

I asked him about Blue America as a bastion of illegal immigrants. "This is dishonest research. You're not approaching the piece in the spirit of an honest reporter," he said. "Is this how you're going to start your career? I mean, really, doing this sort of piece? I used to do 'em, I know 'em, how one starts, but it's just something you'll mature beyond."

I shared with him some more of my research, and asked how he made his observations. On NASCAR name recognition: "My experience going around to people that I know in urban metro areas is a lot of them can't name five NASCAR ... but that's a joke." On Spa Lady locations: "I think that's the type of place where people would get the joke and get the reference." On whether Blue Americans read more books: "That would be interesting, but one goes by one's life experiences."

"What I try to do is describe the character of places, and hopefully things will ring true to people," Brooks explained. "In most cases, I think the way I describe it does ring true, and in some places it doesn't ring true. If you were describing a person, you would try to grasp the essential character and in some way capture them in a few words. And if you do it as a joke, there's a pang of recognition."

BY HOLDING himself to a rings-true standard, Brooks acknowledges that all he does is present his readers with the familiar and ask them to recognize it. Why, then, has his particular brand of stereotype-peddling met with such success? In recent years, American journalism has reacted to the excesses of New Journalism—narcissism, impressionism, preening subjectivity—by adopting the trappings of scholarship. Trend pieces, once a bastion of three-examples-and-out superficiality, now strive for the authority of dissertations. Former *Times* editor Howell Raines famously defended page-one placement for a piece examining Britney Spears's flailing career by describing it as a "sophisticated exegesis of a sociological phenomenon." The headline writer's favorite word is "deconstructing." (Last year, the *Toronto Star* deconstructed a sausage.) Richard Florida, a Carnegie Mellon demographer whose 2002 book *The Rise of the Creative Class* earned *Bobos*-like mainstream cachet, nostalgizes a time when readers looked to social scientists in academia for such insights:

"You had Holly Whyte, who got Jane Jacobs started, Daniel Bell, David Riesman, Galbraith. This is what we're missing; this is a gap," Florida says. "Now you have David Brooks as your sociologist, and Al Franken and Michael Moore as your political scientists. Where is the serious public intellectualism of a previous era?"

This culture shift has rewarded Brooks, who translates echt nerd appearance (glasses, toothy grin, blue blazer) and intellectual bearing into journalistic credibility, which allows him to take amusing dinner-party chatter—*Was that map an electoral-college breakdown or a marketing plan for* Mighty Aphrodite?—and sell it to editors as well-argued wisdom on American society. Brooks satisfies the features desk's appetite for scholarly authority in much the same way that Jayson Blair fed the newsroom's compulsion for scoops.

There's even a Brooksian explanation for why he has become so popular with the East Coast media elite. Blue Americans have heard so much about Red America, and they've always wanted to see it. But Blue Americans don't take vacations to places like Galveston and Dubuque. They like to watch TV shows like *The Simpsons* and *Roseanne*, where Red America is mocked by either cartoon characters or Red Americans themselves, so Blue Americans don't need to feel guilty of condescension. Blue Americans are above redneck jokes, but they will listen if a sociologist attests to the high density of lawn-abandoned appliances per capita in flyover country. They need someone to show them how the other half lives, because there is nothing like sympathy for backwardness to feed elitism. A wrong turn in Red America can be dangerous: They might accidentally find Jesus or be hit by an 18-wheeler. It seems reasonable to seek out a smart-looking fellow who seems to know the way and has a witty line at every point. Blue Americans always travel with a guide.

By Jason Fagone
June 2004

DID DR. NORWOOD GO TOO FAR?

ive him a pencil and a pad of paper, and William Norwood can explain the universe. He'll show you why a circle is perfectly round. He'll prove why sound moves more slowly than light. He'll demonstrate why lasers are useful, and why the golf club he's doodled on his pad is a good design for a golf club. He doesn't think he knows everything, but he believes that he can *figure most things out*. In Norwood's world, there are answers.

This confidence is what made Norwood famous. He is one of the world's best heart surgeons, hailed as a genius by all the People Who Know. Norwood fixes the broken hearts of little babies. Hearts the size of shrunken plums, veins slimmer than angel-hair pasta. A technical virtuoso, Norwood is ambidextrous—he can stitch with both hands. He's also creative. Using that dogged, scientific mind, Norwood has been scribbling new heart surgeries on his pad for 30 years—surgeries that, before, only existed in his brain. At this very moment, surgeons around the world are performing *Norwoods*.

As of February 19th at 12:59 p.m., Norwood was the chief of cardiothoracic surgery at A.I. duPont Hospital for Children in Wilmington, in charge of the Nemours Cardiac Center. In just 5 years, he had almost single-handedly built the center from scratch. It had become one of the most respected in the country. He was at the top of his profession.

And then, at 1 p.m. that February day, it was over. Called into a conference room, Norwood saw the chief operating officer of the Nemours Foundation. For weeks, the FDA and the state of Delaware had been investigating an experimental medical device at the Cardiac Center—a device used in a new type of procedure, performed on Norwood's watch by his chief of cardiology. The hospital said later it believed some medical staffers had "failed to comply with hospital policies regarding informed consent and the use of a medical device." The COO extended his hand and told Norwood the Cardiac Center needed "new leadership."

It wasn't the first time he'd had to go. Norwood breeds naysayers everywhere, because not everyone has Norwood's confidence. Some call it arrogance, but he doesn't care. *Move forward. Advance the field.* Those are the beliefs that keep pushing him, even when colleagues have questioned him and lawyers have sued him. He's been knocked around a little, sure, but he's always made it through. He's always found another hospital only too happy to have a surgeon of Bill Norwood's stature.

But this Nemours situation was different. Not only was Norwood shown the door; he was escorted out of the building by security. This was a great surgeon, his name already in the history books, walking the first part of the lonely quarter-mile corridor at duPont with a rent-a-cop by his side. Oh, this was a sea change, and it would only get worse. He started reading dark tidings in the newspapers, rumblings of future lawsuits over babies who'd been injured or died during his time at Nemours. Now that he was vulnerable, how many of his patients would lawyer up? Had Norwood finally lost the ethical battle he'd been fighting for 30 years—caught in the gap between the human desire for progress and the equally human unwillingness to bear the cost of it?

You want costs? Here's a cost. A great surgeon is sitting in his Wilmington home, doing nothing. *Not* operating. *Not* saving babies' lives. Might as well take a crowbar to Lebron James's kneecaps, a hot poker to Scorsese's eyes, for all the talent that's wasting away. But that's something that bothers Norwood's supporters more than it bothers him. No, the worst thing for Norwood has got to be this: He's finally run smack up against a problem he can't work out. His pad and pencil can't resolve people's fundamental ambivalence about the value of medical risk-taking.

So it's late evening, April 1st—fine day for a cruel joke. Norwood's on the phone from his house. He has nothing to say. Only small talk about his son, William, a golfer on the Hooters tour.

"Hooters is being sued," says Norwood, abruptly. Some "boy-girl sort of thing," he says. Sexual harassment at Hooters—isn't that the whole point? The doctor is incredulous: "*Excuse me?*"

Then, softly, a wounded admission:

"The world is getting tough, you know."

WHEN THE NURSE woke her at 2 a.m., Michelle Madden knew her daughter was dying.

"I'm losing her," Michelle said.

When she got to the Intensive Care Unit at Nemours Cardiac Center, the big double doors swung open, and Michelle confronted her worst nightmare. Mykenzie Madden's heart had stopped. A team of nurses and doctors hovered over Michelle's little "Peanut," trying to restart it. Mykenzie was just seven months old. Michelle started crying.

"You have to be strong," the nurse told her. "If you feel Mykenzie is suffering, you are the only one who can tell us to stop."

Michelle couldn't understand how things had gone so horribly wrong. "We figured we were getting out of the woods," she says.

She had good reason to believe that. When Michelle first came to Nemours in February 2003, Mykenzie was very sick. She had a condition called hypoplastic left heart syndrome (HLHS), which meant the left side of her heart was underdeveloped. If she didn't have three operations, all before she turned about 2 years old, Mykenzie would die. The first, the most difficult, would take place days after Mykenzie was born. That was why Michelle had come to Nemours. She had come for William Norwood—the man other mothers claimed had "hands of God," the man who had invented the operation her baby needed.

Michelle says the doctors at Nemours told her that once Mykenzie made it through the first surgery, she would do fine. Even better, she says, the doctors told her they'd replaced the traditional third surgery with an innovative new procedure that was less invasive. In the new procedure, the heart would be implanted with a tiny tube of platinum called a "stent," which would channel blood between two key structures. She thinks they talked about altering the second procedure, too, to prepare for the third. Michelle doesn't remember details, only that they laid out a plan.

In February, Mykenzie had her first surgery at Nemours. For a while, it was touch and go. Eventually, though, she recovered, and Michelle took her home to South Jersey.

They came back for the Stage Two on August 22nd. Norwood assisted in the surgery. But then fluid started to pool around Mykenzie's lungs—so-called "pleural effusions"—and she couldn't breathe on her own.

After a 12-day struggle, Mykenzie's heart stopped on that terrible night in the CICU. Michelle isn't sure how long she watched the doctors try to restart it. After maybe an hour—it felt like forever—she told them to give up: "I yelled 'Stop, stop, she's gone!' and ran to her—and picked her up in my arms and held her as hard as I could."

Michelle was devastated, but she wasn't angry with the Nemours doctors. "I just figured surgery didn't work for Mykenzie," she says. (The hospital declined to comment for this story.) Then, months later—after the funeral, after the depression, after the Zoloft—she got a call from a friend. Channel 10 had run a TV news segment about William Norwood. The segment said he had been fired over a controversy related to the stent that Mykenzie would have gotten in the third surgery, had she lived. The stent, Michelle learned, was experimental, and hadn't been approved by the FDA.

The next day, Michelle e-mailed some of the moms she'd bonded with during those long hours at the Cardiac Center. They compared notes: All had different stories of what doctors had told them and when. They knew for sure that several babies who had developed serious complications last summer did so after the Stage Two surgery. And they realized they didn't understand why. In fact, they realized they didn't understand much of anything.

And they began getting angry. Because their babies were dead.

IF YOU KNEW he was a physician but didn't know what kind, you'd guess he was a country doctor. The novelty tie, dotted with cartoons of little kids. The neatly combed wave of white hair. The sturdy glasses. The meaty, enormous hands that seem like they'd be liabilities in a high-tech operating room.

But the first impressions are wrong. William Norwood is most comfortable in the OR. He likes it so much, he's trying like hell to get back there—and failing. (Norwood's lawyer is preparing a complaint against the Nemours Foundation.) "It's impossible for me, at my stage and stature, to get a job anywhere," says Norwood. "It's impossible. Particularly under these circumstances." Has he been trying? "Oh, are you kidding? Think I'm sitting on my thumbs? Boy. What would you do?"

He is 63 years old, and it's getting late to start over. He'd like to stay in the area; he's got a house in Wilmington; twice divorced, he now lives with his scrub nurse of 28 years, Jodee Desilets; he has two grown sons (golfer William, 38; and Jonathan, 22, who is in school at the University of Rochester).

But on the morning of April 23rd, Bill Norwood isn't operating. Instead, he's sitting in the cavernous Green Room of the Hotel du Pont in downtown Wilmington, poking at eggs Benedict.

He is out of his element, and it shows:

"Doing heart surgery in these life-and-death situations is…"

He pauses. Five seconds. Ten seconds.

"…not just demanding of dexterity. It is also very emotionally demanding. It is very very very difficult to be in a situation where things don't go very well. The pressure comes from within—not so much…"

He leans forward, puts his hands on his chin, pauses another five seconds.

"…not so much directly or overtly, but…"

Norwood grabs the spoon with his right hand, then the knife. He smooths the tablecloth.

"…it's there."

Norwood doesn't express emotion well. He doesn't think that way. He thinks scientifically, where life is a set of problems whose solutions require only focus, dedication, logic, and time. Look at the era that produced him. Check him out in Los Alamos in the early 1960s, where his father, a chemist, was learning how to make nuclear bombs explode in specific shapes. The Manhattan Project put food on the table. Young Bill dreamed, of course, about becoming a fighter pilot.

After a brief marriage and divorce—and a short stint in the Air Force Academy—Norwood ditched the pilot path and went to med school at the University of Colorado, then became a resident at the University of Minnesota Hospital. That's where he met surgeon Aldo Castaneda, who changed his life.

Castaneda was a pioneering heart surgeon, a man willing to take big chances to make progress. His predecessors were world-renowned for their daring deeds. There was the ballsy German who discovered cardiac catheterization in 1929. Other folks were afraid to try it, so the German cathed his *own* heart—then walked to the x-ray lab to prove it was possible. He was promptly fired—and later won the Nobel Prize. Then there was Robert Gross, a surgical resident in Boston in 1938. Gross wanted permission to try the first-ever closed-heart surgery. His boss said, Hell *no*. But when the boss went on vacation, Gross did it anyway, and made history. He got fired, too. And you can't forget Minnesota's own C. Walton Lillehei, who was still on staff when Norwood arrived—Lillehei, the man who braved rivers of his own patients' blood to invent open-heart surgery in 1954.

"Somebody said a long time ago, 'If I succeed, it's only because I stood on the shoulders of giants, looking forward,' " says Norwood. "And I can *name* the giants I stood on."

Castaneda was a giant. Castaneda could take a kid with zero function—couldn't breathe, couldn't pump blood—and make him normal. "The possibility of that kind of result is what has always driven Bill," says a very close confidant of Norwood's who has known him for 30 years.

After completing his residency and a Ph.D. in biophysics, Norwood followed Castaneda to Children's Hospital Boston. There, the young doctor started hunting around for something big to do that might help him escape Castaneda's shadow. Trouble was, "The easy stuff had all been done," says Peter Lang, a senior associate in cardiology at CHB who was there at the time. Thanks in part to Castaneda's research, doctors could now correct most types of congenital heart defects. One, however, remained a problem: hypoplastic left heart syndrome. HLHS was a real mind-blower. Kids born with HLHS had virtually no left ventricle and a tiny aorta—the two structures that, together, pump blood to the body.

Kids born with no *right* ventricle—well, doctors could fix that. The right ventricle pumps blood to the lungs. By the late 1970s, they had figured out how to reroute the heart's plumbing so the stronger left ventricle would do all the work.

But that wasn't possible with hypoplast kids. With no *left* ventricle, an HLHS baby could turn ashen and die within days, if not hours, of birth. Doctors didn't think they could flip-flop the procedure; how would the weaker right ventricle handle all the pumping alone? But Norwood thought he could do it, could make the right ventricle pump blood to the body *and* the lungs.

"He was trying to figure out some scheme, some set of hookups," says Norwood's longtime confidant. It occupied him 24/7. He would sit at the breakfast table, sketching pictures of the heart. On weekends, when he watched football games on TV, he kept a pad nearby in case inspiration struck.

Finally, it did. Norwood would try to turn part of the baby's pulmonary artery—the one that normally goes from the heart to the lungs—into a "new" aorta. The right ventricle would pump blood to the body through the "new" aorta. If he then created a passageway between the "new" aorta and the original pulmonary artery, some blood would get to the lungs, too.

It was just a temporary solution, meant to buy the baby some time. The baby's single ventricle was now doing double the work. It would stress out. So after this Stage One rerouting—what came to be called the *Norwood procedure*—doctors would perform another surgery, to give the heart a breather. They would take the vena cavas, which normally return oxygen-poor blood to the heart, and detour them straight to the lungs. In those days, surgeons built the detour in one step; they've since split it into two, both open-heart. In the Stage Two surgery, at about six months of age, they reroute the blood from the top half of the body. In Stage Three, by the age of two, they reroute blood from the bottom half.

Norwood *thought* his procedure would work, but he didn't know for sure. He had to dive in. There wasn't much to lose, since 100 percent of HLHS babies were dying anyway.

The first operations, begun in 1979, were tough. It took Norwood a while to get his procedure working, and in the interim, kids died. Peter Lang took care of the first 150 infant patients, overseeing them in the ICU. "We felt terrible," he says. But they knew it was leading somewhere good.

The families knew it, too, even though their babies didn't survive. "They never got upset with him," says Norwood's confidant. "I think there was actually a feeling they knew they had contributed something important, even though it hadn't worked out well for their child." In 1982, after years of fine-tuning, the first patient made it through the surgeries and lived. Norwood and his colleagues published a landmark paper announcing their discovery.

Then a strange thing happened. Instead of being greeted with hosannahs, Norwood was attacked. Doctors said he was prolonging the babies' agony, and that "compassionate care"—letting them die in comfort—was preferable. Norwood stood by his good results.

But even his own colleagues in Boston turned against him. Their resentment had to do, in a strange way, with Norwood's devotion to his work. "I remember [Norwood] in the beginning, sitting in the ICU for days, never leaving the side of those patients," says Paula Bokesch, an anesthesiologist at Emory University who worked at Boston then. Norwood wasn't staying with them out of sentiment—he was afraid other doctors, clueless about the intricacies of the hypoplast kids' alien circulations, would screw things up. If a doctor who wasn't part of Norwood's team tried to tweak a dial, Norwood would tell him to get lost.

"And their response," says Norwood's confidant, "was not 'Okay' — they held it against him personally."

That was the price of progress, but Norwood stood his ground. He used to compare his situation to a line from Don McLean's "American Pie":

The players tried to take the field;
The marching band refused to yield.

There was Norwood and his players, and there was everybody else.

NORWOOD'S troubles at Nemours started with a phone call. Last fall, according to a complaint filed with the FDA, Judith Guinan got a call from a Nemours doctor, asking her to "sign and backdate" a consent form. The *Inquirer* reported that the hospital claimed the original consent form "could not be located." The form said that Judith's daughter, Molly, had been implanted with a non-FDA-approved stent during a heart operation in 2002. "Neither my husband or I recalled ever seeing it before," Guinan declared in her FDA complaint, so she refused to sign.

Concerned, the Guinans filed their complaint with the FDA, which launched an investigation. The state of Delaware investigated as well. According to the state's report, Nemours doctors failed to obtain required "informed consent" paperwork in four cases, failed to follow FDA regulations covering experimental devices, and also failed in 14 cases to get approval from the hospital's Internal Review Board, which monitors experimental devices. Both doctors were fired, along with the Cardiac Center's administrator, John Walsh. (The attorney for Norwood, Walsh and John Murphy, Norwood's longtime chief of cardiology, claims to have the original consent form, which he says is signed by Kevin Guinan. He also says that Murphy had asked the IRB's vice chairman if he needed approval, and the vice chairman told him no.) Since then, at least seven sets of parents have hired lawyers to investigate their cases.

This wasn't the first time questions of informed consent had arisen around Norwood. In 1992, when he was chief of cardiothoracic surgery at the Children's Hospital of Philadelphia, Stephen and Karen Gault took their son Stephen Jr. to him for surgery, not open-heart, to widen his aorta. They signed consent forms to that effect. According to court records, Norwood told them—15 minutes before Stephen Jr.'s operation—that he'd be doing a full-fledged open-heart surgery that the Gaults had been told by another doctor wasn't necessary. Karen Gault later testified that when she asked why, Norwood told her, "I'm the one with the medical background."

During surgery, Norwood stopped Stephen Jr.'s heart using a rapid hypothermic cooling technique he had been investigating in his CHOP research lab. The morning after surgery, Stephen Jr. had a devastating seizure. He's now a quadriplegic and partially blind. The Gaults sued, and in 2000 the jury announced a verdict of $55 million—at the time, the biggest malpractice award in state history. (As it turned out, the parties had reached a settlement of $7.5 million just before the verdict was read, so the verdict didn't stand.) During Norwood's decade-long tenure at CHOP, he was sued at least 25 times, according to court records.

The lawsuits—most settled, some dismissed, and some won by Norwood—didn't seem to sully his professional reputation. The field of pediatric heart surgery is small, and there are maybe 15 big-name surgeons worldwide. Norwood was—is—one of them. Cardiac centers bring in big bucks for children's hospitals, so hospitals try to attract name players like Norwood. "He was a huge money-maker," says Norwood's friend, former hospital administrator John Walsh.

Nemours was lucky to get a marquee player like Bill Norwood. Parents could sense how highly he was valued—so much that some say he created what one mom describes as a "secret society" that prevented their kids from getting the care they needed when things went awry. And they felt this way even before they discovered that the stents used on their kids were experimental. Kevin Guinan's daughter Molly had a stent implanted for a condition similar to HLHS. According to the complaint filed with the FDA, he had trouble getting Molly consultations he thought she needed with specialists outside the Cardiac Center, even though these specialists were at the same location. The center doctors "told us they could handle it," says Guinan. Chris Conway says he tried in vain for four weeks to get his son, Teagh, a GI consult after Teagh received a stent. Conway finally transferred Teagh to CHOP. Both the Guinans and the Conways are now clients of Philadelphia's Beasley Firm.

"All I can say," says Bill Norwood, "is that the people associated with the Nemours Cardiac Center are *so* advanced, and *so* specialized, that they were the best medical care possibilities available." He seems surprised by the families' complaints. "*Excuse me*? Why in the world would we not use all available resources? We did. Always."

But when Julie Kerr brought her daughter to Nemours for the Stage Two in July, she could see that the atmosphere had changed since her first surgery in March 2003. "The nurses, they were all depressed," says Julie. "They were like, 'They're dropping like flies. We haven't seen anything like this since we've been here.'" Julie's daughter died on August 21st. In fact, parents who were at Nemours that summer say between 8 and 10 children died there from July to September 2003.

They wonder why alarms didn't go off.

TO UNDERSTAND, you've got to grasp how the Cardiac Center is unique, and why Norwood set it up that way. Most hospitals are chopped into departments, each with its own chief. Nurses report to the nursing chief, cardiologists to the cardiology chief, and so on. At Nemours, it was different. At Nemours, everyone reported to one man: Norwood. He believes this structure—which he calls the Programmatic Approach—lets doctors and nurses be more focused and work more efficiently. As Norwood described it in the 2002 Cardiac Center annual report, "The esprit de corps is remarkable."

He'd been trying to implement this for decades. He tried for 10 years at CHOP, where he became chief cardiothoracic surgeon in 1984, but he clashed with the hospital brass and couldn't get his hierarchy in place. "There's a tremendous amount of inertia in staid, administrative structure," says Norwood. Finally, in

1994, he left CHOP to start his own cardiac clinic in Genolier, Switzerland, along with his mentor, Aldo Castaneda. But after 2 years, Castaneda developed prostate cancer and became too ill to operate. Meanwhile, the clinic's patient base never materialized, and it couldn't stay afloat.

Norwood started getting offers to come back to the United States. A few "name" places, like the Cleveland Clinic and Case Western, wanted him. But in 1997 he settled on Nemours in Wilmington, according to his friend John Walsh, because Nemours was willing to let him build his dream center.

"What we had here was what we wanted," says Walsh. And what they had was an amazing level of autonomy. They basically wrote their own budgets, and determined their own salaries, which Walsh says were generous but not excessive. Norwood even had a profit-sharing agreement: He was given a pot of money to hand out as bonuses. In 2003, the pot amounted to $2 million, which was distributed among the Cardiac Center's 150 staffers.

For the first time in his career, Norwood had successfully built a "programmatic" center. He had his handpicked team of players. He had control.

But in the end, that control might not have been in his best interest "Everybody's greatest strength is their greatest weakness," says H. Scott Baldwin, an oncologist who worked with Norwood at CHOP. "There was no arguing with him, you know. You either saw it his way or you were wrong."

The way Norwood saw it, stents were the wave of the future. Indeed, he and John Murphy—the cardiologist who implanted the stents, using a catheter that saved the kids from that third open-heart surgery—weren't hiding what they were doing. Norwood wrote about the stents in his 2002 and 2003 annual reports to the Nemours Foundation board; Murphy presented his findings at professional meetings. There was even a picture of the stent on the Nemours website. Norwood and Murphy thought they had a good idea, and forged full speed ahead. As Norwood said in his 2002 annual report, "The efforts of this Center are always directed at setting the mark."

The stent procedure could end up saving lives—most of the kids who've gotten it are doing fine. It could also turn out to be a dead end. But there's no way of knowing until years from now. This is where the ethical equations get sticky with guys like Norwood. How much of a learning curve should a doctor—or parent—tolerate, considering the potential payoffs down the road? Is it okay for Norwood to keep innovating, just as long as it's not on *your* kid?

There are no concrete answers, because surgery isn't regulated, even today. Hospital review boards and the FDA have yet to challenge the surgeon's essential freedom—the ability to modify operations at will. Take three reputable pediatric heart surgeons, ask them how they do a Stage Three, and you'll get three different answers.

"I modify all my surgeries all the time," says Norwood. Regulation, he says, would be "a disaster," and "would immediately stop progress." And progress is what he wants—what he's revered for.

All Norwood needs is permission from the parents of his patients. Case law has established some regulation—a patient's right to "informed consent." But that's not necessarily satisfied by getting a signature on a form. According to Delaware state law, for a doctor to obtain consent, he has to explain "the risks and alternatives to treatment" that a "reasonable patient" would want to know.

Parents, though, aren't always reasonable. Sometimes, they're simply not smart enough to understand, or too emotionally overwhelmed to pay attention. No matter what a doctor tells some parents, they just won't get it—especially with something as complex as congenital heart surgery. Norwood says he gave the parents enough information so they understood what was going on, what the realistic possibilities were. "I'm not out to *deceive* anybody," he says. Anyway, he insists, informed consent "*cannot* involve full disclosure of all possibilities. 'Cause all possibilities are contained in 15 volumes of medical text that we can't teach the parents about in a 15-minute conversation. *Excuse* me?"

Some doctors go to greater lengths to protect themselves. One renowned pediatric cardiac surgeon at a leading institution says that whenever he makes a "significant" surgical modification, he has parents sign a separate consent form. Another heart surgeon, Emile Bacha at the University of Chicago Children's Hospital, says that he's experimenting with a modified HLHS surgery that also uses stents—but Bacha says he makes sure he gives parents any data he has comparing the traditional surgery to the new one. "We didn't want somebody to come back and say, 'My child died, and you were doing something experimental, and why did you do it?'" says Bacha. "We wanted it to be explained. We tell the parents, always."

Even if a doctor goes to great lengths to make sure a family understands, it's impossible to know if they really do, says one heart doctor familiar with consent lawsuits: "That's always going to be the subject of controversy and debate."

"It's almost ridiculous how—things can occur in the world of human nature," he continues. "People will say, in retrospect, 'Well, we didn't understand that.' That's an unfortunate aspect of the system. There's absolutely no way to guarantee anything. You do the best you can."

Still, it's one thing to neglect to tell parents about a surgical complication or a specific risk. It's another altogether to *plan* to alter an operation and not tell the parents about all the potential risks. That's what some parents suspect Norwood did. That's why Julie Kerr, Michelle Madden and three others have hired lawyer Theresa Blanco.

At least one parent, Suzanne Dant, says she wasn't told *anything* about changes to the standard procedures. She brought her day-old son Connor to Nemours in June 2001. She says the doctors gave her a brochure describing the traditional HLHS surgeries—the open-heart kind. After Stage Two surgery, which Norwood performed, Connor developed pleural effusions, the fluid around the lungs. About two weeks later, Suzanne says, she gleaned a disturbing bit of information from a nurse: Connor had been given a "modified" version of the Stage Two. It said so on the hospital's operative report, she says: "I was like, 'What?'"

Other moms, like Julie Kerr and Michelle Madden, say they were told the new procedures would be different, but didn't understand how, exactly, and weren't given a choice. "They were told: This is the way it's going to be," Theresa Blanco says of her clients.

If given a choice, they might have opted for the standard procedures, because those have very low risks, while there's little or no data on the new ones. The mothers say that Norwood never explicitly compared the risks of the standard surgeries with the new ones. "If you tried to do brand-new procedures in patients who are excellent candidates for standard procedures, that's very hard to do," says world-renowned James Lock, chairman of the department of cardiology at Children's Hospital Boston.

The *standard* Stage Three operation—the one Nemours replaced with the stents—is low-risk. At CHOP, only two kids died after the Stage Three between 1994 and 1999. The standard Stage Two is also low-risk. At good hospitals, at least 96 percent of kids survive it. This April, the Children's Hospital of Wisconsin reported results of 85 consecutive Stage Two surgeries—with not one hospital death. Last summer at Nemours, at least four children died who had been given Stage Twos, including one who'd had the surgery 2 years before. It might just have been a bad group, says a leading pediatric heart surgeon. Still, he says, four Stage Two deaths "seems like more than you would expect."

"It's complicated territory," says Norwood. All his surgical modifications, he says, are "designed with a positive purpose." About modifications to the Stage Two, he says, "They don't increase the risks. It's exactly the same."

Without full medical records for the babies in question—which the parents have requested from Nemours—it's impossible to tell whether their deaths were unusual, or to pinpoint what Norwood might have done differently in some Stage Twos. According to partial operative reports for two of the kids and a journal kept by one set of parents, it appears he tried at least two different versions. Even more confusing, Julie Kerr says she was told her daughter's Stage Two would be modified, but the operative report doesn't say it was. Blanco—who says that four children whose parents she represents developed pleural effusions after their Stage Twos—is investigating whether a modified Stage Two might have resulted in the kids' deaths.

Norwood says he didn't do anything to cause the babies' pleural effusions— that his modifications were "not simple, but medically sound." The families and their lawyers, he says, are "so wrong, it's unbelievable."

"LAWYERS WANT money." Another late-evening phone call to Bill Norwood. It's April 28th, a Wednesday. He is…expansive. "I don't think lawyers, in general, have a large-picture societal view of things," he says. "They are in the bidness of their bidness."

He is very perceptive. Over the phone, he hears that the computer keys of his interlocutor stop clicking whenever he's not talking. He doesn't like it.

"You type down what I think," says Norwood, "and you type down what you think, and we continue this....Fair is fair."

"You're right."

"Goddamn I'm right," says Norwood.

"It'll take me longer, but I can do it this way."

"That's okay," says Norwood. "Getting the right out takes time. Getting the *truth* out takes time."

And here's the truth about informed consent, according to Bill Norwood:

"The idea of informed consent from a medical standpoint is wrong. It's a legal term."

But lawyers aren't the only ones pushing for informed consent. Times have changed, and not only in the obvious ways. It's not just that lawyers are in "bid-ness," and the FDA is on a rampage, and the hospital is using the stent contro-versy as a smokescreen for a bureaucratic shake-up—which is what Norwood's supporters believe.

The field has changed, too. Back in Norwood's Boston days, there were still big problems left to solve. It's different now. Today, most heart-defect operations have very good results. "Now, it's a matter of refining the technique—rather than enormous leaps forward," says James Tweddell, chief of pediatric cardiothoracic surgery at Children's Hospital of Wisconsin. The mavericks like Norwood have gone by the wayside. The field is full of fastidious surgeons who have had to become expert at managing risk.

And the families, too, have changed. These aren't the Boston moms of 1979. This is a new breed. The new mom has fewer kids, and may have had to try harder to have the ones she does. And she can eat doctors like Norwood alive.

She may not have time to wade through 15 volumes of medical texts, but she's got DSL Internet and online support groups and all the resources in the world to learn the right questions to ask. She wants to know her kid's pulse ox levels. She wants to be told the published risk figures for certain types of operations. She wants, goddammit, to know if her doctor is doing something new—something he's never tried before. "I think he should be honest with families," says Peter Lang. Especially since the new surgeries, the ones that got Norwood into trouble, were "the kind of things families would embrace," says Lang. "If things don't go well and they feel they've been had, then it becomes bad on many fronts."

Norwood's old colleagues can't believe how bad it's gotten for him. They agree with former Norwood colleague Marco Cavaglia, chief of cardiac anesthesia at a hospital near Milan, who says, "This is just really sad." The controversy, they say, could eclipse the whole of Norwood's career, and they feel he deserves so much more—a worldwide conference in his honor, a medical school dedicated to his legacy. Even the families are sensitive to the pathos of Norwood's situation. When Nemours moms saw his sentimental quote about being fired in Wilmington's *News-Journal*—"I spent half my days crying, and half my days hoping and wishing"—they sympathized.

"That touched me ," says Suzanne Dant, Connor's mom—Connor, who she says was given a modified Stage Two without her knowledge. "I can't imagine what [the doctors are] going through now. But my other thought was, what do you think the *parents* are doing? I have spent a lot of time crying. And my child's *alive*."

Michelle Madden's is not. Nine months after Mykenzie died in the CICU, Michelle is haunted by a problem she can't solve. She thinks she did everything she could for her daughter, but how can she be sure, considering all the gaps in what she knows? According to one operative report, it appears Mykenzie's Stage Two wasn't modified after all. But she knows others were. Michelle doesn't trust the hospital anymore. She doesn't know what might have happened if she'd only done some more Web research, or asked more questions, or transferred Mykenzie to CHOP.

No. Stop.

But she can't stop.

"I keep wondering," she says, "what if things were different? Would my daughter still be here? *What if* has me bothered." For Michelle Madden, the world has gotten tough as well.

By Christopher McDougall
May 2004

WOULD YOU THROW YOUR BRA AT THIS KID?

o gripes from Lang Lang—he knows he's living a fantasy, with his "rubbery fingers" and killer smile and the 20-year-old beauty who'll be waiting backstage for him tonight with orchids and a belly shirt—but there's still this thing, this one thing: He'd love to make a phone call. To Beethoven. To feel that "special connection." And if Beethoven could see him right now, you can bet he'd want to meet Lang Lang—someplace dark, probably, where he could get his stubby hands around the little punk's throat.

Lang Lang has just arrived at the Kimmel Center for rehearsal, looking like he slid from a chopper to kick some archvillain's ass before settling behind the Steinway. His eyes are Polarized onyx ovals; his body is caped in floor-length black calf with even *more* leather underneath, this one a poured-into number that fits like body armor. Just as coffee-sippers in the Kimmel lobby are looking over and realizing *Hey, there's La*—he's gone, wheeling back outside, big stuff obviously breaking on the tiny Motorola jammed to his ear, maybe some flash about his new CD, *Lang Lang Live at Camegie Hall*, which has been on sale for, like, 20 hours and has already bashed past Andrea Bocelli for No. 4 on the classical charts and is clawing hard at mezzo supervixen Cecilia Bartoli for No. 3.

At 21, Lang Lang is the boy prince Beethoven never was, and if you don't think Beethoven would have hated him for it, you don't know about the time

Beethoven tried to hammer a *real* Austrian prince over the head with a chair, or threw a plate of roast beef in the face of a waiter he didn't like, or shredded the title page of his great Third Symphony, the "Bonaparte," when he thought Napoleon was getting too full of himself. He might look all Sex Pistols in those portraits, with the Billy Idol tease and Johnny Rotten snarl, but the truth is, the great composer was a gnarled little ogre who couldn't get laid without a cash deposit, and it made him writhe with envy. He was so short and pudgy he seemed hunchbacked, with cheese-grater smallpox scars and such regrettable hygiene that friends periodically sneaked into his room to replace his filthy clothes.

As for Lang Lang...when he comes through the backstage door a few minutes later, he skins off his layers of leather to reveal slim black jeans and a tapered burgundy shirt. Armani? Could be; he makes it look Armani. Behind him is a silent man in his early 50s, watchful through slim steel frames, who takes Lang Lang's coats over his arm. It's his father, Lang Guo-ren.

"*So* good to see you again," an elderly backstage aide breathes. She pronounces his name fully and correctly—*Lawng. Lawng*—two separate words in Mandarin which together mean "*brilliance of the sky.*" She extends her hand a scootch, subtle as a pickpocket, so Lang Lang can either shake it or ignore it with no embarrassment on either side. Instead, Lang Lang wraps his arms around her.

"I *love* being here," he says. For a moment, the woman's eyes close. If she could choose a moment to die... Then Lang Lang is off, shaking hands down the hall. Bizet's *Carmen* trills from his pants; cell phone again.

For a classical musician, Lang Lang is so magnetic that he makes some music writers squirmy. "Cute as a button and oozing charisma, this kid has a winning combination of graceful athleticism and a Tiger Woods smile that would instantly disarm any audience," one pants. "In 21 years of writing about music, only once or twice has an artist so impressed this writer with the authority, personality and musicality of a performance as pianist Lang Lang displayed Sunday," another reviewer begins, then goes totally gaga: "Now, upon hearing his first live solo recital disc, I'll take it a step or two further. Lang Lang is the single most complete pianist I have ever heard, bar none. And he's only 18!"

But later, as Lang Lang heads to the Kimmel stage for rehearsal, uglier words must be echoing in his mind: *vulgar ... disappointing ... self-indulgent ... slam-bang crass.* For all the reviewers who call Lang Lang "the future of classical music," a more elite cadre remains unmoved and unimpressed. No, check that. They're very moved—to irritation, to insults, and, at least once, to the exit: *New York Times* critic Anthony Tommasini was so irked by a Lang Lang concert, he walked the hell out.

"I lasted through one encore: Schumann's *Träumerei*," Tommasini wrote after Lang Lang's Carnegie Hall performance last November. "It was not easy to hear that wistfully beautiful melody so yanked around. Surely Mr. Lang played many more encores for his adoring fans. But I didn't want to be a party pooper, let alone impede…" Tommasini concludes with a slash at the Lang Lang-crazy crowd—"the future of classical music."

With prison-rape reviews like those over his head, Lang Lang walks toward the piano at center stage. Conductor Christoph Eschenbach mounts the podium, but halts when he sees Lang Lang reaching for a microphone. "Thank you," Lang Lang tells the rows of elderly people who've come for the free rehearsal, including one gent who's still banging down the aisle in a walker. "It means a lot to me that you've come to hear me practice." Smart—before playing a note, he's already got applause.

Then Lang Lang slides behind the piano, closes his eyes, and rolls his head back. His hands rise, slowly, till they're arched above his head like he's just exited a coffin, then drop in a straight plunge to the keys. Every part of his body joins in: His lips pucker in silent sing-along, his free hand paints invisible pictures in the air, he even seems to pump a fist to cheer on the Orchestra.

Theatrics like these make critics like Tommasini crazy. "Mr. Lang's head seems to be so full of his own hype that there can't be much room left for analytic thinking," Tommasini snipes, then chips in a little advice: "If his managers were smart, they would cancel his recordings and concerts for at least next summer and get Mr. Lang to the Marlboro Music Festival in Vermont, where he could spend a couple of months playing chamber works with fine musicians young and old and remember what it means to be a serious performing artist." Montreal's top daily, *La Presse*, called Lang Lang "pianistically imperfect," and after 2002's Ravinia Festival, the *Chicago Tribune*'s John von Rhein got really nasty and dropped the L-bomb: "All he needed was a white sequined suit and a candelabra and Ravinia could have sold him as the new Liberace."

It's not just the piano-bench pyrotechnics that needle them; it's the way Lang Lang, they feel, ignores whatever the music is supposed to express and instead cuts loose with great balls o' fire, turning Haydn into honky-tonk. He puts on one hell of a show, true, but that's the problem: According to a roundtable of *Times* critics who named him one of their top peeves of the year, Lang Lang has created a "cult of personality" that dazzles listeners with charisma, but at the cost of composers' subtler intentions. "After Lang Lang had delivered his blistering account of Liszt's *Reminiscences de Don Juan*—a grand paraphrase of Mozart's *Don Giovanni*—I wanted to buy him a ticket to the opera," wrote the *New York Observer*'s Charles Michener. "To let him in on the secret that the Don and Zerlina's duet, 'La ci darem la mano,' is about seduction, not the apocalypse."

Does this kid have any clue what "wistful" is? Does he get what Beethoven meant by "Suffering is God's greatest gift to man"? Lang Lang's devoted father is always by his side, while Beethoven first learned music from a drunk shit dad who yanked young Ludwig out of bed to play for his drinking buddies, then slammed the piano cover on the sleepy kid's fingers whenever he dongered a note; Beethoven's "immortal beloved" later rejected him to marry his friend, while his attempt to turn a favorite nephew into a protege ended when the boy tried to kill himself. Just when Beethoven found acclaim as a composer, he went deaf. That's why the Moonlight Sonata might be on every "Romantic Favorites" CD, but for Beethoven, the first three notes were modeled after a funeral march. And that's why turning such misery into music takes self-control and interpretative honesty, not just Lang Lang's "unusually rubbery fingers of indescribable fleetness and agility," as one critic put it.

Lang Lang's rehearsal is coming to an end. Eschenbach asks the strings to repeat a passage, then says, "Bravo." The musicians are instantly up and clattering for the door—it's lunchtime, and they've got a concert in a few hours. The elderly audience filters out. Custodians with latex gloves move in, working the aisles for cough-drop wrappers. After a while they disappear, too.

The giant hall is nearly empty—except for Lang Lang, who's back at the piano, and his father, who's silently watching. Lang Lang's head is down, and nothing is moving but his fingers. His focus is so intense, it seems rude to breathe. He's never let on how much the bashing bothers him. He's never publicly answered his critics before. Until tonight.

WHEN BRIGHT Cheng heard what Lang Lang was planning, he hurried to get a ticket. "This is very surprising," says Cheng, a noted composer and professor of musical composition at the University of Michigan. "Beethoven's Fourth is not what I would have expected at this stage of his career. Not at this stage of *any* young pianist's career, really."

Cheng was a concert pianist himself, a protege of the great Leonard Bernstein and a longtime friend of Yo Yo Ma. He gave up performing to compose, and teach, and helped build a composition program at Michigan that can hold up its head with Juilliard and Philadelphia's Curtis Institute. Cheng's been keeping an eye on Lang Lang for years. "He has the talent and arsenal to be the world's next great artist of the piano," Cheng says, then confesses a personal jones: "There's never been a truly great pianist from China. He's certainly making the same splash Horowitz made at that age."

But Cheng is a little worried that tonight Lang Lang may be overreaching. Beethoven's Piano Concerto No. 4 is, debatably, the most perfectly structured concerto ever composed. "This is an old man's piece, not a young man's," says Cheng—meaning most concert pianists test themselves against it only after they've spent decades not only honing their soloist skills and orchestral experience but also, like a Shakespearean actor attempting Lear, learning enough about heartache and personal loss to feel it, not finesse it.

For Lang Lang to play it at all is rather defiant, especially since one of his scheduled appearances is Murderers' Row—Carnegie Hall, where the *New York Times* critics will be sharpening their rhetoric in anticipation of his arrival. "He's certainly making a statement," says Cheng. "I've been wondering whose idea this was." And tonight, before Lang Lang gets to Carnegie Hall, he'll have to perform with one of the world's most demanding Beethoven experts staring down at him: conductor Christoph Eschenbach, an esteemed concert pianist in his own right who first made his name performing Beethoven's concertos.

But if Lang Lang is intimidated, he better let his ass know, because right now it's not showing Eschenbach much respect. A few minutes ago, in a nice show of Philadelphia union hospitality, Lang Lang was kicked off the piano by stagehands who wanted to set up. No prob—he heads back to Eschenbach's chambers so they can rehearse a little four-hand piece he and the Maestro will be performing at a post-concert recital for Orchestra donors. Lang Lang slides behind the piano at Eschenbach's side, courteously giving the conductor so much bench room that one of Lang Lang's cheeks is left hanging. That's okay; once they begin, Lang Lang barely sits. It's only a moderately spirited piece, but Lang Lang is swaying and cantering along, butt-bumping Eschenbach by accident or staring at the side of his head for two ... three ... four beats, waiting for the Maestro to loosen up and join the party.

Eschenbach is cold steel; his body is motionless except for his hands and, occasionally, a bit of lower lip. If every strand of Lang Lang's DNA were removed and chemically reversed, the result would be the anticlone beside him. Eschenbach's hairless dome barely nods while Lang Lang's brush cut is jerking like a car-wash scrubber; Eschenbach's spine is canted a disciplined 45 degrees to the keyboard, while his face ... wow, that face. With those stark cheekbones and bottomless eyes, Eschenbach's face seems imprinted with things he has seen and the rest of us, luckily, never will.

Eschenbach was born in Germany just after the beginning of World War II; by the end, he was orphaned and barely alive, a 5-year-old in an East German refugee camp, sick with typhoid and mute with shock. A cousin finally found him, but it would take more than a year for Eschenbach to begin recovering his health and learning to speak again. His cousin let the mute boy plink at the piano and, when he took to it, somehow managed to get him lessons while fighting for food in the rubble and ruin of postwar Germany.

Today, it's not that he's still shell-shocked; Eschenbach's eyes can dance with mirth, and he's notably gracious and generous. (An Orchestra handler whose assignment is to keep Eschenbach's volunteer commitments within human limits says, "Maestro doesn't know 'yes' has an opposite.") It's just that everything about him seems so spare and exactingly controlled, like he's still surviving on food rations; he even uses minimal oxygen, answering a question with an arched eye, a cocked finger, his own barely perceptible but unmistakably intelligible sign language.

Seeing the two of them at the piano, their styles so contrary that each seems a dogmatic rebuttal of the other, it's a jolt to learn that it was Eschenbach, of all people, who gave Lang Lang his first break. Back in 1999, Eschenbach was music director of Chicago's world-renowned Ravinia Festival. Lang Lang came for an audition, and though Eschenbach usually grants just 20 minutes to each unknown, something about this 17-year-old intrigued him. He asked for more. Did Lang

Lang know any Rachmaninoff? Lang Lang answered with a bit of "Rach 3," the horribly complex concerto that turned David Helfgott into a gibbering maniac in the movie *Shine*. Interesting... how about Chopin? Lang Lang segued into Sonata No. 3. Very impressive. Eschenbach promised Lang Lang he'd keep him in mind and sent him home to Philadelphia.

Three days later, Eschenbach had a major problem. One of his marquee attractions, Andre Watts, was too sick to play. Eschenbach needed a sub, and fast. And not just any sub, but someone who knew Tchaikovsky's First Concerto and... Wait!

Lang Lang flew back to Chicago, and with one day's preparation took the stage for his Ravinia debut. "It's amazing," Eschenbach thought. "In 20 years, I've never heard the same range of colors, nor the same musical imagination, not since I auditioned Tzimon Barto." After his smash debut, Lang Lang was congratulated backstage by Eschenbach and conductor Zarin Mehta. It was already past midnight, but they were curious what else this prodigy was capable of. How about Bach's Goldberg Variations? Even a wonder like Glenn Gould considered Bach's encyclopedic work for harpsichord his definitive challenge. Lang Lang went right back to the piano, and even though he was a teenager who had just endured an exhausting test of nerves and stamina, he played the Goldberg Variations till two in the morning.

Eschenbach and Lang Lang became neighbors after Eschenbach took over the Philadelphia Orchestra last year. By then it had been four years since Lang Lang's "big splash," as Eschenbach puts it, but even though Lang Lang performs 150 times a year (translation: nearly every other day), he still comes to Eschenbach to study new repertoires. For all Lang Lang's flamboyance, Eschenbach finds him an ideal student. "He just lives the theater of the music," Eschenbach says. "Anything I suggest in his ear, he brings it out of the piano in his own way." Eschenbach has no children of his own, nor, in fact, any emotional attachment that anyone is aware of, but with Lang Lang, he feels fatherly: "I worry that he is so driven by the sheer music business, so much travel and so many engagements, that I wonder where his personal life is rooting—if it's rooting in something which might nurture relationships."

He can't help Lang Lang's dating, but there is something he can do about the critics' beatings. "I'm the one who chose the Beethoven concerto for him to play," Eschenbach reveals, and then, in characteristically marvelous understatement, he adds: "I sensed a resentment growing." Yes, one might sense a soupçon of resentment when the *Times* begs Lang Lang to hang it up for the summer and the *Tribune* is sizing him for a Liberace jumpsuit. "This Beethoven concerto is one of the most subtle pieces in the literature," Eschenbach says. "A subtle concerto would be just the thing to mute those voices bashing him."

He says it matter-of-factly, yet the truth is, giving Lang Lang this opportunity is an exceptional act of faith and friendship. Eschenbach, after all, has only been head of the Orchestra for a year; by contracting a very young, very controversial pianist to perform a piece that many would say is beyond his reach, Eschenbach is risking the Orchestra's confidence in his stewardship. If Lang Lang bombs, every classical musician in the world will wonder why Eschenbach gave him the chance in the first place. Even a sympathetic fan like Bright Cheng has to wonder if Lang Lang is up to it.

But unlike his focus a few minutes ago onstage, Lang Lang right now is showing no hint of pressure. He and Eschenbach are racing into the final passage of their four-hand piece, and Lang Lang is still rocking around so much that Eschenbach has to adjust himself with a slight wiggle. Then he wiggles again. And bobs his head. And suddenly, Eschenbach is off his seat, giving a full-on hop. As they bring the piece home, Eschenbach and Lang Lang fly off the bench at the same time and together thunder down the final note.

For a second, both of them remain motionless, perhaps wondering what the hell just happened. Then they crack up laughing. "That was great," Eschenbach says, beaming. "Really great." Then he turns serious. "Rest today. Yes?"

"I'll be ready," Lang Lang says.

WITH THE clock ticking down, it's unfair to expect any more of Lang Lang's time, but I ask anyway. He has a rapid conversation with his dad in Mandarin.

"I was asking if we had any food at home," Lang Lang says. "But why don't we just go to a restaurant. Do you like Chinese food?" I'm pretty sure he's kidding, but he's so happy-go-lucky I can't tell. The three of us grab a cab outside the Kimmel, and a few minutes later, we pull up at 6th and South. Lang Lang cracks up when he sees the window of an adult novelty shop. "'There's sex to be had,'" he quotes. "I've got to remember that!"

Sure enough, he leads us to the Golden Empress Garden, a tiny place off South Street I've always disregarded as a desperation takeout joint. The owner is happy to see one of his country's national heroes, but not surprised. "This is just a few blocks from the house, so we eat here all the time," Lang Lang says. The waiters even know to bring Lang Lang a fork. "I've got to rest my arm," Lang Lang explains. "I know a pianist who injured his arm while he was performing in Beijing and eating a lot with chopsticks."

That's no joke. Lang Lang's mentor, the man who brought him to Philadelphia, is Gary Graffman, head of the Curtis Institute. Years ago, Graffman was the Lang Lang of Brooklyn; he was only seven when he won a scholarship to Curtis, then was selected for personal instruction under those two piano gods, Vladimir Horowitz and Rudolph Serkin. Eugene Ormandy invited Graffman to debut with the Philadelphia Orchestra when he was 18, and for the next 30 years, he remained in constant demand by the world's top orchestras. To this day, his recordings of Prokofiev's piano concertos have never been equaled.

But in 1979, when the 48-year-old Graffman was just hitting his peak, burning flashes began cramping his right arm. He was diagnosed with "focal dystonia," an especially painful form of repetitive-stress symptom that can feel like a hammer blow to the funny bone. Graffman would never regain full use of the hand and had to give up performing. His personal tragedy became his alma mater's windfall; Graffman returned to Curtis, and soon began attracting piano students from around the world who were dying to study with the man who had inherited fire directly from Mount Olympus.

"Gary was one of the main reasons I came to Curtis," Lang Lang says, while his father is ordering a frightening amount of food. ("You like scallops? You like pork?" Lang Lang keeps asking. "Greens? Tofu?") Curtis was created in 1924 by Mary Louise Curtis Bok, heiress of the Curtis Publishing fortune, who housed her pet project on a full city block smack in the tenderloin of Rittenhouse Square. Mary Louise's school soon earned a rep as a musical X-Men Academy—kids with extraordinary powers could enter as early as they liked, stay as long as they liked, and never pay a cent. Play piano, and you get a free Steinway grand in your apartment; arrive from Kazakhstan, and you'll get an English tutor.

Getting in, however, is the tricky part. Curtis has only 160 students at a time, just enough for a full orchestra with, on the side, about 25 opera vocalists, 10 piano soloists, maybe the odd harpsichordist and a few composers. That's it. Auditions are only held when a spot opens; until the current tuba student graduates in about 4 years, none need apply. When Curtis does open its doors for applicants, up to 1,000 will gather from around the world for 30 or 40 spots. It's brutal, but once in, Curtis students never flunk out; the school's mission isn't to create great musicians, but to nurture geniuses who already are.

"You always hear about Juilliard and the Royal Academy, but Curtis, in my view, is much better," Lang Lang says. "We were very poor, and Curtis gave us *everything*. It was like a dream." Our food has arrived, and Lang Lang's father is taking charge of the table, filling our plates with garlicky shrimp and scallops, tofu in spicy bean sauce, sautéed pork with greens. He speaks very little English, but when he hears his son repeating "Curtis," he gives an oddly serious smile and a deep head-bow, an Eschenbach-worthy sign of gratitude.

Lang Guo-ren had always hoped to be a world-touring musician himself; he devoted his teen years to mastering the Chinese erhu, a rare and tricky two-stringed instrument that can sound like a ghostly human voice. But China's Maoist government assigned him to a military ensemble, and Lang Lang's mother, an aspiring dancer, was turned into a phone technician. Before Lang Lang was even born, his parents began transferring their thwarted dreams to him: His pregnant mother listened to hours of classical music, hoping it would somehow be woven into her developing fetus's genetic makeup.

And damned if it didn't work. When Lang Lang was two, his parents exhausted half their annual income on a piano, and discovered their son could plink out a snatch of Liszt's "Hungarian Rhapsody" after hearing it on a Tom & Jerry cartoon. "I had my first professional teacher at three, and my first recital at five," Lang Lang says. The crucial moment, however, came at age six: "I had to start practicing four hours a day, instead of two, because I needed to start learning the repertoire—Bach, Mozart, Chopin, Chinese folk music." Most young musicians fall away at this point, when toodling the keys turns into work.

But something was different with Lang Lang, and it would become his defining characteristic: While other kids were toiling, he was having a blast. "When I'm playing the piano, I'm on another planet," he says. "It's crazy. It's great." Wherever Chopin took him, it had to smell better than home: When Lang Lang was accepted at age nine to China's top conservatory, he and his father had to leave their northern province and move to a tiny, unheated shithole in Beijing, surviving off his mother's meager salary and sharing, with four other families, a literal shithole down the hall.

Within a few years, though, a bit of Lang Lang buzz began to spread when the kid from the Beijing tenement won the International Tchaikovsky Competition for Young Musicians in Japan. A critic who's seen video of Lang Lang's prize-winning rendition of Chopin's Piano Concerto No. 2 was struck to witness "a rapture that's rare in a 13-year-old" and "an imagination that somehow brings forth fresh phrase readings at every turn."

Two years later, Lang Lang and his father came to Philadelphia to test that rapture before the Curtis admissions board. Lang Lang's mother kept her job and apartment in China, just in case.

Right from his audition, however, the 15-year-old became Curtis's resident star. Graffman personally instructed him, which gave Lang Lang a chance to witness one of the gutsiest and most remarkable comebacks in musical history: In 1993, after 15 years away from the stage, Graffman began performing again—using only his left hand. He started with a series of works written for Paul Wittgenstein, who'd lost his right arm in World War I, but once colleagues saw what he was attempting, they began to compose new music for him. To master this fresh repertoire, Graffman had to work harder than ever; he used to learn one concerto a year in his prime, but in his 70s, he learned three new concertos in one year, and performed five.

Graffman's return was inspirational in a way only a young virtuoso like Lang Lang could appreciate: For a teenager who spent weeks and hours in solitude, memorizing scores and fingering chords over and over, it validated the monastic lifestyle. It proved that no matter what happened later, even if you lost an arm, you'd still have your music and a chance to triumph.

But, oddly, I could never hear this from Graffman himself. For months, I'd been trying to speak with Graffman about Lang Lang, but he wouldn't return my calls. Finally, I got this peculiar message from Curtis's PR director, Emily Cheramie: "When it comes to Lang Lang, Gary values him as a student and a friend, but now he feels he has to focus on current students. There are students here who are just as talented as Lang Lang, and they could feel slighted."

"O—" I drawled, completely confused, "—kay." Her response was so divorced from simple fact, it sounded insane: Were any *other* Curtis students being called "the future of classical music," or topping the charts between Bartoli and Bocelli? Besides, Lang Lang wasn't even a student anymore.

But even more poignantly, was any other Curtis student being abused as badly in the press, or more in need of a champion? Especially a champion who knew Lang Lang had no family and few close personal friends who could speak up for him? I had to wonder if Graffman's silence had anything to do with the fact that Lang Lang's face is smiling down from giant posters in Borders and Tower Records all over the country, while Graffman's tremendous accomplishment has gone largely unnoticed. I couldn't get a copy of Graffman's recording of Ned Rorem's "Piano Concerto for Left Hand" anywhere in town. ("I don't think we've ever carried it," a Tower clerk said.) I could only find it at an online specialty store; his autobiography is long out of print and equally hard to find.

"You will enjoy great success—*in bed!*" Lang Lang is saying, as his father hands out fortune cookies. "Open yours."

You should have good health.

"In bed!" Lang Lang cracks up. "All Chinese do that with fortune cookies."

"So," I ask, "what's your relationship like these days with Gary Graffman?"

"Great. I call him all the time before I depart somewhere. He always helps me a lot. It's kind of funny, though—"

"What's that?"

"He's always saying, 'Lang Lang needs a girlfriend, and I know a lot of girls like him.'" For the first time, Lang Lang seems a little uneasy. He picks up his unused chopsticks and peels the wrapper, then compulsively curls and uncurls it. "I like girls very much, but ... I don't have time for a girlfriend right now."

I decide not to mention that Graffman won't return my calls. Maybe it's not jealousy, exactly; maybe there's a subtler explanation that connects a man in his 70s who goes back onstage with one hand, to a conductor who's spent his life alone, to a 21-year-old with no love life who can't record by himself. As *Inquirer* critic David Patrick Stearns observed of Lang Lang: "He needs listeners in the room in order to perform. An entire recital sits in the Telarc vaults ... most of which died for lack of audience stimulation." After that fiasco, a studio audience was always dragooned.

The monastic life may not only create a lifelong gift, but a lifelong love: A first love, between the performer and an audience, that never dies. Seven-year-old Gary Graffman spent his days practicing in a Brooklyn apartment, then years on the road; Lang Lang left home at nine, and his homeland at 15. He's been separated from his mother ever since—although his parents are still married, his mother has gotten used to sacrificing her marriage for her son's career, and now spends most of the year in Hong Kong. None of these pianists have siblings. All they've had, from the time they were toddlers, was their audiences. Maybe the reason Graffman won't speak up for Lang Lang is because, in crude terms, when your ex-wife remarries, you don't give her away. By keeping quiet while Lang Lang experiences the first critical abuse of his life, his first strained relationship with listeners who'd always adored him, Graffman is giving Lang Lang a taste of something Beethoven knew very well—what it's like to be alone.

ESCHENBACH comes onstage and immediately starts apologizing. This can't be a good start. He's swapped the order of the performance, he announces: instead of coming on first, Lang Lang will follow the Orchestra's version of *Transfigured Night*, the Arnold Schöenberg composition that so annoyed its debut audience in 1902 that they rioted. "Please," Eschenbach says. "Give it a chance." No, not good at all.

But the audience laughs politely at Eschenbach's mock pleading, and not only refrains from torching the lobby, but actually applauds warmly as the turbulent piece ends. Eschenbach walks offstage as the clapping fades, and the Kimmel settles into silence. The first violin tings a string, then the whole string section thrums to life.

Eschenbach returns, and before anyone has time to react, Lang Lang appears, marching straight to the piano. What happens next … well, the best account will come several nights later, when Lang Lang performs the same piece at Carnegie Hall, and a *New York Times* reviewer scrutinizes each movement like the rounds of a title fight:

Christoph Eschenbach brought the Philadelphia Orchestra to Carnegie Hall on Tuesday, Allan Kozinn will write, *and judging from the emotionally weighty scores by Schöenberg and Mahler, he clearly had the most sober intentions. So he was taking a chance when he invited Lang Lang along as the soloist in Beethoven's Fourth Concerto.*

Surprised applause ripples through the audience at Lang Lang's sudden entrance, but dies when he doesn't look up. He flips his tails over the bench. At lunch, he'd told me he was going to perform in one of his gorgeous Chinese tunics, but he must have thought better and kept it conservative. He keeps his head down now, apparently deep in thought. Eschenbach, baton in hand, watches him.

There was perhaps a bit of playacting here: the pianist as the deaf Beethoven, turned in on himself and oblivious to the rude intrusions of the external world.

Before he wrote Piano Concerto No. 4, Beethoven was going to kill himself. He penned a death-note confession to his brothers, revealing his secret: "Though born with a fiery, active temperament, even susceptible to the diversions of society, I was soon compelled to withdraw myself, to live life alone," Beethoven wrote. "If I approach near to people a hot terror seizes upon me, and I fear being exposed to the danger that my condition might be noticed." Rather than admit he was losing "the one sense which ought to be more perfect in me than others," Beethoven lived in snarling seclusion, keeping even his brothers at bay.

"With joy I hasten to meet death," Beethoven wrote. But one thing made him hide the note and hold off: If he could endure a bit longer, he suspected, he might be truly great. His tragedy had one bitter benefit—he could try anything and never fail, because who would blame a deaf man for a flawed symphony? So when he sat to write Piano Concerto No. 4, all rules were off. He made his hero Orpheus, whose music could charm demons and open the gates of hell, but whose human frailty made him lose his love and life. This would be Beethoven's personal statement, his wordless confession, so he'd speak first: For the first time in the history of the piano concerto, the soloist begins, while the orchestra sits silent.

Lang Lang drops his hands to his lap and takes a breath. He seems regretful, as if he doesn't really want to begin. Eschenbach waits. And then cadences begin wafting from the piano, softly, without Lang Lang seeming to move. The first movement has "an almost unearthly quality"—Orpheus soothing the hounds of hell—and as Lang Lang plays, his free hand floats and drifts with the ghostly notes.

... [H]e was the picture of calmness, Kozinn will note, his only notable mannerism being a tendency to conduct or draw pictures in the air with his left hand while playing Beethoven's running lines with his right.

"When people say I'm showing off," Lang Lang explained over lunch, "it's because they don't see me when I'm alone. I play the same way, because I'm having *fun*. Music tells me a story, full of characters, and I love to bring them to life." He hated *Shine*, which made the piano seem like torture; when Lang Lang recorded the "Rach 3," he posed for the album cover with a nonchalant lean and a grin saying *This shit ain't tough*.

That urge to have fun is why, with the first movement behind him, Lang Lang faces a personal challenge in the second. Technically, the first movement is more demanding, but it lets him set his own tempo and tone. Now, though, the orchestra is entering, and Lang Lang's responses have to be hushed and subordinate to its cadence. If he can control himself, if he can suppress his urge to turn loose the power, he'll help create what's been called "the most remarkable dialogue in instrumental music." This is the moment every trained ear in the audience is listening for.

... [T]here was a keen musical intelligence at work, Kozinn will note approvingly, and a real give and take between Mr. Lang's piano line and Mr. Eschenbach's shaping of the orchestra.

From the tempo challenge in the second movement, Lang Lang passes to a new danger in the third. Instead of holding back, he's asked to cut loose in "triumphant jubilation"—just his kind of thing. But the key here is *elegance*; if he takes those forte markings as license to pound, he'll save Kozinn some work by allowing him to reuse *slam-bang crass* and a Jerry Lee Lewis dig.

... [H]e remains a supremely gifted wild card, Kozinn will conclude. But...

Backstage that night, violinist Jason DePue will get a little heated. "You have people who are really harsh on him. Know what they don't get? He's a pure red rose. Perfect. Ready to bloom. Leave him the fuck alone. I'm going to tell him, soon, if you ever need a friend, I'll be there." Another friend is also waiting; Xiao-

Yin Zhu, a 20-year-old harpsichordist, has shown up with an armful of flowers to sit with Lang Lang's father. She's at Curtis now, also being groomed for stardom. With her Bond Girl beauty and prodigious talent on a magnificent instrument, she's a record promoter's dream. She'll go home alone tonight; Lang Lang will be so absorbed that he'll forget to even walk her to her door.

But...

When Lang Lang leaves the stage, he has the same look he had when he entered, his head low and his smile rather sad. The standing ovation will still be thundering, and two elderly women will help each other find words. "My God," one begins.

"It's like he's in..." the second falters.

"Yes," says the first.

"Ecstasy."

"Yes."

But in purely musical terms, Kozinn concludes, *this was an uncommonly beautiful performance.*